MASTERPLANNING THE ADAPTIVE CITY

D1338793

Computational design has become widely accepted in mainstream architecture, but this is the first book to advocate applying computational urbanism to create adaptable masterplans for rapid urban growth, and urban heterogeneity. Practitioners and researchers here discuss ideas from the fields of architecture, urbanism, the natural sciences, computer science, economics, and mathematics to find the means with which to manage urban change in Asia and developing countries throughout the world. Divided into four parts—the historical and theoretical background, our current situation, methodologies, and prototypical practices—the book includes a series of essays, interviews, case studies, and original research to accompany chapters by editor Tom Verebes, giving you the most comprehensive overview of this approach.

Essays by Marina Lathouri, Jorge Fiori, Jonathan Solomon, Patrik Schumacher, Peter Trummer, and David Jason Gerber.

Interviews with Dana Cuff, Xu Weiguo, Matthew Pryor, Tom Barker, Su Yunsheng, and Brett Steele.

Case studies by Zaha Hadid Architects, James Corner Field Operations, XWG Studio, MAD, OCEAN CN, Plasma Studio, Groundlab, Peter Trummer, Serie Architects, dotA, and Rocker-Lange Architects.

Tom Verebes is Associate Dean for Teaching and Learning in the Faculty of Architecture at the University of Hong Kong, and Director of OCEAN CN Consultancy Network.

University of Strathclyde
Dept of Architecture
Library

D307.1216
VER

EDITED BY
TOM VEREBES

MASTERPLANNING THE ADAPTIVE CITY

COMPUTATIONAL URBANISM IN THE TWENTY-FIRST CENTURY

Routledge
Taylor & Francis Group
LONDON AND NEW YORK

First published 2014
by Routledge
711 Third Avenue, New York, NY 10017

Simultaneously published in the UK
by Routledge
2 Park Square, Milton Park, Abingdon, Oxon OX14 4RN

Routledge is an imprint of the Taylor & Francis Group, an informa business

© 2014 Taylor & Francis

The right of the editor to be identified as the author of the editorial material, and of the authors for their individual chapters, has been asserted in accordance with sections 77 and 78 of the Copyright, Designs and Patents Act 1988.

All rights reserved. No part of this book may be reprinted or reproduced or utilized in any form or by any electronic, mechanical, or other means, now known or hereafter invented, including photocopying and recording, or in any information storage or retrieval system, without permission in writing from the publishers.

Trademark notice: Product or corporate names may be trademarks or registered trademarks, and are used only for identification and explanation without intent to infringe.

Library of Congress Cataloging in Publication Data
Verebes, Tom.
Masterplanning the adaptive city : computational urbanism in the twenty-first century / Tom Verebes.
pages cm
Includes index.
1. City planning--Data processing. 2. Urbanization--History--21st century. I. Title.
HT166.V463 2013
307.1'2160285—dc23 2012046308

ISBN: 978-0-415-53479-6 (hbk)
ISBN: 978-0-415-53480-2 (pbk)
ISBN: 978-0-203-42805-4 (ebk)

Typeset in Gothic
by Keystroke, Station Road, Codsall, Wolverhampton

Acquisition Editor: Wendy Fuller
Editorial Assistant: Laura Williamson
Production Editor: Jennifer Birtill

Printed in Spain by GraphyCems

Dedicated to Dean Ralph Lerner

CONTENTS

xi FOREWORD >Mark Burry

xiii PREFACE AND ACKNOWLEDGMENTS >Tom Verebes

1 INTRODUCTION >Tom Verebes

5 **PART I >CONTEXT: ENDURANCE, OBSOLESCENCE, AND CHANGE—A THEORETICAL FOUNDATION**

7 CHAPTER 1 >THE CITY AS CULTURAL AND TECHNOLOGICAL EXPRESSION >Tom Verebes
7 1.1 Globalization and Networks
13 1.2 The Edge of Chaos
15 1.3 The Associative Logic of Urbanism

20 CHAPTER 2 >PROJECTIVE ARCHITECTURES: THE QUESTION OF BORDERS IN A CONNECTED WORLD >Marina Lathouri

23 CHAPTER 3 >CONVERSATION 1 >Dana Cuff with Tom Verebes

28 CHAPTER 4 >THE NEW NEW >Tom Verebes
28 4.1 Ancient China and The New
30 4.2 Urban Europe: A Brief History of Its Industrialization and Planning
34 4.3 The Paradigm of the New World Instant City
36 4.4 The Dubai Mirage

40 CHAPTER 5 >INFORMAL CITY: DESIGN AS POLITICAL ENGAGEMENT > Jorge Fiori

48 CHAPTER 6 >CONVERSATION 2 >Xu Weiguo, Xu Feng and Gao Yan

54 CHAPTER 7 >URBANIZATION AND ERASURE >Tom Verebes
54 7.1 The Trouble with Speed Freaks
57 7.2 Ghosts of the Past
60 7.3 An Ecological Model for Twenty-First Century Urbanism
62 7.4 The Problem of Functionality, Endurance, and Obsolescence
64 7.5 Time, Change, and Adaptation

68 CHAPTER 8 >PUBLIC-SPHERES: ATMOSPHERE AND ADAPTABLE SPACE IN HONG KONG >Jonathan D. Solomon
69 Something in the Air
71 Hong Kong's Public-Sphere
73 The City as Natural Artifice

75 CHAPTER 9 >CONVERSATION 3 >Matthew Pryor with Tom Verebes

80 CASE STUDY >QIANHAI MASTERPLAN, SHENZEN, CHINA >James Corner Field Operations

82 CASE STUDY >FLOWING GARDENS, INTERNATIONAL HORTICULTURAL EXPO, XI'AN, CHINA >Plasma Studio

85 **PART II >CONCEPTS/PARADIGMS: NEW PARADIGMS AND PRACTICES IN URBANISM**

87 CHAPTER 10 >THE DEATH OF MASTERPLANNING IN THE AGE OF INDETERMINACY >Tom Verebes
87 10.1 Planning and/or Emergence
92 10.2 Teleological Fallacies of the Masterplanner
95 10.3 Principles of Uncertainty: Planning after the Global Financial Crisis
99 10.4 Complex systems, Equilibrium, and Emergence
106 10.5 Parametric Patterns and Models of Evolutionary Urbanism

118 CHAPTER 11 >FREE-MARKET URBANISM: URBANISM BEYOND PLANNING >Patrik Schumacher

123 CHAPTER 12 >Conversation 4 >Tom Barker and Tom Verebes

129 CASE STUDY >ONE NORTH SINGAPORE SCIENCE HUB, SINGAPORE >Zaha Hadid Architects

132 CASE STUDY >URBAN CHINA RESEARCH >OCEAN CN

135 CASE STUDY >KAILI ETHNIC CULTURAL COMPOUND, GUIZHOU, CHINA >dotA and Shanghai Tongji Urban Planning and Design Institute

139 **PART III >METHODOLOGIES: TOOLS AND MOVING TARGETS**

141 CHAPTER 13 >A NEW TOOLBOX FOR ADAPTABLE MASTERPLANNING > Tom Verebes
141 13.1 Models as Information
144 13.2 Parameter Space, Solution Space, Urban Space
148 13.3 Simulation and Gaming Environments as Management Systems

153 CHAPTER 14 >MORPHOGENETIC URBANISM: TOWARD A MATERIALIST APPROACH TO MASTERPLANNING >Peter Trummer
154 The Aggregated Figure
156 The Ground as Matter

158 CASE STUDY >PARAMETRIC PEARL RIVER DELTA >OCEAN CN

162 CASE STUDY >SERIAL SYSTEMS: REMODELING HONG KONG HOUSING >OCEAN CN

165 CASE STUDY >DENSITY AND OPENNESS REVISITED: RECODING BUILDING BULK IN HONG KONG >Rocker-Lange Architects

168 CHAPTER 15 >COMPUTATIONAL URBANISM >Tom Verebes
168 15.1 The Evolution of Computational Methodologies and Urbanism
175 15.2 Automation, Optioneering, and Optimization
180 15.3 Parametric Urbanism

186 CHAPTER 16 >PARAMETRIC URBANISM REDUX: URBAN DESIGN AND COMPLEXITY IN AN AGE OF INFINITE COMPUTING >David Jason Gerber

193 CHAPTER 17 >CONVERSATION 5 >Su Yunsheng with Tom Verebes

CONTENTS

198 CASE STUDY >YAN JIAO HUA RUN 4D CITY, HEBEI PROVINCE, CHINA > dotA and OCEAN CN

205 CASE STUDY >MICA URBAN PICTURESQUE, GENEVA, SWITZERLAND > Group8 Architects and Kaisersrot

209 CASE STUDY >THE MEGABLOCK AND ITS POPULATED FIELD, AND THE AGGREGATION OF STREETS >Peter Trummer, Associative Design Program, Berlage Institute

214 CASE STUDY >ENDURANCE AND OBSOLESCENCE TOOLBOX: STUDIES OF ADAPTABLE MASTERPLANNING >The University of Hong Kong

221 PART IV >PROJECTIONS: PROTOTYPING MULTIPLE FUTURES

223 CHAPTER 18 >ENDURANCE, OBSOLESCENCE, AND THE ADAPTIVE CITY > Tom Verebes

223 18.1 New Prototypical Practices

226 18.2 Typological Variants and Topological Transformations

230 18.3 Icons and Innovation

232 18.4 Control, Resilience, and Change

237 CASE STUDY >DEEP GROUND: REGENERATION MASTERPLAN FOR LONGGANG CENTER AND LONGCHENG SQUARE, SHENZHEN, CHINA >Groundlab

241 CASE STUDY >XIN TIAN DI FACTORY H, HANGZHOU, CHINA >Serie Architects

245 CASE STUDY >REGENERATION OF PHOENIX SHOPPING STREET, BEIJING, CHINA >XWG Studio

248 CASE STUDY >ORDOS MUSEUM, ORDOS, INNER MONGOLIA, CHINA >MAD

253 CASE STUDY >LIANTANG/HEUNG YUEN WAI BOUNDARY CONTROL POINT PASSENGER TERMINAL BUILDING, HONG KONG SAR/SHENZHEN, CHINA >Hong Kong Parametric Design Association, dotA, and OCEAN CN

259 CASE STUDY >COUNTERPART CITIES: FUTUREPORT, HONG KONG SAR, SHENZHEN, CHINA >The University of Hong Kong Research Team, Led by Tom Verebes

266 CHAPTER 19 >CONVERSATION 6 >Brett Steele with Tom Verebes

273 CONCLUSION >Tom Verebes

275 BIBLIOGRAPHY

283 NOTES ON CONTRIBUTORS

291 INDEX

FOREWORD

Economic uncertainty, the birth of a transdisciplinary urban design agenda, divergent reactions to conspicuous resource depletion, and affordable access to massive computing power all combine to encourage us to seek new ways to theorize on and practice the design of our cities, with a fresh set of assumptions. It is time to put away our comfortable preconceptions of the ideal city: resplendent in the eternal sunshine of an untroubled existence—and completed. We know that cities are never finished, rely on differences of wealth and status as a weird kind of motivating dialectic, require constant regeneration and rethinking, and cannot dreamily be assumed to evolve into a utopian existentialism. We have no successful precedent for the ideal city, but we have plenty of experience and understanding now of what does not work, and that includes any master plan incapable of nimbly adapting to rapid shifts in population growth, wealth, climate, and consumer expectations.

Masterplanning the Adaptive City is being published in distinctly volatile times. Against a backdrop of arguably the most serious and comprehensively disastrous global financial crisis ever, for the first time in history over 50 percent of the world's population are now citizens rather than rural dwellers. We are truly urbanized, meaning that the basics of life now need to be conveyed long distances to where the majority live rather than the majority clustering around convenient local sources of water and food. Human settlements once sited in predominately defensible places that afforded ready trade and transport, inter alia, conformed to unwritten rules of sustainability. We seem to be presumptuously urbanizing today in ever greater numbers, confident that food sources will be secure, water abundant, global warming abated by means other than human agency, potential pandemics readily checked, and fuel always available at affordable prices pending the invention of free energy. On that basis we continue to plan most of our cities' expansion in much the same way that postindustrial society has massively urbanized in the past—through the inexorable commandeering of peripheral agricultural land for the purposes of building over. Or going up and up, thereby swelling the numbers drawing on the relief offered by ever-scarcer public space. How is this possible?

If times are volatile in terms of sustainability, they are also volatile in terms of trying to maintain the status quo of the traditional approaches to increasing population sizes in our existing towns and cities and to the design of new ones. Consider the seven decades since the conclusion of World War II, and the challenges and opportunities for postwar reconstruction. Politicians, planners, sociologists, and architects confidently set the agenda in a strange fusion of the prewar early modernist urban theory, applied originally to accommodate natural growth but then used to mitigate the extraordinary circumstances of smashed cities requiring massive and rapid repair. The lack of a sense of civitas that has tainted so much of the resulting urban fabric, regardless of continent, does not reflect lack of imagination but rather a complex set of deficiencies that no single profession or discipline can fully admit to. The complexities of the dynamics involved and the speed at which they operated successfully frustrated earnest efforts to draw resplendence from the wastelands of war, slums, brownfield sites, *terrain vague*, and uncontrolled immigration. It is improbable that any single theory from any single discipline is equal to the task; Le Corbusier's "radiant city" has never emerged to specification, even when a tabula rasa is accompanied by apparently inexhaustible funds—the rows and rows of worker huts in the desert glare outside Doha are testament to the inevitability of exclusion for a proportion of a city's population.

A beauty of this book is that it sets out to augment rather than sniff at or snuff out any movement or theoretical base that has gone before. The authors do not claim a "right answer" based on a particular theory or realpolitik and a highly selective body of evidence. Joel Kotkin may well be right about the universal desirability of suburbia and a natural instinct for personal and not collectivized conveyance, and therefore reliance on the ability of the market to set the agenda. Jane Jacobs's conviction that we need to retain the past in order to help explain the future may be as valid as Le Corbusier's densification created at the expense of whatever formerly occupied the site. Christopher Alexander's pattern language might be the key to accommodating the individual's core sentiments through rules, systems, and generative processes rising above the master plan at any scale. Henri Lefebvre's Marxist humanism and community engagement may be as valid as Gordon Cullen's cityscape appropriate for any age and anywhere, and Kevin Lynch's image of the city might always be the "right" one. What the pioneers of modern urban renewal and expansion have in common are deeply held convictions that urban planning needs guiding principles.

Theories from so many disparate disciplines with an interest in urbanism are inevitably oppositional. Principles of market-led self-organization can work across the economic spectrum, for example in the dockland redevelopments in London and Melbourne, and in the favelas of Brazil—unexpectedly functional slums that are not necessarily chaotic failures of unplanned human agglomeration. Such principles are incompatible with top-down masterplanning, whether state driven or developer led. *Masterplanning the Adaptive City* transcends any disciplinary sectarianism by nimbly leaping away from consideration of the evolving city as plan (as in "planning") and into the city as volume (space), and in considering spatiality the chapters are not limited to a cute three dimensions. Design computation recognizes neither disciplinary boundaries nor Cartesian space. As a means of enabling rich conversation across all urban design intelligences, access to massive and rapid design computation can deal with complexity in entirely new ways. This book facilitates novel and nonpartisan speculation on the nature of the adaptive city in ways not remotely possible in the predigital age. Alternate theories can be tested without fear or favor, whatever their provenance, and this is far richer in implication than testing alternative solutions. In this context, the term "masterplan" has an entirely different set of meanings, all of them positive.

Mark Burry
Design Research Institute Director
RMIT University
Melbourne

PREFACE AND ACKNOWLEDGMENTS

This book was triggered by my ongoing research at the University of Hong Kong (HKU), within a funded research project titled "Endurance and Obsolescence: The Problem of Rapid Urbanization in China", started with a University Grants Council (UGC) Seed Grant in 2009. I am grateful to the late Dean Ralph Lerner for his clear vision, which lured me to HKU. This book is only one of numerous projects which Ralph sadly could not see to its conclusion. In this light, I also thank Dean David Lung for his ongoing support, which has allowed me the time and space to complete this book.

To track my personal engagement with the central themes of this research, it was Jeffrey Kipnis's persistence in 1993, when he set out to discover "a New Architecture at the Architectural Association," which so enticed me. Kipnis, together with Barham Shirdel and a team of thirteen grad students at the AA, set out to boldly sketch a vision for a new sixty-four-square-kilometer city in Hainan Island, China. That experience has helped to shape my interests and ambitions ever since, and this book is in many ways a culmination of a twenty-year journey of experimentation in urbanism. It is not a coincidence that I am in Hong Kong twenty years later, researching issues associated with Chinese urbanization. I am grateful to many other teachers, including Donald Bates and Ricardo Castro, who helped shape my interests as a young graduate in the 1990s.

Thanks to those who contributed essays: Patrik Schumacher, Jonathan Solomon, Marina Lathouri, Jorge Fiori, David Gerber, Peter Trummer; to those whose conversations have been transcribed for this book: Brett Steele, Dana Cuff, Tom Barker, Xu Weiguo, Su Yunsheng, and Matthew Pryor; and to the many architects and urbanists whose projects are included in this theoretical endeavor.

My time spent at the AA, including sixteen months as a graduate student and then thirteen years teaching and codirecting the Design Research Lab (DRL), was a time that nurtured experiments now consolidated in the thesis of this book. My invaluable collaborations with Brett Steele, Patrik Schumacher, Christopher Hight, Yusuke Obuchi, Hanif Kara, Tom Barker, Bob Lang, Laurence Friesen, Alisa Andrasek, Theo Spyropoulos, Jeroen van Amejde, Marta Male Alemany, and many others will be challenging to parallel. Our conversations, discussions, and great intellectual arguments, especially those on computational design and the city, during the years of our Parametric Urbanism agenda, are sublimated in this book. Others, including Mohsen Mostafavi who hired me as a kid and countless former AA colleagues, are also recalled in these pages.

Thanks to my valued colleagues at HKU, who have helped to shape this position in a new and challenging context, giving their vital feedback in discussions, studio reviews and juries, especially Jonathan Solomon, David Erdman, Yan Gao, Christian Lange, Jason Carlow, Kristof Crolla, Dorothy Tang, Vincci Mak, Oliver Ottavaere, Cole Roskam, Eunice Seng, Joshua Bolchover, Wang Weijen, Juan Du, among others.

There are several authors, architects and urbanists without whom, and without whose research, which foregrounds this book, the outcomes of this project would not be possible. These include Manuel De Landa, Sanford Kwinter, Steve Johnson, Kevin Kelly, Juval Portugali, Michael Weinstock, Rem Koolhaas, Lewis Mumford, Reyner Banham, Christopher Alexander, Stephen Marshall, and Michael Batty, among too many others to list in these acknowledgements. They had sketched out, before me, the foundation for an evolutionary understanding of the city.

Many thanks to my research assistants with whom I collaborated on various stages of this book, including Li Bin, who helped kickstart the initial research and its first formulation at the 2009 Hong Kong-Shenzhen Bi-City Biennale. Nathan Melenbrink was an invaluable collaborator on research into computational urbanism, working nonstop for months in the "big middle" of a research project. Kenneth Sit Hoi Chang helped to cohere some of the strands which have been woven together in this book. Thanks, too, to Vivian Ho for her transcriptions of the recorded conversations that appear here.

I cherish my various colleagues and collaborators, partners and codirectors over the years at OCEAN UK Design Ltd., ocean D, and now OCEAN CN, especially Yan Gao and Felix Robbins who have been my coconspirators in helping shape the thesis and design research outcomes included in this book. Lastly, my thanks are due to my wife Nicole, and to Rubin, Samson and Elisha for their patience throughout 2012!

Tom Verebes
Hong Kong, 2013

TOM VEREBES > INTRODUCTION

> A clean sheet of paper has no blotches, and so the newest and most beautiful words can be painted on it.
>
> Mao Tse-tung, 1966[1]

A pertinent introductory question may be: why write a book on the topic of adaptable masterplanning and evolutionary urbanism, and why at this time? It has become a cliché in recent years to underscore statements on contemporary urbanism with the caveat that more than half the world now lives in cities. The equivalent of the population of Europe has been urbanized in China in the last thirty years. Given this current context of rapid and extensive global urbanisations, this book is neither an academic treatise on urbanism, nor a pro forma manual on "how to" engage as a designer with the contemporary field of computational urbanism. Positioned between discourse and technology, ideas and techniques, theory and practice, this book uses the written word, or discourse, as a vehicle for articulating the ambitions, achievements, and innovations of design work at the cutting edge of the discipline.

> We no longer know where to look to find the glorious ensembles and performances that we once called the "city."
>
> Sanford Kwinter[2]

While this book is about cities, the term "city" has become antiquated, lacking both sufficient precision to describe twentieth-century urbanity and specific relevance to the vast urbanization occurring in this century. The attributes of the "city of tomorrow" of this century may not be comprehensible through the lens of the nineteenth-century European and North American metropolis. Patrick Geddes first used the term "world city" in 1915,[3] and the city taxonomy of the twentieth century includes the "megalopolis,"[4] "global city,"[5] and "megacity,"[6] each term aiming to encapsulate the qualities of expanding urbanization. In his research studios at Harvard Graduate School of Design, Rem Koolhaas initially titled his endeavor "The Center for the Study of (what used to be) the City," which later became known by the shorthand "The Harvard Project on the City." In order to comprehend the contemporary city, it seems it first needs to be renamed.

Contemporary urbanism requires new conceptual and methodological apparatus with which to address the complex qualities of interaction, communication and exchange that characterize the twenty-first-century city.[7] Any book about urbanism within the context of rapid urbanization in the early twenty-first century must inevitably address two preconditions in its formulation: first, the ongoing instability of the global economy and its political, social, and urban ramifications; and second, the planet earth's changing climatic environment and the imminence of ecological crises. Contemporary design and prototyping methods, prevalent in architectural milieus, have not as yet been fully explored as tools to be applied to mass customization on the scale of the city. Challenging the paradigm of the repetitive and uniform Fordist production which guided much of the twentieth century in Europe and the Americas, the ramifications of our new design approaches are not stable and singular but rather dynamic and multiplicious. *Masterplanning the Adaptive City* aims to interrogate the changing and diverse qualities of urbanism today across a global field of contexts, histories and contemporary practices.

Cities are in continuous transformation, even if ever so slowly. Investigating the social logic of stable, long-lasting spaces within the phenomena of urban transformation, this compilation of projects, texts and conversations aims to chart a trajectory of conceptual and methodological apparatus in order to empower the designers of cities. Speculating on alternatives to conventional planning, the approach that is unfolded follows a survey of the historical disciplinary background to the understanding of urban complexity. This book explores the evolutionary nature of cities, addressing issues associated with the duration and obsolescence of architecture and urbanism through a projective account of how contemporary computational methodologies have the capability to manage urban change. Far from a celebration of impermanence and ephemerality, this book probes the paradoxical tension between the need for contemporary architecture to endure culturally, socially, environmentally, and economically, and a seemingly more urgent need for cities to adapt to dynamic contextual conditions and evolve. There is another paradox here, between visionary urbanism, the scope of which is grand if not totalizing, and the thesis of evolutionary dynamics, whereby adaptations emerge locally and grow incrementally. Through the chapters of this book—the essays, conversations, and projects it presents—a range of investigations into aggregate, incremental, and time-based models of urban growth will correlate top-down and bottom-up methods with which to confront and to mitigate the paradox of planning for urban growth and change.

Regarding the inherent, inevitable obsolescence of buildings and cities, it may be necessary to relinquish to some degree the assumption that all architecture must be permanent, and wholly functional, forever. The history of urbanization chronicles how cities become dysfunctional, decline, and die, as a symptom of political, economic, demographic, environmental, and other contextual changes. The emphasis of this book is not on the history of cities, but rather on methodologies aimed at heightening the potential of the city to adapt to the changing forces which shape it. We aim to sketch out strategies for avoiding the primacy of short-term ambitions in favor of adaptive mechanisms which enable the city to evolve to meet current and future needs and desires.

The central aim of this book is to articulate the goals and means by which to pursue adaptive models of designing, managing, and maintaining the dynamic nature of cities. The book is also a theoretical and a rhetorical response to a previous generation that theorized the complexity of the city—the contributors to this endeavor can be identified by scanning the citations and bibliography. It is also a contribution to an evolutionary model of urbanism being formulated by a small yet growing demimonde of instigators, also too numerous to list in this brief introduction.

BOOK STRUCTURE

The book is comprised of four sections, each with a dense mix of formats and a breadth of topics and contributions from a range of specializations. It is intentionally *urban*—intense, heterogeneous, congested, even cacophonous

—mirroring the contemporary metropolitan experience. Each section has subchapters containing a narrative text by the author, punctuated by a series of six contributed essays and six transcribed conversations with experts, as well as case studies of eighteen recent design projects by a series of leading avant-garde practices, other experimental research teams, and academic studios.

Section 1, "Context: Endurance, Obsolescence and Change—A Theoretical Foundation," charts the historical and theoretical foundation of the inherently dynamic, associative and evolutionary nature of the city. Cities in an era of globalization express culture and technology through networks. Via a survey of the successes and pitfalls of past models of urbanization, and the standardization and mechanization of cities, the conditions for new adaptive models of urbanization in Asia are elucidated.

In Section 2, "Concepts/Paradigms: New Paradigms and Practices in Urbanism," the discursive foundation for speculations on alternatives to teleological modes of development is presented, in which principles of uncertainty, complexity, and emergence are embraced in what is termed the "age of indeterminacy." The tension between top-down planning and informal, emergent urbanization helps to explicate the concepts associated with computational approaches to adaptable masterplanning.

Section 3, "Methodologies: Tools and Moving Targets," outlines the new information-based toolbox of the contemporary architect and urbanist, and assesses the potential for associative design models to inform city design using dynamic, emergent processes through which the performance of multiple design options can be simulated and evaluated. The design methodologies outlined in this section aim toward an ordered sense of spatial differentiation, diversity, and difference.

Lastly, Section 4, "Projections: Prototyping Multiple Futures," critiques the legacy of standardization of material practices and repetitive modes of production. Prototyping and customization are investigated as the basis for harnessing urban complexity, as an experimental mode of testing multiple urban futures. An argument for heterogeneity and high-quality architecture aims to strike a balance between endurance and change, longevity and adaptability.

Masterplanning the Adaptive City traverses conventional disciplinary boundaries between architecture, urbanism, critical theory, complexity science, the natural sciences, mathematics, computer graphics, and programming, among others. This speculative research project should be judged by the future impact of the paradigms outlined, and not on the perceived incongruity or imprecision of its promiscuous disciplinary references.

NOTES

1 > Quoted in J. Grasso, J. Corrin, and M. Kort (1991) *Modernization and Revolution in China* (New York: M.E. Sharpe), 27.

2 > S. Kwinter (2011) *Requiem for the City at the End of the Millennium* (Barcelona: Actar), 93.

3 > P. Geddes (1915) *Cities in Evolution* (London: Williams & Norgate).

4 > J. Gottmann (1961) *Megalopolis: The Urbanized Northeastern Seaboard of the United States* (New York: The Twentieth Century Fund).

5 > S. Sassen (1991) *The Global City* (Princeton, NJ: Princeton University Press).

6 > M. Castells (1996) *The Rise of the Network Society* (Oxford: Blackwell).

7 > T. Verebes (2009) "Experiments in Associative Urbanism," in *Digital Cities*, ed. Neil Leach (London: Wiley), 25.

I

CONTEXT

ENDURANCE, OBSOLESCENCE, AND CHANGE—A THEORETICAL FOUNDATION

CHAPTER 1

TOM VEREBES >THE CITY AS CULTURAL AND TECHNOLOGICAL EXPRESSION

This chapter charts the historical and theoretical foundation for an understanding of the city as inherently dynamic and evolutionary in nature. Globalization is understood as arising from a deep connection to the proliferation of networks. The emergence of megacities is a feature of the radically changing conditions of urban earth. What follows is a critique of the prevalent western bias in the history of urbanization, focusing on pertinent issues at stake in the urbanization of Asia. The associative logic inherent to urbanism is introduced as a fundamental shift from a mechanical paradigm to one guided by an understanding of life.

1.1 GLOBALIZATION AND NETWORKS

The city is everywhere. The local is now global. What happens here may affect what happens elsewhere. No one is alone. Nowhere is isolated. We will be concerned with the future of urban earth in later pages of this book. Initially, our investigation focuses on the ancients.

From the first sedentary settlements, over half the world's population now lives in cities, a process which has taken 12,000 years. What explains this rate of global urbanization? Man as a social animal? Is it our apparent need to exchange knowledge, resources, and goods? Cities are at once an expression of the cultural practices and technologies of the present. The shift from an agrarian, migratory civilization toward an increasingly sedentary one over time evolved into urban civilization, and the origins of globalization. Just as infrastructural networks and communication technologies have evolved, so have the civilizations they serve. The beginnings of globalization are located in the relation of the urban population of the planet—now in the majority—to the interface of man-made technological endeavors, and their instrumentality as infrastructure and networks.

Urbanism has its roots in the taming of nature. The first widespread territory to be altered irrevocably by mankind was the Nile delta, the irrigation canals of which spawned one of the first sedentary regions. Similarly the draining of swampland or the taming of the wild tributaries of the Euphrates and Tigris rivers in Mesopotamia represent the will of mankind to dominate and conquer nature on a large scale. It is not surprising that natural waterways were the first locus of urbanity, as the rise of the city was "contemporaneous with improvements in navigation," and this newfound mobility provided the city with "command over men and resources in distant areas," thus proving the means with which to procure and distribute goods beyond the locale.[1]

Cities grew. They were not designed. Before there were cities (without wishing to make any claims about when this threshold occured), villages and towns comprised a new kind of sedentary settlement, "a permanent association of families and neighbors, or birds and animals, of houses and storage pits and barns, all rooted in the ancestral soil, in which each generation formed the compost of the next."[2] Urbanization, as defined by Kingsley Davis, is "the increase in the proportion of the population that is urban as opposed to rural."[3] Lineated inscriptions of sedentary agricultural patterns are evidence of how "the plough radically changed the way the Earth's surface was utilized."[4]

The Neolithic revolution, arising from greater security, the abundance of food, and higher survival rates, marked the shift from stone-age nomadic groups to sedentary agricultural societies and was, for V. Gordon Childe, the first of three revolutions. It was followed by a second, "urban" revolution, in which trade and manufacturing enabled more complex and hierarchical organization of the roots of urbanity, between 3000 and 4000 BC. Later we will investigate Childe's third revolution, the industrial revolution of the eighteenth and nineteenth centuries.[5] A fourth revolution—the information revolution—has since taken place and has permeated contemporary urbanity.[6]

It is at the stage that man's evolution shifts from the transient huts of hunting and gathering societies to more permanent, sedentary societies that "the basic prerequisites are reached for the birth of urban settlements." Prior to longer-lasting dwellings, presumed by historians to be permanent, housing had evolved, as outlined by Norbert Scheonauer, from "ephemeral or transient dwellings," to "episodic or irregular temporary dwellings," to "periodic or regular temporary dwellings," to "seasonal dwellings," and to "semi-permanent dwellings."[7]

The origins of urbanity remain largely inaccessible, and few physical remains exist prior to the civilizations of Mesopotamia and Egypt. This account is less concerned with an analysis and reconstruction of the basis of former civilizations than in the reasons for their emergence, their growth, and their demise. The endurance of civilization is a misconception, evident in the history of sequential failed empires and civilizations.

The Roman Empire was a systematic city-building endeavor. It created 5,627 cities in Europe, North Africa, and the Middle East. Aelius Aristides told the Roman Emperor in AD 144, "you have cast a net over the totality of the inhabited world." The Romans had systematized the principles and sequences for establishing and growing a city by the Roman system, "as a manual, a repertory, a how-to book, a dictionary, an anthology of quotations—a compromise between a treaty (indeed a manifesto) and a book of procedures."[8] In his *Ten Books of Architecture*, Vitruvius detailed a logic of a set of performance criteria and their parameters to be balanced in the city. Environmental orientation, exposure, altitude, climate, and flora are set out as the basis for locating the city to create optimal conditions for health. Military defences, roads, and sea ports are also initial considerations in setting out the position and height of defenses, and the location and design of the buildings and spaces of the city.[9] The Roman guidelines for the desirable location of a city had predictably led to "simple societies [being] found in the least desirable regions, and more complex societies claim[ing] more favourable regions."[10] Joseph Rykwert, in his narrative analysis of Rome, laments "the transition from topological and ritualistic town-making to the imposition of the geometric grid" and its effects.[11] Nostalgia aside, the grid was a device for the domination of land, and a tool of globalization.[12] The Harvard Project on the City studio describes the Roman System as the first pro forma for urban globalization, its systematic deployment of infrastructural, financial, and military networks across a vast territory demonstrating the operation of networks enabling vast connectivities.[13] Rome propagated technology and culture through networks.

The Scottish ecologist Patrick Geddes, in his 1915 book *Cities in Evolution*,[14] described how the specific topography of cities helped to shape them, in relation to "where food and water supplies came from [and] where the settlement was established."[15] Geddes defined the period of industrial development as "paleotechnic" followed by "neotechnic." Mumford added another term for the era between 1000 and 1750, calling it the "eotechnic" period, which he saw as the dawn of modern technologies.[16] This era maintained the balance between industry and agriculture, between nature and man. The industrial revolution was to interfere with this balance.

> In the case of primordial settlements, three different path systems develop: The territorial path network makes searching for food easier, the settlement path network connects individual resting places and houses. The central point is the water source. The long-distance path network connects places of habitation and is used for interregional migrations.
>
> Frei Otto[17]

Globalization did not happen suddenly nor did it occur recently, rather it has been ongoing for centuries, even millennia, beginning in earnest with the opening up of trade routes in the fifteenth century. Before large-scale and long-distance shipping created the roadmap for globalization, ancient trading routes facilitated exchange among far-distant societies, and the development of the world's infrastructures solidified land transport, canals, and railways, as well as longer distance transport by sea and air. Networks enable the flow of people, products, information, and knowledge. The building of canals and railways in industrial Europe enabled transport of resources and goods, and connected localities in a web of industrial relations.[18] Shipyards later emerged for the building of large ships for the European empires, and car transport, while it did not immediately inscribe a whole new network onto industrialized regions, brought about more independent and spontaneous movement. The proliferation of air travel and high-speed railways, coupled with telephony and the internet, are collapsing time, shrinking space, and again creating possibilities for global communication to unforeseen extents.

The term "city" has become inadequate to describe twenty-first-century Asian urbanism. Patrick Geddes was one of the first urban theorists to argue for the history of cities being one of continual, but not constant, evolutionary change. Geddes had little hope for the future of the city: he mapped urbanity from the "polis" in Greece to the "metropolis" and the emergence of the "megalopolis," to what he called the "parasitopolis" and the "patholopolis," and through to the terminus, the "necropolis."[19] Geddes, who used the term "world cities" as early as 1924, foreshadowed the current generation of urban theorists grappling with the interconnectedness of urbanization in the twenty-first century.[20] The sociologist Jean Gottmann coined the term "megalopolis," in his book *Megalopolis: The Urbanized Northeastern Seaboard of the United States* (1961).[21] "Megalopolis" refers to the condition of the city when it becomes so large it cannot be conceived of nor managed as one single city, or when multiple smaller cities grow into expansive territorial conurbations. Gottman's research focussed on the "enormous scale jump that had occurred in an urban agglomeration stretching from Boston to Washington," which connected thirty-two million people in 1961, and fifty-six million today.[22] These figures pale in comparison with the extent of urbanization in Asia in the last half-century.

Today's growing "megacities" are of interest both for their global economic influence and as "magnets for their hinterlands . . . as a function of their gravitational power toward major regions of the world."[23] It is the formlessness of the megacity which allows its expansiveness. The metropolis of the twenty-first-century city has no single center, nor any edges. The emergence of megacities represents "the shift of the urban centre of gravity, in terms of global urban population, away from Europe, towards Asia and Africa."[24] Our current era is defined by an "abundance of information technologies and the associated increase in the mobility and liquidity of capital."[25] Henri Lefebvre in his seminal book *The Urban Revolution* (1970) "anticipated the 'generalisation' of capitalist urbanisation processes through the establishment of a planetary 'fabric' or 'web' of urbanized spaces."[26] Steven Johnson, in *Emergence* (2001), writes how "technological and geopolitical changes obviously have a tremendous impact—killing off entire industries, triggering mass migrations, launching wars, or precipitating epidemics."[27]

Urbanity is undergoing profound change as a repercussion of accelerated globalization and the increasing ubiquity of information and communication technologies. The softening, or in some contexts the entire disappearance, of borders and the unit of the nation state are the result of the fluidity created by deregulated economies, leading to a transcendence of the national unit and, in turn, the isolated self-sufficient city. Far from heralding the end of cities, Saskia Sassen sees the result as being "transnational urban systems," in which the reciprocal logic of concentration and dispersal that occurs in large metropolitan centres also happens across interconnected networks of global cities.[28] The global city relies on transnational flows from city to city, through financial, electronic, and other networks. No city is therefore independent. All is interconnected; as Sassen states, "there is no such thing as a single global city—and in this sense there is a sharp contrast with the erstwhile capitals of empires."[29] The global city, according to Castells, "cannot be reduced to a few urban cores at the top of the hierarchy," rather cities and their regional and local territories become connected at a global level.[30] At another scale, cities are now vulnerable to the forces of the global economy. A downturn in one part of the world can quickly affect cities elsewhere. From this perspective, current urban planning techniques can neither predict nor resist economic fallout and its impact on the city. Conveniently, when urban growth and economic booms coincide, planning takes credit and validates its regimes.

> The information age is ushering in a new urban form, the informational city. Yet, as the industrial city was not a worldwide replica of Manchester, the emerging informational city will not copy Silicon Valley.
>
> Manuel Castells[31]

Steven Shaviro summarizes Castell's three "material layers" of the space of flows. The first layer is our new "physical layer of electronic hardware and software, the technology that has to be deployed in order for the network to function at all . . . or what McLuhan calls the medium." The second material layer is constituted by the "nodes and hubs" of its physical geography, which is how megacities expand and become "differentiated into heterogeneous zones." The third layer is the "rarified and homogenous space in which the global financial and political elite lives, works, and travels."[32] The global network of business centres requires the "back-end" infrastructure to feed the physical flow of cargo and people. The "logistic landscape" as defined by Charles Waldheim and Alan Berger arises from a global economy that has become increasingly distributed internationally. Logistic landscape territories spawn "new industrial forms based on global supply chains" and accommodate the "shipment, staging, and delivery of goods," shifting from concentrated organization to an increasingly decentralized and distributed logic of production and flow of goods.[33]

The centrality of a single national city is a residual colonial model. Economic, cultural, and technological networks have played a role in shaping the status of the city as an important economic unit. City-to-city networks facilitate relationships which render nations not so much moot as secondary. This new kind of associated urbanism relies on information and communication technologies, as well as the persistently expanding flow of people. A distinction can be made between centralized and decentralized power and decision making, regarding the ways in which "energy flows through a city—that is with respect to the city's distribution systems." "Hierarchical structures with conscious goals and overt control mechanisms" differ from "cross-border networks," spontaneous self-organized patterns of interaction between people forming loosely organized, short-term affiliations.[34] Cities remain integral to globalization, and to telecommunications and other network technologies. Given the "denationalizing of urban space," Sassen asks the question: "Whose city is it?"[35]

> In principle, the new information and communication technologies have the technical capacities to alter—and indeed eliminate—the role of centrality and hence of cities as economic spaces.
>
> Saskia Sassen[36]

In the past, teleology defined ideality as the betterment of society, but today's world is more sinister. "The principal aim of the new 'liberalism'—the ideological belief in the free, or self-regulating, market—is to legitimate, through democratic institutions, the removal of democratic control over economic life." The neo-liberal idea of a self-regulating, "intelligent" market "is but a cynically recurring contrivance that, contrary to its claims, relies on a significant amount of enforcement." If the market is to be "left 'unfettered,' as though it is separate from society," globalization is complicit with global capitalism and its intellectual hegemony.[37]

The model of Sassen's global city or Castells's megacity presupposes that all cities operate within global networks. The city is an expression of the technology of the present. The notion of the city as a machine is implicity created from modernist architectural paradigms of the twentieth century, and most often referred to at a domestic scale in Le Corbusier's idea of the house as a "machine for living in." It is arguable the city in the twentieth century was also conceived as a machine for living in. Following Futurism's declarations one hundred years ago, cities are today more closely aligned with natural processes than with paradigms of mechanical efficiency.

> They [the Metabolists] really believed in technology, in mass production; they believed in systematic urban infrastructure and growth . . . . [T]he Metabolists had no scepticism toward their utopia.
>
> Arata Isozaki[38]

In contrast with paradigms of mechanization, *Metabolism 1960: The Proposal for New Urbanism* was a momentary manifesto for a varied movement with an original argument, rooted in biological analogies of growth, adaptation, and regeneration. Noboru Kawazoe's introduction to the book announced the name of the movement, "Metabolism," and claimed "human society as a vital process—a continuous development from atom to nebula." The reasoning for using the biological term "metabolism" was the group's belief that "design and technology should be a denotation of human vitality."[39] The Metabolists were responding to the contingencies of accelerated urbanization in Japan, and their vision of the future city was one in which "advanced technology exist[ed] in parallel with an untainted nature—a techno-utopia."[40]

The western cousins of the Metabolists, Archigram, also assigned technology a supporting role in a new model of networked urbanism. Although not constructed, the group's *Plug-In City* of 1965 has had considerable influence on the conception of the city as an essential armature, which the inhabitants' interactions change in small, locally specific interventions. Cedric Price's *Fun Palace* (1960–1965), a "paper" project for an obsessively programmed urban interior, was one of the precedents which propelled Archigram's fascination with programmatic complexity, self-organization, mobility, and technology in the quickly changing culture of the 1960s. Half a century ago, architects were projecting a city—and even a world—in which inhabitants were imagined occupying the "nodes and links" of network systems, where "you never leave the structure of the web."[41]

> If cities can generate emergent intelligence, a macrobehaviour spawned by a million micromotives, what higher level form is currently taking shape among the routers and fiber-optic lines of the internet?
>
> Steven Johnson[42]

In the midst of the current technological revolution, the information revolution, we are entering an age of "near-infinite connectedness."[43] Anthony Burke delineates three types of linked but distinct networks: "network as symbol, network as organizational diagram or [network as] geometry," each participating in a schizophrenia of freedom and control, and the myth of a relation between the connectivity of networks and democracy.[44] Networks are not neutral; they have power to connect, deliver, inform, propagate, control, and censor. Networks create new forms of collective organization. It is through the emergence of bottom-up organization that the stasis and apparent solidity of institutions could be mobilized through the interaction of a multitude of agents, who possess the power, if not to overthrow institutions, at least to transform them.

The increasing ubiquity and accelerated speed of transmission of information contribute to the globalization of urban culture. Networks pervade the way we now think about the world as intelligent and highly distributed. Our understanding of network phenomena, such as the interdependent ecology of a rainforest, informs our understanding of the connectedness of the global capitalist network, which libertarians insist is natural and organic. As a development of the cybernetic theories of the 1940s and 1950s, today's networks are assumed to be "self-generating, self-organizing, self-sustaining systems" which function through multiple feedback loops, and "induce effects of interference, amplification, and resonance." Networks, despite their dynamics and interactivity, "create local stability and maintain internal homeostasis in far-from-equilibrium conditions."[45] For over half a century architects, through seminal projects such as eastern and western Metabolism, have been trying "to draw a life in which everything is computerized," "as if people actually live in the circuitry itself."[46] The hyperconnected, mobile, adaptive, and responsive condition of today's urbanity, facilitiated by information networks, instantaneously connects us to all cities, everywhere.

In the last century, modernization was equated with the application of technology to resolve, even to "cure," problems, bring efficiency as a hallmark of technocracy, and to innovate and make progress. The counterpoints to this legacy, deeply ingrained in the ways in which modernist positivism unfolded, are still taking shape. New technologies intensify existing networks or supplant them with new systems in today's increasingly distributed forms of intelligence.

In the past the city was a symbol of the world. Now the world has become a city.[47]

1.2 THE EDGE OF CHAOS

Despite a latent and lingering belief in utopianism, the city can no longer be conceived of or maintained as an ideal construct. The complexities of urban change should be facilitated rather than constrained by the mechanisms of masterplanning. We now understand the city as complex, dynamic, and inherently difficult to manage and control. In effect, cities in the twenty-first century will benefit from the embracing of complexity, as opposed to the persistence of the notion that planning prevents the apparent chaos of unplanned urban growth. How, then, do we manage change and evolution while also investigating the design implications of the greater cultural, social, economic, and environmental endurance of cities and buildings? Cities can endure for great intervals, but how does history explain their fragility and unpredictablility? Cities are complex entities that are never entirely stable, always in a state of flux, growing, decaying, or dying. The paradigm of the city as a machine is increasingly being rejected in favor of biodynamic analogies.

> There is no such thing as the ideal city, but there are such things as technical criteria and there are such things as causative natural conditions.
>
> Frei Otto[48]

We lack theories to explain the rise and fall of ancient cities, or the growth, establishment, and decline of past empires. Many cities, however, have "repeatedly outlived the military empires that seemingly destroyed them forever," including, for example, Damascus, Baghdad, Jerusalem, and Athens.[49] The seeming endurance of urbanity meant many cities were not abandoned in the face of war, destruction, or decimation, due to the constant flow of rural populations flooding to the city.

This was true of biblical cities and of European cities in the middle ages, and in the new world of the Americas.

Stability, as understood in classicism and neoclassicism, depends on fixed part-to-whole relationships. This can be exemplified by the relations between building elements (columns, architraves, pediments, and so on), as well as by the building blocks of the city—buildings—to the city itself. By their nature cities seem stable, yet history proves the contrary. Steven Johnson raises the question "why cities took so long to emerge, and why history includes such long stretches of urban decline."[50] Remarkably, Rome, the population of which peaked at one million inhabitants, was repeatedly sacked, and by the eighth century had a meagre population of seventeen thousand.

What paradigms, if any, can be pursued to generate, guide, and explain tomorrow's urbanism? In a "conversation" between Koolhaas and Kwinter, in various texts over several years, the city was retheorized as by located at the edge of chaos. If there is to be a "new urbanism" or even the possibility of a future for urbanism, Koolhaas asserted in 1994, "it will not be based on the twin fantasies of order and omnipotence."[51] Kwinter follows up to explicate a "new" urbanism, as "a *soft* urbanism, a liquid urbanism of grazing, perpetually interacting forces, free of hard control, certainty, predictability or permanence."[52] In his *Requiem for the City at the End of the Millennium*, Kwinter asks, "What do we get in return for the surrender of control?" It seems mankind is engaging in a last-ditch effort to gain control and mastery, but instead of continuing the quest to conquer nature mankind needs to learn to ride with dynamics, and to design flexible and adaptable control systems to engage with a world in flux. Deleuze credits Foucault as the first to say that "we're moving away from disciplinary societies . . . toward control societies that no longer operate by confining people but through continuous control and instant communication."[53] The discourses surrounding electronic data collection systems, sensing and feedback systems, smart materials, intelligence, and interactivity and responsiveness all pertain to a "control society" in which information is "immediately fed back into the system" in real time. Urban planning as a regulatory regime urgently needs to catch up to this networked, technologically proficient, more supple and adaptable model of control.[54]

> The reawakening of the vital and the organic in every department undermines the authority of the purely mechanical . . . . The clue to modern technology was the displacement of the organic and the living with the artificial and the mechanical. Within technology itself the process, in many departments, is being reversed: we are returning to the organic. At all events, we no longer regard the mechanical as all-embracing and all-sufficient.
>
> Lewis Mumford, 1934[55]

Aristotle's philosophy can be thought of as being more akin to biology than mathematics. Whereas Plato's understanding of the polis was based on stable hierarchies which resisted change, Aristotle understood the city through an analogy of the diversity of species and the wonder of life. For Aristotle, the ideality of the city "was not a rationally abstract form to be arbitrarily imposed on the community: it was rather a form already potential in the very nature of species, needing only to be brought out and developed."[56] The notion of controlled growth in Aristotle's musings is akin to concepts in biology for limits on the size of the parts or whole of an organism. Greek colonization struggled with the limits of the land and resources available to feed its population, and begs the question whether there are natural limits to the city. Given today's expanding urban population and the reliance on resources from far beyond the confines of the city, the issue of limits and controlled growth is now a moot one.

Kisho Kurokawa believed Metabolism aimed to make sense of "the shift from a mechanical to a biodynamic age."[57] At the same time, in Europe, visionary architects were speculating on the ways in which technology could become more lifelike. Yona Friedman's *Ville Spatiale* (1958) hovered above the natural earth as a three-dimensional freeform city in the sky, while Konrad Wachsmann proposed a modular model of organic growth, and Constant Nieuwenhuys' *New Babylon* (1959–1974) aimed to "put an end to the separation of city and landscape" in a new symbiosis. The massive challenges of the damage to the world's natural ecology demand such a sensibility.

A mechanistic paradigm of order can be seen as an effect of the repercussions of the origins of modern science, starting with Descartes in the mid-seventeenth century.[58] Through the isolation of a physical process its analytical basis can be summarized, or reduced, to a machine-like linear mapping which behaves according to specific rules. We have been witnessing a remarkable yet slow transformation throughout the twentieth century, a "superseding of the physics model of space and the adopting of a biological model of explanation."[59] Fascination with the complexity sciences and natural sciences was preceded by postmodern reactions to an ancient yet persistent, mechanistic view of matter, one with its origins in the seventeenth century, but called upon to act as the conceptual foundation of modernism. Science does not fail to provide a model of the world to adequately explain how things form and how they work, but the science of modernism was still propped up by old science. Positioning design as part of what we identify as nature explicates the fundamentally intertwined order of the world. Nothing comes into being without association with other systems or a context. A particular order is therefore dependent on an environment providing the specific conditions for it, and processes in nature do not follow linear paths toward fixed, uniform outcomes each time the rules are played out. Rather, emergence, though not life in the strict sense of living biological systems, helps to explain how nothing is unconnected, yet not everything is connected.

Less concerned with the social logic of stable, long-lasting spaces than with the phenomena of urban transformation, the challenge for architects and urbanists in this century will be to specify and instrumentalize the theoretical and practical apparatus with which to confront massive urban change, and to chart new, as-yet unforeseen trajectories. The associative logic of urbanism is a product of the capacity for urban self-organization, amid the hierarchies which plan and maintain cities as a defense against descent into chaos and disappearance.

1.3 THE ASSOCIATIVE LOGIC OF URBANISM

Historically, the tools used to shape the city evolved in parallel with the changing contingencies of the city. Military defenses help us to understand the evolution of relational urban form, and the changing nature of urbanism raises questions of the city's complex, adaptable—and organic—attributes.

What is presented here is not a unified theory of the city, nor an approach to urbanism which can be applied ubiquitously, yet this thesis has its basis in recognizing the relationality between global tendencies and specific, localized attributes. The city is now located at the juncture of technology and culture, networks and populations, interfaces and information.

> Houses make a town, but citizens make a city.
>
> Jean-Jacques Rousseau[60]

Man is a tool-making species, and civilization has been an ongoing construction project since the making of primitive utensils, tools for agriculture, and machines which facilitate labor. The growth of cities is paralleled by the development of machines and tools. Karl Marx argues for the historic mission of the inventions of each particular era having a deep connection to the social order.

The relationship of technology to nature and culture can be explicated through a history of war machinery. Manuel De Landa notes the origins of the "arms race between projectiles and defensive walls" can be traced back to developments in agriculture in the Neolithic Period, when defenses were built to protect surplus food. The citadel, burg, or walled city as a self-contained round plan has a long history in Europe, with the form developing as a means of defense. The parametrics of military defensibility were for perhaps eight thousand years the principal criteria used in the building of the perimeter of a city.[61] The origins of the planning of cities can thus be found in the evolution of military plans as the basis for city design. Leonardo da Vinci recapitulated and consolidated art, science, technology, and military engineering: his manifold inventions adapted existing technologies for new applications; the late fifteenth century saw artillery technology advance, rendering the previously impregnable fortified city vulnerable to invasion and decimation; and the "arms race" is evident in the plastic variation and evolution of city plans in the sixteenth century.

Many urbanists have argued for the delimitation of neighborhood units and functional precincts based on vocation and interest.[62] Medieval European towns had a basis for such limits of size, arrived at naturally through the motivation for self-sufficiency of the town. Medieval towns were highly distributed, with their separation based on pedestrian limits from market towns. They were also small. The period of concentration around larger cities was to follow in the eighteenth and nineteenth centuries. The medieval city articulates a fundamental break with the countryside. The city becomes artificial, through ever greater fortifications, "thus contributing to separating the city from the countryside by a no-man's-land of glacis and moats," infrastructure which would shield the city not only from invasion but from rural life as well.[63]

The development of larger armies in the Europe of empire, in the eighteenth century, was facilitated by the standardization of the production of weaponry, facilitated by the new techniques of machining in factories.[64] As the seemingly impregnable ramparts of European cities were removed in the nineteenth century, in response to the diminished threat of invasion and the vulnerability of the walls to modern means of warfare, the inherent associative logic of cities morphed again. Throughout history, military technologies and their associated dictation of defensive spatial positioning have informed the organization of the city. Given the removal of threats of invasion from the boundaries of cities to longer distances away, or to within, the notion of intelligence, as misunderstood as it still is, has invaded all aspects of urbanity.[65]

In the case of Paris, Georges-Eugène Haussmann intervened in the largely evolved medieval urban fabric with the superimposition of a new network of grand avenues. Haussmann's vast reorganization of the city's infrastructure in the latter part of the nineteenth century was motivated partly by hygiene, sanitation, and safety, but also by the military objective of preventing invasion by enabling vast troop movements within the city, and control of the population through greater surveillance and presence of the authorities on the ground. Dominance, power and control may not have been the explicitly stated goals of Paris's transformation, but they were undeniably the effects which it gave rise to, and Haussmann became the archetypical planner.[66] In another case of militarily motivated urbanism, Beijing's series of ring roads was conceived to control movement toward the political centre of the city, the area surrounding the ancient seat of the emperors, the Forbidden City. Thus advances in military technology have shaped the "norm" in many civilian—and civic—systems. The notion that the city developed for military and economic reasons misses out an essential component, however: it is the sharing of culture, or for that matter the evolution of culture, which is the city's great achievement.

After the expansion beyond defensive city walls, an interconnected Europe was forecast by Arturo Soria y Mata in his concept of the *ciudad lineal* (linear city) in 1892—a "roadtown" based on a perpendicular street grid laid out along an inter-urban or even transcontinental network, conceived as potentially connecting all of Europe. As an inadvertent prototype for urban sprawl along the strip, the linear city may seem extreme, yet nearly all rapidly growing cities expanded along railway lines, and later along roads.

Though facilitated by the proliferation of affordable cars and the seeming abundance of petrol, it is now well known that the U.S. military's evacuation plans for the centers of cities in the event of nuclear war contributed to the sprawl of suburbia, away from downtown city centers. Wright's *Broadacre City* concept, first published in his 1932 book *The Disappearing City*, depicted the sprawl of America across the expansive Jeffersonian grid. Hilberseimer's 1949 project *The City in the Landscape* sees the city from the air, as a "continuous system of relational flows" more than a composition of objects such as buildings and land subdivisions.[67]

Conventional contemporary masterplanners continue to deploy two-dimensional plans as a basis on which to pursue stability and order. The intention in this book is to conceive of a four-dimensional mode of "planning" in which time is the context for the negotiation of a set of dynamic processes. Inevitably the notion of the organic arises. Over a century ago, Patrick Geddes wrote on the organic, biological attributes of cities. While cities can transform with seeming lifelike behavior, it is questionable whether the city is indeed like an organism. The city as an organic entity is more than mere metaphor.[68] Expanding this narrative from architecture, which is presumed to be fixed and enduring, to the city, requires the metaphor of the organic to be not only convenient but also relevant.[69] The argument presented here does not contradict earlier formulations of the city as a living, changing entity, but rather supplements these. In the work of Ebenezer

Howard, Lewis Mumford, Frank Lloyd Wright, Jane Jacobs, Christopher Alexander, Aldo Rossi, the Krier brothers, and numerous others the paradigm of the organic is a persistent theme, initially as an undercurrent in modernism, and can serve to guide urbanism in a century of massive urban change.

Beyond simplistic metaphors, the behaviors of the mechanisms deployed in the city are sensitive, responsive, and adaptive.[70] One of the central questions raised in later chapters is the inherent, paradoxical debate between notions of "collective intelligence" as a means of understanding and producing urbanism, versus a single masterplanner or designer responsible for urbanism's present and future. The city is a new kind of man-made nature, increasingly understood and modelled according to the associative logic of natural and biological systems.

NOTES

1 > L. Mumford (1961) *The City in History* (San Diego: Harvest/HBJ Book), 58.

2 > Mumford, *The City in History*, 13.

3 > K. Davis (1965) "The Urbanisation of the Human Population," in *The City Reader*, eds. R.T. LeGates and F. Stout (London: Routledge), 20.

4 > F. Otto (2009) *Occupying and Connecting: Thoughts on Territories and Spheres of Influence with Particular Reference to Human Settlement* (Stuttgart: Edition Axel Menges), 58.

5 > V. Gordon Childe (1925) *The Dawn of European Civilization* (London: Kegan Paul).

6 > R.T. LeGates and F. Stout, (1996) "Introduction to Part One: The Evolution of Cities," in *The City Reader*, ed. R.T. LeGates and F. Stout (London: Routledge), 31.

7 > N. Schoenauer (1982) *6000 Years of Housing* (New York: Norton & Co.), 9.

8 > J. Attali (2001) "The Roman System, or the Generic in All Times and Tenses," in *Mutations*, ed. R. Koolhaas, S. Boeri, S. Kwinter, N. Tazi, and H.U. Obrist (Barcelona: Actar), 22.

9 > Vitruvius (1914) *The Ten Books on Architecture*, trans. M.H. Morgan (Cambridge, MA: Harvard).

10 > N. Schoenauer (1982) *6000 Years of Housing* (New York: Norton & Co.), 12.

11 > J. Burry and M. Burry (2010) *The New Mathematics of Architecture* (New York: Thames & Hudson), 158.

12 > J. Rykwert (1976) *The Idea of a Town: The Anthropology of Urban Form in Rome, Italy and the Ancient World* (Cambridge, MA: MIT), 188.

13 > A. Andraos, R. El-Samahy, P. Heyda, et al. (2001) "How to Build a City: Roman Operating System," in *Mutations*, ed. R. Koolhaas, S. Boeri, S. Kwinter, N. Tazi, and H.U. Obrist (Barcelona: Actar), 11.

14 > P. Geddes (1915) *Cities in Evolution: An Introduction to the Town Planning Movement and to the Study of Civics* (London: Williams).

15 > D.G. Shane (2011) *Urban Design Since 1945: A Global Perspective* (London: Wiley), 28.

16 > L. Mumford (1934) *Technics and Civilisation* (New York: Harvest), 108–110.

17 > F. Otto (2009) *Occupying and Connecting: Thoughts on Territories and Spheres of Influence with Particular Reference to Human Settlement* (Stuttgart: Edition Axel Menges), 55.

18 > A. Picon (2010) "Nature, Infrastructures, and the Urban Condition," in *Ecological Urbanism*, ed. M. Mostafavi and G. Doherty (Baden: Lars Müller), 520.

19 > L. Mumford (1986) *The Lewis Mumford Reader*, ed. D.L. Millner (Athens, GA: University of Georgia Press), 231.

20 > R.T. LeGates and F. Stout (2011) "Editor's Introduction," in *The City Reader*, ed. R.T. LeGates and F. Stout (London: Routledge), 599.

21 > J. Gottmann (1961) *Megalopolis: The Urbanized Northeastern Seaboard of the United States* (New York: The Twentieth Century Fund).

22 > D.G. Shane (2011) *Urban Design Since 1945: A Global Perspective* (London: Wiley), 22, 140.

23 > Shane, *Urban Design Since 1945*, 254.

24 > Shane, *Urban Design Since 1945*, 254.

25 > S. Sassen (2001) "The Global City: Introducing a Concept and its History," in *Mutations*, ed. R. Koolhaas, S. Boeri, S. Kwinter, N. Tazi, and H.U. Obrist (Barcelona: Actar), 105.

26 > N. Brenner and R. Kiel (2011) "From Global Cities to Globalised Urbanisation," in *The City Reader*, ed. R.T. LeGates and F. Stout (London: Routledge), 600.

27 > S. Johnson (2001) *Emergence: The Connected Lives of Ants, Brains, Cities and Software* (London: Penguin), 106.
28 > S. Sassen (2011) "The Impact of the New Technologies and Globalisation on Cities," in *The City Reader*, ed. R.T. LeGates and F. Stout (London/New York: Routledge), 556.
29 > S. Sassen (2001) "The Global City: Introducing a Concept and Its History," in *Mutations*, ed. R. Koolhaas, S. Boeri, S. Kwinter, N. Tazi, and H.U. Obrist (Barcelona: Actar), 105.
30 > M. Castells (1996) *The Rise of the Network Society* (Oxford: Blackwell), 380.
31 > Castells, *The Rise of the Network Society*, 398.
32 > S. Shaviro (2003) *Connected, or What it Means to Live in the Network Society* (Minnesota: Regents), 134.
33 > C. Waldheim and A. Berger (2008) "Logistics Landscape," *Landscape Journal* 27, no. 2: 220.
34 > Castells, *The Rise of the Network Society*, 151.
35 > S. Sassen (2001) "The Global City: Introducing a Concept and its History," in *Mutations*, ed. R. Koolhaas, S. Boeri, S. Kwinter, N. Tazi, and H.U. Obrist (Barcelona: Actar), 113.
36 > S. Sassen (2008) "Disaggregating the Global Economy," in *Shanghai Transforming*, ed. I. Gil (Barcelona: Actar), 84.
37 > S. Kwinter (2011) *Requiem for the City at the End of the Millennium* (Barcelona: Actar), 31–33.
38 > Quoted in H.U. Obrist (2011) "Introduction," in *Project Japan*, R. Koolhaas and H.U. Obrist (Köln: Taschen), 18.
39 > R. Koolhaas and H.U. Obrist (2011) *Project Japan* (Köln: Taschen), 187.
40 > Obrist, "Introduction," 18.
41 > M. Wigley (2007) "The Architectural Brain," in *Network Practices: New Strategies in Architecture and Design*, ed. A. Burke and T. Tierney (New York: Princeton), 36.
42 > Johnson, *Emergence*, 113.
43 > Johnson, *Emergence*, 113.
44 > A. Burke (2007) "Redefining Network Paradigms," in *Network Practices: New Strategies in Architecture and Design*, ed. A. Burke and T. Tierney (New York: Princeton), 56.
45 > S. Shaviro, *Connected*, 10.
46 > Wigley, "The Architectural Brain," 36.
47 > Mumford, *The City in History*, 74–75.
48 > F. Otto, *Occupying and Connecting*, 110.
49 > Mumford, *The City in History*, 13.
50 > Johnson, *Emergence*, 110.
51 > R. Koolhaas (1995) "Whatever Happened to Urbanism?" in *S, M, L, XL*, OMA, R. Koolhaas, and B. Mau (Rotterdam: 010).
52 > Kwinter, *Requiem for the City*, 81.
53 > G. Deleuze and F. Guattari (1988) *A Thousand Plateaus* (London: Althlone), 174.
54 > Shaviro, *Connected*, 3.
55 > Mumford, *Technics and Civilisation*, 372.
56 > Mumford, *The City in History*, 184.
57 > In Koolhaas and Obrist, *Project Japan*, 58.
58 > A. Perez-Gomez (1986) *The Origins of Modern Science* (Cambridge: MIT Press).
59 > Kwinter, *Requiem for the City*, 74.
60 > Quoted in Mumford, *The City in History*, 93.
61 > Otto, *Occupying and Connecting*, 41.
62 > Mumford, *The City in History*, 310.
63 > A. Picon (2010) "Nature, Infrastructures, and the Urban Condition," in *Ecological Urbanism*, ed. M. Mostafavi and G. Doherty (Baden: Lars Müller), 520.
64 > Mumford, *Technics and Civilisation*, 90–93.
65 > Burry and Burry, The New Mathematics of Architecture, 11.
66 > Mumford, *The City in History*, 172.
67 > C. Waldheim (2010) "Weak Work," in *Ecological Urbanism*, ed. M. Mostafavi and G. Doherty (Baden: Lars Müller), 118.
68 > S. Marshall (2009) *Cities, Design, Evolution* (New York: Routledge), 124.
69 > M. Burry (2011) *Scripting Cultures: Architectural Design and Programming* (Chichester: Wiley), 159.
70 > Marshall, *Cities, Design, Evolution*, 124.

CHAPTER 2

MARINA LATHOURI > PROJECTIVE ARCHITECTURES

THE QUESTION OF BORDERS IN A CONNECTED WORLD

The question of forecasting and regulating urban change and growth in order to manage the indeterminacy of forces—economic, political, cultural, social, environmental—is not new; it is a historical process immanent to the development and planning of the modern city. So is its connection with the idea of mobility and connectivity. However, the principle of flow, resting on the dynamic nature of contemporary processes of economic and cultural activity, which often engender novel forms of citizenship and urbanity, transforms the city, paradoxically, into a permanent frontier zone. Though the problem of the frontier has always arisen in the political economy of urban territoriality, at a time when the urban enclave and the rise of global alternatives coexist, multiple and changing demarcations of the singular and the multiple, the individual and the collective, the private, the public, the national, and the transnational emerge. It is in precisely these internal territories that the various regimes of the architectural project, as unfolded in the economy of the new design technologies, can play a role in the articulation rather than management of indeterminacy.

A particular challenge in the work of identifying contemporary dynamics and practices is that they are too often absorbed into conceptual frameworks which obscure their historical settings. The search for design methodologies and techniques which embed the dimension of time and the element of change is not new. That is to say, the attempt to forecast and regulate urban change and growth in order to manage the indeterminacy of forces—economic, political, cultural, social, environmental—is a historical process immanent to the development and planning of the modern city. In fact, this was precisely the meaning of the term "planning" in the nineteenth century: to delineate future developments within a present plan. The term was associated with the French terms *distribuer*, meaning "to apportion between several," and *disposer*, "to arrange, to put things in a certain order." These definitions may seem simple, but their implications are complex. The first is that planning, as a discipline of space, embraces different scales—everything, from the tiniest physical entity to an entire territory, can be arranged, put in a certain order; one can claim that the effects of such ordering are potentially global.[1] The second implication is that any "disposition" is an active process, not just the analysis of what happens. That is, it is at once an analysis of what happens and a program for what should happen, to bring about what Ludwig Hilberseimer described as "the transition toward a desired end."[2] Framing this way of conceiving and programming things in a more contemporary manner, it accommodates the transfer of existing arrangements (and old capabilities) into new organizing logics.

Reflection on the town was historically situated in a space of geographical, economic, and administrative relations, and not solely on the basis of the symbolic and aesthetic relationship between a smaller, geometrical figure, which is a kind of architectural module, and the territory. It was in the nineteenth century, however, that the city came to be thought of as an open and dynamic system, its planning essentially linked to patterns of distribution of land and population, and forms of spatial organization over a larger territory—in short, there occurred the formalization of a type of urban development. It is worth recalling at this point the study *Teoria General de la Urbanización* (*General Theory of Urbanization*, 1867) which Ildefonso Cerdá wrote to support his 1859 project for the Barcelona Extension, and in which the term "urbanization" first appeared. The objective was to develop a plan with no definite limits that would embrace the entire region while outlining the future growth of the city of Barcelona. In these terms, planning became the focus of endless discussions that form a broad field of knowledge, made up of a complex of disciplines and practices ranging from statistics to sociology, economics to geography, science of finance to administration, design to engineering. The CIAM debates on the city (1928–1959), to take another example, placed themselves squarely within this field of knowledge. An interplay of spatial and temporal scales runs through the negotiation of relationships between different programmatic categories such as "typical dwelling unit," "urban organism," "region-city" and "ecological field." The primary rationale in these categories, expanding from the scale of the intimate to the scale of geography, is "capitalizing a territory" over time rather than structuring space contained within a defined programmatic (functional) field.[3] The latter understanding usually supports the readings and critiques of these debates. Yet, in principle, they indicate spatial arrangements that connect the individual to a number of multiplicities, systems of inhabitation to processes of production of a larger territory. Leaving aside the strictly utopian aspect of these arguments and projects, it is interesting that a number of specifically urban agencies and variables appear as the fundamental problem of design, which aims to formulate "principles which give the evolving organism consistency and unity" and a "method of applying these principles."[4]

The idea of the spatial, economic and social effectiveness of territorial distribution and urban structuring has always been linked to the idea of mobility and connectivity. The problem of circulation has been the most instrumental in planning, and the imagery of flow, integrating a natural economy, efficiency, and potentially the question of construction, its most desirable effect. Though the structuring function of both involves fastening together and mutually reinforcing a multiplicity of territories and operations, circulation systems and flows are inscribed within these territories and therefore involve geographical and social divisions.

In a more precise sense, the principle of flow, resting on the open and dynamic nature of contemporary processes of economic and cultural activity, which often engender novel forms of citizenship and urbanity, transforms the city, paradoxically, into a permanent frontier zone. This is not to repeat that there are invisible borders everywhere and nowhere. But implicit in the urban imagery of flow is not a smooth continuity which only connects, but the ceaseless moving of the boundaries, which actually represents a very literal disruption of the relation between people and territory, between a system of legality and territory.

Continuing urban growth, on the one hand, has prompted elaborate arguments on economic policies, new organizational models, environmental strategies, and sustainable development patterns. On the other, digital technologies of communication are forming new social domains and knowledge spaces. Yet, considering the characteristics and implications of both, there seems to be a lack of reflection on the fundamental question of the city as the constitution of a public (social) spatio-temporality and potentially a political space (although it may be difficult even to arrive at a current definition of the term "political"). Before we embark, however, on any programmatic act, we need to work out and develop the conceptual practices which will capture the distinctiveness of, and thereby advance, the new design methodologies and novel forms of practice. In particular, within what tends to emerge and operate as a transboundary, often notional, public sphere, which can bypass administrative and institutional apparatus at the urban and (inter)national level, to reposition the question of the border as a critical actor, as a means to articulate the intersection and interaction of these technologies with social, place-bound, and other material conditions, is crucial.

This question—the definition and marking of the border—is unavoidably engendered in the political economy of urban territoriality. A significant example is the role that *termini*, which could be translated as "boundary stones," played in the early foundation rites of the city of Rome. These stones served not only to mark the boundary of a property but also to demarcate the limit, the *limen*, within which all things were under the authority of Rome and therefore subject to Roman law. Thus the stones in effect delimited the sovereign field.

At a time when the urban enclave, a form of withdrawal from the collective, and the rise of global alternatives coexist, it seems that the dynamic nature of urbanity is not "deprived of any limit" in its processes. In contrast, multiple and changing demarcations of the singular and the multiple, the individual and the collective, the globalized local and the localized global emerge. Thus within the constantly negotiated transactions between private property, public spaces, corporate domains, material arrangements, and systems of regulation, the need for a strengthening through articulation of borders and thresholds—economic, juridical, social, cultural, and spatial—is fundamental. It is precisely in these internal territories that the various regimes of the architectural project, as unfolded in the economy of the new design technologies, can play a role in the articulation rather than the management of indeterminacy.

NOTES

1 > See Pierre Merlin and Francoise Choay, eds. (1988) *Dictionnaire de l'Urbanisme et de l'Aménagement* (Paris: Presses Universitaires de France).

2 > Ludwig Hilberseimer (1955) *The Nature of Cities* (Chicago: Paul Theobald), 257.

3 > Michel Foucault (2007) *Security, Territory, Population: Lectures at the Collège de France, 1977–1978*, ed. Michel Senellart (New York: Picador, first published Paris: Editions du Seuil/Gallimard, 2004), 17.

4 > Alison and Peter Smithson (1967) *Urban Structuring* (London: Studio Vista), 29.

CHAPTER 3

CONVERSATION 1

DANA CUFF (DC) WITH TOM VEREBES (TV)

TV Dana, I would firstly like to thank you for your enthusiasm to have this conversation. Our planet is becoming urbanized faster and to a greater extent than ever, and I would like to hear your thoughts on the most effective current and past models of urbanization, citing their successes and even their failures. I'm keen to discuss the extent to which masterplanning can manage and, perhaps, even forecast the future. Given your expertise as an urbanist, can you reveal whether you define yourself as a masterplanner?

DC I have in fact publicly stated that masterplanning is dead, so the last thing I would call myself is a masterplanner. From your question though, it seems you are interrogating the concept of masterplanning more than a singular homogenous image. The era of the masterplan was the modernist era, which had demonstrated the limits and possibilities of that way of thinking about the city. Neither have the models that have evolved since then taken advantage of the strengths that masterplanning might offer, and nor have they formulated a strong enough alternative to stand against masterplanning. It is interesting now, in particular, to question the masterplan, partly because of rapid urbanization but also because the models pursued after modernism have been so flawed, the most well-articulated of those being the new urbanist prescriptive model of form.

TV Can you elaborate more on the modernist model of the masterplan?

DC In the modernist period, the strengths and limitations of the masterplan were made very apparent. To say masterplanning is dead is an intentional overstatement. The notion that a centralized authority can pursue and implement a single goal is patently false. No masterplan has ever been implemented, and that in and of itself should be an indication of a problem with masterplanning. So to refer to your first question concerning the most effective methods of masterplanning, and if by that you mean the most effective way to implement a plan, then I would say there are none. If, however, you're talking about other goals that you might have through planning strategies, regimes, or processes, we could probably find interesting, effective models.

TV We share the disbelief that we can fully manage and control an entire design process of urbanism to completion, to a teleological end. Whether the term "masterplanning" is too loaded, we still need to design for the future and to manage change effectively. I believe the tools of conventional masterplanning are incapable of managing the fundamental indeterminacy of the ways in which cities develop, grow, and change. Even the daily complexities of interactions within a city can no longer be represented nor forecasted by static images. This raises several questions. To what extent, then, are we able to design and forecast with some level of certainty within a world which is quite indeterminate? How can we harness complexity and begin to manage change differently than with the models and processes of the twentieth century, which bias the finality of a design outcome? In which ways do you think the methodologies now available to us have potential to bridge relations between top-down regulatory planning processes and more bottom-up emergent conditions?

DC I think there is a false dichotomy between the so-called top-down masterplan, which has a quasifascist level of control, versus the bottom-up emergent model, which is a populist, anything-goes model with no need for architecture or urbanism. Architects and urban designers more specifically have an important role to play in formulating the way in which a city will grow and change. The way I've been working on this, in all the projects we take on at CityLab at UCLA, is through the umbrella structure of scenario planning. These are strategies which target the gap between the masterplan and bottom-up citizen-activism. This involves working with forces of interest from a number of ways, including economies, ecologies, or demographies, as a means to determine likely scenarios that could emerge in a particular city. What we always look for are the places where design can act as a lever that enables a different and better kind of city to emerge over time. It is this kind of structure that has some predictive value about economic, the environmental, and cultural systems, which would make one scenario more likely than another.

TV Multiple scenarios for urban design and city planning is an approach which aims to confront the ideological bankruptcy of masterplanning, while also not giving in entirely to a laissez-faire mode of urban development. If we surrender all control, the complexity of the city will overwhelm. Here lies a paradox, because all cities have some degree of planning. Another paradox involves the process and sequence of how cities are built and undergo change in time—whether incrementally and slowly, or in totality and quickly. If we unravel the short history of the evolution of cities, which is between 6,000 to 12,000 years, we find cities inevitably adapt by remaining responsive to the demands of the forces that shape them, either from bottom up or from top down. Here, though, I find a paradox between the evolutionary logic of the formation and accretion of cities, to the parallel necessity for endurance of the city's material fabric. Within today's short-term investment models, cities and buildings are not built to last very long. Do you see this as problematic?

DC By contrasting the notion of a dynamic emergent city and endurance, do you literally mean cheap building techniques and the fact that they crumble, versus preservation?

TV This paradox has different implications in different contexts and material histories in the world. Perhaps in Europe or North America, to argue for the need for cities to endure seems that of the conservator's prerogative for material and cultural continuity. Within the rapidly urbanizing context of Asia, particularly in China, buildings are poorly built in a model of investment with equally short-term vision. In China's vast urbanization, construction standards have generally led to buildings having a short design life, indicating a distinct lack of material, and environmental and ecological sustainability.

DC You're right to distinguish between what's happening in different parts of the world. Los Angeles developed in what people consider to be unplanned growth, sprawl, and short-term thinking. I'm not sure how much I can speak to the parallel between China and the southwest of the U.S., as similarities in kind or in degree, but the way cities are growing in China seems like a totally new phenomenon. From an architectural perspective, and not that of an urbanist, the question for me is: What role does the material environment play, and design more particularly, in the tension between the expression of politics and economics, and urban transformation? Take for example the New York City grid, which came about from a decision by the city council in 1811 to restructure land in the city and provided a physical and formal infrastructure of the particular street pattern that New York adopted that then allowed for a variety of transformations for the next two hundred years. There are complaints about that grid but it turns out to have actually been flexible and adaptive, and had produced a captivating cosmopolitan form. Was that something that was predicted? It might be called a successful scenario model which looked at the farmland patterns to the north of Manhattan, but the grid was not seen initially as a way to create an urban design model, or as a machine for city building thereafter. People could grasp the political repercussions and they could see its economic advantages, despite the short-term economic disadvantages as it transformed property boundaries. There was also an ecological or environmental model built into the organization of streets and building plots. That seems to me not quite a masterplan but something like a scenario-form with material infrastructural components that have an ability to adapt within it. So the grid has been very enduring but also intrinsically flexible. To compare the New York City grid to the New Urbanist prescriptive form models, which are used more like deterministic masterplans, and are thus less capable of flexibility and cannot operate over the long periods of time which cities need to evolve. The problem of Mazdar in Abu Dhabi is the same as Seaside, ironically, because it lays down at a single moment in time the vision of what the city is intended to be, which is inherently inadequate, because there will inevitably be different economic and political conditions in the future. So instead of laying out a scaffolding or an infrastructural originating point, it lays out the entire formula.

TV We share a belief in the emergent nature of urbanism, however the new urbanists might argue for the exact opposite of your summary of the objectives of new urbanism. Traditional vernacular urban form grows incrementally, and the gradualism of this older urban model did have the openness you value in the Manhattan grid, or sprawl as an unplanned condition, which can indeed generate heterogeneity and grow and change gradually.

DC Let's be careful about any romantic models of vernacular urbanism because they are also planned, but the issue is the time increment of planning. Medieval or Renaissance walled cities were more strictly top down and absolutely formal than Brazilia or Chandigahr. The question to ask is: What is a proper increment of planning? In some of my recent projects I have been looking at how large-scale interventions in the city fit within existing urbanism, as a moderately utopian plan. For example, the public housing schemes or new-town planning of the 1950s, 60s and 70s in the United States and Europe dealt with increments which in my mind were clearly too big to lead to reasonable urban design formulations. As designers, we are condemned to try to operate at a large scale, yet we ought to be critical about scalar models in which you cannot make design material, formal, and architectural design propositions. Instead, we can formulate infrastructural and developmental scenarios, and strategies for subsequent development.

TV The grid has also had different manifestations in different parts of the world, arguably with mixed levels of success. If one contrasts the openness of the Jeffersonian grid in what it creates in the historic American context to the way in which the grid is used in China's contemporary urbanization, the rolling out of the megablock grid can be understood to bring homogeneity through overly standardized planning methods. Does the instrument of the grid overly delineate and segregate the disciplinary tasks of designers from that of planners?

DC I was making reference to the Manhattan grid from which to learn lessons, but instead let's talk about grids as infrastructural formations. The grid as is currently used in Chinese cities is a perfect case of the wrong infrastructure for what cities could become. In Albert Pope's work about the end of the city of form, the point is well taken that we haven't built a city in United States with the grid since World War Two. Automobile and vehicular infrastructure has very little resemblance to the romantic ideas that we had about nineteenth century cosmopolitanism. I'm interested at the moment about the future of infrastructure with the high-speed rail networks that are being planned across Europe, China, and the United States. If we think of the high-speed rail network as the contemporary equivalent of how Manhattan city council had thought about the grid in 1810, what kinds of new urban forms can grow around high-speed rail stops? My research has been concerned with scenarios of how particular cities might evolve with the arrival of the high-speed rail stations and what they would do to instigate positive urban effects. My experience of Xi'an [China], is where people walk for a mile and what you get is another identical giant block; another giant Walmart, Starbucks, eight stories of shopping, and it's unclear why one would ever leave that one block.

TV You are raising two kinds of forces of globalization, the first of which has been going on for hundreds of years, in the ways in which infrastructure connects people and cities. We are now connected through the flow of bits of information that allows for a conception of the city as instantaneously globalized. And the other kind of globalization you talked about, of which Walmart and Starbucks are emblematic, is the homogenization of the world. For one megablock in China to be identical to the next megablock is, I believe, deeply problematic. It is not clear to me whether this is rooted in the limits of the organizational model or whether homogeneous cities continue to be linked to a model of standardized production. I'm interested in how homogeneous urbanism can be countered through the ways in which architecture has embedded design and production methodologies aiming toward increasing heterogeneity. Computational tools and methods have permeated every architect's office, teaching studio, and research lab worldwide, but the ways in which we make cities and the kinds of cities we make have been less affected by computation. If we can make a distinction between a building and a city, or between an architect and an urbanist, how might you imagine city planning being altered by contemporary design and production technologies, which have become well rehearsed in architecture, but are as yet not fully tested in urbanism?

DC At the moment there is a fracture between computational models of urbanism and scenario planning, yet I see these eventually being complementary models. In computational urbanism it seems, at present, the notion of contingency can be better built in. In scenario planning, politics and economics are absolutely the contingencies that are understood to play a strong role and through design you can elucidate economic and ecological alternatives and contingencies. I recall joining your final reviews at the [Design Research Lab at the] AA years ago, and the models that were emerging were super interesting because they allow the visualization of urban algorithms that are so complex one could never have imagined them before. This is less strong in scenario planning, since the logic of representation is not so fundamentally built into the logic of the planning itself. In computational urbanism there is a bond between methods and representations, which is its strength. Now, the question is: Can you build in enough uncertainty and contingency in computational urbanism to avoid it becoming a gaming strategy, for instance? There are some interesting applications of this going on now in California related to various kinds of growth scenarios. In community planning models where, for instance, if you want fewer greenhouse gases and more public transportation, a series of diagrams about the city can be generated for people to make choices about. If you want everyone to live within a quarter mile of a park, the urban form can be constrained to evolve toward this goal. This kind of applied computational urbanism becomes less interesting in terms of design but is highly relevant in terms of promoting new debates about the city, if you think of the city, as I do, as political, economic, and design processes. I question, however, whether there is enough capability for idiosyncrasies in the current status of computation.

TV Dana, it is through communication infrastructures that we have connected our voices and thoughts, between Los Angeles and Hong Kong. I'm grateful for your time to discuss and debate models and methods of urbanism at this important juncture.

CHAPTER 4

TOM VEREBES >THE NEW NEW

This chapter selectively probes ancient and modern history for the successes and pitfalls of various models of urbanization, relating experiences in Europe, the Americas, the Middle East, and Asia. The industrial revolution brought about the standardization and mechanization of cities. Concepts of the new and the phenomenon of the instant city are recurrent, and the prevalence of the erasure of heritage and sprawling development are the warning signs of Modernist history repeating itself in China. The paradox of top-down planning alongside informal, emergent, and unintended urbanization is framed not as a crisis but as an opportunity to rethink masterplanning in the twenty-first century.

4.1 ANCIENT CHINA AND THE NEW

> The city, as one finds in history, is the point of maximum concentration for the power and culture of a community.
>
> Lewis Mumford[1]

In exploring the roots of modern Chinese urbanization, it is helpful to look at China "with blue eyes," meaning from the outside, as a foreigner.[2] Through a successful revolution in 1911, Sun Yat Sen defeated the Qing Dynasty to establish modern China. This first revolution marks the first of four prominent and turbulent eras of change in modern China. Throughout a history which is often forgotten, this ancient culture has confronted modernity again and again. In the twentieth century, and more than ever today, change is the only constant.

Before the twentieth century, two paradoxical tendencies are discernible in the history of the Chinese city: moving existing cities to new locations, and building entirely new cities from scratch. The imperial era in China gave rise to three millennia of building walled cities, symbolizing and ensuring state authority while exemplifying the will for insularity and permanence.[3] In a response not unique to China, as we have seen, the building, rebuilding, altering, and extending of city walls was carried out according to military, administrative, economic, demographic, and religious parameters specific to the country's development. From the seventeenth to nineteenth centuries, a great period of development of walled cities provided security and more effective governmental control.[4] The second tendency to note during the imperial era was for emperors and central and local governments to unilaterally remove entire cities to new locations, indicating a view of the city as impermanent, ephemeral, and open to radical change.[5]

In Mao's vast urbanization program, the *danwei*, or work unit, was the preeminent basis for organizing society, industry, in a low-rise model of insular, aggregate urbanism. Not wholly new, "the *danwei*'s spatial logic borrowed from 'ancestral' forms of Chinese urbanism—especially the courtyard house, which in turn miniaturized many of the spatial design principles seen in larger scale in Chinese walled cities."[6] At its peak, ninety percent of China lived in some form of collective work unit.

Fastforwarding to the turn of the millennium, it has taken China only two decades to urbanize a population and landmass equivalent to those of Europe, which had endured several centuries. The instant city is not an entirely new phenomenon. Former Chinese Communist Party Chairman Deng Xiaoping's infamous "one country, two systems," communist–capitalist hybrid has driven great cultural change over the last two decades. Although the ancient Chinese city was based on the emperor at the center of the universe, today's Chinese cities are far from centralized—in fact they are highly decentralized and laterally extensive. Even the courtyards of Hutong and Siheyuan housing were limited by walls dividing internal, private, domestic space from the public realm beyond. Today's Chinese cities have lost the boundaries demarcating what is inside and outside the city, private and public space, the urban and agricultural.

Liang Sicheng, whose efforts were central to the planning of modern China, argued for the preservation of China's heritage, protection of "the beautiful bodies" and "orderly disposition of her environmental settings," wishing to avoid destruction of the "integrity of the whole" by the introduction of "unharmonious things."[7] The Old and Dilapidated Housing Renewal (ODHR) program, initiated in the 1990s, sought to rehouse existing residents in situ, but the powerful economic forces of the times still got the better of Beijing's physical heritage. Between 1990 and 2002, an estimated forty percent of the Old City was erased. Demolition was unleashed for the sake of the new, with buildings conceived and executed for today, not tomorrow. The failure of urban renewal in America, for decades the mantra for slum clearance, has parallels in modern China, where in the last decade some of the imminently dispossessed residents became famous as "stubborn nails"—people who refused to leave their homes, drawing attention from all over China and the world, with viral internet photos of single remaining houses surrounded by vast construction pits.

If the rapid urbanization of today's China is without precedent, within China or anywhere else, what is the tradition upon which this urbanism is built? Is it Hong Kong or Singapore? Is the "Eurostyle" a passing phase or will it in due course create its own vernacular?[8]

> Architecture seems to be squirted against facades like sauce from a squeeze pack.
>
> Neville Mars, *The Chinese Dream*, 2008[9]

Xin Tian Di—literally, "New Heaven and Earth"—is a partial restoration and conversion of Li Long housing, mixed with some faux historic architectural interventions, in the French Concession in Shanghai. It is an urban phenomenon which has now been exported all over China. Despite Xin Tian Di being a postmodern stage set, its great achievement has been to "make history cool—and prove that reclaiming the past can be big business." Xin Tian Di is where the past can be consumed and the future remains in abeyance. Campanella summarizes Xin Tian Di as where "China goes to see the West and the West goes to see China, where the old go to see the future and the young to see the past."[10] Different to the top-down planning and investment model of Xin Tian Di, another model of urbanization is taking hold in Shanghai, in the district of Tai Kang Lu. A bottom-up model, Tai Kang Lu is an area of pedestrian alleyways in which government housing tenants sublet their properties (sometimes several times over) to owners of small restaurants, bars, galleries, and boutiques. Caught up in leisure and shopping, but also a generative regeneration, Tai Kang Lu is an expression of urban gradualism, a model of newness without erasure.

In the last decade Shanghai has expanded in a polycentric model of urban growth, with a series of nine satellite centers taking shape around the periphery of the city. Some of these "new towns," including Thames Town (England), German Town, and Swedish Town, are modelled on national architectural characteristics of pre-twentieth-century Europe. Although these efforts to model Shanghai's urban expansion on European historical models is misguided, the greater challenge for Chinese urbanization in the coming decades is to negotiate the clash between the forces of new urbanization and the historic fabric of Chinese cities, which has consistently been deemed obsolete, valueless vernacular residue, of which little remains today. Shanghai, largely due to its complicated colonial history, is today the preeminent locus in China for the negotiation of clichéd oppositions of east and west, old and new, history and the future, tradition and innovation. Unlike other colonial set-ups, where locals were confronted by one single invader and occupier, Shanghai's modern history is based on the presence of seven concurrent occupying nations, from the nineteenth until the first half of the twentieth centuries.[11]

What is the character of wholly new cities in China? While gridded planning of streets and subdivisions has its roots in the ancient world, the specificity of the grid to imperial city planning must be clarified before dismissing it from a western perspective. Its key principles include "orientation to the cardinal compass points; symmetrical rectilinear layout with a palace complex at the center; a north-south cardinal axis or 'ritual way'."[12] Modern China is made by the ubiquity of grids. The two-dimensional plane of the ground plan is used to order plans based on infrastructural hierarchies, "megablock" land subdivisions, buildings, residual spaces and landscapes. With respect to the instrumentality of the plan, it is not an implicit instrument of planning but rather a means of mapping the current and projective state of the city in its primitive, reduced form, and, in turn, it is both an analytical device for understanding spatial relations and the ultimate form of representation of the city.

As an urban subdivisional, massing, and programmatic typology, the megablock is reliant on vehicular transport and most often its organization is based on highway arteries, local infrastructure, and a disconnected interior. The megablock is often comprised of "disconnected big box malls, stores and towers, behind which low rise development" creates isolated enclaves.[13] Deeply embedded as it is in patterns of land procurement and investment on a large scale, the subdivision of Chinese cities into megablocks means megabucks for both suppliers of and investors in land. As organizational models and mechanisms for planning, the grid and the megablock seem adequate as ubiquitous and general tools, yet inadequate to project the specificities of the vast scale of China's future urbanism.

4.2 URBAN EUROPE: A BRIEF HISTORY OF ITS INDUSTRIALIZATION AND PLANNING

The world's current propensity to aspire to betterment, in terms of finances, health, and sanitation, can be traced back in western philosophy to Aristotle, who accounted simply for why cities emerge and grow.

> Men come together in the city to live; they remain there in order to live the good life.
>
> Aristotle

What is lost in the migration to the city, at the expense of material gain and comfort?[14] Today's wish for the "good life" may be insidiously connected to globalization and consumerism, yet, for the present and future, utopianism in the twenty-first century is a project about amelioration, not ideality.

The classic utopia was most often designed as an "outopia" (no place) or "eutopia" (good place), as elucidated by Patrick Geddes in his reading of Thomas More's *Utopia*.[15] In this light, utopia lies between nothingness (or nowhere-ness) and goodness. Since the industrialization of Europe, utopianism has taken a different, more context-specific approach, toward visions which seek to renovate, regenerate, and reconstruct the existing city. With industrialization, utopia became a social project, fused with literature, philosophy, and political treatises rather than with religion. In Tafuri's reading, ideology, to remain relevant and "in order to survive," had to "negate itself as such, break its own crystallized forms, and throw itself entirely into the 'construction of the future'."[16] Utopianism thus became, and possibly still is today, a project about amelioration, about changing the present, about transformation in general, and was no longer about a vision of a new, previously unseen, ideal, and potentially unknowable future. Utopia now aims to undo the mistakes of the past, and to heal the ills of the present.

The demise of the powerful Roman Empire unfolded over hundreds of years. Following the sacking of Rome by the Visigoths in 476, the organizational system of Europe shifted from "a network of cities and towns to a scattered, unstable mix of hamlets and migrants, with the largest towns holding no more than a thousand inhabitants," a state in which Europe remained until the first signs of the Enlightenment five hundred years later.[17] The reemergence of urban Europe in the Middle Ages, after a long hiatus, has largely been attributed to technological innovations in farming. The next wave of urban development was driven by a similar acceleration in energy flows, "this time arising from the exploitation of fossil fuels—[which] propelled another great spurt in city birth and growth in the 1800s."[18] Out of this technological phase transition there evolved new kinds of cities—industrial cities such as Manchester, as well as the massive new urban centres of the nineteenth century, in London, Paris, and New York.

The Industrial Revolution encapsulated a great period of urbanization in Europe, which led the entire continent away from an agrarian society toward the irreversible dominance of urbanity. Linked to the expansion of European cities during the nineteenth century was the economic basis of colonialism, which fuelled the factories of industrialists, providing a seemingly endless source of raw materials in the expanding colonies, cheap labor from the countryside, and ever expanding consumer markets. Within the unholy history of European urbanization, and this ever-so-brief summary of the reasons behind it, it must be noted that it took about 350 years to reach its current stable condition. Paris was in fact the first city to have a birth rate higher than its death rate. By the mid-eighteenth century, large cities had achieved "a changing relationship with microbes," which had the effect of transforming them "from death traps into net producers of people."[19] Compared to the rate of recent Asian urbanization, Europe changed at a snail's pace. Beijing, for example, was larger than any European city for hundreds of years, before it was surpassed by London and Paris.

> Men had become mechanical before they perfected complicated machines to express their new bent and interest; and the will-to-order had appeared once more in the monastery and the army and the counting-house before it finally manifested itself in the factory.
>
> Lewis Mumford[20]

The machine age started much earlier than the European Industrial Revolution, in the tenth century, and it was followed by a steady rise in mechanization until the eighteenth century. The routinized order of the monastery was transferred to the mechanical routines of bureaucratic processes. Modern science emerged, heralded by Alberto Perez-Gomez as the introduction of a *scientia universalis*, marking for him an era in which poesis was lost through the dominance of mechanization.[21] As much as one cannot deny European civilization's shift from a totalizing sense of religiosity, this is a deeply troubling, nostalgic epistemology, which can only look backwards for its inspiration, justification, and resistance.

An important paradigm which emerged as a result of the Industrial Revolution was the assembly line model of production. This new ability to standardize and repeat components of products through mass production made for mass consumption and pushed aside the notion of the bespoke, one-off product, made by a single craftsman for a single consumer. As an effect of mass production, the industrial cities began to take on repetitious qualities, both within themselves and increasingly through shared characteristics.

Rationalist epistemologies, however, continued to be touted throughout the period of first-world modernization. For Banham, the twentieth century was marked by "faint echoes of a far from faint-hearted epoch when men truly tried to come to terms with 'the Machine' as a power to liberate men from ancient servitudes to work and exploitation."[22] The Futurists wanted to destroy material heritage in celebration of speed and new machinery; Frank Lloyd Wright's *The Art and Craft of the Machine* (1901) presented an argument for mechanization and the machine aesthetic, while laboring through a hangover of a Berlagian craft movement. Modernism's aversion to the "supposed excesses of personal wilfulness" in Art Nouveau and Jugenstile places the mechanistic in opposition to the organic, which can also be seen as opposition to Ruskin's anti-technology position.[23] The Deutscher Werkbund in 1907 was foregrounded by its rejection of Art Nouveau and the Arts and Crafts Movement. The Werkbund proposed standardization as a new virtue, and the divorce of aesthetics from material qualities. The new standards emerging in the twentieth century formed the basis of a new aesthetic zeitgeist, a new model of uniform production.[24]

Mechanization, as an ontological orientation for industrialization, had little space for the organic world. Instead, the standards and conventions of repetition and routinization led from the introduction of machinery toward the underpinnings of all aspects of urban life being industrialized, and in due course mechanized. The mining town of the nineteenth century represents the extreme of this un-building of social organization and the human condition.

Industrialization seemed to bring on rapid urbanization, evident in the coal towns of the era. The literature of Charles Dickens best captures the decrepit, filthy, vice-ridden qualities of the industrial nineteenth-century city. In his *Hard Times*, the fictional Coketown was described as a new kind of city, which rested on three main pillars: "the abolition of the guilds and the creation of a state of permanent insecurity of the working classes; the establishment of the open market for labour and the sale of goods; and the maintenance of foreign dependencies as sources of raw materials."[25] The horrid hygienic and moral conditions of the early industrial cities and the disparities between rich and poor are not limited to the industrial Europe and America of the eighteenth and nineteenth centuries. The current industrialization and urbanization of Asia has also created massive economic divisions between urbanites and the rural population, and between workers in cities and the emerging wealthy classes.

In the late nineteenth century, suburbs represented the means of escape from the degenerated, congested, unhygienic, and unsafe conditions of urbanity.

Perhaps no other cause addressed the ills of the Industrial Revolution so directly as the garden city movement, exemplified by Ebenezer Howard's concept of the "balanced community." The garden city model engaged with the "archaic and false opposition" of the city and country, and aimed to lessen the extreme bipolar condition of man divorced from nature, and to humanize the city and relativize it to the country town.[26] Philanthropic in spirit, Ebenezer Howard believed growth was planned by civic authorities, not driven solely by the initiative of private investment. Tafuri has critiqued the garden city and city beautiful movements, questioning the relevance of "urban naturalism, [as] the insertion of the picturesque into the city and into architecture" as an attempt to mask the then-obvious "dichotomy between urban reality and the reality of the countryside."[27]

The proclaimed "self-sufficiency" of the garden city is a compelling idea with relevance for today's ecologically motivated initiatives, however questionable its claims may have been. This idea was based on limiting the size of the domestic and neighborhood unit, and its optimization to contain a mixed of functional zones. Mumford asserts that "the worst sin of zoning is that it violates an essential social characteristic of neighbourhood planning, namely, that each unit must be balanced—it is the city writ small."[28] Howard's garden city movement was based on creating smaller urban centers, with these limits rooted in a "lack of confidence in metropolitan self-regulation."[29] This performance model of urbanism, requiring limits on size in order to achieve a balanced functionality, raises the question of where the threshold between a town and a city lies.

Shifting the scale of armature from nineteenth century infrastructure to vast boulevards and superblocks, mid-century Soviet-era urban designers modelled the expansion of Moscow and other Soviet cities after Howard's garden city prototype, with programmatic self-sufficiency based on smaller urban units.[30] The garden city model sees the city as a mosaic of cellular towns, and may be limited in its relevance to the vast scale of urbanization occurring in the developing world. Hilbersheimer similarly proposed the deployment of the modular "settlement unit" in a model of the city which functions as an organism, exemplified in his Rockford city plan.

Le Corbusier's vision of the *City of Tomorrow*, translated from his 1925 book *Urbanisme*, achieved great impact, in that it conjoined two paradoxical concepts of modernism: "the machine-made environment, standardized, bureaucratized, 'processed,' technically perfected," and "the natural environment" of open space, sunlight, air, green foliage, and views. Mumford criticized Le Corbusier's vision, accusing him of two mistakes: "the overvaluation of mechanization and standardization," and "the theoretical destruction of every vestige of the past," which he claimed eliminated lessons learnt from previous errors.[31]

The growth of large cities was a nineteenth-century phenomenon in Europe. In 1800, not one European city had a population of over one million. Despite its low rate of urbanization up until the 1980s, Beijing was the largest city in the world for centuries, with a population exceeding one million in the 1700s.[32] By 1850 London's population had reached two million, and Paris's one million. By 1900 there were eleven cities with populations greater than one million, including Berlin, Chicago, New York, Philadelphia, Moscow, St. Petersburg, Vienna, Tokyo, and Calcutta. By 1930, there were over thirty-seven such cities, now on every continent.[33] In 1975 only one-third of the world's population lived in cities; by 2007, urbanites made up half the world's population; and according to projections the fraction will be two-thirds by 2050.[34] At the time of writing, official census figures put the number of cities in China with populations of over one million at more than 170.

Given the speed of the onset of urbanization today, and the speed and extent of transformation in cities such as Manchester, New York, and Chicago, in what ways can lessons from the cities of the Industrial Revolution inform the blueprints for Asia's instant cities?

4.3 THE PARADIGM OF THE NEW WORLD INSTANT CITY

At the time cities such as Manchester were mushrooming in Europe, the rate of growth of cities in the new world was perhaps even more electrifying. Preindustrial colonial cities such as New York, Boston, Philadelphia, and Montreal underwent retooling, expansion, and densification, while a wholly new city emerged at the confluence of transportation routes—of the railroads of the Midwestern United States and routes for seafaring shipping on the Great Lakes, via the St. Lawrence Seaway. This was Chicago, the ultimate nineteenth-century instant city. A new world city, Chicago charged ahead after the Great Fire of 1871 to become the fastest growing city in America. Its status as an infrastructural hub is the reason for its apparently isolated position, and for its rapid growth.[35] As a locus for the sorting, storage and redistribution of "grain from the west, lumber from the north, and cattle from the southwest," Chicago only existed because of industry and trade, and its infrastructural machinery.[36]

As Friedrich Engels called Manchester a "shock city"—emerging quickly with great force—so Chicago was a city which emerged rapidly, and while both European and American instant cities are "often considered as though they were unique and discrete phenomena, . . . the first phase of industrial urbanism proved to be merely the beginning of a long process of urban adaptation and transformation."[37] During the eighteenth century, Protestantism, industrialization, capitalism, and colonialism drove the rapid emergence of cities and created the conditions for a system of flows of capital, resources, and goods. Le Corbusier marveled at the pure formal elegance of the grain silos of the American urban landscape, ignoring the "railway connections to the vast agrarian hinterland of the Great Plains," from where the grain emanated.[38]

In the United States, the Urban Renewal Act (URA) of 1948 enabled federally funded projects, yet vast swathes of the historic fabric of New York were razed in the name of slum clearance. Renewal, regeneration, adaptive reuse, and preservation, as understood today, provide a spectrum of ways in which to deal with dilapidated, defunct, or obsolete urbanism. In her seminal book *The Death and Life of Great American Cities*, Jane Jacobs advocated the neighborhood as a unit having the capacity for emergent self-organization, through local interactions focussed around the street as the locus of urban activity. Jacobs was critical of the erasure of historic neighborhoods as a side effect of the goals of the URA. According to Mumford, her "assault on current planning" rested on her view of the nature, function, and structure of great cities, which valorized the "unplanned casualness" of the sidewalk, street, and neighborhood, yet was underpinned by a "preoccupation that [was] almost an obsession, the prevention of criminal violence in cities."[39] Jacobs was reacting to the ills of modernization, and of modernism. The deep conservatism of her position prevented her from addressing urban renewal, or urbanization, on any terms other than her own, which were confined to a definition of a well-functioning city as comprised of polite, well-organized, and vibrant neighborhoods dependent on "human-scale" urban typologies promoting interpersonal relations and a sense of "belonging." Jacobs saw the symptoms of urbanization as being "disorganization and excessive congestion," and converted them into a remedy in which "congestion and disorder [are] normal, indeed the most desirable, conditions of life in cities." In 1962, one year after Jacobs published *The Death and Life of Great American Cities*, Mumford wrote a scathing critique of her simple position: given cities have continuously vibrant and active city streets, they establish homeostasis and remain safe as social spaces. Mumford's assault on Jacobs can be summarized in his view of the sense of belonging as resting "not on a metropolitan dynamism, but on continuity and stability."[40] The space of flows creates proximity and instantaneousness. These new networks create "serendipitous encounters between strangers" or what Jacobs called "contact," in which chance encounter rules over predictable routines.[41] Jacobs was critiquing an approach to urban renewal which was "a decidedly top down approach," in which large-scale modern housing projects in American inner cities "tried to deal with the problem of dangerous city streets by eliminating streets altogether."[42] To some extent Jacobs's spearheading of a grassroots movement against the top-down planning of slum clearance and large infrastructural projects such as those championed by Robert Moses failed to recognize some of the ills of American society—principally those of a racially divided country and the "white flight" of middle-class educated Caucasians to the suburbs, leaving the inner cities to poor African Americans and lower income immigrant groups. Jabobs in her writings makes little mention of such phenomena, which no doubt contributed to American cities becoming dangerous and depopulated, and generally in decline.

Jacobs's position is limited as a universal thesis in its inability to explain why some vast modern cities are in fact safe places to be. Why does Tokyo, a city of over thirty million inhabitants, have a negligible crime rate? What explains the safety of public housing estates in Hong Kong and Singapore? And what, then, are the self-regulatory control mechanisms of urbanism? In Rem Koolhaas' 1978 treatise on metropolitan life, *Delirious New York*, the author argues that what he terms "the culture of congestion" is an essential precondition of metropolitan life. Stripped of sentimentality over the loss of the neighborhood in the "great" American city of the mid-twentieth century, *Delirious New York* celebrates disorder as a feature of saturation and the complexity of urbanity.[43]

For the topic of neighborhoods to be relevant for urbanization in Asia, its discourses need to be situated in the vast metropolis. Chicago, as we shall see, was the "Shenzhen of the nineteenth century."[44] The new cities of the twenty-first century need to be conceived according to long-term rather than short-term visions.

4.4 THE DUBAI MIRAGE

Chicago also has parallels to Dubai, as an isolated hub which grew with great speed out of the interchanges of global networks. Few places exemplify the model of the instant city better than Dubai. Before the Global Financial Crisis of 2008, this section might have had a tone of concurrent exuberance, marvel and disbelief. Dubai's harbor was dredged in the 1970s with the ambition of making the city a major cargo hub. Now tourists outnumber the residential population of Dubai fivefold, and ninety-six percent of the residential population is foreign.[45]

As an experiment, Dubai seems highly unlikely to become a standard, repeatable model for urbanization elsewhere. We will see later some of the risks of decay, demise, and extinction caused by such fragile, and shallow, foundations for urbanism as have been laid in Dubai. The UAE produces nothing except oil, but this emerging economic wonder has generated enormous wealth by tapping into the flow of international capital. Koolhaas accuses the western reading of the "Model Dubai" as "not being immune to Wall Street's toxic corruption" as "lazy."[46] More investigation is needed, then, of the historical and current organizational parallels to other cities in the past, present, and future.

Dubai, unlike many contemporary cities, is based on an "enclave-and-armature system in its starkest form, [in which] each enclave is closed and controlled, air-conditioned and policed, connected by the highway along the coast."[47] Dubai echoes another city in the desert, Las Vegas. Though not based on the liberalization of gambling, Dubai is a vehicle-based, low-density model of urbanization, wholly irresponsible in ecological terms, and grown out of global networks. The American strip, celebrated by Venturi and Scott-Brown in the mid-1960s, represents the ultimate vehicular space—neither city nor suburb. In this light, Los Angeles also represents an extreme model of low-density sprawl, based on the private car as the prime mode of movement. Further parallels between Las Vegas and Dubai surface in how both cities have marketed themselves as "leisure meganodes" in global travel and entertainment networks. Organized on programmatic narratives related to theme parks, the urbanism of Dubai is meant to "dazzle and awe" through media spectacle and the artificiality of its place-making. This model of urban development requires staggeringly high energy inputs, as it places its quotidian survival, and more importantly its longer term endurance, in a fragile condition entirely dependent on intense fossil fuel consumption for its cars and air conditioners.

Dubai's status as a global hub can be correlated to another city of gold in the desert, Timbuktu—the ancient, fabled city in Mali, the obsolescence of which was brought about by the emergence of cargo shipping between coastal sub-Saharan

Africa and North Africa during the early colonial period.[48] Timbuktu maintained a population exceeding one hundred thousand—larger than any European city—for nearly five hundred years, until the end of the seventeenth century. The city was rediscovered by a European, for the first time in over three centuries, in 1826. Timbuktu is credited with having the world's first university, and commercially it was the centre of the gold and salt markets. It was also implicated in transporting, over centuries, between nine and thirteen million black African slaves to North Africa.[49] Like Dubai, Timbuktu did not produce anything. It was a city of contractors and merchants, serving as a node for the warehousing and distribution of goods transferring to and from the boats of the River Niger and the camel caravans through the Sahara. The Dubai model of the instant city follows a similar pattern, with wealth generated from the exchange of goods and services. Both cities risk extinction through threats from harsh climatic and geographical environments, and the fragility and potential unsustainability of their economies. The difference between the two cities is that Timbuktu endured as a thriving city for half a millennium. Dubai is, in urban years, still a baby.

In what seems tantamount to a warning, Campanella has claimed that "the only place remotely comparable to China today is Dubai . . . but China is a hundred Dubais [in population terms], with a thousand times its ambition."[50] In terms of future urbanization, Dubai is not an isolated anomaly—rather it might be called the regional edition of China's model of twenty-first-century urbanization. Cities as "green" as Dubai (in the durational rather than ecological sense) often cannot be judged, as they "need time to prove themselves as substantial condensers of civilization," and are usually the result of a "coalition between geography, human settlement, available labour, wealth, and natural resources." Despite the difference in size between the Gulf and China, and between their energy-based and labor-based models of economic development,[51] both have great imbalances of wealth and large populations of migrant workers. Both lack resources. The Gulf–China parallels seem convergent on too many fronts. In the future the history of these parallels will be told.[52]

In the future, to what extent will the urban model of Dubai, and all it represents in economic, ecological, and social terms, be revealed as just a mirage? Can it sustain itself? Will an alternative energy source save it from extinction? Will it disappear as a general model if there are shifts in the global network of consumer, financial, and travel flows? If the global demand for oil continues to rise, as resources diminish, will Dubai, again as a general model, adapt to its challenges, or will it perish? More than nearly any other contemporary city, Dubai may turn out to be the place which provides clues to answering the questions posed in this book concerning urban change, adaptation, and evolution—or conversely obsolescence, abandonment, and even disappearance—and to ways of meeting the urgent challenges facing urban earth.

Investigations of urban growth and expansion must also consider the long history of abandonment of cities. The balance which must be struck in order to maintain and sustain a city is a precarious one. We have seen how suburbanization led to the de-densification and depopulation of city centres in the twentieth century, and throughout urban history. "Desertification" of cities is a real and serious risk.[53] In Reyner Banham's 1971 book *Los Angeles: The Architecture of Four Ecologies*, [54] the author's position on the abandonment and demolition of downtown Los Angeles—which since the 1960s has been revived—is not entirely clear. Detroit is a city which is either, optimistically, in decline, or has all but died. It is often cited as a casualty of the shift of the automotive industry to the East, as well as an emblem of the racial division of American cities, and white flight. At one time the Motor City, as it is known, was a symbol of capitalist supremacy and of the automobile industry, but as "the largest capitalist machine in the history of civilization, its viability lasted barely a few decades . . . . [T]he city came and went in less than a hundred years."[55] Today much of the city is in ruins and seems quite close to abandonment, despite the presence of one of America's wealthiest suburbs, Grosse Point, just across the city's "8-mile line."[56] In fact Detroit's city council is reviewing legislation to change the zoning in parts of the city from residential or commercial to farming, thereby de-urbanizing it.[57]

Coming full circle, one of the centers of the Industrial Revolution, London's Docklands, suffered desolation in parallel with the decline of the British Empire and changes in British manufacturing, and also due to the removal of shipping from the River Thames to better seaports. The redeveloped Canary Wharf was prematurely deemed a failure in its first few desolate years, only for it to grow into a global center of finance. Similarly, Manchester and Liverpool also decayed on all fronts in their postindustrial, postcolonial, and postwar conditions, only to be regenerated by government investment coupled with an extended property boom in the 1990s and 2000s.

Do these cities represent a warning about how urban decline can lead to eventual abandonment, or do they simply attest to urban change as a given? Is imbalance the new paradigm? Models of urbanization which lack basic self-sustaining capabilities and resilience seem wholly inappropriate for export, especially to China. Far from a mirage, Dubai came about through the consolidation of real flows of energy, goods, people, and capital. These dynamic flows, when understood as bottom-up interactions of the type which all cities need to maintain themselves, took place within a top-down model of planning, urban design, and architecture. With its laissez-faire economic model, Dubai, as a freak of desert urbanism, persists, but for just how long?

NOTES

1 > L. Mumford (1986) *The Lewis Mumford Reader*, ed. D.L. Millner (Athens, GA: University of Georgia Press), 104.

2 > M. Hulshof and D. Roggeveen (2011) *How the City Moved to Mr. Sun* (Amsterdam: SUN), 309.

3 > T. Verebes (2010) "Endurance and Obsolescence: Instant Cities, Disposable Buildings, and the Construction of Culture," in *Sustain and Develop: 306090, Vol. 13*, eds. Jonathan Solomon and Joshua Bolchover (New York: Princeton Architectural Press).

4 > J. Grasso, J. Corrin, and M. Kort (1991) *Modernization and Revolution in China* (New York: M.E. Sharpe).

5 > W. Skinner (1977) *The City in Late Imperial China* (Stanford, CA: Stanford Press).

6 > T.J. Campanella (2008) *The Concrete Dragon: China's Urban Revolution and What It Means for the World* (New York: Princeton Architectural Press), 191.

7 > Campanella, *The Concrete Dragon*, 103.

8 > N. Mars (2008) "Cities Without History", in *The Chinese Dream*, eds. N. Mars and A. Hornsby (Rotterdam: 010), 525.

9 > Mars, "Cities Without History," 534.

10 > Campanella, *The Concrete Dragon*, 277.

11 > D. Scott Brown and R. Venturi (2008) *Shanghai Transforming*, ed. I. Gil (Barcelona: Actar), 66–71.

12 > Campanella, *The Concrete Dragon*, 94–95.

13 > D.G. Shane (2011) *Urban Design since 1945: A Global Perspective* (London: Wiley), 53.
14 > L. Mumford (1961) *The City in History* (London: Harcourt Brace Jovanovitch), 111.
15 > See Mumford, *The Lewis Mumford Reader*, 217.
16 > M. Tafuri (1976) *Architecture and Utopia: Design and Capitalist Development* (Cambridge: MIT), 50.
17 > S. Johnson (2001) *Emergence: The Connected Lives of Ants, Brains, Cities and Software* (London: Penguin), 110.
18 > M. De Landa (1997) *A Thousand Years of Nonlinear History* (New York: Zone), 83.
19 > De Landa, *A Thousand Years of Nonlinear History*, 150.
20 > L. Mumford (1934) *Technics and Civilisation* (London: Harvest), 3.
21 > A. Perez-Gomez (1985) *The Crisis of Modern Science* (Cambridge, MA: MIT), 11.
22 > R. Banham (1960) *Theory and Design in the First Machine Age* (Oxford: Butterworth-Heinemann), 12.
23 > Banham, *Theory and Design in the First Machine Age*, 44.
24 > Banham, *Theory and Design in the First Machine Age*, 72, 76.
25 > Mumford, *The City in History*, 447.
26 > S. Kwinter (2010) "Notes on the Third Ecology," in *Ecological Urbanism*, eds. M. Mostafavi and G. Doherty (Baden: Lars Müller) 94.
27 > M. Tafuri, *Architecture and Utopia*, 8.
28 > Mumford, *The Lewis Mumford Reader*, 171.
29 > Johnson, *Emergence*, 147.
30 > Shane, *Urban Design since 1945*, 91.
31 > Mumford, *The Lewis Mumford Reader*, 177, 182.
32 > Shane, *Urban Design since 1945*, 9, 87.
33 > Mumford, *The City in History*, 529.
34 > UN HABITAT, World Urban Forum III.
35 > R.E. Park, E.W. Burgess, and R.D. McKenzie (1996) "The Growth of a City: An Introduction to a Research Project," in *The City Reader* (London: Routledge), 165.
36 > R.T. LeGates and F. Stout (1996) "Editor's Introduction," in *The City Reader* (London: Routledge), 161.
37 > R.T. LeGates and F. Stout (1996) "Introduction to Part One: The Evolution of Cities," in *The City Reader*. (London: Routledge), 18.
38 > Shane, *Urban Design since 1945*, 140.
39 > Mumford, *The Lewis Mumford Reader*, 184–189.
40 > Mumford, *The Lewis Mumford Reader*, 192–194.
41 > S. Shaviro (2003) *Connected, or What it Means to Live in the Network Society* (Minnesota: Regents), 133.
42 > Johnson, *Emergence*, 50.
43 > Koolhaas, R. (1978) *Delirious New York: A Retroactive Manifesto for Manhattan*.
44 > Campanella, *The Concrete Dragon*, 281.
45 > R. Koolhaas (2007) *The Gulf* (Baden: Lars Müller), XVIII.
46 > R. Koolhaas (2011) *Volume 23: Al Manakh Gulf Continued*, ed. T. Reisz (The Netherlands: Archis), 5.
47 > Shane, *Urban Design since 1945*, 157.
48 > T. Verebes, "Endurance and Obsolescence."
49 > F.T. Kryza (2006) *The Race for Timbuktu: In Search of Africa's City of Gold* (New York: Harper Collins), xiii.
50 > Campanella, *The Concrete Dragon*, 15.
51 > J. Jiang (2011) *Volume 23: Al Manakh Gulf Continued*, ed. T. Reisz (The Netherlands: Archis), 494.
52 > O. Bouman (2011) *Volume 23: Al Manakh Gulf Continued*, ed. T. Reisz (The Netherlands: Archis), 180.
53 > S. Boeri (2010) "Five Ecological Challenges for the Contemporary City," *Ecological Urbanism*, eds. M. Mostafavi and G. Doherty (Baden: Lars Müller), 451.
54 > R. Banham (1971) *Los Angeles: The Architecture of Four Ecologies* (London: Pelican).
55 > S. Kwinter and D. Fabricius (2001) "Houston," in *Mutations*, ed. R. Koolhaas, S. Boeri, S. Kwinter, N. Tazi, and H.U. Obrist (Barcelona: Actar), 594.
56 > Shane, *Urban Design Since 1945*, 141.
57 > Shane, *Urban Design Since 1945*, 261.

CHAPTER 5

JORGE FIORI >INFORMAL CITY

DESIGN AS POLITICAL ENGAGEMENT[1]

For decades now the debate around and approaches to the informal city have been profoundly despatialized. Since the mid-1990s, however, a new generation of policies, programs, and projects for the informal city have returned to the role of architecture and design in addressing the scale of informality and of the social needs associated with it. A rich spectrum of experiences of different scales and ambitions has emerged, but no systematic assessment of their significance and impact has yet been undertaken. This short text reflects on some of the arguments of the recently created research cluster on Urbanism and the Informal City within the Architectural Association School of Architecture (AA) regarding the direction and contribution of those experiences.

The concept of the "informal" emerged in the developing world in the early 1970s to describe of a set of socioeconomic and spatial processes—predominantly urban—which combined irregularity with very low levels of productivity in the production of goods, services, and the built environment, in ways that were often associated with conditions of poverty and destitution. The concept also related to spatial configurations that did not conform to the expected and desired forms of the modern city. It referred to conditions which were not at all new and not dissimilar to those which had existed in developed economies long before; what was new was the expansion and growing articulation of these conditions with the very processes of development and economic growth which were supposed to eliminate them, and the perception that the spaces of informality were not devoid of potential but in fact full of resourcefulness and creativity which required support rather than eradication. Over four decades, the concept of informality acquired enormous importance, gaining multiple forms and rapidly spreading in its application far beyond the cities of the developing world, to become both a central feature and a functional tool in the new forms of internationalization of capital at a global scale. From Lagos to New York, the informal became increasingly constitutive of the urban condition in general.

The fact that vast amounts of people, activities, and built structures central to the life of cities across the world happen to be outside their rules and institutions undoubtedly represents a massive challenge for policy makers, city planners, and urbanists. Is this a threat, a reflection of the illegitimacy of current institutions, or just another way of producing and "planning" cities? Can these different ways of producing and appropriating cities, with their different logics and sets of rules, coexist? What is the spatiality of the informal and of its articulation with the "formal" city? Above all, can spatial strategies and design address both the encounters of these different logics and contribute to the redesigning of the urban institutions that frame such encounters?

The AA has played an important role in shaping the international debate on self-produced informal cities and the formulation of strategies to deal with them. The seminal works of Otto Koenigsberger and John Turner have been immensely influential. Many others associated with the AA at different times and in different capacities have made important contributions to both analyses and policies relating to the informal city. However, in line with much of the debate over the years, these contributions were predominantly focussed on the social aspects of informality rather than on questions of space and design. Recent work by the Housing and Urbanism program at the AA Graduate School and by the AA research cluster on Urbanism and the Informal City has sought to give continuity to this legacy while focusing on the potential of architecture and urbanism as tools of political engagement in the transformation of the informal city and the social conditions associated with it. Central to this interest is not only the view that the widespread nature of informality makes it a very important issue for urbanists everywhere but also the belief that the informal city challenges the traditions of urbanism and urban design. Masterplans, land-use plans, and all the conventional tools of spatial planning are of limited use in the context of the informal city, and in some cases are truly irrelevant. Addressing the informal city is ineluctably about rethinking the discipline of urbanism itself—its methods, tools, and instruments of spatial design and intervention. Indeed, that is one of the reasons why the informal has attracted the attention of so many leading architects and urbanists.

Seldom do new ideas and concepts translate quickly into policies. In the case of informality, however, policies focussed on informal housing, informal settlements, the informal economy, and so on, emerged soon after the concept was first formulated. Four decades of debate have been accompanied by four decades of strategies and policies to address the conditions of informality. The concept was soon appropriated by different disciplines, theoretical perspectives, and ideological positions, leading to different understandings of the causes of informality and to different policy and planning responses. However, in terms of addressing the scale of the informal or of the social needs associated with it, we can say without fear of error that, despite the considerable innovation in policy approaches, there were also four decades of failure. The reasons for such failure are multiple, complex, and far beyond the scope of this short text. However, we believe that one contributing factor in this failure has been the almost complete despatialization of the debate on the informal city and of the strategies for dealing with it.

A critique of modernist planning and architecture that apportioned considerable blame to design for previous failures in urban and housing policies; a growing valorization of organic and self-produced cities "without architects" and "without planners"; and the very pertinent emphasis on the socioeconomic and political dimensions of informal processes have increasingly led to the fading away of any preoccupation with space and design. The search for means of addressing the scale of "the problem" emphasized, in line with the different theoretical and ideological persuasions involved, the political, the social, or the economic dimensions as being central to a logic of "scaling up." In the 1970s, policies that attempted to combine state-driven, low-cost "site-and-services" and "slum upgrading" programs and projects with "community participation" led almost invariably to introverted, disconnected, and fragmented interventions devoid of any sense of urbanism or of the city itself. In the 1980s and early 1990s, guided by the by-then dominant neoliberal orthodoxy, the focus shifted toward institutional reform, deregulation, and minimization of the state in order to unblock markets as the central mechanism for scaling up. Deregulation, in turn, would supposedly have the added benefit of dissolving and removing a central feature of informality: its irregularity. However, the fact is that throughout these decades the informal kept growing in size, diversity, and complexity.

Toward the mid-1990s, when the shortcomings and the socioeconomic costs of the neoliberal recipes were becoming more evident, a new generation of ideas and policies began to emerge in connection with issues of urban development in general, and urban informality in particular. Alongside this, a new understanding of scaling up surfaced, one that saw scaling up as a much more complex, fragile, and contradictory process which is inescapably multi-dimensional in nature; and one that recovered the spatial as a necessary and relevant dimension. Scaling up was increasingly seen as a result of multidimensional, multisectoral, and multiscalar processes; as not a quantitative process but a change in the quality of

Landscape and Urban Agriculture
The Fabrica de Música and the landscape act as one building, each one interacting with the other to form a comprehensive whole.
Grass
Highly permeable grass is used to retain the steep landscape, absorb excess stormwater and reduce the required construction on site
Grass Pavers
Permeable material to mitigate runoff and erosion
Agriculture
Introduces fresh produce, agricultural education, and micro economies into the favela
Wetlands
Passively filter rainwater for gray water applications and irrigation for agriculture
Cabbage / Kale
Carrot
Beet
Onion
Squash

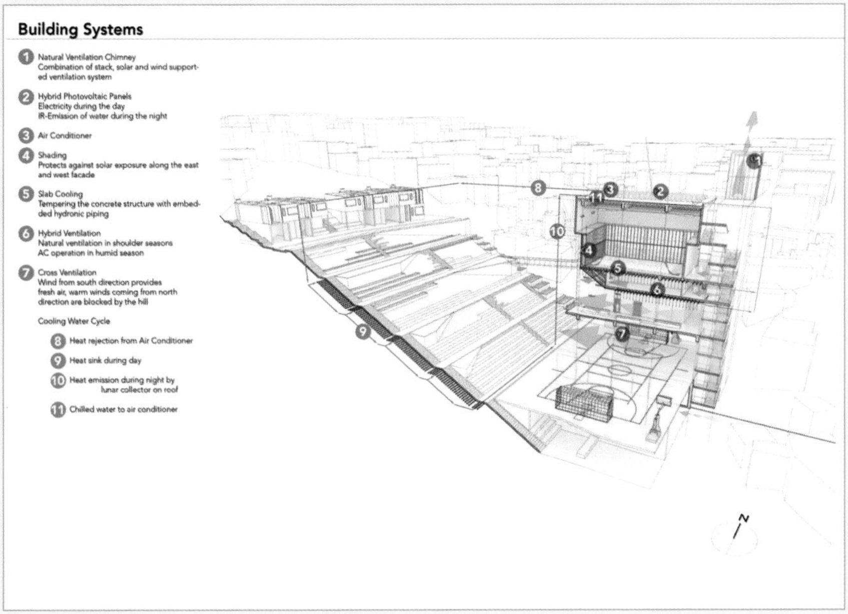
Building Systems
1 Natural Ventilation Chimney
Combination of stack, solar and wind supported ventilation system
2 Hybrid Photovoltaic Panels
Electricity during the day
IR-Emission of water during the night
3 Air Conditioner
4 Shading
Protects against solar exposure along the east and west facade
5 Slab Cooling
Tempering the concrete structure with embedded hydronic piping
6 Hybrid Ventilation
Natural ventilation in shoulder seasons
AC operation in humid season
7 Cross Ventilation
Wind from south direction provides fresh air, warm winds coming from north direction are blocked by the hill
Cooling Water Cycle
8 Heat rejection from Air Conditioner
9 Heat sink during day
10 Heat emission during night by lunar collector on roof
11 Chilled water to air conditioner
N

(opposite and left)
Caracas metro Cable (U-TT), indicating landscape and other systems, and the proposal inset into the context.

the city itself and in the nature of its political institutions; and as a political restructuring of urban institutionalities through synergies and contradictions across processes operating at multiple dimensions and scales, including social, economic, politico-institutional, and spatial.

In this context, debate on the project for the informal city gained new impetus. For many, this project—whether focussed on housing or any other sectoral concern, whether small or large—was now seen as necessarily urban in its ambition. The emphasis was increasingly on integrated urban projects, multidimensional, multisectoral, multiprogrammatic, and multiscalar in nature—"extroverted" projects that understood the requalification of site as inherently related to the requalification of its multiple articulations with context and ultimately with the city. This was redesigning site as redesigning the city, through a multiplicity of "footprints" operating in multiple dimensions and at multiple scales. From this perspective, scaling from the project level "upwards" would be the result of the articulation of the multiple footprints of multiple projects—small and large—operating at multiple scales and across multiple periods of time. This was a perspective that posed an almost impossible challenge, while at the same time enabling an understanding of the true and full complexity of the endeavor.

It is not accidental that within this overall debate there should have been a return to discussions on the role of architectural and urban design in addressing the spatial dimension. Among policy makers, academics, and practitioners, governments, international organizations, and NGOs, there was a growing acknowledgment of the relevance of "good design." A spectrum of experiences, programs, and projects across the world—and particularly in the developing world—started to address the issue of design more explicitly. However, these developments still reflected different understandings of the informal, of the meaning and relevance of scaling up, and of the exact role of design. In our view, despite the new openness to the role of design, many of the previous misconceptions regarding the nature of the informal and the challenge of scaling up were unchanged. It is difficult to elaborate on these differences in a short text, but it is our contention that the one dividing line among those experiences and projects that is particularly relevant to this discussion is to do with the understanding of the relation between site and context, and of the relevance of multiscalarity.

On the one hand, there are projects that aim to requalify site in quite small, localized, often monoprogrammatic interventions that do not use spatial design as an instrument to irradiate transformations beyond the location. These can be referred to as microprojects. On the other hand, there are projects—small, large, and very large, and almost invariably multiprogrammatic and multisectoral—that, in line with the ideas formulated above, seek very explicitly to impact beyond site, articulating and connecting different and multiple scales.

Microprojects have often been associated with an understanding of the informal as the negation of planning—as unplannable, unpredictable, and in continuous mutation, as nonsystemic—hence there is no place in this perspective for the concepts of scaling up or of multiscalarity. Indeed, it argues that scaling up amounts to an attempt to reintroduce the logic of homogenization through the imposition of the dominant formal system of relations and rules, and the dissolution of the informal in all its potential. While often romanticizing the spatial qualities of the informal, this perspective acknowledges the potential of architectural and urban design in very small "doses." In our view, this is a perspective that returns to the dilemmas of previous approaches to the informal, and can lead down a blind alley. One of the most interesting exponents of this perspective is the Brazilian architect Paola Berenstein Jacques.

However, there are other microprojects—perhaps the majority of them—which are not informed by the same analysis of informality, but motivated by a search for high-quality interventions at an affordable level and scale. Often community-based, almost invariably focussed on provision of housing, these projects tend to be limited in scale and have limited urban ambitions more out of necessity than as a matter of principle. They are frequently associated with a desire for scaling up through a quantitative replication of a successful formula in ways not dissimilar to early understandings of scaling up. Good examples of such projects would be *Elemental*—an approach to incremental housing initiated by the architect Alejandro Aravena in Chile—or the experience of community-based housing projects by CODI in Thailand.

While many microprojects have shown considerable inventiveness and often good architectural design, their contribution to an urbanism relevant to the conditions of informality is very limited.

On the other side of the dividing line is what we might call "open urban projects" with the explicit ambition of multiscalar impact. Often reflecting an understanding of the informal as "another way of planning," they also see the informal as being part of systemic relations. Or, to be more precise, part of a network of multiple systems of informality that interconnect and interpenetrate at multiple levels and scales with the formal city. It is this understanding that makes it possible to talk about scaling up and to use terms such as "footprints," "acupunctures," or "benign metastasis" to describe the ambition of impacting beyond site on a larger system of relations, and indeed across systems.

Such projects over almost two decades have encompassed interventions of very different sizes and scales, from small to extremely large. At the small end of the spectrum, interventions are mainly on an architectural scale, introducing one or few buildings within an area of informality. The impact beyond site and the ambition of scaling up is often linked to the ways in which buildings are inserted into the informal fabric, to the creative mixing of programs, to the explicit attempt to connect to a network of existing or future plans for the area, and to the adoption of a new set of rules and institutional arrangements that take account of the informal ways of doing things and informal rules.

A project that became emblematic of this type of urban acupuncture is the *Vertical Gym* by the Urban Think Tank (UTT) in Caracas, Venezuela. Its success, not only as a sport facility, led to the creation of many new multipurpose gyms in Caracas. Similarly, the proposal by UTT for a *Modular Music Factory* that can provide all the resources for the musical training of around a thousand children a day in sites as small as 1200 square meters follows an analogous logic of insertion in the informal urban fabric. The library Santo Domingo by Giancarlo Mazzanti, at the top of a squatter settlement in Medellin, Colombia, is another instance often cited. Some interesting examples of this type of small-scale intervention are provided by the architectural practice of Teddy Cruz at the border of Tijuana,

Mexico, and San Diego. A well-known illustration is that of *Casa Familiar*, which through the involvement of local communities came up with a new mix of types and uses that challenged very directly the existing regulations and institutional arrangements for housing provision. It is precisely this articulation between local social practices, a design strategy, and the redesigning of rules which propels these experiences beyond site into the realm of urban transformation.

At an intermediate urban scale there have been many very interesting experiences, providing the best examples of attempts at implementing integrated projects of a multidimensional, multisectoral, and multiscalar nature. The paradigmatic case is Favela-Bairro in Rio de Janeiro, Brazil—a slum upgrading program for settlements of up to 2500 families. It combined the provision of infrastructures of connectivity, the introduction of services, and the requalification of the public realm with the production of housing for those residents that needed relocation, the provision of clinics and educational facilities, and job creation initiatives. In spatial and design terms it placed particular emphasis on the treatment of the edges of the sites and the articulation with the surrounding areas by overlapping the infrastructures of access and circulation with public spaces and the introduction of new services.

At the very large end of the spectrum of interventions within the informal city are examples such as the upgrading of the favela Rocinha in Rio de Janeiro, with a population of more than one hundred thousand inhabitants, or, even more striking, the proposals for the upgrading and redevelopment of Dharavi, a large slum in Mumbai, India, with a population of almost one million inhabitants. The challenges posed by these types of sites are much more complex and require a combination of spatial tools. The proposal of HOK for Dharavi is very interesting in its attempt to combine masterplanning with a flexible approach to progressive development and upgrading.

What these experiences have in common is that, whether small or very large interventions, they are all projects formulated within conditions of almost complete informality, often only connecting spatially with the formal city at the edges of their sites. A new generation of large projects has emerged in the last few years, however, which explicitly addresses large territories encompassing a variety of informal and formal conditions. We believe that these projects pose bigger challenges, but also carry much greater potential for transformation at the scale of the city. This is the case not only because these territories are much more representative of the city condition as a whole in their multiple articulations of informal and formal, but also because the resolution of the challenges they pose—institutional as well as spatial—connects more explicitly with the scale of the city. Some recent instances of this type of project have been driven, not accidentally, by the introduction of large transport infrastructures. The Metrocables of Medellin (by architects Edison Escobar and María Patricia Bustamante) and Caracas (by the Urban Think Tank) are interesting examples. Another project of similar scale and complexity is the Complexo da Mangueira (by architect Jorge Jáurequi) in a central zone of Rio, which encompasses favelas, large transport infrastructures, significant sports facilities such as the Maracanã Stadium, green areas and parks, formal residential areas, commercial amenities, and many important institutions.

At the core of all these experiences lie, in our view, three central challenges. First, the need to combine with great flexibility and sensitivity the preservation of many of the qualities of the informal with the eradication and redevelopment of conditions that are socially and economically undermining and ethically unacceptable. This is a fine, complex and often extremely conflictual balance to achieve, as it touches on a variety of entrenched positions and interests. Second, the need to formulate spatial strategies that can enhance the productivity of the territory, since low productivity is not only a defining feature of the informal but one that is directly associated with the conditions of deprivation and poverty within the informal. Here, questions of connectivity and articulation of multiple economic scales is central to any lasting increase in productivity. Third, and most important, there is the need to develop spatial strategies that engage very explicitly with the politics of institutional transformation. The articulation of spatial design with the redesign of urban political institutions and regulations is an unavoidable challenge, and the cornerstone of any spatial strategy that aims to contribute to the creation of inclusive cities capable of accommodating a variety of logics of city production, appropriation, and use.

The examples given here are not in any way intended to provide an illustration of best practice, rather they show the range of what has now become a vast and rich experience of designing for and with the informal city. Not only have the tools of design been insufficiently analyzed, but the impact of these integrated projects and their spatial strategies has not been assessed in any meaningful manner, not least because the methodologies of impact assessment are too limited to give an account of the complexity and multiplicity of levels and scales of impact. We believe, however, that almost two decades of projects for the informal city, in contrast to prior responses, reflect the emergence of a different understanding of site, of context, of connectivity, of scale, and of the articulation of design with the productivity of the territory, with the social organization and mobilization of informal producers and dwellers, and with the politics of institutional redesign.

It is in line with this belief, and with the arguments formulated here, that the AA research cluster on Urbanism and the Informal City has identified the questions we consider central to uncovering the potential of such projects:

- What is the place and role of design in addressing the scale of the informal city and of the social needs associated with it?
- What is specific about designing for, with, and in the informal city? What are the appropriate tools, instruments, and methodologies of design?
- In what ways does design contribute to the research, analysis, and understanding of the informal?
- How does design contribute to enhancing the productivity of a territory?
- How does design articulate with the redesigning of urban institutions and political processes in the city?

NOTE

1 > This text presents a condensed version of the introduction to the symposium of the same title, organized by the AA research cluster on Urbanism and the Informal City, which took place in February 2012. The research cluster is coordinated by Jorge Fiori, Elena Pascolo, and Alex Warnock-Smith.

CHAPTER 6

CONVERSATION 2

XU WEIGUO (XWG), XU FENG (XF) AND GAO YAN (GY)

GY Xu Weiguo, can we discuss your thoughts on the greatest successes, and also some of the failures, of China's rapid urbanization during our era?

XWG I believe the primary challenge for China in recent years, as well as its greatest achievement, has been to provide sufficient housing for its huge population in such a short period of time. The growth of cities is inherently triggered by the increase of urban residents, and this is the foundation before discussing anything else. Currently, 40 percent of the population of China is urbanized, and the future target is 70 percent. At the beginning of Open Door Policy in the early 1980s, the urban population was only 10 percent. Here in China, everything has to be superfast. We develop rapidly at first, and then we rectify our wrongdoings. The speed of our development was too fast to get things right in the first place, which inevitably led to poor quality. When old buildings become obstacles for development, they are knocked down and replaced. In recent decades, it was impossible to build high-quality and high-density buildings due to the poor economy and limited availability of building technologies. People flooded into cities and higher-quality buildings would have taken much longer time to construct at a higher cost.

There are parallels between the Chinese experience and Germany immediately after World War Two. There were great demands for housing, and Germany applied a modernist approach to achieve their goals, which was seen as functional, efficient, and economic. There are, in fact, unique characteristics to how contemporary Chinese cities are produced. In this context, new knowledge is being generated. For instance, domestic practitioners as well as foreign architects have learned how to quickly satisfy clients' requirements. The way architecture is practiced in China is worthy to be acknowledged and evaluated. You can also find many examples of new technologies developed for construction, for example ingredients for increasing the drying speed of concrete. Hence my view is that we should reexamine the history of China's rapid development in the past twenty years. We can't simply ignore the achievements and magnify the criticism of poor quality and the short lifespan of buildings.

XF For me, the greatest achievement of rapid urbanization in China has been the aggregation of resources which used to be distributed, and the densification of urban facilities. The causes of the current status of urbanization in China are economic and political forces. Offices, housing, and retail spaces are built for consumption and for economic profit. Under such circumstances, architecture is just one link in the entire economic chain. From a political perspective, governors need to make the best of their years in their post, meaning the more visible their achievements, the more likely they might be in line for a promotion at the end of their term. This explains the five-year cycle and government plan throughout China. This also reflects the dominance of top-down development policies in China.

GY What about the negative impacts of rapid urbanization?

XF Rapid development has destroyed much of the authentic and original physical fabric and their associated social community relationships in many cities, replaced by generic architecture. This explains why people say Chinese cities all look the same.

XWG Regarding the old city, I have a different view. Take Beijing, for example. Although I agree that much of the historical heritage should be preserved, when keeping the old conflicts with need of development, what shall we do? This is a sensitive question. Many western scholars who argue for historic preservation do not take into account problems of poverty, starvation, and homelessness. When fundamental needs have yet to be satisfied, development takes priority over the protection of old buildings. Urbanization is pursued for citizens to live a better life. Of course, architecture with historical value should still be preserved, but not everything old is worthy of preservation, for several reasons. Unlike western historic cities such as Paris, London, and Barcelona, Beijing's courtyard fabric is very low density, making it a very inefficient use of land. Had we stubbornly kept all courtyard houses and hutong, it would have stunted the development of Beijing. The second reason is the unacceptable living standards of courtyard houses. Without proper drainage systems nor hygiene facilities for basic human needs, people who live in old hutongs all wish to move to spacious, bright, and clean buildings elsewhere.

GY I lived in a courtyard house and I fully appreciate your views on the living conditions. Most of the people now living in hutongs are migrants from other cities. The hutongs are disordered, dirty, and lack environmental and infrastructural administration. The old city center has deteriorated significantly in the past decade.

XWG Not only in Beijing, but also in many other cities, historic city centers have become the least desirable areas. The original local residents prefer to rent out their properties in the city center and move to newly built outskirts. Returning to my point: under these circumstances, the conservation of old buildings should give way to development.

GY Criticism of massive demolition as a result of development should be discussed more broadly rather than zooming in to the issue of cultural and historical loss. It is not that the decision makers had not appreciated the cultural value of the old city, but rather they had to balance the importance of heritage with the urgency of development.

XWG What I cannot accept is the views of those who irresponsibly exaggerate the importance of preservation without understanding the real needs of citizens and the most urgent problems for Chinese cities. Many western scholars who blame the savage development of China by rejecting demolition of the old buildings need to be more impartial and objective.

XF This also brings up other issues from another perspective. As we know, Chinese urbanization is not driven by architects, nor planners, nor scholars, but by the policies of the government and profit motive of developers. Architecture in China has seldom escaped these two constraints. A great amount of housing has been built, which has to some extent improved the quality of life, however we need to downplay the commercial and political value of architecture, and rather emphasize social, architectural, environmental values to build better cities.

GY Let's shift the discussion to masterplanning, which aims to manage, control, and forecast singular future design goals. In China, city planning is based on top-down decision-making processes, often carried out without adequate feasibility studies due to apparent time constraints. Perhaps the mechanisms of city planning need to be fundamentally questioned.

XWG City planning is still crucial to provide guidance for development for the urbanization of China. Without planning, Chinese cities would be even worse. We all know that cities undergo change. Without city planning mechanisms able to adapt to changes in the future, a one-off plan will soon be obsolete. Hence, urban planning needs to be flexible and dynamic with a view to the future. Concerning visions of the future, CIM [City Information Modeling] is a more information-based, flexible platform for urban planning and design.

GY Definitely. A number of companies in China have been invested in city modeling for years. Various products and applications have been available, but these technologies need to be coordinated in a more systematic way.

XF I agree with XWG that urban planning methods were valid for China's urbanization in the past, but planning proposals are often measured primarily by efficiency. A common conception of planning is actually for the purpose of selling land for higher profit. Current urban planning does not give sufficient consideration for the benefit of the public. Historically, Beijing was organized around the social relations of the Han ethnic group outside the city walls, where the urban fabric was less planned and grew naturally, while only the Eight Flat members (Man ethnic group) were allowed to live inside the planned city. Current urban planning can be improved to take into account more bottom-up approaches, in top-down decision making processes.

GY XF's point actually reflects XWG's earlier comment on CIM. Rather than planning for the purpose of an instant result, we should shift our focus to the mechanisms which organize physical spaces and artefacts according to evolving circumstances of four-dimensional planning. This can be realized through information-based modeling techniques such as CIM. In other words, a city plan can avoid becoming easily obsolete and can therefore be more durable to guide future development through flexibility and adaptability.

Can we shift toward a discussion of the sustainable city?

XWG The form of the sustainable city has specific definition, which should include energy, environment, society, and so on. What interests me most are the formal implications of sustainability, i.e. organic urban forms related to nature. Before humans built cities, our living environment was surrounded by natural and organic forms. With the emergence of artificial cities, we began to live in opposition to nature. Artificial forms are overly geometrical and are inconsistent with natural order. I am interested in a new kind of urban form, which will reconcile the conflict between human consumption and natural resources, more organic rather than geometric. Can we conceive of the city as a continuation of nature? Secondly, space flows continuously between interiors and exteriors, and architecture becomes a porous medium facilitating the exchange between natural and artificial environments. Thirdly, new kinds of artefacts emerge between nature and architecture, connecting smoothly and coherently with natural forms. These seem to be the consequence of digital technologies in the city, which in turn shift workflows from parametric design systems, through digital fabrication, to eventually digital construction.

GY You are hinting at the influence of digital technology on urban form. One can interpret your ideas as references to eastern philosophy, i.e. the integration of mankind and nature, harmony between artificial environments and natural beings.

XWG Yes. It actually echoes the traditional Chinese philosophy of Daoism, which regards nature and human as a singular entity. This should begin to influence the way we build and rebuild our cities.

XF The introduction of computational design and manufacturing in China is creating many new opportunities for urbanism to define new kinds of nonstandard architectural and urban forms. In China, nonstandard architecture has often been limited to implying iconic buildings.

GY Do you think computational approaches open up new possibilities to relate multiple buildings to each other, therefore creating new urban spaces? In spite of our understanding of the significance of organic morphologies, to clients, these design approaches can serve to satisfy their desire for iconic buildings to stand out from the background, hence fulfilling their economic and political objectives.

XF Iconic buildings can also often perform as urban catalysts.

GY Despite our shared goal of making organic and natural cities, and putting aside what an organic city might look like, let's look at other alternative approaches. For instance, many Japanese architects, such as Toyo Ito, Kengo Kuma, and Sou Fujimoto, share the same view of architecture as a medium between human and nature, whereas they address this ideolology without computation. So, is computational design only one of many methods to achieve more natural cities?

XWG I think the core values of freedom, democracy, and equality, concern humanity, yet most architecture is counter to humanity. Architecture should adapt to human behavior through constant change and evolution. Architecture needs its own identity, but the replication of the identical types is still prevalent. High-quality architecture in the future will rely more on nonstandard approaches and technologies, and will lead to the expression of more specific, and more widely accepted, architectural identities.

GY The defense of iconicity in architecture reflects a desire for humanity through architecture despite criticisms of the superficiality of iconic buildings.

Moving to another topic, do you believe there to be contradictions between how cities change, and the need for architecture to [reflect] cultural, social, environmental and economic continuity?

XWG I recall Bernard Tschumi's and Rem Koolhaas' ideas of architecture resulting from emergent activities, as a basis of an understanding of flexible architecture, rather than as a static sum of rigid spaces. But how can we design for long lifecycles while the city continues to develop? Architectural design should be based on an understanding of the dynamics of urban contexts.

GY So you think the inherent paradox between long lifespan and urban change can be reconciled?

XF This is a complex question. Computational design inevitably needs to address current requirements with fixed forms. Nevertheless, our new design methods allow designers to embed variable parameters which may reflect changes in the future as various scenarios. To reconcile this paradox, a balance of bottom-up and top-down processes will need to emphasize social, political, and economic factors.

GY Regarding the design life of buildings, how can buildings be conceived to be more adaptable, rather than becoming quickly obsolete, resulting in wasteful demolition? For example, can feasibility studies become more future oriented to generate adaptable design briefs?

XWG Alejandro Zaera-Polo has theorized how the architectural is about surface, as the architectural surface has the most direct relationship to the city. Surface houses open spaces which are autonomous and independent from the skin. Such interior spaces can satisfy current needs, but also can adapt to changes in the future.

GY Many cities in Europe have taken this approach to transform historical buildings, by hollowing out the interior and leaving only the façade to maintain the street appearance.

XWG This trend of façadism addresses ways of designing with the past for present and future needs.

XF Architecture in China cannot escape short design life unless its status as a commodity will be diminished. The government now grants seventy-year leases for housing in China. No one knows what will happen in seventy years. Even some governors have officially stipulated the design life of buildings to be only thirty years. The short design life of architecture is deeply rooted in the country's political and economic policies. I don't think the short lifespan of buildings is necessarily a bad thing. Architects and planners should have a vision toward a variable future. Buildings can be classified, for example, for some to be demolished, some to be upgraded, some to be renovated, some to be expanded.

GY In other words, architecture in China should be more than a vehicle for generating profit or political face. Architecture needs to satisfy other measurements for the benefit of the community, the users, and the environment.

The last question I would like to raise is: How can architecture and urbanism achieve a more durable architecture for more sustainable cities?

XWG I would like to come back to the exciting prospects of CIM, in parallel to BIM. There is great potential to develop intelligent buildings in city information models, which can adjust the distribution of energy sources for the city according to the dynamic behavior of individual buildings. If we expand the way we control buildings through artificial intelligence based on BIM models, we can control urban complexity as well. Firstly, there are many layers in a neighborhood, including, drainage, water supply, waste discharge, vehicle circulation, air conditioning, etc. All these systems are linked parametrically in a city information model, so an entire neighborhood can be managed efficiently. If we expand this to a district of a city, the immediate benefit is to mediate different design options based on the simulation of the information model.

GY This represents a significant research endeavor to investigate.

XWG Definitely! We are still focussing on research at an architectural scale. The city needs to be investigated in greater depth.

GY The more I think about it, the more exciting this seems, because decisions about urbanism can be validated with more scientific rigor. What the digital pioneers have achieved formally, in computational design and parametric urbanism, is only the tip of the iceberg of immersive computation in urbanism.

XWG I agree that the most significant value of parametric design is beyond creating irregular forms. The potential of associative tools to manage the city is unlimited. Architects determine relatively little.

CHAPTER 7

TOM VEREBES >URBANIZATION AND ERASURE

Given the unprecedented rapidity and extent of urban growth occurring in China, some of the side effects include the erasure of material heritage, haphazard, uncontrolled growth, and low-density sprawl. Cities have become homogeneous through repetitive and poorly built architecture. There also seems to be an urgent need for new paradigms in the face of imminent global ecological crisis. The paradox of the endurance of architecture and its inevitable dysfunctionality and possible obsolescence creates the conditions for new adaptive models of urbanization. This chapter presents an evolutionary approach to urban development, in which change is the only constant.

7.1 THE TROUBLE WITH SPEED FREAKS

We are currently in an unprecedented era, in which the greatest extent of city building that has ever occurred in any part of the world is taking place. China has the goal of urbanizing a further four hundred million people within the next twenty years. Rapid urbanization has manifold side effects, including badly constructed buildings with little cultural value or longevity, pointing toward a crisis in cultural, social, economic, and environmental sustainability.

In recent years, with booming economies fuelling accelerated global urbanization, the phenomenon of the instant city has often been the subject of celebratory commentary. It seems as though rapid urbanization has been set on automatic, while we marvel passively, powerlessly, and remotely, like a movie audience, at its impressive, awesome force. Far from being innocent, the architect who honors or condones this mass—or mess—of urbanization can be seen as being implicated in a myopic frenzy of short-term production. In this light, should the architect be credited or blamed, or rendered impotent because of the state of our buildings, our cities, and our planet?[1]

In the chapter entitled "A Contemporary City" in his 1929 book *The City of Tomorrow*, Le Corbusier announces his project for a city of three million people, arranged in identical housing blocks on vast, blank fields of modern space. His scheme for "skyscrapers in the park" located in the centre of Paris made claims of "eliminating congestion in the centre" and providing "open spaces which are the lungs of the city."[2] One of the twentieth century's most recognized projects, criticized as emblematic of modernism's denial of history and its ruthless drive to erase and replace all remnants of the past with a sanitized and standardized future, the *City of Tomorrow* is the ultimate prototype for tabula rasa urbanism, having as a precondition the obliteration of the equivalent footprint of the old Paris.

Two pronounced effects of the speed and scale of urbanization are evident: erasure and sprawl. Following a model of low-density sprawl, China's cities have undergone "lateral expansion," often beyond the city boundaries—a phenomenon colloquially referred to as *tan da bing*, or "making a big pancake."[3] Tabula rasa modernism is widely practiced in contemporary Asia, with the state-sponsored apparatus of urban change wielding great power and carving a relentless path into the future with as much certainty as it eradicates the past. The speed of change, as Thomas Campanella asserts, can be stunning, but it can also be stupid, and can come at the cost of "quality, longevity and even safety."[4]

Much has been written in recent decades on European and North American cities in the postwar era of the 1950s and 1960s. Given the rapid technological progress of this period, the dysfunctionality of many existing cities in terms of their infrastructure and building stock became evident. Countless cities embarked on missions to retrofit themselves, establishing new, radically incompatible schemes that superimposed the new world order onto the existing city, thus obliterating it through erasure. The western notion of tabula rasa contrasts the new world with the old, whereas for the Metabolists the concept of erasure was born out of the fragility of urbanity in the natural environment; it was the force of earthquakes and tsunamis, as well as wars, that led to this alternative, eastern notion of erasure.[5]

Modernism's urban program sought to erase traditional, incrementally grown urban morphology, citing its inadequacy for new functions, discarding figural approaches to urbanism in favor of formal abstraction. Modernization in China, according to Jiang Jun, occurred in three stages: initially there was the Westernization Movement of the 1870s; this was followed by the development of national industry in the 1920s; and in the 1950s the Great Leap Forward.[6] A fourth, ongoing stage, as yet without a name, is the largest urbanization project ever undertaken.

Despite being predominantly rural until the 1980s, China has had an urban population for over five thousand years. One of the first serious studies of contemporary Chinese urbanization by a foreign research team was carried out by Harvard GSD's Project on the City, led by Koolhaas, in their 1996 study on the Pearl River Delta (PRD), published as *Great Leap Forward* in 2001.[7] As a treatise based on gonzo-journalistic techniques, *Great Leap Forward* can be seen as a celebration of urbanization—in all its crassness. Part historical record, part documentary photojournalism of the state of urbanization in the PRD, Koolhaas celebrated China's victory over the past—a past it had already forgotten. The future was not the focus of Harvard's PRD research, rather it targeted the dynamism of the present and the speed and ruthlessness with which the past can be altered, if not erased entirely, forever.

Mistakes made by permitting the widespread demolition of China's cities and towns—while now gaining in the public consciousness, as well as that of professionals, investors, and the government—are irreparable. Images of the Chinese character *chai* (拆, meaning "destruction") painted on doorways across the nation are a reminder of how history, in its manifestation in the architecture of the city, can be erased.[8]

拆

As analyzed by Zhang Tinwei, China's rapid urbanization has four characteristics: "huge size, a fluctuating trajectory, a rapid growth rate since the 1980s, and an uneven distribution pattern."[9] The unevenness of China's urban history is marked by a large, relatively poor rural population, despite large urban centres having existed throughout its history. The Shanyang Reform of nearly 2500 years ago set up a free peasant economy as the basis of the unification of rural China; the current context of rapid urbanization has marked a paradigm shift.[10] From 1978 to 2008, China planned and built 468 new cities, and saw over half a billion people move into its cities, representing the fastest rate of urbanization ever.

Another imbalance is the tiered zones of "first cities" along the eastern seaboard, with second- and third-tier cities located inland in the northeast, middle, and west of China. The China Western Development Strategy, or "Go West," is an ongoing policy enacted in 1999 by the central Chinese government as a mission to (re)develop the central and western regions of China, to "increase connectivity with the coastal provinces, redress economic disparities, and thus ensure social stability"[11] and to promote "'balanced development' across the nation."[12] One particularly noteworthy city, Chongqing, was detached from Sichuan Province in 1997, and on paper it became the largest municipality in the world, with a population of thirty-two million, though its urbanized population was several million less than the total population of the municipality. Through relaxation of the Hukou system for Chongqing, with the aim of registering up to ten million migrant workers to live in the city between 2010 and 2020, it is likely to become the largest single city in the world within a generation.[13] Like all second-tier Chinese cities, especially those located west of the eastern seaboard, Chongqing is on the cusp of a tremendous wave of development and transformation.

China's emblematic instant city must be Shenzhen, the country's first Special Economic Zone (SEZ), declared by Deng Xiaoping in 1990. A small fishing village of twenty thousand people in 1980, Shenzhen's population is now in excess of fourteen million, about twice that of its sister city just to the south, Hong Kong. Unlike other cities, "where population growth is a result of natural birth of permanent residents," Shenzhen has grown principally due to "an inflow of floating residents."[14] In spite of the boundary between mainland China and the Special Administrative Region of Hong Kong, it is plausible that Hong Kong and Shenzhen might merge in the future, becoming one vast megacity.[15] The Pearl River Delta is likely, according to Manuel Castells, "to become the most representative urban face of the twenty-first century," the "Southern China Metropolis," a continuous urban agglomeration comprising Hong Kong, Shenzhen, Guangzhou, Macau, Zhuhai, and other cities. Megacities connect multiple cities in a region, making the influence and impact of urbanism pervasive and ubiquitous. In Castell's terms, the megacity is a current trend which can be traced back to the joining of Tokyo–Yokohama–Nagoya with Osaka–Kobe–Kyoto, creating "the largest metropolitan agglomeration in human history, not only in population, but in economic and technological power." The distinctive feature of the new urban form of megacities is "being globally connected and locally disconnected, physically and socially."[16] In contrast to the metropolitan, high-density urbanism of Hong Kong, across the boundary the urbanization of the PRD is modelled on low-density, vehicle-based "mass suburban developments," created as enclaves for industry, commerce, or residential programs.[17]

In the last thirty years, Asia has established new terms for the city, the articulation of which will be defined in the decades to come. The megacity, the newest of which is the Southern China Metropolis, poses new challenges, and promises great opportunity. To meet these challenges, "the planner's dilemma is becoming more and more visible: cities and megacities seem to be unplannable."[18] Opportunity does not come without the risk of mistakes, regrets, and possible failure; opportunity is a game of uncertainty.

7.2 GHOSTS OF THE PAST

The trouble with the modernist architecture of the twentieth century was not that it created spatial order by repeating building elements, but rather that the effects of mass production led to monotony in cities. The demise of modernism also led to disillusionment with the production processes which had underpinned it. Standardization, as the outcome of a presumed rationalization and reduction of difference, drove modernist architecture toward the proliferation of homogeneity, vastness, erasure, and sprawl.

To what extent is homogenization a side effect of globalization? Koolhaas posed a related question in 1994, asking whether homogenization of urbanity was in fact an "intentional process, a conscious movement away from difference toward similarity."[19] The "generic city" was seen as a celebration of mediocrity, with boredom as the background to life's spectacle, and was ultimately understandable as simultaneously any place and no place. Later, in 2001, the "city of exacerbated difference" was recognized as a feature of contemporary Chinese urbanism, perhaps even as a contradiction of the generic city, involving the "greatest possible difference between its parts," rather than the "balance, harmony, and . . . degree of homogeneity" of more traditional forms of urbanism.[20] This struggle to come to terms with specificity and the generic continues. Koolhaas, perhaps today's preeminent theorist of sameness, remarks on the uniformity of cities in a recent interview in the *Journal of International Affairs*, claiming globalization gives rise to "profit-driven repetition" which "causes anxiety about identity".[21] Opposing the generic, here is a plea for uniqueness over sameness, difference over repetition, identity over blankness. Is this also indicative of a "natural" evolution of local influences, in which globalization "naturally produces indigenous phenomena and vernaculars"?[22] Sassen's concept of the global city challenges "the more diffuse homogenizing dynamics we associate with the globalization of consumer markets".[23] Global urbanization, and its flow of goods, services, cultures, technologies, and ideologies, is a force of homogenization. Despite having heralded the virtues of the generic city, Koolhaas now argues that the need for cities to promote their identifying uniqueness is paramount. Sameness always requires difference to striate its smoothness. Globalization, for Koolhaas, "designates a general schema of the hybridization of thought and action."[24] Increasingly the cities of tomorrow will negotiate the homogenizing forces of globalization according to the particularities of local issues, policies, and practices. This is not a call for the revival of Kenneth Frampton's critical regionalism, yet it may be a call for specificities to win out over generalities. This can be restated as the desire to promote difference through differentiation caused by local influences.

The tabula rasa is a questionable approach to the redevelopment of existing urban areas, as well as for rural agricultural land and villages in China, which are also being razed flat. This dominant paradigm for development in Asian cities over the last two decades is no longer a viable option for urbanization in this century. How will Chinese cities achieve their anticipated growth and densification without relying on tabula rasa strategies? Confronting the forces of urbanization which are quickly homogenizing nearly all cities in China, the central question here concerns how to achieve more performance-based, context-specific architectural and urban design.

Modernist principles of planning are still prevalent, as the default mode of urbanization in China with respect to the development of transport infrastructures, zoning, and land subdivisions. With regard to the successful management of urban growth in this critical, "Asian" century, transplanting traditional, evolved European or American models of urban growth to Asia would be tantamount to taking a neocolonialist approach. Although ubiquitous, such problems must be addressed in specific ways, according to local issues. The effect of globalization on China is evident in the emergence of Shanghai as a center for multinational companies, and its position "at the intersection of major global manufacturing, trading and real estate circuits."[25] China will in due course usurp the west. What seems a potential impediment to this "progress" is the model of urbanization itself, which is freighted with the potential to repeat mistakes made elsewhere in the past.

> The paradox of this period of rapid "urbanisation" is that the city itself is being effaced.
>
> Lewis Mumford, 1938[26]

Cities in China are being constructed quickly and linearly, with a blueprint for completion and no operating manual. This approach leaves little scope for mutation according to a more gradual model of development. Rapid urbanization has often led to economies in which goods are willingly consumed and disposed, and an urban order in which infrastructure is often inadequate, and architecture is often shoddily built for short-term gain. There is a drive to produce goods (or buildings) for short-term profit, and little motivation to produce goods that will endure.

In 2001 there were still eleven million bicycles in Beijing, but since then Beijingites have been buying nearly one thousand cars per day.[27] Despite the fact that typical densities of Chinese urban sprawl are much higher than those of America, suburban settlements in China are often gated and insular, perhaps because of traditions of courtyard housing, as well as Mao's *danwei* system of cooperative workers' settlement units. Sprawl in China and the U.S. do, however, have some traits in common. Both countries "consume an immense amount of productive agricultural land," and in both patterns of urbanization are "a function of rising car ownership."[28] Not only is the move to suburbia in China an expression of a new socioeconomic desire for material gain and the luxury of space, and of a wish to leave the "noisome city" behind, it is also a move away from the former communist collectivism of the *danwei*.[29]

Chinese cities seem to have some of the familiar shortcomings of American urbanism—decentralization, and hence sprawl, based on a model of private vehicular transportation. Peter Rowe has identified four modes of contemporary urbanization in China: first, "independent urban expansion"; second, urbanization along infrastructural corridors; third, centralization through consolidation of various urban entities; and fourth, the model of decentralization with new satellite cities, as in Shanghai's One City, Nine Towns model.[30] One of the urgent questions, if the mistakes of urbanization are to be pre-empted in China, is what alternatives may there be to urban decentralization, low density and sprawl? Combating the diffusion of a suburban model of development and extension of the city, Shanghai's polycentric model is characterized by "limited, governed, and selective densification in nodes in which public transport is a deterrent for car use," yet there is scope to further densify the existing city, through "reuse, substitution and implantation."[31] Asian urbanization has presented such problems and opportunities for several decades, and now demands contextually specific approaches.

In the 1960s, western modernism's grand and radical crescendo gave rise to disillusionment. Big problems were thought to require big ideas. Conceptions of the future will have—and perhaps ought to have—aspects of science fiction. In the "space age" of the 1960s, the belief in technology as the vehicle for the discovery of new potentials for society, if not entirely new worlds, drove a generation of architects to challenge prevalent notions of the city. In an article in 1960, Fumihiko Maki defined the term "megastructure," yet he also theorized "group forms"—small-scale village-like groupings—as viable alternatives to a pure metropolitan urban model.[32] The megastructures of the mid-twentieth century created an entirely new urban order, "in the form of a finite, whole, single building, designed and executed in a single architectural project."[33] Megastructures were often conceived, designed, and built in one single effort, thereby constraining their capacity to absorb change. Jonathan Solomon's essay in this book, "Public-Spheres," explicates his research into the interior urbanism of Hong Kong's fused shopping and infrastructural spaces, demonstrating how large-scale urban armatures can be grown or evolve over time, rather than designed as a singular whole. In this sense, the technologies of modernism created new kinds of networks from which the city gains new potentials to behave in plastic, indefinite, responsive modes.

> Bigness no longer needs the city: it competes with the city; or better still, it is the city. If urbanism generates potential and architecture exploits it, Bigness enlists the generosity of urbanism against the meanness of architecture.
>
> Rem Koolhaas, 1995[34]

Mumford summarizes the quest for "bigness," or urbanism, as agency against architecture. Christopher Alexander set out two "major problems" for architects to address: first, "the very large," referring to large-scale public and urban projects; and second, "the very small."[35] In today's parlance, "object-oriented design" addresses how small interactions and associations can aggregate to form larger, more complex wholes.

> In short, every successful institution of the metropolis repeats in its own organization the aimless giantism of the whole . . . . The organic, the qualitative, the autonomous were reduced to a secondary position, if not obliterated in every department.
>
> Lewis Mumford, 1934[36]

As part of an ongoing conversation, Kwinter states in relation to Koolhaas's texts "Bigness"[37] and "Whatever Happened to Urbanism"[38] that architecture's "unwillingness to confront the primary shaping forces of our time, modernisation and urbanisation" is of paramount concern.[39] Bigness is therefore a threshold "that bears at best an indirect relationship to size alone and a far more precise and direct relationship to the object's complexity." Koolhaas's seminal essay championed the "relinquishing of hard control."[40] Relinquishing to what? Kwinter asks, before answering "relinquishing to complexity, we learn [of] the shaping force that hovers like a cybernetic ghost at the edge of that surfer's wave."[41]

Size matters in Asia's global urbanization. Asian megacities are much larger and more densely populated than other megacities in other parts of the world. The vastness of the project of erasure and sprawl may in fact haunt the planet for years to come.[42]

7.3 AN ECOLOGICAL MODEL FOR TWENTY-FIRST CENTURY URBANISM

> A City! It is the grip of man on nature.
>
> Le Corbusier, *Towards a New Architecture*, 1921[43]

We face immense challenges concerning the future ecological viability of our cities. If alternative approaches are not researched, developed, and implemented soon, the current techniques of urbanization and their associated obsolescent, disposable architecture may contribute to future ecological disasters. Contemporary discourses related to "sustainable design" need to be reassessed and expanded for the cultural, social, and economic endurance of cities and buildings. Confronting short-sighted, haphazard, investment-driven urban development, this approach emphasizes public and cultural issues related to urban and societal evolution. In question is the legitimacy of low-quality building techniques, which result in buildings with short design life, and "throwaway" architecture. Key to achieving increased design life is the maintenance and preservation of existing social structures in new urban conditions, and the harnessing of new potentials for sensitive urbanization integrating existing architectural heritage.

As an alternative to disposable architecture, the economic benefits of high-quality design emphasize innovation in computational and material research, aiming for increasing the capacity of cities to evolve and adapt to dynamic contextual conditions. In addition, questions of the duration (design life) of individual buildings are concerned with how buildings can be conceived, built, used, and adapted for the long term, rather than becoming quickly obsolete, resulting in wasteful demolition and new construction. In the mid-twentieth century, Mumford lamented the "economic establishment" for how it was more likely to "destroy [a] product outright than to give it away or to limit the output at source."[44] In 1972, the first Club of Rome warned of the imminent limits on urban growth.[45] Later, in the 1990s, in *The First Global Revolution*,[46] the group claimed the world requires a common adversary to unite people, and this common enemy has become "global warming, water shortages, famine and the like." Regardless of culture, the planet's natural emergencies demand attention, everywhere, without exception.[47] Throughout history, man's technological achievements have often registered as domination of nature rather than sensitive adaptation to it. Discoveries are sought perhaps selfishly, in pursuit of control through short cuts. Mankind seeks to command rather than to grow, to control rather than to allow form to emerge.[48]

For decades society has called on contemporary architecture to be more "sustainable," more "green," more "eco-friendly," with an increasingly loud voice. Only recently has the call for reform in the face of crisis extended to cities. In Reyner Banham's 1969 book *The Architecture of the Well-Tempered Environment*, a new paradigm for environmental performance was sketched,[49] yet larger issues are at stake than well-tempered buildings. In their 1960s projects, *World Resources Inventory* and *World Game*, Buckminster Fuller and John McHale documented "the unequal distribution of world resources and population on 'Spaceship Earth'."[50] Fuller now seems one of a few anomalous personalities in architecture who focussed on global environmental issues imminently challenging the next generation. His influence can be understood as an "apotheosis of [the] combination of nature and network" in which the global logic of the planet was seen as our collective responsibility.[51] The future, as understood by those who conceived and designed Expo 1970, was something that urgently needed to be projected. World Fairs and Expos of the 1950s to the 1970s were broadcast to the world to describe the architecture, urbanism, infrastructures, and products of the future. Technology, the environment, and man make up a three-fold relationship which, due to imbalances in the world, is most often an asymmetrical relationship. The opposition man versus nature is a false distinction; in fact humans are a fundamental part of nature. James Lovelock's and Lynn Margulis's Gaia hypothesis, formulated in the 1970s, views the earth as one single "self-managing" ecosystem. The "deep ecology" movement (a term coined in 1973) also saw man as part of nature, not as its opponent.[52]

While some see the merging of an ecological sensibility with urbanism as the basis of the discipline of landscape urbanism, this is only one avenue for remediation of the presumed split between man and nature.[53] The integration of the natural and the artificial was a central theme guiding the Metabolists. Marshall suggests that "in recognizing a city as an ecosystem it naturally accommodates the biological and non-biological"[54] and does away with false dialectics of nature and artifice, organic and inorganic . . . . This concept of a complex, dynamic whole differs from the idea of a city designed as a finite and fixed object, and raises several questions about how to design, plan, or predict with certainty the inherently malleable order of the city. Balance needs to be discovered, urgently.

The scale of East Asian and South Asian urbanism demands a more robust and practical approach to the future of cities. The ecological and social implications of China's recent revision of Socialism—now "Socialism with Chinese characteristics"—and its adoption of a market economy at a local, national, and global level, are extreme and irreversible. Damage to the environment and vast migrations of workers are the two most challenging side-effects of urbanization in China. Although the dialectic of "nature and society" is principally a western one, the realities of vast urbanization and their associated challenges have been most prevalent, in recent decades, in the East.[55] It now seems urgent for China to find a role in leading the world in creating cities which not only thrive economically but that are more ecologically sensitive, and achieve a better social and economic balance between urban and rural populations, industry and agriculture, man and nature.

Paradigms of technological progress, scientific achievement, mechanistic positivism need to be evaluated. As alternatives to the tenets which drove modernist ideology, the concept of the city as an ecology which grows and changes over time, following a soft, evolutionary mode of growth, development, selection, and adaptation, seems at once a natural argument and a wholly artificial ambition. The paradoxes inherent in man's legacy of dominance over nature are acute, given the increasing scarcity of natural resources, including food and water. In various guises, there are calls for cities to go "back to nature." In some sense, this is a literal ambition for designers, planners, and policy makers "to foresee spaces for a nature that is close to us and yet not controlled, toned down or artificial".[56] The equilibrium of the environment requires balancing man and nature, urban and rural, and also industry and agriculture. More than ever urbanity needs to find the dynamic equilibrium inherent in biological and physical processes. An opposition such as the artificial versus the natural denies a model of urbanity in which interrelated systems and agents form a continuously dynamic concept of matter. The paradigm of the city as an ecology is not limited to the simple understanding of organic matter in the city. Ecological concepts involve "the interrelation and causality in hierarchical systems, a heuristic interest in development pathways and behaviors, and a sensitivity to temporal pattern and the subtle but inexorable process of 'spontaneous' formation, particularly in technological milieus."[57] Cues offered by natural systems, which are self-organized and take shape without a designer, will help to elaborate the complexity of urbanism.

7.4 THE PROBLEM OF FUNCTIONALITY, ENDURANCE, AND OBSOLESCENCE

Form does not always follow its intended function. Functionality does not have any ideal, stable state. Fitness for purpose is questionable. All buildings eventually become dysfunctional, even though functionally fit on opening day. A balance needs to be struck between fulfilling a stated purpose and allowing for the capacity of a building to adapt to future criteria. What is the status of cities with regard to their functionality? What triggers cities to adapt, evolve, and be continually renovated to fit the contingencies of the present?

The first machine age, the age of mechanization which culminated with the modernist movement, reflected a thoroughly positivist ideology, in which technology was seen as the catalyst for change, supported by blind belief in modern science. This certainty waned with mid-twentieth century 'revisionist' modernism, and functionalism was deemed an inadequate paradigm to drive and substantiate architectural culture. Reyner Banham viewed the inadequacy of functionalism as lying "not in the extent to which functionalism as a theory had pushed architecture in the direction of mindless mechanization, but in the extent to which functionalism, as practiced, had failed to go anywhere near as far as developing technology could carry it."[58] Functionalism, perhaps largely through the influence of Le Corbusier, was seen as interchangeable with rationalism. Recall Hilbersheimer's sanitized images of a pure matter–function approach to urban life. Modernists, with their wish for mechanical order, confused "mere formalism and regularity with purposefulness, and irregularity with intellectual confusion or technical incompetence."[59]

The challenges in this current century are in part the result of the unprecedented scale of urbanization, and also perhaps of uncertainty over the basis upon which cities can be planned. Do we even have the right terms, yet, to describe the task of designing dynamic patterns of interaction in space? Space is not immutable, but is rather responsive to shifting demands. This, then, is the central task of planning—and its intrinsic paradox—to design that which changes over long periods of time.

The paradox of endurance and impermanence is evident in Metabolism's fascination with impermanence, which has cultural roots in the making of temporary structures. The Ise Shrine in Japan, meticulously rebuilt every twenty years since AD 690, is perhaps the emblematic example of temporality as a device for instilling cultural continuity, involving the ritualized inheritance of the cultural and technological knowledge required to reconstruct the shrine precisely as it has been for centuries.[60] The theme of endurance can, however, be misconstrued as a reactive, even reactionary position, fundamentally at odds with modernization and urbanization. Considered as a model for contemporary Asian urbanization, the ideas of Jane Jacobs are "lost in translation," lacking pertinence for the unprecedented extent of urbanization in Asia. Jacobs's arguments, if not obscured by sentimentality, might be made tangible in the last ditch effort of preservationists, who are desperately seeking to save some of the existing traditional fabric of Chinese cities, most notoriously the Hutongs in Beijing and the Lilong housing of Shanghai.

Koolhaas, in an interview with Arata Isozaki, has claimed there were two tendencies in the Metabolist movement, "one is very formal, and very harsh, the other shapeless and undefined." Fumihiko Maki's notion of "group form" grew out of his observations of "recurring vernacular patterns in different parts of the world." His interest in organic urban growth runs counter to the hard masterplanning sensibility of late modernism, and specifically to that of some of his Metabolist peers. Related to the organizational concept of group form is the principle of "slow-growth urbanism," which counters what Maki labels "a product of absolute power from the past or a by-product of some techno-utopia future expressed by everyone from Le Corbusier to Yona Friedman to Kenzo Tange."[61]

Marshall has observed that "some traditional urbanism can have functional order without planning while some Modernist planned urbanism is dysfunctional despite planning"[62] While a distinction between planned cities and unplanned cities is helpful in highlighting historical differences in urbanism, these are not options to choose between. Historically, cities grew as aggregates, emerging from local, small-scale architectural interventions which collectively shaped the whole.

As a side effect of a larger ecology of matter, the lifespan of a building is directly related to the severity of the climate, the extent of maintenance, and the inherent resilience of its materials. Decay and failure of materials can lead to ruination.[63] Although time will ensure a building undergoes continual material change, its use also often changes. In this sense, a building becomes obsolete if it is no longer suitable for its intended purpose. Users might, however, alter uses or introduce wholly new uses to buildings to make them relevant. What is the equivalent of these architectural issues in urbanism? How can cities function well over long periods? How can they adapt and remain relevant, and thrive?

7.5 TIME, CHANGE, AND ADAPTATION

Let us revisit the paradox of planning for urban growth through the investigation of the endurance of cities, and how urbanism can mature over long periods, and allow for growth, change, evolution, and transformation over time.[64] A set of oppositions have been interrogated, including the relation between flexible design approaches and singular solutions; permanent or long-lasting buildings versus adaptable or reuseable buildings; and how cities can be planned to be complete versus patterns of urban growth and change. Within the various theoretical stances of contemporary urbanists, many will agree that "there is a certain looseness in urbanism, and a certain fixity and rigidity in architecture."[65] Whether it manifests as flourishing or as decay, when we try to understand how cities take form and how they transform over time, change is the only constant. This is a call for new techniques to address what is articulated here as the surrender to the forces of time. Although time, as its relation to movement is a prominent theme of the twentieth century, in art, literature, cinema, some arenas of avant-garde architecture, reconsidering "materialist" approaches to space, will serve to explain the formation and functioning of modernity.[66] The only inevitable and unavoidable fact of urbanism is that space is not fixed, but changes through time.

Le Corbusier, among other modernists, was fascinated by traditional urban fabric, and sketched in particular the white villages of the Mediterranean. This fascination with grown or evolved morphology may have been a complement to the top-down modes in which he projected urbanism in his day job; or is it a paradoxical aberration? Perhaps the modernists, with their will to make the world anew, lacked the tools with which to negotiate the morphological integration evident in these villages.

Regarding an understanding of complex systems, Christopher Alexander made an important distinction between "generated structures" and "fabricated structures."[67] He cautioned, however, against "gradualism" as a basis for understanding step-by-step processes, akin to "evolutionary adaptation," as "making the same mistake that the early adherents of Darwinism made in biology—to assume that small steps alone, modification coupled with selective pressure, would be sufficient to get a genotype to a new state, hence to create entirely new organisms."[68]

Marshall contrasts a paradigm of evolutionary urbanism with a "creationist" model, in which the city is designed as an object, and a "developmental" model, in which the city is understood as a growing organism.[69] Despite the religious metaphor, "creation" remains a prevalent model for masterplanning, with the "master" planning the city as a prescribed outcome from a position of authority and omnipotence. Metaphors aside, the "developmental" model was argued for by Christopher Alexander, albeit metaphorically.

The creationist and developmental paradigms are helpful in characterizing the reciprocity between design as a form of omnipotent control, and the inevitable adaptation of the city, and they set up the argument for an evolutionary understanding of the city, in which "designers and planners are only ever partly—only temporarily—in control."[70] In his book *The Nature of Order: The Process of*

Creating Life, Alexander delineates a distinction between "living structures" and "non-living structures." The classification does not make a strict distinction between organic and inorganic matter, but aims to explain, and possibly excuse, artefacts which, "for the first time, introduce[d] a type of structure on earth which nature itself could not, in principle, create."[71] The understanding of order, then, is rooted in the processes of its formation.

Urban culture, social order, and technological change can be said to evolve alongside each other. These longer-term transformations inherent in urban evolution involve "a combination of variation, reproduction and selection," and take place over successive iterations of adaptation.[72] Interestingly, Mumford equates the "human heritage" of cities with permanence, when evidence of the changing, evolutionary nature of cities suggests otherwise.

> The mark of the city is its purposive social complexity. It represents the maximum possibility of humanizing the natural environment and of naturalizing the human heritage: it gives a cultural shape to the first, and it externalizes, in permanent collective forms, the second.
>
> Lewis Mumford[73]

In his book *Design with Nature*, Ian McHarg outlined ways in which nature and culture can better coexist.[74] Planning, traditionally seen as a discipline which seeks to forecast stable, predictable order, is today faced with the immense challenges posed by global warming, the effects of which, given a minimum rise in temperature of two degrees Celsius, include "drought or flooding in many parts of the world, and a sea level rise of several metres within a century and much more after that."[75] A roadmap to mitigate such conditions is beyond the scope of this book. A central concern, however, is the investigation of ways in which urbanity can adapt to the changing global environment, with local pertinence as a basis for planning for an uncertain future. A new model for planning requires a response to global warming, and "an evolutionary step forward in humanity's ability to plan for and manage its future."[76] Some urbanists, landscape urbanists, environmentalists, and others insist that neither mitigation nor adaptation can be effective planning strategies unless there is a massive transformation of the economy, its mode of using resources and its basis in disposable manufactured goods, buildings, and cities. As a prerequisite for such change, society must begin to accept the natural complexity of the world, and to learn to better adapt to it.

A series of oppositions characterize the evolutionary mechanisms of urbanism, including history and the future, convention and innovation, endurance and ephemerality, permanence and change. All of these help to explicate the concept of evolution in cities, society, and culture.

NOTES

1 > T. Verebes (2010) "Endurance and Obsolescence: Instant Cities, Disposable Buildings, and the Construction of Culture," in *Sustain and Develop: 306090, Vol. 13*, eds. Jonathan Solomon and Joshua Bolchover (New York: Princeton Architectural Press).

2 > Le Corbusier (1929) *The City of Tomorrow and Its Planning* (London: Dover), 138.

3 > T.J. Campanella (2008) *The Concrete Dragon: China's Urban Revolution and What It Means for the World* (New York: Princeton Architectural Press), 190.

4 > Campanella, *The Concrete Dragon*, 282.

5 > R. Koolhaas and H.U. Obrist (2011) *Project Japan* (Köln: Taschen), 57.

6 > J. Jiang (2009) "Go China's Sustainability: Asynchronous Revolutions," in *Sustain and Develop: 306090, Vol. 13*, eds. Jonathan Solomon and Joshua Bolchover (New York: Princeton Architectural Press), 136.
7 > C.J. Chung, J. Inaba, R. Koolhaas, and T.L. Sze (2001) *Great Leap Forward* (Köln: Taschen).
8 > Campanella, *The Concrete Dragon*, 159.
9 > T. Zhang (2011) "Chinese Cities in a Global Society," in *The City Reader*, eds. R.T. LeGates and F. Stout (London: Routledge), 590.
10 > W. Pan (2008) "Utopian Cities, or How the Author Solves the Problems of Rural China," in *The Chinese Dream*, eds. N. Mars and A. Hornsby (Rotterdam: 010), 466.
11 > J.C. Brazier and T. Lam (2009) "Go West, Go Big, Go Green? A Journey through China's 'Great Opening of the West'," in *Sustain and Develop: 306090, Vol. 13*, eds. Jonathan Solomon and Joshua Bolchover (New York: Princeton Architectural Press), 85.
12 > Zhang, "Chinese Cities in a Global Society," 594.
13 > M. Hulshof and D. Roggeveen (2011) *How the City Moved to Mr. Sun* (Amsterdam: SUN), 81.
14 > Zhang, "Chinese Cities in a Global Society," 597.
15 > D.G. Shane (2011) *Urban Design since 1945: A Global Perspective* (London: Wiley), 29.
16 > M. Castells (1996) *The Rise of the Network Society* (Oxford: Blackwell), 404.
17 > Shane, *Urban Design since 1945*, 44.
18 > H. Haken (2000) "Foreword" in *Self-Organisation and the City*, J. Portugali (Berlin: Springer-Verlag), v.
19 > R. Koolhaas (1995) "The Generic City," in *S, M, L, XL*, OMA, R. Koolhaas, and B. Mau (Rotterdam: 010), 1248.
20 > Chung et al., *Great Leap Forward*, 29.
21 > R. Koolhaas (2012) Interview with Paul Fraioli, *Journal of International Affairs*, April.
22 > S. Kwinter (2011) *Requiem for the City at the End of the Millennium* (Barcelona: Actar), 34.
23 > S. Sassen (2001) "The Global City: Introducing a Concept and Its History," in *Mutations*, eds. R. Koolhaas, S. Boeri, S. Kwinter, N. Tazi, and H.U. Obrist (Barcelona: Actar), 114.
24 > J. Attali "The Roman System, or the Generic in All Times and Tenses," in *Mutations*, eds. R. Koolhaas, S. Boeri, S. Kwinter, N. Tazi, and H.U. Obrist (Barcelona: Actar, 2001), 21.
25 > S. Sassen (2008) "Disaggregating the Global Economy," in *Shanghai Transforming*, ed. I. Gil (Barcelona: Actar), 81.
26 > L. Mumford (1986) *The Lewis Mumford Reader*, ed. D.L. Millner (Athens, Georgia: University of Georgia Press), 109.
27 > Campanella, *The Concrete Dragon*, 220–221.
28 > Campanella, *The Concrete Dragon*, 293.
29 > A. Hornsby (2008) "Hey Fuck! Where'd the City Go?" in *The Chinese Dream*, eds. N. Mars and A. Hornsby (Rotterdam: 010), 206.
30 > P.G. Rowe (2008) "Urbanising China," in *Shanghai Transforming*, ed. I. Gil (Barcelona: Actar), 79.
31 > S. Boeri (2010) "Five Ecological Challenges for the Contemporary City," in *Ecological Urbanism*, eds. M. Mostafavi and G. Doherty (Baden: Lars Müller), 449.
32 > Shane, *Urban Design since 1945*, 259.
33 > S. Marshall (2009) *Cities, Design, Evolution* (New York: Routledge), 83.
34 > R. Koolhaas (1995) "Bigness, or the Problem of Large," in *S, M, L, XL*, OMA, R. Koolhaas, and B. Mau (Rotterdam: 010), 515.
35 > C. Alexander (1980) *The Nature of Order, Book 2: The Process of Creating Life* (Berkley: CES), 557.
36 > L. Mumford (1961) *The City in History* (London: Harcourt Brace Jovanovitch), 531.
37 > Koolhaas, "Bigness, or the Problem of Large."
38 > R. Koolhaas (1995) "Whatever Happened to Urbanism?" in *S, M, L, XL*, OMA, R. Koolhaas, and B. Mau (Rotterdam: 010).
39 > Kwinter, *Requiem for the City*, 78.
40 > Koolhaas, "Bigness, or the Problem of Large."
41 > Kwinter, *Requiem for the City*, 80.
42 > Shane, *Urban Design since 1945*, 332.
43 > Le Corbusier, (1921) *Towards a New Architecture.*
44 > Mumford, *The City in History*, 545.
45 > D.H. Meadows, D.L. Meadows, J. Randers, and W.W. Behrens III (1972) *The Limits to Growth: A Report for the Club of Rome's Project on the Predicament of Mankind* (New York: Universe Books).

46 > A. King and B. Schneider (1991) *The First Global Revolution: A Report by the Council of the Club of Rome* (New York: Pantheon Books).
47 > R. Koolhaas (2010) "Advancement versus Apocalypse," in *Ecological Urbanism*, eds. M. Mostafavi and G. Doherty (Baden: Lars Müller), 67.
48 > L. Mumford (1934) *Technics and Civilisation* (London: Harvest), 37–43.
49 > R. Banham (1969) *The Architecture of the Well-Tempered Environment* (Chicago: University of Chicago).
50 > Shane, *Urban Design since 1945*, 29.
51 > Koolhaas, "Advancement versus Apocalypse," 62.
52 > S. Kwinter (2010) "Notes on the Third Ecology," in *Ecological Urbanism*, eds. M. Mostafavi and G. Doherty (Baden: Lars Müller), 104.
53 > C. Waldheim (2010) "Weak Work," in *Ecological Urbanism*, eds. M. Mostafavi and G. Doherty (Baden: Lars Müller), 118.
54 > Marshall, *Cities, Design, Evolution*, 116.
55 > N. Mars and E.W. Schienke (2008) "The Green Edge," in *The Chinese Dream*, eds. N. Mars and A. Hornsby (Rotterdam: 010), 151.
56 > S. Boeri (2010) "Five Ecological Challenges for the Contemporary City," in *Ecological Urbanism*, eds. M. Mostafavi and G. Doherty (Baden: Lars Müller), 447.
57 > Kwinter, *Requiem for the City*, 81.
58 > R. Banham (1960) *Theory and Design in the First Machine Age* (Oxford: Butterworth-Heinemann), 11.
59 > Mumford, *The City in History*, 302.
60 > Koolhaas and Obrist, *Project Japan*, 19.
61 > Koolhaas and Obrist, *Project Japan*, 37, 295, 304.
62 > Marshall, *Cities, Design, Evolution*, 217.
63 > M. Mostafavi and D. Leatherbarrow (1993) *On Weathering: The Life of Buildings in Time* (Cambridge: MIT), 5.
64 > M. Hensel and T. Verebes (1998) *Urbanisations* (London: Black Dog).
65 > R. Koolhaas (1996) "Architecture against Urbanism," in *Managing Urban Change*, eds. Y. Verwijnen and P. Lehtovuori (Helsinki: UIAH), 121.
66 > S. Kwinter (2002) *The Architecture of Time* (Cambridge, MA: MIT), 214.
67 > Alexander, *The Nature of Order, Book 2*, 180.
68 > Alexander, *The Nature of Order, Book 2*, 198.
69 > Marshall, *Cities, Design, Evolution*, 255–256.
70 > Marshall, *Cities, Design, Evolution*, 255–256.
71 > Alexander, *The Nature of Order, Book 2*, xiv.
72 > Marshall, *Cities, Design, Evolution*, 218.
73 > L. Mumford (1986) *The Lewis Mumford Reader*, ed. D.L. Miller (Athens, Georgia: University of Georgia Press), 104.
74 > I. McHarg (1995) *Design with Nature* (London: Wiley).
75 > S. Wheeler (2011) "Urban Planning and Global Climate Change," in *The City Reader*, eds. R.T. LeGates and F. Stout (London: Routledge), 460.
76 > Wheeler, "Urban Planning and Global Climate Change," 460.

CHAPTER 8

JONATHAN D. SOLOMON >PUBLIC-SPHERES

ATMOSPHERE AND ADAPTABLE SPACE IN HONG KONG

"This is truly a surreal place," begins the Discovery Channel's special on Ski Dubai, a 22,500-square-meter indoor ski arena in Mall of the Emirates.[1] Ski Dubai opened in 2005 and includes a four-hundred-meter long, eighty-five-meter high run, and four other slopes of varying difficulty. While even among the world's indoor beaches and ski slopes the climatic differentials at Ski Dubai are extreme—the average high temperature in Dubai in August is forty-one degress Celsius, while the temperature in Ski Dubai varies from between one degree below zero in the day and six degrees below when snow is produced at night—they are not necessarily unexpected. In fact none of the manipulations of program, of topography, or of climate at Ski Dubai are outside the reality of the contemporary urban experience or the definition of public space in cities, from colonialism through globalism.

Like Dubai, Hong Kong is a city of the unexpected and improbable. Its complexity denies stable relationships between public and private spaces and distinctions between formal and informal operators that are the traditional purview of the masterplan, in favor of evolutionary processes, mutations of code, or accidents that produce new species. Nowhere can this better be seen than in the changing role of atmosphere in forming and organizing the city. The complexes of interconnected, air-conditioned interiors spreading in three-dimensional networks for kilometers across the territory appear at a scale suggesting planed implementation, but their slow growth in a series of incremental and often unforeseen moves reveals substantively different origins; their remarkable effects on public life in the city reveal equally unanticipated consequences.

Networked atmospheres in Hong Kong are neither the result of formal masterplanning nor of informal solution finding, rather these networks have developed aformally, as a result of processes neither entirely informal nor entirely formal, but through collaborations between comprehensive planning and bottom-up solution finding, resulting in unique divergences.[2]

The accident that begins this particular divergence is the invention of the modern air-conditioner, introduced into the city broadly beginning in the 1960s. For a century after its founding, urban form in Hong Kong extended and blurred distinctions between inside and outside, working to cool through strategies ranging from shade trees on public streets to deep, high-ceilinged arcades protected from the sun by bamboo screens, to cross-ventilated interiors. With the introduction of the air-conditioner this boundary space was radically reduced, to the thickness of a pane of glass. At the same time the energy differential between interior and exterior climates was radically increased, an increase that feedback would only further, as hot exhaust from the interior was routinely vented directly into the street.

Mutation of this atmospheric boundary brought about new spatial products. Artificially cooled interiors became a new space for commercial activity, proving popular and outgrowing the small building footprints of the city's colonial grid. Footbridges, beginning as privately funded projects to increase the profitability of second-level arcades in the1960s, gradually formed a network. As the network proved commercially successful, with linked properties largely owned by the developer Hong Kong Land renting at the same or even higher rates than those on the street, the government began constructing more links to improve connections to transit facilities. Exterior fringe belts, often older street networks lined with small shops with an atmosphere of their own, reconfigured as projects like the 1994 Central and Mid-Levels Escalator and brought new crowds. In the late 1990s and 2000s, the air-conditioned interior arcade linking train station to shopping mall to office or home became the organizational framework of Hong Kong's urban life in comprehensive developments such as the International Financial Center and Quarry Bay Center, or, further afield, developments over the Olympic, Sha Tin and Kowloon stations of the city's Mass Transit Rail (MTR) stations. The mutation became the norm. Hong Kong's public sphere is a public-sphere: an atmosphere of public life.

SOMETHING IN THE AIR

Atmosphere fascinates architects because, like the soul, it is simultaneously intangible and primal. Mark Wigley neatly explores these contradictions in his 1998 "Architecture of Atmosphere."[3] Since the modern period, atmosphere has been portrayed as equal parts powerful and ephemeral, from Reyner Banham's "well-tempered environment" to, in a more contemporary context, Sylvia Lavin's "kiss" and Jeff Kipnis's "blush."[4]

Footbridge on Chater Road linking air-conditioned shopping arcades in the Mandarin Hotel and Prince's Building, 1965. Photograph courtesy of the Government of the HKSAR.

Atmosphere has become equally alluring to studies of the origins of modern civic space in urbanism and political theory. David Gissen describes the works of architects Pierre Patte and Eugene Henard, engineer Jean-Charles Adolphe Alphand, and civic planner Georges Haussmann, who, in his words, “ensnared water, gas, trees, stone, and animal and human ablutions into a circulatory vision of an urban streetscape . . . designed to circulate both nature matter, ‘bourgeois’ concepts of leisure-nature, and state-capitalist notions of nature (nature furthering real estate investment, among other economic aspects).”[5] German philosopher Peter Sloterdijk has described the history of artificial atmosphere as beginning with the 1848 Palm House at Kew Gardens, designed by Decimus Turner and engineered by Richard Burton. Heated by coal boilers in its basement that fed water pipes under iron gratings in the floor, the Palm House combined active and passive environmental management to sustain an environment suitable for the keeping of various species of exotic palms being returned to Britain from colonial possessions. To Sloterdijk, the Palm House “marked a clear caesura in the history of building,” by recognizing that “organisms and climate reference each other, as it were, a priori.”[6]

A network of publicly and privately developed footbridges join diverse programs in Central, 2010. Photo by Jonathan D. Solomon.

There is rich interest in the creation of atmosphere in contemporary art and architecture practice, much of which embodies both a pursuit of adaptive morphology and spatial effects and a critique of static definitions of the public. Olafur Eliasson's 2003 *Weather Project* at the Tate Modern in London manipulated humidity, heat, and light to conflate the boundless experience of the exterior within the enclosed. An Te Liu's 2008 *Cloud* at the eleventh Venice Architecture Biennale, is an assembly of air purifiers, ionizers, washers, humidifiers, and ozone air cleaners running continuously. "*Cloud* is read" writes Mason White, "as a machined equivalent of an actual cloud abstracted into its components of moisture processing, air exchanges and atmospheric densities and imagines the potential, as with snow-making machines, of generating entire weather conditions at will, . . . its own bubble of processed air dissipating into the larger space, an invisible zone of purity shape-shifting with the interior microclimates."[7] Diller Scofidio + Renfro describe their 2002 Blur Building on Lake Neuchatel, Switzerland more simply, as "an architecture of atmosphere."[8] Utilizing water as a building material, 31,500 high-pressure mist nozzles emit fog generated from the water of the lake below. The Dutch Pavilion at Expo 2000 in Hanover actualizes what Sloterdijk refers to as "an operational unit of the sprawling triad of space station, greenhouse, and Human Island." "A hybrid form between botanic garden and large residence," he writes, "this brilliantly bizarre building, a kind of vertical plant-tower, offers a contemporary comment on an expanding definition of dwelling spaces of biotopic diversity under conditions of high urban density."[9]

A review of projects collected by Zoe Ryan for the 2006 exhibition *The Good Life* at the Van Alen Institute in New York reveals a particular fascination with the adaptability of atmosphere to structure the public realm. Rebar's *(PARK)ing* (2005) converts San Francisco parking spaces into urban parks using sod and potted plants; Greyworld's public art projects in the UK, Ireland, France, and Germany (1996–2005) convert street furniture and guard railings into musical instruments; Takano Landscape Planning Company's *Takachi Ecology Park* in Obihiro City, Japan (2006) includes inflatable domes to simulate weightlessness and a "fog and water environment that changes constantly depending on the weather conditions"; temporary urban beaches convert highways to recreational spaces in Paris, Amsterdam, Brussels, and Rome.[10]

While atmosphere generates broad interest, it has remained largely a boutique project for urbanism. With the exception of projects such as Masdar, the zero-carbon city in Abu Dhabi masterplanned by Norman Foster, comprehensive solutions remain elusive. Evolved and adaptable conditions such as those in Hong Kong therefore offer rich opportunities for study.

HONG KONG'S PUBLIC-SPHERE

Hong Kong is an ideal testing ground for how atmosphere catalyzes and organizes public life at an urban scale. The city lacks any of the figure–ground relationships that traditionally bring order to public space in either the western or eastern tradition: there is no axis, edge, or center. Even the ground itself, and the streets, courtyards, and squares that populate it, are elusive.[11] In their place, microclimates of temperature, humidity, noise, and smell constitute entirely new social hierarchies. Welcome to the public-sphere.

Cool air, whether actively generated or encouraged passively through shading, rescripts circulation and redefines gathering spaces. At sites where a masterplan would call up an axis, a formal solution to the representation of state power, the free circulation of multiple modes of travel and movement of services, and the armature of the public sphere, Hong Kong's evolutionary development drives aformal responses. Take the new headquarters of the Government of the Hong Kong Special Administrative Region, located on a parcel of land named Tamar, after a British ship that once docked in the area of the harbor from which it was reclaimed. The Tamar site has no formal context in the city. Even its major architectural feature, a huge gateway formed by two office slabs, leads nowhere but into another, earlier office slab. The connection between the Tamar site and Hong Kong Park is in no way axial, but it is no less active in the traditional role of the axis. The path leads down a partially enclosed escalator and through a high-end shopping mall, Pacific Place, across a footbridge over Queensway, a busy eight-lane highway, and through Queensway Plaza, a shopping mall originally built by the government and now leased to the luxury department store Lane Crawford, through the lobby of the Admiralty Center office towers, down an escalator past the entrance to the MTR, up another escalator to a footbridge over Harcourt Road, another express artery, before accessing Tamar via a landscaped roof deck. Passing through interior and exterior atmospheres, public and private spaces, and changing constantly in dimension and direction in three dimensions, the path is an unplanned anomaly, but one that is uniquely adapted to suit the needs of the city.

At Admiralty, in Central, or at Taikoo Place and other dense subcenters throughout the city, it is common to find pedestrians streaming through corridors routed through corporate lobbies, above public parks, or under streets rather than at grade in order to stay cool or dry. Perfumed air distinguishes distinct cultural and economic strata that are spatially contiguous and largely indistinct from one another. Central, a high-end shopping mall branded by Armani, is distinguished from an adjacent and connected mall catering to Filipina foreign domestic workers by, among other things, prodigious scents. Just across a footbridge over Chater Road, varying access to natural light affects retail rents at the Landmark Mall. Up the hill along the Central and Midlevels Escalator, tourists and western expatriates gather on a street of steep steps in much the same way. Cool air is not the only sphere generated by Staunton's, the adjacent pub: the smell of beer and cigarettes and grilling beef and the sounds of generic rock and roll, English chatter, and clinking glasses form a microclimate distinct from the local street market just a block away.

The public-sphere is so interesting precisely because it is a catalyst for adaptability. The incremental growth and change of aformal armatures, the articulation of private and public spaces (and what is permissible in both extremes), and the atmospheric properties of spaces substitute for the "planning" of buildings and space in their conventional senses. The result is a far more adaptable urbanism.

Generally appreciated for its exquisite detailing and inventive engineering, Norman Foster's 1985 HSBC Main Building sits adjacent to one of the last remaining colonial public spaces in Hong Kong, Statue Square. Both the square and the building, with its open ground plan below suspended banking halls, are

Footbridge network in Central Hong Kong overlaid with a gradient of ambient air temperature. Drawing by Adam Frampton, Jonathan D. Solomon, and Clara Wong.

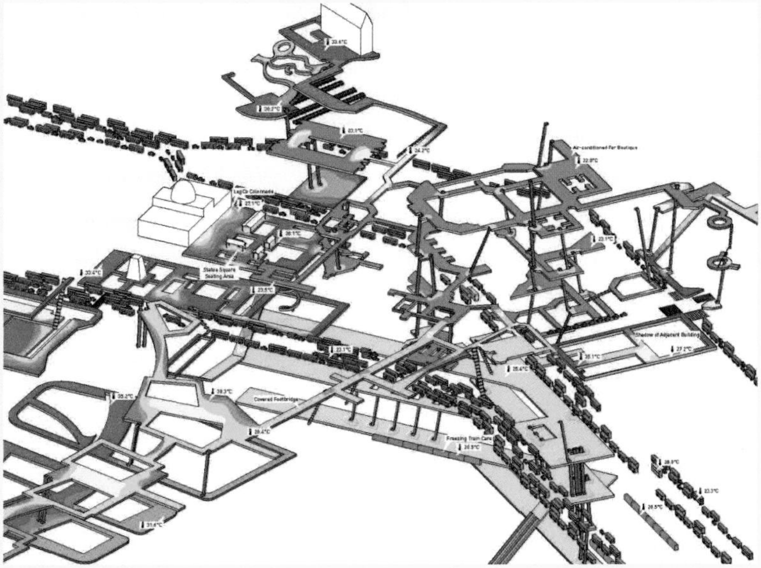

host on Sundays to foreign domestic workers gathering on their government mandated day off. David Howes uses this space, and the larger weekend occupation of footbridges outside shopping malls, as an example of the influence of atmosphere on the city's public sphere. Referring to the work of urban ethnographer Lisa Law, he describes how the sounds and scents of the foreign workers, mostly Filipina, establish temporary cultural boundaries between their "Little Manila" and the financial center. "This conflict within Hong Kong society," writes Howes, "over the sensuous (re)construction of space by the migrant workers during their leisure hours, testifies to the politics of differing sensory strategies for making sense of the same place, and calls attention to the multicultural tensions embedded in the city's urban fabric."[12]

Although the atmospheres of the contemporary city are highly planned by MEP Engineers, they are limited to distinct spatial boundaries. The bounded interior marks a new kind of threshold space in the city, aformal armatures mediating between the artificially cooled, scrubbed, formally planned interiors of the city's offices, shops, and homes, and the hot, messy, informal life of the street.

THE CITY AS NATURAL ARTIFICE

What is the code and what is the mutation? This question is fundamental to understanding the emergence of new forms of civic space in the contemporary city. The public-spheres of Hong Kong attest to the malleability not only of urban space and its patterns of use, but also of our own notions as citizens of the natural and the artificial. Consider examples such as Hong Kong's Cheung Kong Garden. Opened in 2002, Cheung Kong Garden is managed by Cheung Kong Holdings but accessible to the public, an amenity provided by the developer to maximize the floor area of the adjacent tower, Cheung Kong Center. Despite the verdure, Cheung Kong Garden is a fabrication; complete with cement formed into the shape of rocky outcroppings and artificially circulated watercourses, it sits atop a parking garage. Contrast this with Cheung Kong Center, designed by César Pelli and opened in 1999, which boasts the cities cleanest (most filtered) interior air. Conditioned via TAAS, or Totally Adaptive Air-conditioning System, it could not be less natural, and yet it is the most "pure" of atmospheres in Hong Kong.

Unlike formal public spaces, public-spheres do not rely on coded relationships between space and meaning. They work in broad strokes: the creation of cool air, whether by the planting of shade trees or the running of air-conditioning, will engender subjective readings of the city's structures, leading some to treat the space as a thoroughfare, others as a plaza, others as a café. At the extreme, a tube of air kept below freezing in the desert can engender, or at least allow the possibility of, a ski slope. Precisely because of their aformal and asymbolic construction, public-spheres are agents for the adaptable city.

ACKNOWLEDGEMENTS

The author's research was supported by the University of Hong Kong's Small Project Funding grant scheme. An early draft was presented at The City and Public Space in Asia workshop, organized by the author and Gregory Bracken with the Delft School of Design International Institute for Asian Studies and the University of Hong Kong. The author's research is an elaboration of themes explored with Adam Frampton and Clara Wong in *Cities without Ground* (Oro Editions, 2012). Airtek Hong Kong provided early support of the measurement of temperature differentials in Hong Kong malls.

NOTES

1 > Discovery Channel, "Ski Dubai World." Accessed July 7, 2012. http://dsc.discovery.com/videos/really-big-things-season-2-shorts-ski-dubai-world.html

2 > Jonathan Solomon (forthcoming) "Hong Kong: Aformal Urbanism," in *Shaping the City: Studies in History, Theory and Urban Design*, 2nd ed., eds. Rodolphe El-Khoury and Edward Robbins (New York: Routledge).

3 > Mark Wigley (1998) "The Architecture of Atmosphere," *Daidalos* 68: 18–27.

4 > Reyner Banham (1969) *Architecture of the Well-Tempered Environment* (London: The Architectural Press); Sylvia Lavin (2011) *Kissing Architecture* (Princeton: Princeton University Press); Jeffrey Kipnis (1997) "The Cunning of Cosmetics," in *El Croquis: Herzog & de Meuron* (Madrid: El Croquis).

5 > David Gissen (2010) "APE," in *Design Ecologies: Essays on the Nature of Design*, eds. Lisa Tilder and Beth Blostien (New York: Princeton Architectural Press), 65–66.

6 > Peter Sloterdijk(2009) "Atmospheric Politics," in *Space Reader: Heterogenous Space in Architecture*, eds. Michael Hensel, Christopher Hight and Achim Menges (London: Wiley), 173–174.

7 > Mason White (2009) "99.7 Per Cent Pure," *AD Architectural Design* 79, no. 3: 21–22.

8 >"Diller Scofidio + Renfro." Accessed July 7, 2012. http://dsrny.com/

9 > Peter Sloterdijk (2009) "Foam City: About Urban Spatial Multitudes," in *New Geographies 0*, Harvard University Graduate School of Design, 136–143.

10 > Zoe Ryan (2006) *The Good Life: New Public Spaces for Recreation* (New York: Van Allen Institute), 29, 31, 56, 61.

11 > Adam Frampton, Jonathan D. Solomon, and Clara Wong (2012) *Cities without Ground* (San Francisco: Oro Editions).

12 > David Howes (2005) "Architecture and the Senses," in *Sense of the City*, ed. Mirko Zardini (Baden: Lars Mueller), 326–327.

CHAPTER 9

CONVERSATION 3

MATTHEW PRYOR (MP) WITH TOM VEREBES (TV)

TV This book's core thesis questions the legitimacy of conventional masterplanning techniques to address the complexities of urban growth and transformation, and in particular to rapid urbanization occurring at the pace it is in China. As a landscape architect based in Hong Kong for so many years, and given your experience of working within multidisciplinary masterplanning teams alongside your teaching and research, I am interested to hear your views on the preeminent models and methodologies from which urbanization takes shape and the extent to which masterplanning can deal with the speed and complexity and quantity of urbanization taking place, especially within the context of the unrelenting and unprecedented urbanization occurring in Asia. What do you believe to be the merits and pitfalls of top-down centralized planning processes, and by what means can bottom-up emergent processes be developed and engage local constituencies, issues, and desires, to generate local specificities within global models?

MP Your question doesn't have a yes/no answer to it, so I'll start by briefly outlining my experience in urbanization. I came to Hong Kong in 1991, and I was involved in the latter end of the New Town Development program in Hong Kong, and the new airport in Hong Kong. Within this part of the world masterplanning seems to be a mainstay of private consultancy in the planning, architecture, and engineering fields. Most of the masterplans I've been involved in have been driven by very much top-down, large-scale planning methods, and I think the largest masterplan I've worked on was for six to seven hundred thousand people, but I know that doesn't even compare with the size of some cities being developed.

Approaches to masterplanning range from the very basic laying out of roads, building massing, and land uses to highly sophisticated techniques which use computer models to test the sustainability of proposed development against various sustainability indicators, e.g. energy efficiency, waste, etc. These masterplans have tended to be premised on the basis of accommodating a certain population with the requisite commercial, infrastructural, institutional, industrial facilities, within a given area, as a response to migration from surrounding areas, or commonly from the speculative opinion of a developer or governmental organization. Up until about the mid-1990s it was just about laying it all out, as evident in the New Town layout plans, which are highly engineered.

From the latter half of the 1990s, masterplanning teams were becoming more sensitive to the fact that it should be more than just an urban fabric of roads and the buildings: there was a soft component to new urbanization. You need to have community facilities to actually make places for people. Yet this is very difficult for masterplanning teams to achieve that because they're coming at it from the wrong angle. They largely deal with physical form and they do not have a connection to engage with community, and nor do they have the capacity to create community. So masterplanning becomes a one-moment-in-time view of what the city should be, a snapshot. The masterplan is built, yet who is it given to and how do they occupy, take ownership, and modify it? In the last ten years, the landscape architect has been moving slowly to the front end of the development process, from being a designer of the green elements or the beautification of masterplans to somebody who has a stronger connection with the existing environment and potential social community. Landscape architects have interests and skills in helping communities to develop and find balance with their environment.

TV You raise some questions concerning masterplanning as a purely goal-oriented process. In the history of urbanization, all cities grow, change, transform, and some even die out. Within the context of Asian urbanization, there has been so much building, destruction, and rebuilding, which has already proven the inadequacy of masterplanning and the limited value of the resulting architecture, and then the whole process starts again almost from scratch, as a cyclical tabula rasa mechanism. Landscape architecture sketches out ways in which the city is understood as a paradigm of ecology, and more precisely that of literal growth and change, learning from analogies to natural ecologies. There is a prevalent belief that the inorganic matter of the city grows and dies, adapts and changes in relation to the symbiosis with literal organic ecological process. When you describe the role of a landscape architect, or a sustainability expert or an ecologist, it seems there is much to learn from disciplines whose expertise on the pre-existing environment or the natural environment can help to guide the relationship of the organic stuff and the inorganic crust that we build. In which ways can masterplanning begin to take on the approach that sees city design as necessitating a longer-term view of how cities grow, change, and mature as an evolutionary model? Also, in which ways can this paradigm enable designers, planners, and policy makers to carry out masterplanning as a process which embeds indeterminacy that can shepherd the city to adapt and change in time?

MP I certainly see the role of the masterplanner as facilitating change rather than instigating whole new urban structures. The idea of ecology as a potential framework for understanding urbanization has been of great interest to landscape architects. It is important to be careful to avoid a partial understanding of ecology, which is about life, organisms, growth, and sustainability. The central ecological concept of "carrying capacity" pertains to how many of a species can live in an area and be supported by its natural systems. How does this play out in relation to the human population in a given urban area? My area of interest is in the sustainability of cities, and the city is indeed a strange vehicle to look at sustainability. Students ask me if Hong Kong is "sustainable" and I reply by saying that if you want to put seven million people in this box then yes, it's probably a pretty good model, but why put seven million people into this box? This box is probably only capable of supporting seventy thousand. The footprint of this city is not just its physical fabric—it goes all over the world, and everything tells us Hong Kong is an unsupportable model in terms of a sustained population. So ecological urbanism ultimately only touches the surface of it, and a fundamental ecological concept such as carrying capacity, or how much a city or region can reasonably support, would be a more durable paradigm through which to approach urbanism.

TV Is the term "sustainability" so ill-defined that one can level a judgment on a city such as Hong Kong that it has, in your definition, a hundred times more people than it can locally sustain itself? In this sense, is there such a thing as a "sustainable" city, or is it a misnomer if one accepts the impossibility for contemporary cities to sustain themselves, in terms of self-sufficiency with respect to its resources, water management, food production, the minimization of its footprint, etc.? Most cities are inherently environmentally unsound, and therefore in the many definitions of sustainability, cities can be deemed unsustainable. Other definitions of sustainability might challenge short-term construction, and short life span of buildings. Would cities be more sustainable if cities were built to last longer, rather than to be disposable? Does this raise a paradox for the mechanism by which we design and manage cities to concurrently better embed capabilities to adapt to urban change, and the material and possible social sustainability given that cities were built to endure?

MP "Sustainability" is a widely appropriated term, used for whatever particular argument people want to put forward, without a commonly accepted definition. The term "sustainable" is not a superlative but rather a comparative when referring to cities, which can be more sustainable or less sustainable. I don't think cities can be fully sustainable, in terms of my working definition, which is a "no-footprints" view of sustainability. I don't think any form of city can leave no damage or create no negative impact, simply because of the resources it takes to support cities. Going back to the point about population, urban populations generally far outstrip available resources. We tend to export our impacts; by gathering food resources from far afield and exporting our waste to other regions we can give ourselves the impression the city is manageable. In the long term I have no confidence that we can find a sustainable city model. We can make cities more sustainable through making systems more effective and efficient, through increased density, green building technologies, the use of public transport rather than private transport, and all sorts of other ways, but I don't think we can make a city that leaves no footprints. Cities have big footprints in their physical form and huge footprints in the unseen network that's required to support them, so I won't say cities are sustainable.

TV On one hand, we are discussing cities in opposition to the natural processes of the planet. In another sense, we are witnessing a diminishing distinction between the natural and the artificial worlds. Technology has developed a biological nature, as we see with the simulation software that you alluded to earlier. Without much technological positivism, we now have increased skills to generate, monitor, analyze, and provide feedback through technologies that are increasingly symbiotic with nature. Do you perceive potential for a greater fusion between the natural and artificial world coming from a greater understanding and application of technology to problems which are, broadly speaking, environmental?

MP I certainly see the potential for it, and I'm optimistic. Cities are based on technological advances, and we seem to be getting more intelligent in the ways we use technology, but I don't believe in an ultimate technological fix for all the problems created by the city. There is a historical arc of technology that supported the city and continues to support the development, sophistication, and complexity of the city. The potential for solving or for creating a more balanced sustainable system seems to get subsumed by the inspiration, innovation, and excitement of doing something new, which in turn just creates more demands on the system. I think there will need to be a fundamental change in attitude. I rather suspect that, if we want truly sustainable communities, we will have to revert to a simpler mode of life, and become antitechnological, antisophisticated. I believe that the biggest settlement unit that is sustainable is the village. Cities are too big. The city is pushing us faster and further toward depletion. We will find a better, more sustainable city model, but at the moment I see us heading toward disaster.

TV You sketch an imminent, dystopic future.

MP The future is indeed dystopic.

TV Speculations and fictions aside, there might be consensus among most people within the professions that deal with the future that we have massive challenges ahead, to say the least. Perhaps we should question whether we will have cities in the future.

MP Yes, it's a bit of a dark note. There seems to be such a strong presumption for development, and I don't see it leading anywhere but a greater, faster, more damaging depletion of the environment that we live in. I don't see technology as a solution but rather as part of the problem. It is the presumption for continuous development that I find so worrying.

TV There has never been a stage of urbanization of such huge proportions as has happened in China in the last twenty years, and will continue to happen over the next couples of decades. This has occurred principally because of the centralized policy to urbanize people from rural lands, which has a number of political, cultural, and social motivations and implications. Asia seems far from any semblance of stability, and this massive urban project needs to challenge the limitations of conventional ways of addressing urbanization.

MP What I find interesting is the decision-making process: Who is making the decisions about Chinese urbanization? Is it the government, or is it big corporate entities? In the development of megablocks in China, developers clearly recognize that the city is not working, so they build a city within a city as a self-contained unit. This top-down approach is not working, but at the other end, individuals feel they have no capacity to influence the city.

TV At stake in this argument is how smaller-scale emergent conditions can generate patterns of activity and use by empowering people to make decisions, and how this can be brought toward more top-down processes of masterplanning. This seems to be an immense political challenge to the ways in which cities are being developed in China. While I am hopeful for this model, it is unlikely to be installed as a mechanism for the foreseeable future. Cities need ways of generating design schemes as part of more emergent processes, where the rules of the game can be established without knowing how the game ends.

MP I share your view. Neither the big corporation nor the individual can come up with a perfect solution, but the corporation can provide a flexible framework which is then occupied by individuals in the community with the freedom to adapt and change the city on many scales and levels. One of the things I very much appreciate is Hong Kong's ability to reinvent itself, to knock things down and put up something new. After his recent lecture at HKU, I spoke with Rem Koolhaas about one of the old blocks in Kowloon where immigrants used to arrive, settle down for couple of years, and then move on. He had identified the building as a vital element of the cultural heritage of Hong Kong, and saw the need to preserve it and the story behind it. In the conversation were some locals who were aghast at this idea, and thought it much better to knock it down, put up something bigger, and make more money out of it. One could say preservation is a western ideal. In Hong Kong there seems to be a ready willingness to exploit and redevelop the city, rather than to accept it and live with it.

TV It's a complex problem to address the endurance of the social and cultural order of the city. The paradoxes of continuity and change, old and new, tradition and innovation are found in their most extreme sense in the contemporary urbanization in China. Hong Kong has gone through these changes many times and there is, however, great regret by Hong Kong's people, their politicians, architects, and others, of the persistence of an overarching goal of progress. This throws into question the value placed on the material heritage of the city and its social and cultural life. The history of Hong Kong will hopefully remain an influence on policy makers, masterplanners and design teams in China, to avoid the pitfalls of past projects of urbanization.

MP The city is the people, who are nested between those who govern and those who invest.

TV And somewhere in the mix are the designers who give shape to political dreams and business plans!

CASE STUDY

JAMES CORNER FIELD OPERATIONS >QIANHAI MASTERPLAN, SHENZEN, CHINA

2011

Design Team: James Corner, Richard Kennedy, Hong Zhou, Hang Cheng, Biyoung Heo, Brad Goetz, Stephanie Ulrich

This masterplan for a major new urban zone of Shenzhen prioritizes water as both the functional and qualitative driver for urban design. Water City is an innovative, sustainable model of development for a rapidly urbanizing region. The masterplan creates a large-scale water-treating framework that incorporates fine-grained, human-scale spaces, resulting in a hyperdense, ecologically sensitive urban territory with an iconic waterfront, diverse building stock, cultural and recreational destinations, and unique public open spaces that are accessible from any point within Qianhai.

Aerial view of the proposed masterplan.

Masterplan proposal.

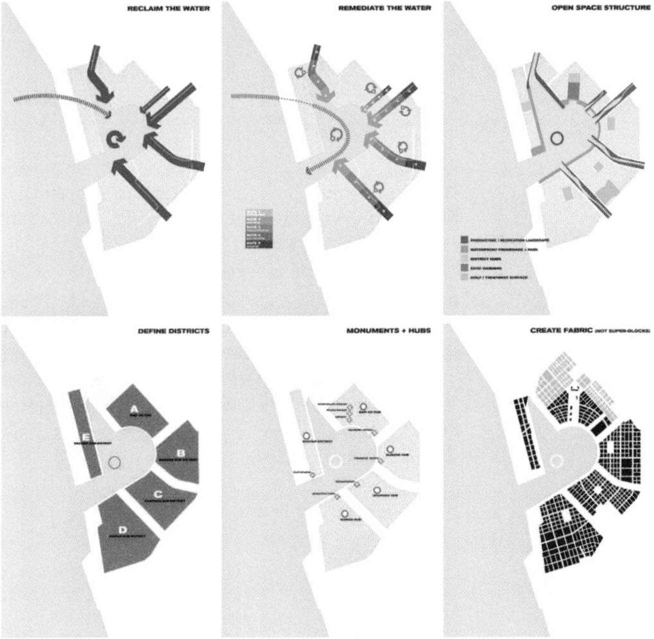

Diagrams indicating the relationship of the urbanism to the ecological corridors.

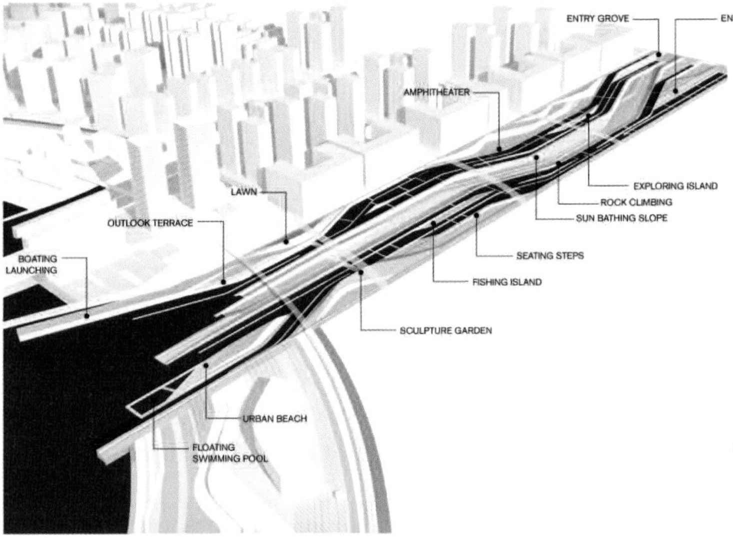

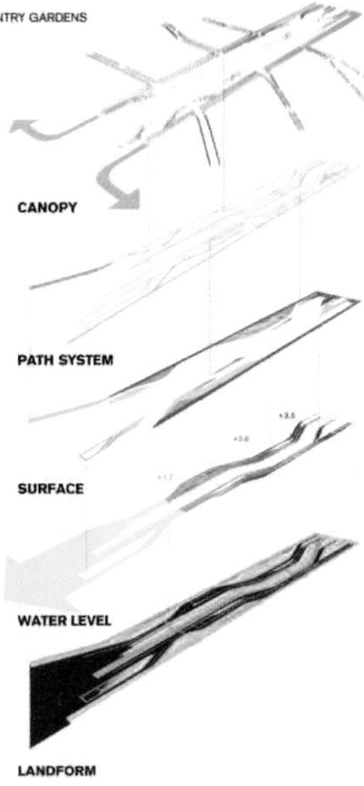

Diagrams indicating the aquatic and flora systems of an ecological corridor for treating water and for public use.

CASE STUDY

PLASMA STUDIO >FLOWING GARDENS, INTERNATIONAL HORTICULTURAL EXPO, XI'AN, CHINA

2011

Plasma Studio collaborated with BIAD, Arup, and John Martin and Associates on the building design, and with Groundlab, Laur Studio, and the Beijing Forest University on the landscape design.

Design Team: Eva Castro, Holger Kehne, Mehran Gharleghi, Evan Greenberg, Xiaowei Tong; with Tom Lea, Ying Wang, Nicoletta Gerevini, Peter Pichler, Benedikt Schleicher, Katy Barkan, Danai Sage
Landscape: Groundlab (Eva Castro, Holger Kehne, Sarah Majid, Alfredo Ramirez, Eduardo Rico)
Client: Chan Ba Ecological District, Xi'an

The project, titled *Flowing Gardens*, was generated as a synthesis of horticulture and technology, where landscape and architecture converged in a sustainable and integral vision, comprising a 5,000-square-meter exhibition hall, a 4,000-square-meter greenhouse and a 3500-square-meter gate building sitting in a thirty-seven-hectare landscape. *Flowing Gardens* creates a consonant functionality of water, planting, circulation, and architecture as one seamless system. At the major intersections of the pathways lie three buildings, each standing independent of yet interconnected with the landscape. The gate building is created at the junction of public meeting space, landscape, and circulation; entering the site along the major axis of *Flowing Gardens*, it creates framed vistas of the gardens. An exhibition centre is formed at the seam of landscape, circulation, and water. Lastly, a greenhouse sits at the top of the South Hill, connecting various landscape features. The greenhouse allows one to experience the beauty of *Flowing Gardens* from across the lake while appreciating plants and flowers from four different climatic zones.

Aerial photos of the built Xi'an Expo site.

Aerial view of the site, indicating the complexity of its organization, and its integration into the existing infrastructures and landscapes of the city.

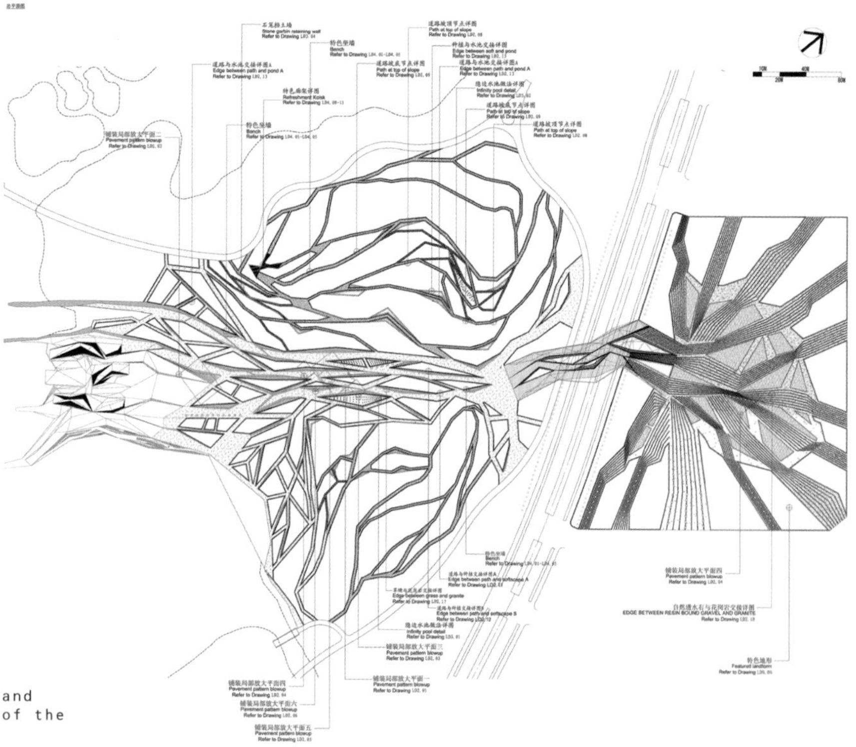

Plan of the flows and subdivision zones of the site.

II

CONCEPTS/ PARADIGMS

NEW PARADIGMS AND PRACTICES IN URBANISM

CHAPTER 10

TOM VEREBES >THE DEATH OF MASTERPLANNING IN THE AGE OF INDETERMINACY

This chapter explicates the discursive foundation for speculations on alternatives to teleological modes of development, with principles of uncertainty, complexity, and emergence embraced in the current era, termed the "age of indeterminacy." The chapter surveys the multidisciplinary discourses associated with an understanding of the city as fundamentally dynamic, and as having a future that is never fully determinable. It also elucidates concepts associated with computational approaches to urbanism, the methods and applications of which will be further elaborated on in later chapters. Finally, the theoretical lineage of the study of dynamic patterns is investigated as a fundamental issue in evolutionary urbanism.

10.1 PLANNING AND/OR EMERGENCE

> Planners can certainly force a city into a particular form. In fact, planners have to give their forms, as the old self-optimizing process, requiring no planner, no longer functions. In spite of this, self-optimization processes can be encouraged, but only if one knows how they work and how to initiate them. The recognition of self-developing processes in our time enables us to create prognoses for the future, as urban development processes are long-term in nature.
>
> Frei Otto[1]

Informal urban growth often shows evidence of evolutionary patterns of formation, due to its incremental, grown rather than planned nature. The attributes of unplanned or informal urbanism can be understood as the outcome of emergent processes. Cities exemplify "how well-adapted designs emerge from what appear to be the countless uncoordinated decisions generated from the bottom up that produce order on all scales."[2]

Architects are often enamoured of evolutionary patterns of urbanization, of urban entities that appear as though they were not designed but rather just happened, with some seemingly invisible intelligence at work. Medieval European towns and cities appear as though they were not designed, but evolved gradually through the playing out of the rules of a dynamic game. Such cities, "far from being messy, disorganized forms, have rather well defined spatial structures."[3] Though often viewed as undesirable from social, political, economic, and hygiene perspectives, slums grow according to the conditions set by minimal resources and topographically constrained sites. The contrast between highly planned parts of cities and adjacent slums, and the corresponding contrast in relative wealth or poverty, is perhaps greatest in South American cities. In such slums, these relations between minimal material means, highly constrained dimensions, and extreme topographies determine the location of buildings and flows of movement in what is a set of endogenous processes, in other words a set of small, local actions which accumulate to form a coherent whole. Although systems are not being deployed as regulatory mechanisms by a central planner, local interactions of massing, routing, access, topography, hydrology, and other parameters tend to result in coherent, compelling organizational features, with a high degree of local differentiation.

Bernard Rudofsky's 1964 book *Architecture without Architects* demonstrated how informal urbanism grows and can become, in due course, permanent. Christopher Alexander understood favelas as "small-scale self-organizing systems with local codes" with which architects or lay people could interact.[4] Avoiding romantic longing for a world before designers in which the cities we created had coherence, functionality, and beauty, today's favelas can give clues as to how to negotiate a new planning model, between "bottom-up self-help and top-down management.[5] In the 1970s, "officially unrecognized informal settlements" made up sixty percent of Latin American cities.[6] The United Nations in 2010 estimated that "one third of the [world's] urban population of 3 billion people now live in shanty towns."[7] Vast informal settlements, for example those in Caracas, Venezuela or Dharavi, Mumbai, qualify as cities in themselves, equivalent in population to the London or Paris of the mid-nineteenth century. The phenomenon of the urban village is particular to China. These enclaves are pockets of residual, older fabric, yet in the case of Shenzhen, for example, are under thirty years old. Perhaps the most extreme example of planned urbanism being infiltrated by the "wild" is Hong Kong's Kowloon Walled City, demolished in 1993–1994 after a long eviction process, begun in 1987.[8]

Is the favela a model of freedom within the regulatory regimes of planning? Will cities in the future be "a mixture of the emergent and the planned, the biotic and the geometric"?[9] The means by which oppositions such as planning versus informal urbanization, top-down versus bottom-up growth, control versus deregulation might successfully be negotiated perhaps forms the underlying motive for this book—to find a balance between mechanisms and processes, between man and nature. Despite the undesirable qualities of slums, they are interesting for their associative organizational logic, which results from algorithmic generative principles. These evolutionary processes suggest higher orders of complex information are involved in the formation of non-planned cities, and could in fact be used to rethink masterplanning via the mediation of the paradox of planning and emergence.

The medieval core of Venice, "whose labyrinthine structure was the unintended product of many personal decentralized decisions," has been contrasted by Manuel De Landa with Versailles, "a city planned to the last detail by centralized decision-makers in the French government."[10] Modern city planning can be seen to be "founded on the premise that 'unplanned' settlements are more disordered and dysfunctional than planned ones."[11] When did modern city planning actually begin? The Renaissance? With Soria y Mata's *ciudad lineal* ("linear city")? Howard's garden city movement? Tony Garnier's *Cité industrielle* of 1917? Le Corbusier's *Ville radieuse* (1933)? In Baroque planning, the notion of finality and omnipresence is evident in the propensity for geometric fixity. Descartes observed the "indiscriminate juxtaposition, the consequent crookedness and irregularity of the streets" of ancient cities, and concluded that their arrangement was guided by something other than "human will guided by reason."[12] Pierre Charles L'Enfant's plan for Washington, DC is emblematic of planning in which the final state of the city is planned beforehand, in its entirety.

Mumford claims that L'Enfant "forgot, in fact, that time is a fatal handicap to the baroque conception of the world: its mechanical order makes no allowances for growth, change, adaptation and creative renewal."[13]

If planning is synonymous with control, then what comes of the absence of planning?[14] A plan is an itinerary to follow, or, more architecturally, a plan can also be a drawing used to organize future construction. Planned and emergent forms of urbanism can be considered opposites, as emergence "has always been about giving up control, letting the system govern itself as much as possible, letting it learn from the footprints."[15] The potential to fully "plan" is reduced as scale increases, and uncontrollable phenomena and events may intervene. Jane and Mark Burry have identified a "cosmological, organizational and geometric shift in perspective to engage with the city from the bottom-up, from the discrete granular forces from which it unfolds, rather than top-down, in the manner familiar from 19th century planning, and even more so, Modernist planning."[16] During the Victorian period, the term "without design" celebrated the apparently natural order arising in the man-made disorder of the industrial town.[17]

In the absence of planning, is control over the future of urbanism relinquished? Conversely, to what extent can wholly planned urbanism adapt to future challenges? It is, however, an oversimplification to assume that adaptive, evolutionary urbanism lacks all planning. The opposition of formal, planned cities and informal, unplanned urbanism is set against the notion of the unplanned city being shaped by small-scale, bottom-up interventions, and the idea of masterplanning as the domain of large-scale hierarchical actions is challenged as romantic. A masterplan can benefit from "contamination" by the mechanisms of informal urbanization, which operate at multiple spatial scales and speeds, never finished, nor pretending to completeness. To assume that traditional urbanism is the result of a "natural" set of characteristics, in contrast to the rational and technologically driven regimes of modernist planning, is to color the issue with nostalgia.

The coherence of the traditional city is the result not of a lack of overall design but rather of smaller, local decisions which amalgamate to create a whole which exceeds the sum of its parts. Rather than seeking a cure for modern ills in traditionalism and preservation, can the grown and evolved urbanism of Marrakech or Isfahan be simulated and created? Here is a challenge: to reconcile the grown and evolved processes of traditional cities, with the superimposition of the new on the existing order of the world.[18]

Scholars of the late modern period, including critics of modernism such as Jane Jacobs, Kevin Lynch, and Christopher Alexander, have sought to correct what they assumed to be the errors of the modernist project by reexamining the merits of the premodernist fabric of the city. At this juncture, an assessment of postmodernism, neotraditionalism, and new urbanism is needed. Despite the prevalence of these tendencies and movements, especially in North America, they represent a reactionary reversal of the utopian models of the twentieth century. Lacking all confidence to chart out the future, and symptomatic of a reliance on a return to the past, these positions are ideologically bankrupt. Vernacular architecture can inform the mechanisms for formation of emergent, self-organized order, yet simplistic replication of its appearance is inadequate.

Houston, a city with a near absence of any zoning control in the conventionally understood sense, is the antithesis of planning—it is wild.

Venturi and Scott Brown celebrated the infiltration of pop culture through the suburbanization of the city in their seminal *Learning from Las Vegas* (1972). Sprawl, according to Albert Pope, is the aggregation of spine units, and he claims sprawl is not an uncontrolled, unplanned condition, but rather an extensive spatial model.[19] Marshall argues that "ad-hoc Modernism and post-planning sprawl is the true evolutionary inheritor of unplanned organic urbanism" without giving judgment on whether neotraditional urbanism or postmodernism is preferred—yet he leaves practically no other alternative paradigm or tendency to pursue. In the American context, postmodern and neotraditionalist movements can be dismissed as reactionary fallout from the radicalness and single mindedness of orthodox modernism.[20]

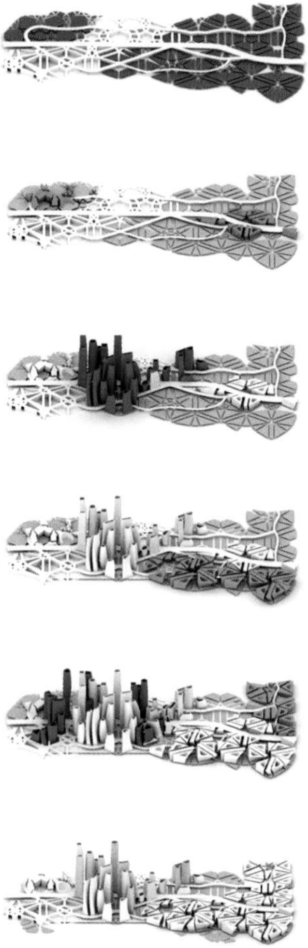

Series of masterplanning interventions in which the site is always complete, yet always able to gain further density in the future. (Studio Tutor: Tom Verebes; Students: Lindsay Bresser, Claudia Dorner, Sergio Reyes Rodr guez; Architectural Association, 2009)

> Form, in the usual sense of the word, is the result of the accumulation of many local accidents.
>
> René Thom, 1975[21]

Self-organized, emergent systems in biological and physical processes parallel the ways in which collective human activity unfolds in real time, including how cities grow and evolve over the years, decades, or centuries. Emergence, in Kevin Kelly's terms, "requires a population of entities, a multitude, a collective, a mob, more. More is Different."[22] Kelly was here echoing the now-famous edict of Philip Anderson, a Nobel Prize–winning scientist, that "more is different," which refers to phase change within an emergent system. By the addition of "more energy, or information, or mass, or whatever, . . . a system will reach a critical point and jump into a new regime [and] new patterns of organization can emerge spontaneously."[23] In this sense, emergent order occurs precisely when control is relinquished, and here lies the essential contradiction between planned cities and evolutionary forms of urbanism.

In his short but seminal book, *An Evolutionary Architecture*, John Frazer proposed an alternative methodology for design, in which "the model is adapted iteratively in the computer in response to feedback from evaluation."[24] One of the aims here is to sketch out an evolutionary approach to urbanism, and in fact these concepts can be mapped back to Metabolism, in which architecture is seen as part of living processes. "An evolutionary architecture will exhibit metabolism, as a thermodynamically open relationship with the environment in both a metabolic and a socio-economic sense."[25] Norbert Wiener, the father of cybernetics, believed that the intelligence of all species lies in their capacity to act as machines to process information from stimuli, and to learn from feedback. The study of metabolisms opens architecture up to a range of concepts and methodologies which are "strongly correlated to the organisations and systems of the natural world."[26] Manuel De Landa argues for bottom-up processes, which, if modelled by "a top-down analytical approach that begins with the whole and dissects it into its constituent parts (an ecosystem into species, a society into institutions)," will fail to capture the emergent qualities of complex interactions.[27] City forms, as Michael Weinstock defines them, are "material constructs" which "emerge from regional variations" of localized systems and patterns of settlements.[28]

Christopher Alexander posits that traditional society was not aware of what he delineates as "living structures" and "non-living structures," and that, "although traditional society was filled with human-created processes—human inspired and human invented—it was dominated by living processes."[29] Alexander's aims in his seminal *Nature of Order* do not include explaining the forms of cities, either traditional or contemporary, in terms of how living things form, develop, and evolve; rather he sees the traditional, premodern city as existing prior to the distinction of nature from artifice, living from nonliving, grown from designed, and so on. Despite the risk of nostalgia in positing or valorizing the inherent attributes of the formation of the traditional city, the argument here is distinctly against a return to traditional formal order or spatial articulation. The "structure-preserving transformations" of traditional cities, Alexander argues, resist the tabula rasa, obliteration approach in urbanism, which dominated so much of the twentieth century and which persists in regions currently undergoing urbanization on a vast scale.

Echoed again and again in recent years by complexity scientists and writers, Alexander's fascination with patterns observed in natural systems and his conviction that design can be connected with the "natural" world resonate deeply and pervasively, and raise many questions about the characteristics of man-made order as part and parcel of, for lack a better term, life. For Alexander, life is a metaphor for order—order is not an operative quality of the processes of artificial formation—rendering moot the distinction between nature and the artificial. What is of interest here is the process of formation of the city. Today's computational approaches to urbanism are unleashing processes which involve interactive rules that create variable outcomes, thereby simulating the ways in which emergent systems create unexpected yet coherent organization.

Conventional techniques of masterplanning, as we have seen, are inflexible in the face of changing requirements and limited in their adaptability to new contextual criteria, and therefore less intelligent than they ought to be. The most-used planning tools inherently lack feedback mechanisms, or the ability to process information and learn from input–output relationships. And it is an oversimplification to set top-down design in opposition to bottom-up growth and development of urbanism—both approaches understand and project the city as a coherent whole. The central question to address is how coherent, compelling evolutionary patterns can be embedded in our existing planning processes.

10.2 TELEOLOGICAL FALLACIES OF THE MASTERPLANNER

> There are questions that one chooses to ask and other questions that ask themselves.
>
> Henri Poincaré, 1890[30]

Cities are at once an expression of the present, and hopelessly retrospective in their inability to meet current demands and expectations. Cities are forever in need of maintenance and renovation. If the city is never fully adequate, never functionally fit for the requirements of the present, then it is logical to conclude that urbanism will in time lead to obsolescence. The problematics of urbanism include fulfilling the apparent needs and contingencies of the present, as well as those of what amount to predictions of the future. Regardless of whether one is considering rarefied visions of urbanism—utopias—or the prosaic yet brutal, tenacious yet transformative tasks of the masterplanner or urban designer, the future is not entirely knowable.

Diagrams indicating possible evolutions of urban densification in a peripheral site in Shenzhen, China. (Studio Tutor: Tom Verebes; Thesis Student: Guo Jia; MArch Thesis, The University of Hong Kong, 2011)

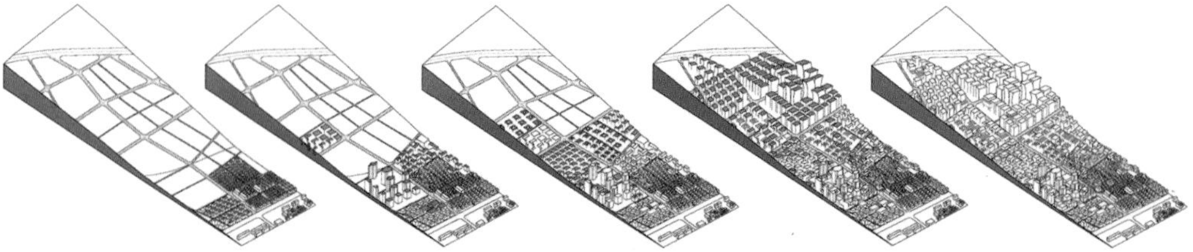

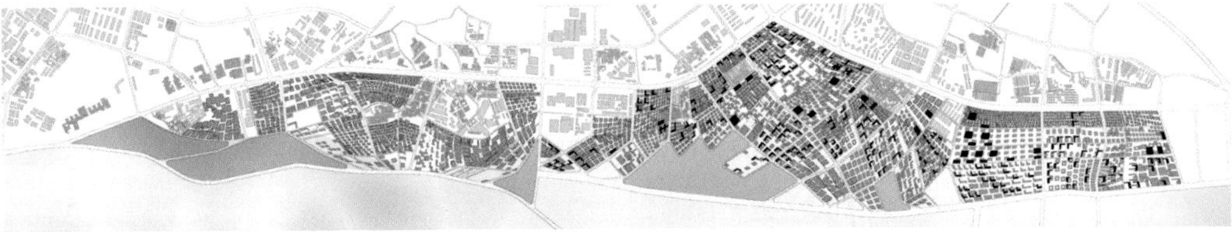

Figure ground and programmatic masterplan for a peripheral site in Shenzhen, China. (Studio Tutor: Tom Verebes; Thesis Student: Guo Jia; MArch Thesis, The University of Hong Kong, 2011)

The conventional tools and techniques of city design are fundamentally unable to manage change. Static plans have traditionally been one of the primary communication tools for presenting images of the city, as final, completed, and stable urban organization, often several years in the future. During recent years, as part of the race for global urbanization, the preeminent form of representation of future urbanism has been rendered images of three-dimensional digital models, also depicting a teleological outcome. This overreliance on narrow, singular, inflexible pictures of the future ignores the inherent complexity of the modern world, and the manifold forces, agents, and contingencies which shape the future. During the course of implementation of a masterplan, the basis upon which decisions are made in response to apparent requirements tends to evolve, or even shift catastrophically, for example according to economic or demographic changes, and hence the process of planning for a stable endgame is ideologically and practically flawed. Despite this, every effort is made to embed the dynamics of the past, the contingencies of the present, and forecasts of the future. The fallacy of determinism is perhaps the greatest challenge for the masterplanner in the twenty-first century.[31]

The inclusion of the term "master" in the title "masterplanner" implies not only a coordinating role, as "master" of a team, but also "mastery," the control of a design outcome—the masterplan. The suppression of indeterminacy here reflects the "dominant cultural expectation that buildings must be built for eternity when in fact most buildings are built to persist for only a short time."[32] Far from celebrating obsolescence, the contemporary world's apparent lack of appreciation of the endurance of material culture begs the question, why is contemporary architecture seemingly so unable to adapt? Are designers engaging in the design process without enough time-based information to embed greater intelligence into design artefacts?

The cybernetician Gordon Pask wrote in 1969 about the discipline of urban planning as being a practice which "usually extends over time, periods of years or decades and, as currently conceived, the plan is quite an inflexible specification."[33] Optimistically, Pask believed that urban development need not be inflexible, but rather could adopt goals which are less to do with permanence and endurance than with what he calls a "reactive environment," with inhabitants in constant dialogue with the mechanisms of design, or "environmental computing machines." He describes the role of the designer as being focussed on "the interaction between the designer and the system he designs, rather than the interaction between the system and the people who inhabit it."[34] In this sense, the designer is no longer conceived of as the controller, or "authoritarian apparatus" of the final product, but rather the designer of the apparatus which will result in the product. The role of design, rather than a form of control, becomes an "odd mixture of catalyst, crutch, memory and arbiter."[35]

Echoing this viewpoint, Christopher Hight has categorised contemporary parametric design as having two principal orientations, the first of which applies computational tools and techniques as a form of drawing, and can be seen as "a genealogy of discourses about architectural ordering that has periodically dominated the field since the Kantian revolution displaced recourse to transcendental or divine similitudes."[36] In this sense, the contemporary architect designs the "drawing machines," or interfaces with which to draw. The other orientation classified by Hight focusses on "simulation of tectonics and material performance, typically structural and more recently environmental."[37] Here is a significant shift from designing as an immediate authorial action, done by hand on paper, to coding for a "back-end" modeling environment, with a "front-end" user interface engaging the designer to produce not one "original" but potentially a series of outcomes, through the negotiation of relationships in a constraints-based experimental approach to design.

Relevant to this argument is the inadequacy of conventional design tools for managing temporal change and spatial differentiation. The philosopher of science, Thomas Kuhn, has described the relationship between scientific knowledge and the fitness-for-purpose of the tools used to explore it:

> So long as the tools a paradigm supplies continue to prove capable of solving the problems it defines, science moves fastest and penetrates most deeply through confident employment of these tools. The reason is clear. As in manufacture so in science—retooling is an extravagance to be reserved for the occasion that demands it. The significance of crises is the indication they provide that an occasion for retooling has arrived.
>
> Thomas Kuhn, 1991[38]

Kuhn suggests that a widely accepted theory is "always based upon more than a comparison of that theory with the world. The decision to reject one paradigm is always simultaneously the decision to accept another, and the judgment leading to that decision involved the comparison of both paradigms with nature and with each other."[39] If one extends this thesis to masterplanning the city, then the inadequacy of the preeminent concepts and methodologies of masterplanning in dealing with an unstable, dynamic world suggests that techniques need to be developed to provide new interfaces of dynamic control.

In his speculative 1994 book, *City of Bits*, William Mitchell challenges the idea of the endurance of the city. He correctly predicts the effects and transformations resulting from the increasing embeddedness and ubiquity of

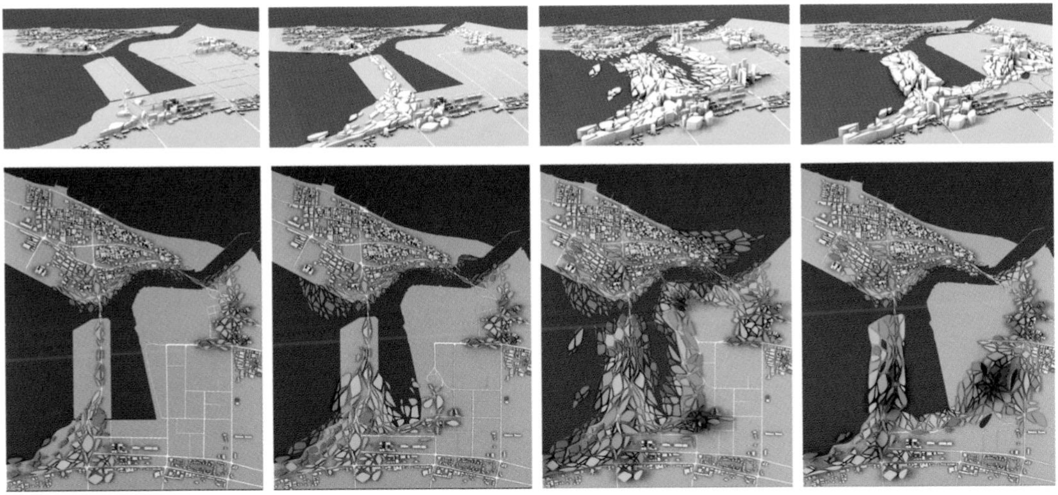

Four scenarios of potential masterplanning for Ras Al-Khaima, UAE, generated from an adaptable information lattice below, and indicating the corresponding massing organizations above. (Studio Tutor: Tom Verebes; Students: Rochana Chaugule, Yevgeniya Pozigun, Ujjal Roy, Praneet Verma; Architectural Association, 2009)

digital communication and information technologies in architecture and the city: "The very idea of the city is challenged and must be reconceived."[40] Given its inherently revolutionary nature, "technology, as has always been the case, lies at the core of the examination of new working protocols in architecture and building."[41]

Nevertheless, we are not the first to seek a paradigm shift, or to be "constrained by the technologies and epistemes at hand."[42] Moving away from the notion of the city as a man-made artefact in opposition to nature, we are forced to accept the accelerative presence of humanity on the planet, and with it a demand for "integrat[ing] technology more smoothly within nature's dynamics."[43] In a world which is increasingly uncertain, information about the world can be embedded in cities and buildings, giving them a metabolic capacity to absorb and process it, and hence to change in relation to dynamic contextual or environmental conditions. In a century when urbanization is occurring at unprecedented rates, the notion of the masterplan as a conclusive document with which to determine the future is in crisis. Uncertainty can indeed be integrated into planning methodologies, though the predominant tendency in nearly all past approaches to urbanism has been to eliminate indeterminacy.

10.3 PRINCIPLES OF UNCERTAINTY: PLANNING AFTER THE GLOBAL FINANCIAL CRISIS

A central theme of this book is the paradoxical nature of planning for an increasingly uncertain world. In the aftermath of the economic meltdown of 2008, and despite the increasingly frenetic pace at which new cities have been established in recent years, many of the cranes were idle, the shipping containers empty, the banks broke or bailed out, and the architects unemployed. The world economy and the entire theoretical basis of neocapitalism lay in shambles; the so-called natural environment had been damaged to the extent that scientists predicted imminent, man-made environmental catastrophes. This is the new twenty-first century: nowhere to run and hide, only our demons to confront.[44]

In relinquishing some control, and moving away from teleological, essentially deterministic predictions of the future, uncertainty becomes the hallmark of all pertinent, prescient approaches to urbanism, along with an increasing understanding of urban development, the global economy, and the environment as being interdependent. Uncertainty can in fact be modelled, most often using a Gaussian "bell curve," which tends to smooth out irregularities and anomalies. This approach to randomness assumes a form of probabilistic thinking in which risk can be computed, and other thresholds of uncertainty cannot. Interestingly, "scalable wild randomness" is often modelled using Mandelbrotian fractals.[45] (Fractal mathematics help to explain patterns which appear to be random, yet which have similar or selfsimilar attributes at different scales.) Dealing with uncertainty is the domain of statistics, with its "standard deviations" related to the averaging of probabilities distributed along a bell curve. Randomness, described as "incomplete information," is simply what cannot be guessed as the "knowledge about the causes [is] incomplete, not necessarily because the process has truly unpredictable properties."[46] Whether these statistical methods are applied to the economy, weather forecasting, geological dynamics or any other complex system, there are parallels to an understanding of the city, which is also complex, in flux, and deeply connected to other dynamic systems.

Forecasts for systems such as stock markets or the weather more often than not contain prediction errors. Concerning economic models, Nassim Taleb writes that "our predictors may be good at predicting the ordinary, but not the irregular, and this is where they ultimately fail."[47] The objective here is not to promote a scientific methodology for planning in an uncertain world, but rather to explicate the difficulty, even impossibility, of completely accurate prediction. Predicting the outcome of a masterplan seems as misguided as predicting the financial markets years in advance, and indeed there is a high degree of interdependence between urbanization and the economy. Our control systems therefore require greater suppleness in their projective capabilities. Design at the scale of the city is less a practice of control than a simultaneous confrontation with and embracing of uncertainty.

> It is no longer the thermonuclear bomb, with its particular modes of geopolitical rationality, that is shaping consciousness, but a new numeric-parametric one: the Market.
>
> Sanford Kwinter[48]

The man-made systems we invent—the global economy, the internet and other dynamic infrastructures—all have their own natural dynamics, which are seemingly integrated with the evolutionary conditions of planet earth. Everything is connected. This thesis is predicated on the acceptance of uncertainty, indeterminacy, and randomness as inherent in the global financial system which has seen so many sequences of boom and bust. Within the world's wild economic system, "the city is not just where we are; it is who we are."[49]

These causal relations and methods of assessing dynamic patterns were brought to the fore in the fallout from the Global Financial Crisis of 2008, when innumerable architectural projects were cancelled across the world. The causal effects of the economy on architectural practice, and inevitably on masterplanning, were more evident than ever. How direct is the effect of a laissez faire economic model, which is widely understood to have become less regulated, on a model of urbanization which is dependent on the will of investors? Does civilization drive "the market," or do "markets now decide what is good, useful and true, so long as the elements are free to fluctuate (that is remain indeterminate and unstable for continuous redeployment)"?[50] Answers may be found through interrogation of the preeminence of laissez faire urbanism and the phenomenon of the instant city, as well as that of the ghost town, which so often follows the pattern of boom and bust.

George Soros, one of the first hedge fund managers, with a lifetime of practical experience in forecasting financial markets, notes that a conception of markets as "self-correcting and tend[ing] toward equilibrium remains the prevailing paradigm [for] the various synthetic instruments and valuation models," yet he claims that this paradigm is "false and urgently needs to be replaced."[51] Kwinter protests: "the idea of the market itself has come to intellectually dominate us."[52] Models based on knowledge alone do not provide for the actions of protagonists based on their perceptions of events. Challenging economic models based on the belief in a self-healing economy, one with a tendency to equilibrium, the prevalent new understanding of the economy, and perhaps of urban development, is rather that it has a tendency to peak and crash, and is in fact subject to great instability. It is in this context that we must move toward a new model of urbanism in which the tools and techniques of forecasting take account of change, as a foundation for design.

> The future is fundamentally unpredictable; and broadly speaking, the longer the timescale for prediction, the less predictable the outcome. This makes cities—which are about as long term as physical products get—intrinsically unpredictable.
>
> Stephen Marshall[53]

Over ten years ago, long before 2008's Global Financial Crisis, Kwinter and Fabricius proposed that contemporary urban development would follow one of two trajectories, to become either a "continuous predatory stop-gap activity of 'efficient market theory' or the 'fast, cheap and out of control' breeder logic of self-regulating capital."[54] Although one outcome of the Global Financial Crisis was disillusionment with the idea of markets as "smart," self-regulating mechanisms in a deregulated economy, blind urban development based principally on a model of short-term economic and political gain is alive and proliferating. Manuel Castell wrote in the 1990s that global markets are organized in "networks and flows, using the technological infrastructure of the information economy."[55] Beyond the indeterminacy of the economy, which drives urbanization, planet earth faces immense ecological challenges, given increases in our petroleum and plastics–based economy, and diminishing resources, including looming food and water crises. According to Manuel De Landa, "cities appear as parasitic entities, deriving their sustenance from nearby rural regions or, via colonialism and conquest, from other lands."[56]

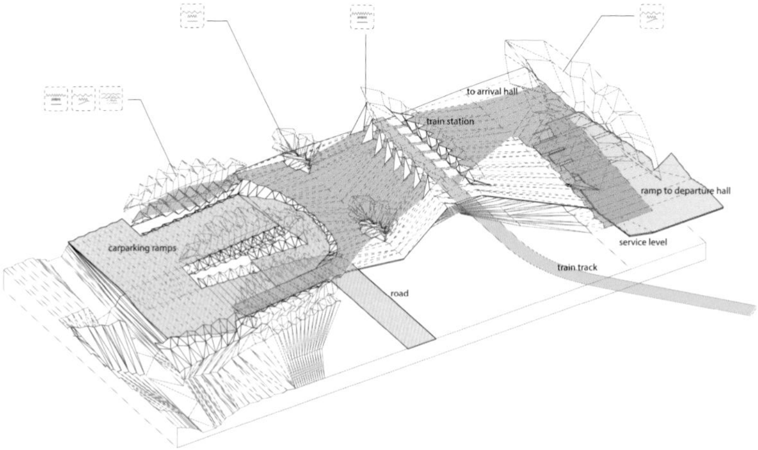
to arrival hall
train station
ramp to departure hall
carparking ramps
service level
train track
road

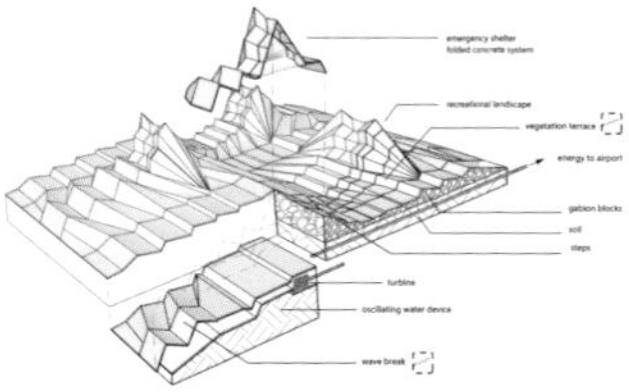
emergency shelter
folded concrete system
recreational landscape
vegetation terrace
energy to airport
gabion blocks
soil
steps
turbine
oscillating water device
wave break

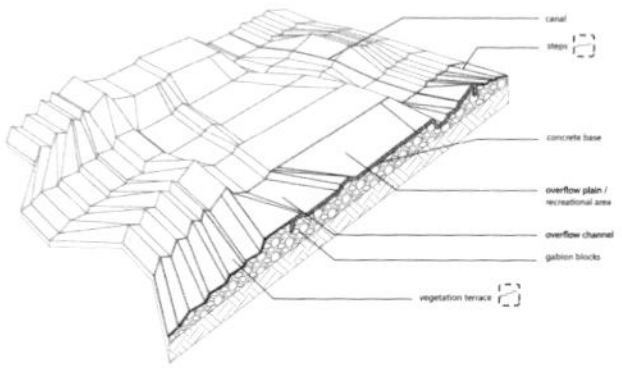
canal
steps
concrete base
overflow plain /
recreational area
overflow channel
gabion blocks
vegetation terrace

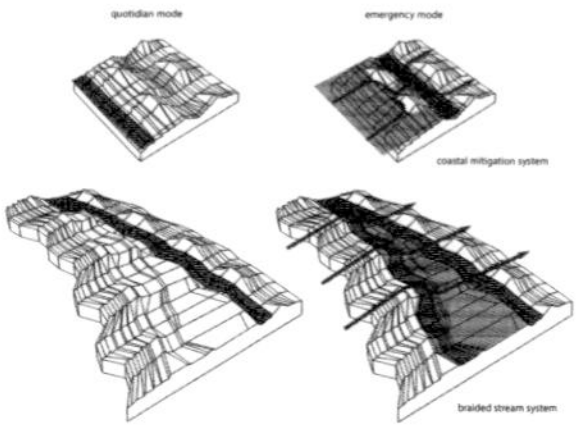
quotidian mode
emergency mode
coastal mitigation system
braided stream system

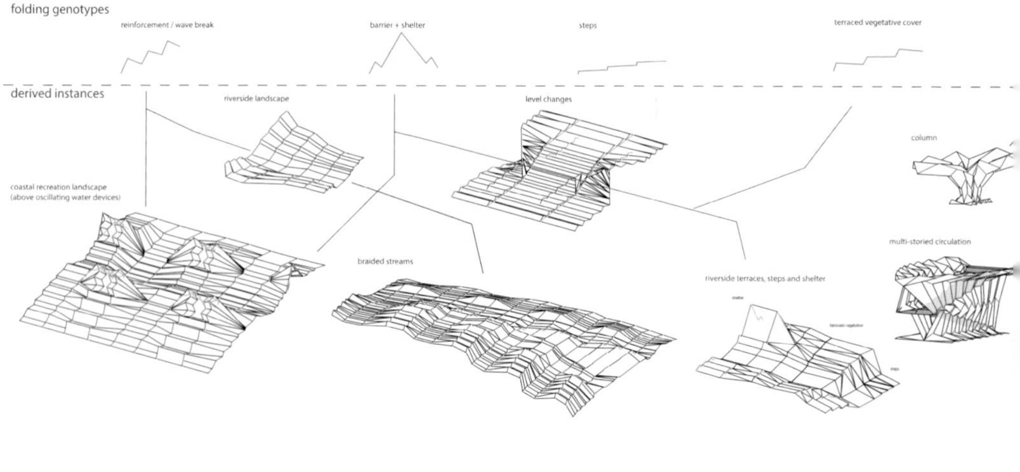
folding genotypes
reinforcement / wave break
barrier + shelter
steps
terraced vegetative cover
derived instances
riverside landscape
level changes
column
coastal recreation landscape
(above oscillating water devices)
multi-storied circulation
braided streams
riverside terraces, steps and shelter

The world's expanding urban population is placing great pressure on agricultural land. Among other countries, China is facing a food crisis, and is quickly developing food colonies in Africa. In this context, it is becoming increasingly necessary to model environmental dynamics. Changing contexts are reflected in an emerging ecological paradigm, in which the city is not in opposition to the "natural" environment but rather in a symbiotic relationship with it. The conventional design tasks of the architect exemplify how the processing of information has come to dominate contemporary design disciplines. Herbert A. Simon asserts that design lies at the boundary of the natural and the technological. The paradox of the city is located precisely at this boundary, a man-made artifice behaving as though it were a living entity.[57]

10.4 COMPLEX SYSTEMS, EQUILIBRIUM, AND EMERGENCE

> When I imagine the shape that will hover above the first half of the twenty-first century, what comes to mind is not the coiled embrace of the genome, or the etched latticework of the silicon chip. It is instead the pulsing red and green pixels of Mitch Resnick's slime mold simulation, moving erratically across the screen at first, then coalescing into larger forms. The shape of those clusters—with their life-like irregularity, and their absent pacemakers—is the shape that will define the coming decades. I see them on the screen, growing and dividing, and I think: That way lies the future.
>
> Steven Johnson, 2001[58]

Computational approaches to design and architectural space increasingly connect biological systems and artificial computational systems, giving rise to questions about what constitutes architectural form, now understood less as permanent, fixed, material compositions than as mobile, dynamic forces and interactions. The

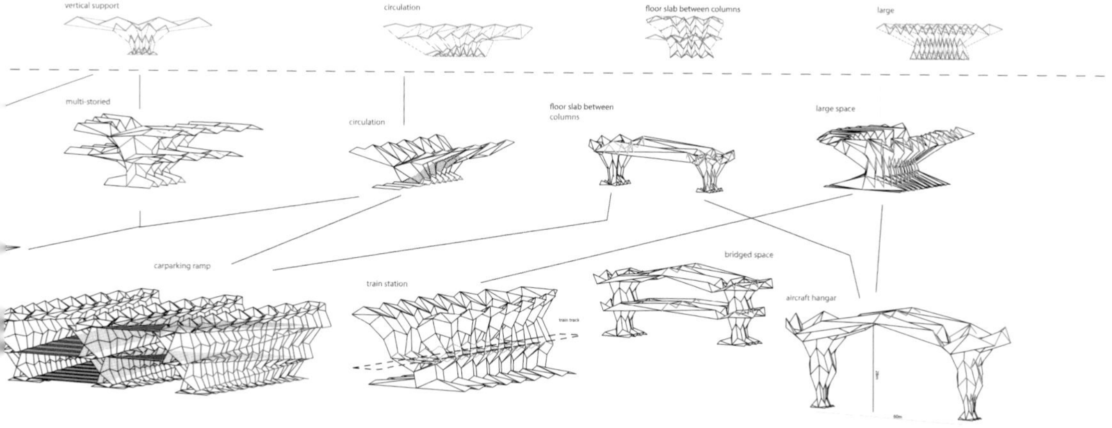

Models of various infrastructural and landscape systems with which to bolster coastal Japan after the Tohuku earthquake and tsunami. (Studio Tutor: Tom Verebes; Students: Chan Yat Ning Chester, Yu Man Fung Jonathan; MArch II Studio, *Projective Design Manual for Rebuilding Coastal Japan*, The University of Hong Kong, 2011)

increasing application of computational coding to design has led to a renewed interest in these kinds of evolutionary processes.

Theories of complex natural systems have proliferated in the discipline of architecture. Nature is so complex, "there is no single 'natural landscape' to be found, no ideal state of nature that can be reconstructed or modelled."[59] Far from finding analogs in the behaviors of species, and hence being isolated from the behavior of "man-made" constructs, systems, and networks, cities have behaviors similar to other complex natural phenomena. In principle, the interactions within a city, or across the global network of cities, are analogous to models in which "interacting individuals can respond to the information gathered by just a few."[60] In the history of urbanity, which spans six millennia, cities have evolved to be "the largest and most complex material forms constructed by humans." Any understanding of enduring civilizations and the evolutionary nature of cities requires an alternative theoretical apparatus: "[monuments] are the most static and enduring constructions of cities, but a chronology of monumental architecture and emperors, of cathedrals and kings, will not serve to unfold the complex interactions of the systems of nature and civilisation."[61] The parallels between natural systems and civilization, according to Michael Weinstock, are such that "all forms of nature and all forms of civilization have 'architecture,' an arrangement of material in space and over time that determines their shape, size, behavior, and duration, and how they come into being."[62]

Over the last two decades, natural systems have increasingly been seen as a source of inspiration for the formal organization of design work, drawing on parallels between natural geometries and their equivalents in three-dimensional modeling environments. Computation is also opening up new design arenas for working with material performance, forces, and effects, which "marks a significant transformation from the primacy of representations to the use of computation as a simulation and map of performativity."[63] The potential of performance-driven computation for urbanism is yet to be theorized, yet there has been some research and practice based on an understanding of the growth of the city, as well as its quotidian routines, as essentially dynamic. Ecological systems give clues to a new view of systems for urbanism, questioning pervasive classical science, which "began to discover that many of its systems were not in fact 'simple' but 'complex,' . . . a new paradigm grappling with the essence of such systems began to emerge."[64]

The paradigm of dynamic equilibrium, a term associated with thermodynamics, can be interrogated for equivalence within discourses on urbanism. The ancient history of urbanization indicates a pattern of shifting from an agricultural society to an urban one. Manuel De Landa has identified the physicist Arthur Iberall as perhaps the first "to visualize the major transitions in early human history (the transitions from hunter-gatherer to agriculturalist, and from agriculturalist to city dweller) not as a linear advance up a ladder of progress but as the crossing of nonlinear critical thresholds (bifurcations)."[65]

A central issue in dynamics is the idea of equilibrium; and in contrast to the idea of the city has having a stable, enduring nature, "In fact, disequilibrium [is the] more characteristic state of urban systems."[66] The term "far-from-equilibrium" originates from the field of thermodynamics, where it has come to refer to "the special states of a system in which it is most likely to produce radical, productive

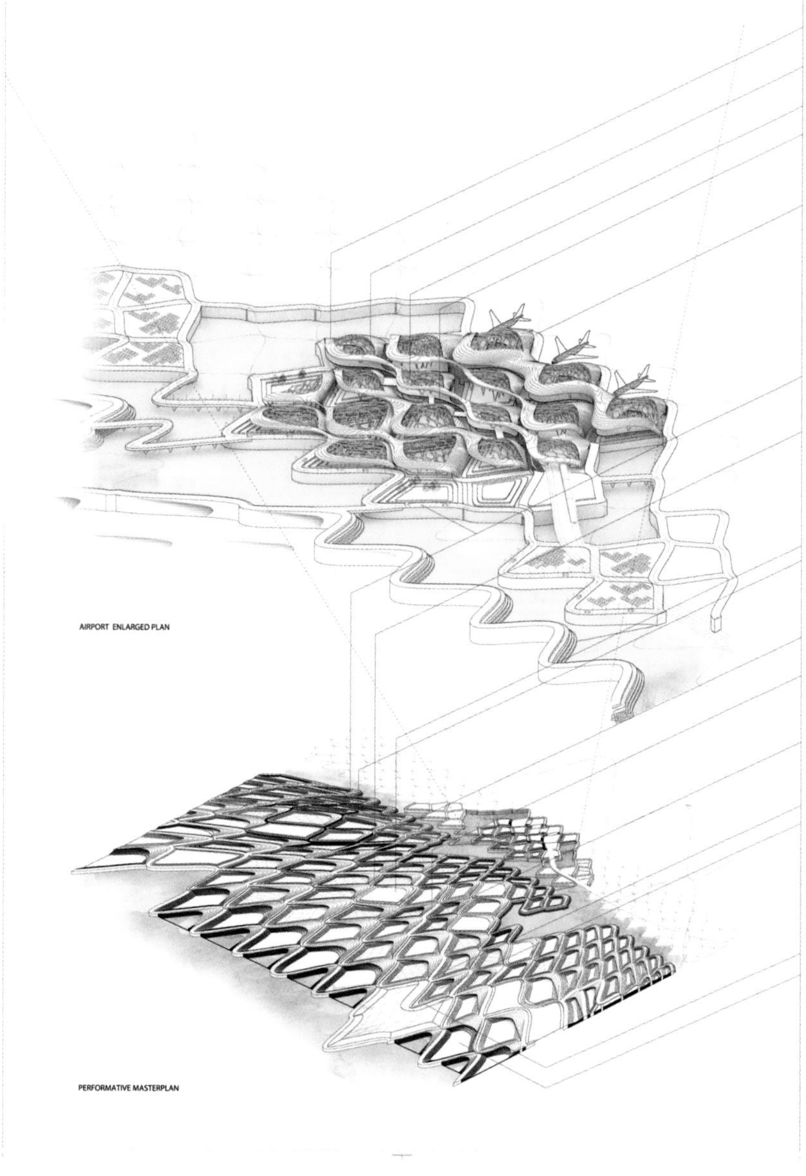

Airport proposal for Sendai (above) and the new coastal landscape (below). (Studio Tutor: Tom Verebes; Students: Ho Lai Ki Nikki, Tang Wai Kwong Danny; MArch II Studio, *Projective Design Manual for Rebuilding Coastal Japan,* The University of Hong Kong, 2011)

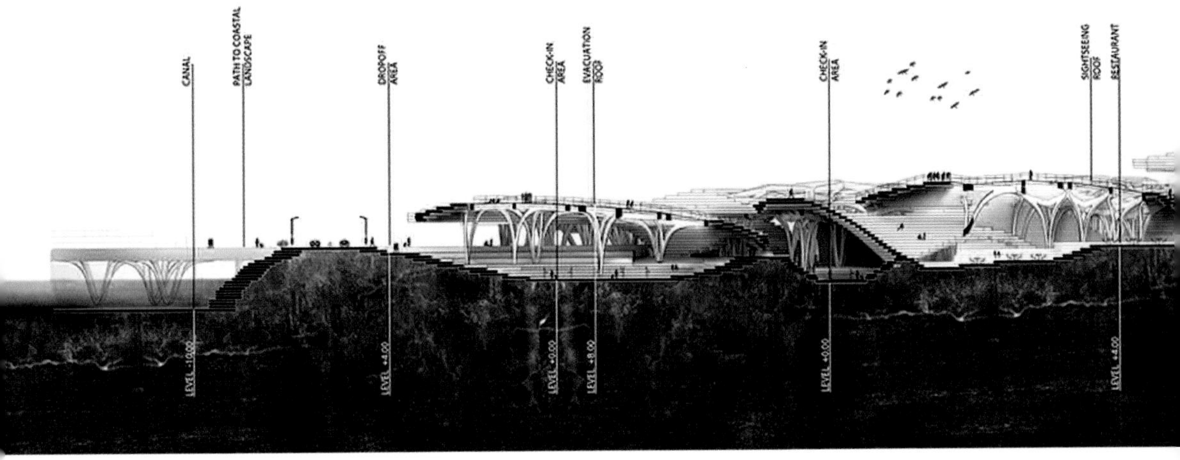

Section of proposed Sendai Airport. (Studio Tutor: Tom Verebes; Students: Ho Lai Ki Nikki, Tang Wai Kwong Danny; MArch II Studio, *Projective Design Manual for Rebuilding Coastal Japan*, The University of Hong Kong, 2011)

and unforeseeable behaviours. When close to equilibrium, the disturbances, anomalies and events passing through a system are easily absorbed and damped out; but as a system is moved further from its rest places it becomes increasingly disordered and differentiated."[67] One of the key concepts in complexity theory "is that of small, simple parts, which are replicated, combined or changed, following simple rules," which through iteration become varied and less predictable.[68] Michael Batty describes how images of the city at any particular point in time "reflect a system far-from-equilibrium, in disequilibrium, whose elements are changing at different rates and whose impact is diverse across different spatial scales and time spans."[69] Whether viewed in real time or over longer historical durations, the city is far from dead, inert, and enduring, rather it is alive, active, and volatile.

Any evolutionary approach to urbanism relates the making of the city to the forces which create form, which in evolution is called morphogenesis. The generative principles of morphogenesis have to do with the formation of shape, "based on laws that describe how forms are initiated in systems with particular types of space–time organisation."[70] Symmetry-breaking processes, pattern initiation, and formation of morphogenetic fields are explained as the "capacity of all life forms to develop ever more baroque bodies out of impossibly simple beginnings."[71] Complexity in architecture has for some time been understood in light of a new appreciation of complex geometric articulation. As much as geometrical complexity provides a potent arena for investigation, static conceptions of geometry can also be limiting. With respect to emergent complexity, without adaptation "it is like the intricate crystals formed by a snowflake: it's a beautiful pattern, but it has no function."[72] Emergent behaviors have the "distinctive quality of growing smarter over time, and of responding to the specific, changing needs of their environment."[73] In such a "lifelike" approach to organization, formal geometric complexities in organization matter less than the capacity for change, which roughly provides a definition of intelligence—the

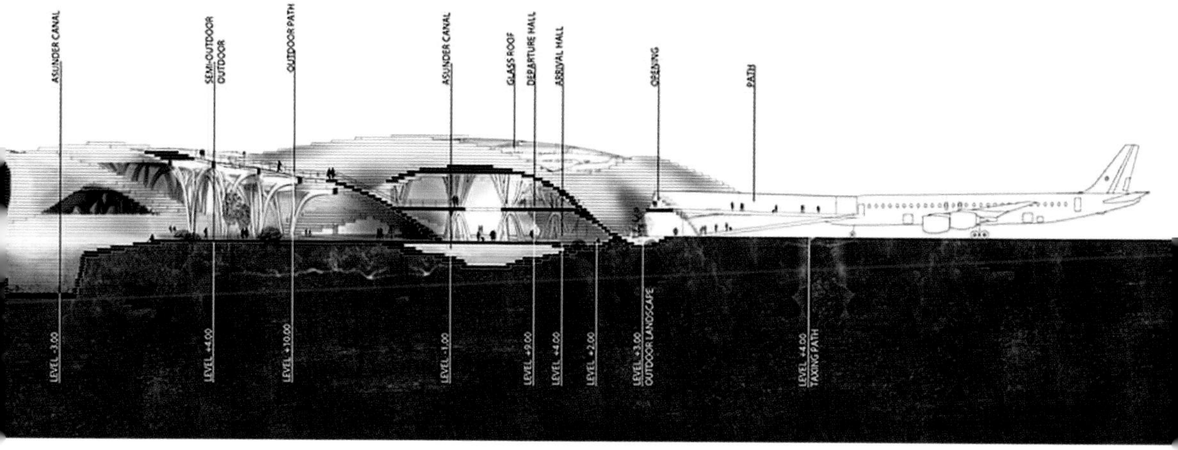

capacity to learn and to embed knowledge in decision-making processes. One of the more compelling innovations in computer science is the U.S. military's development of artificial intelligence for war machinery, which "creates new ways for machines to 'learn' from experience, to plan problem-solving at different levels of complexity."[74]

The cybernetician Gordon Pask argues that conventional architecture is limited to descriptive taxonomy, or prescriptive documentation, but "does little to predict or explain."[75] Pask believed that "urban development can be modelled as a self-organizing system and in these terms it is possible to predict the extent to which the growth of a city will be chaotic or ordered by differentiation."[76] Collective behaviors of organisms create coherent, self-organized formal arrays of dynamic interaction among the individual organisms. Flocks of birds, schools of fish, colonies of ants, and so on all seem to be controlled through a distributed form of intelligence, acting without a central leader.[77]

Juval Portugali claims cities are "to a large extent unpredictable and therefore unplannable," yet adds a caveat, stating that "the perception of cities as chaotic and unpredictable entities is becoming more and more a basic sensation of life" in this century.[78] He sketches out how self-organization is a "conceptual and mathematical theory about complexity" which can teach us how to "control the complexity of our chaotic self-organized cities, how to predict their behaviours, plan their future and thus tame them."[79]

Self-organizing systems "raise questions of control" and of the position of the designer.[80] Self-organization is a compelling understanding of the city, for the ways in which dynamic systems arise from rule-based component parts, and simplicity gives rise to a coherent but complex whole. In establishing new paradigms and practices with respect to the self-organization which occurs within all cities, De Landa argues that "what matters is not the planned results of decision making, but the unintended collective consequences of human decisions," arguing that the "best illustration of a social institution that emerges spontaneously from the interaction of many human decision makers is that of a pre-capitalist market, a collective entity arising from the decentralized interaction of many buyers and sellers."[81]

It is necessary to clarify that an interpretation of emergent behavior as a lack of design intention "is a misunderstanding of fundamental principles of ecology."[82] It is possible to draw parallels between the self-organizational principles of development and evolution in biological forms of life and the emergence of cities—both are produced by "material processes that are ultimately reducible, however long and tortuous the sequences, to the laws of physics."[83] Although the word "emergence" is used in everyday language as a synonym for "appearance," in the sciences it refers to "the production of forms and their behaviour, by systems that have an irreducible complexity."[84] As used in this sense, "emergence" refers to "the properties of a system that cannot be deduced from its components, properties 'emerge' that are more than the sum of their parts."[85] Emergence explains how order is created, but not specifically why a particular form of organization is created.

The principles of evolution in biological systems outline the ways in which order relates to a set of functional criteria, and through successive generations the order is adjusted toward increasingly optimal configurations. According to Marshall, "When we say that evolution has happened, we mean that there was a transformation, via successive intermediates, or descent with modification."[86] Marshall's thesis indicates that evolution is a "generic effect" of a series of non-biological processes of adaptation and transformation, allowing readings of the city to be dissociated from a notion of it as a living organism. In this light, he argues for the idea of design as an evolutionary process, for an approach to design which assumes evolution is linked to "adaptive emergence," as the process of change reflecting incremental local decisions and actions. The term "evolution" is thus used loosely to denote dynamic transformative processes. Questions arise as to whether it can be used to refer to non-biological processes of variation and selection through descent. If "evolution" can be described as any process which aims for long-term transformations resulting from selection and adaptation, to what extent can it be applied to a discussion about urbanism?

The development of complex systems from simple origins is often presented as "a series of major transitions or transformations that are triggered when a critical threshold is passed."[87] Self-organization also refers to "the emergence and development of forms over time—in some cases it is simply used as the description of the sudden appearance of order."[88] Steve Johnson sketches out three phases of inquiry into self-organization: in the first phase, researchers struggled to comprehend the forces which lead to self-organization; in the second, self-organization became a cross-disciplinary focus of study, gaining momentum in research centers such as the Santa Fe Institute; in a third and contemporary phase, Johnson claims "we stopped analysing emergence and started creating it. We began building self-organizing systems into our software applications, our video games, our art, our music."[89]

At the scale of architecture, or a single building, "there is a new sensitivity to the 'life' of buildings, and an understanding that performance and behaviour can be inputs to the process of design rather than functions applied later to a form."[90]

In his seminal, early-adopter essay of 1993, "Soft Systems," Sanford Kwinter called for architecture to learn from the complexity sciences across a variety of disciplines, including environmental, planetary, genetic and geometric instances explicating properties of self-organization. Distinguishing the additive qualities of linear systems, he stated, "nonlinear systems are known primarily for their capacity to change in indeterminate ways over time, continually manifesting new properties, forms, and patterns."[91]

All dynamic systems and collaborative models arise from rule-based component parts which contribute to the coherence of complex entities. The logic of swarm systems as the basis for complexity is not limited to examples from species of fish, birds, or insects; it is equally the basis of crowd behaviors and other mass human interaction. It does not simply reflect a jump from the animal kingdom to the human species; rather the inherent intelligence of swarms can explain much of how highly networked forms of urbanism function. The contemporary global city merges inert physical material with the underlying control of decentralized clouds of computational systems. More than the reality of the cybernetic functionality of the contemporary world, the magnitude and intricacy of urbanism necessitates alternatives to reductive systems of control. Fordist models of clockwork efficiency are inadequate in a world in which the forces that shape the conditions for urban development are complex, vast, and unpredictable. The adaptable and evolutionary qualities of swarm models enable more flexibility in designing the future, a future which is never fully knowable. It is this kind of agility in reacting to and inducing continuous feedback in real time which defines swarm intelligence.

> What we call "life" is a general condition which exists, to some degree or other, in every part of space: brick, stone, grass, river, painting, building, daffodil, human being, forest, city. And further: The key to this idea is that every part of space, small or large—has some degree of life, and that this degree of life is well defined, objectively existing, and measurable.
>
> Christopher Alexander[92]

Christopher Alexander proposes a roster of "fifteen fundamental properties of life," and enlists each property as a means of judging design to be either "good" or "bad." A design is deemed good if it has a "center," which seems to be a simplified definition of a "living" thing, and in turn this notion is contradicted by the property of "deep interlocking and ambiguity," connecting part to part, or center to center, or the whole to its environment. The list of properties climaxes with the fifteenth property, the "non-separateness" or connectedness of things, which "melt into one another and become inseparable"; in effect, this is "a quality which is brought about by the degree to which [things are] connected to the whole world."[93] Alexander believed in creation as a religious concept, as well as in the architect as the creator; but the city cannot be fully "created," as it is constantly evolving.

Shifting from the classical mechanical paradigm which provided cosmological models for half a millennium, biological models more readily explain the integrated dynamic complexity of the world. They help to substantiate the conception of the city as a living, dynamically changing entity, not in opposition to nature but part of the dynamic processes of the planet. Cities are not organisms, nor species of organisms. These terms, however, are transferable; more than metaphors, they can provide models, principles for urban development and evolution, and the basis of an understanding of the city as an ecology, not entirely analogous to natural systems but embedded in relation to them, designs in which local decisions (as in swarm systems, for example) effect the coherence of the whole. In this light, traditional urban morphologies in their growth show similar attributes, and, through the design of simple individual buildings, emergent order of the larger field is achieved over time. The natural world and the man-made must forge greater symbiosis and harmony.[94]

10.5 PARAMETRIC PATTERNS AND MODELS OF EVOLUTIONARY URBANISM

> Systems, notably cities, grow and develop and, in general, evolve. An immediate practical consequence of the evolutionary point of view is that architectural designs should have rules for evolution built into them if their growth is to be healthy rather than cancerous.
>
> Gordon Pask, 1969[95]

The history of urbanism can be comprehended through diagrammatic patterns, codes, and conventions. Urban patterns most often play out various constraints related to the interface between technological and cultural conventions. As described, the city is the result of the association of multiple systems which negotiate each other; in other words, the city is inherently a product of parametric processes. Continuing to explore the paradox of planning versus evolution through "the notion of 'complexity,' which shows that sophisticated forms and patterns may emerge spontaneously from a miasma of interactions," raises questions about how to embed emergent, evolutionary spatial properties in design processes.[96] It seems that the potential to create complex orders inherent in computational design systems can be correlated with the patterns of evolutionary urbanism.

> Each pattern describes a problem which occurs over and over again in our environment, and then describes the core of the solution to that problem, in such a way that you can use this solution a million times over, without ever doing it the same way twice.
>
> Christopher Alexander, 1977[97]

Christopher Alexander was an early adopter within architecture of the appreciation of processes which create patterns, and which are not formulas but mechanisms of variation operating within a specific set of generative rules. In "A City is Not a Tree"[98] he argues for the complexity of the ordering of the city to result from criteria for its functionality. Although Alexander's theories and methods of recognizing patterns of use and configuration are still (or are again) compelling, he rejects informal urbanization as overly simple, and a contradiction arises in his thesis on patterns, in which he favors design over emergence as the generator of a pattern. Marshall posits that the city is "more like a forest of trees—a collective entity—something that may grow indefinitely . . . . [B]etter even than a forest, perhaps, a city is like a whole ecosystem."[99]

Although pattern for Alexander is more a tendency of repetitive use and interaction, or a particular recurrent formal arrangement, for contemporary architects pattern has "an element of mystery and wonder, of intrigue and hope: patterns that can be known by their generators, but never known top down in a stultifying or all encompassing way—their manifestation by its nature unpredictable, offering visual and aesthetic sustenance."[100] Robert Woodbury defines pattern as "a generic solution to a well-described problem."[101] From space-filling, to packing, to models of expansive growth, these new spatial concepts are more fields than they are mathematical objects. In *A Pattern Language*,[102] Alexander sketched out numerous patterns, or conventions, as the basis for an understanding of tendencies. Despite this seemingly unimaginative approach to generating "solutions," Alexander recognized the algorithmic bases of architectural design. He was, however, reticent about, and even dismissive of, the potential to actualize his theoretical interests with computers.[103]

Some of Alexander's ideas about design patterns were furthered by computer scientists, who at the time were "experiencing a paradigm shift caused by what are known as object-oriented programming languages." Algorithmic design is by nature (so to speak) generative of unanticipated outcomes from simple local rules and codes "used to solve, organize, or explore problems with increased visual or organizational complexity."[104] Emergent design, then, is not about repetitive solutions, as in Alexander's "design patterns," but about systems which generate differentiated abstract patterns in relation to inputs and environmental stimuli.[105]

This notion of static, familiar norms is antithetical to a systemic approach to urbanism, where, as in any emergent system, "the city is a pattern in time."[106] According to Philip Ball, patterns are created from "groups of features," whereas form is "the characteristic shape of a class of objects."[107] Gestalt cognitive processes allow our brains "to organize a field of similar shapes into a pattern, so they are adept at somehow discerning commonalities of form between diverse objects—although we find it . . . hard to explain exactly why."[108]

Contemporary design tools are greatly expanding the range of possible patterns we can simulate and invent. A current definition of pattern might be "a sequence, distribution, structure or progression, a series or frequency of a repeated/repeating unit, system or process of identical or similar elements."[109] Traditional concepts of patterns are stylistic, material, ornamental, and decorative, while "the most innovative are now the stealthier patterns of the contents, contexts and consequences of space on ourselves and our world."[110] Shifting from surface effects to the innovative deployment of patterns is "driving a revolutionary type of more accurately patterned and intelligent spatial design that goes beyond the old notion of pattern [and that] can include, but also exceed and extend, its historical and limited scope as purely style, ornament and decoration."[111] Koralevic and Klinger recount how "the infatuation with complex geometry in the mid-1990s soon was replaced by the exploration of highly crafted, non-uniform surface effects based on complex patterning, texturing or relief."[112] This shift from surface to pattern represents "an aesthetic shift [which] led to the re-emergence of the discourse related to ornament and decoration, out of favor with architecture for the large part of the twentieth century."[113] Form, then, is an enterprise which has not as yet been exhausted, yet the simulation of patterns of growth, densification, and change remains a vast, unresolved arena for research.

Within modernism there was a distinct absence of theories or models dealing with how cities grow, and how spatial organization emerges and becomes established. Michael Batty contends that "most theories of urbanism were either based on the science of systems and their optimization and efficiency, or alternatively, on the static spatial patterns designed through the planning and design process."[114] More recently, contemporary notions of the city understand the city as performing "through temporal dynamics is almost entirely absent from conventional models of urbanism."[115]

Alexander marveled at the "dazzling geometric coherence" of natural living systems and species, but stated that "this geometry which means so much, which makes us feel the presence of order so clearly—we do not have a language for it."[116] Since the 1960s the study of pattern has led designers to pursue increased

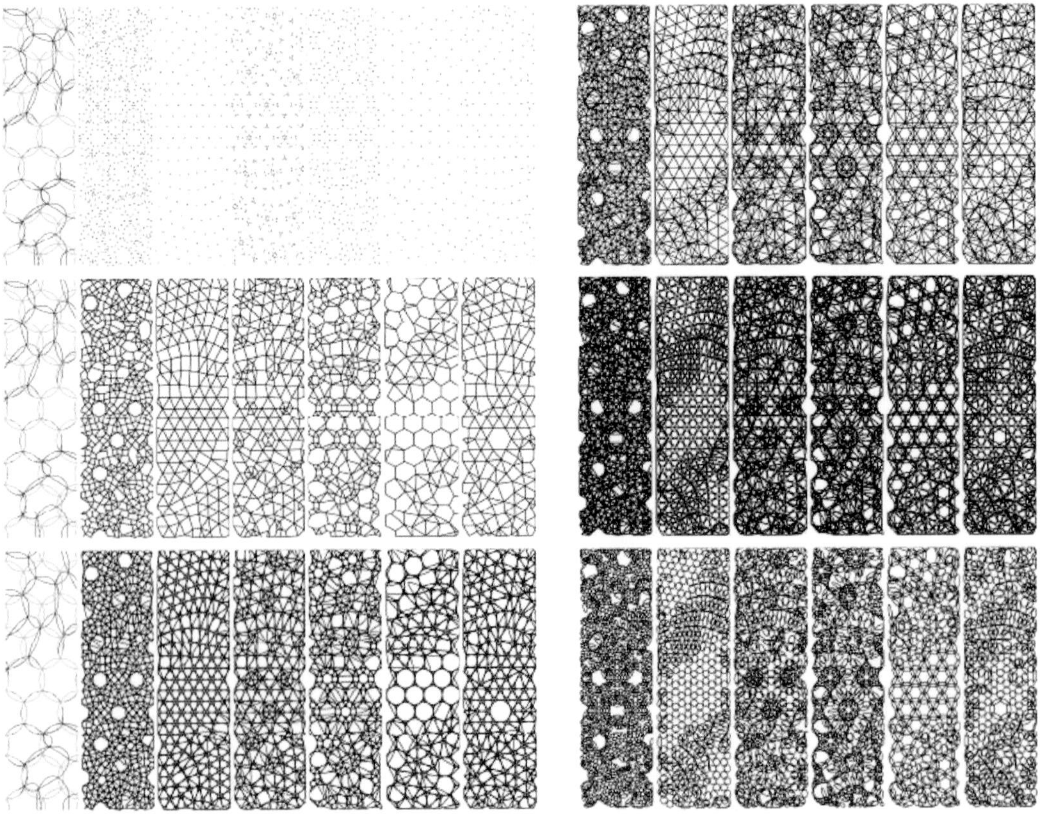

Spatial patterns generated from deformation and interference of regular lattices. (Studio Tutor: Tom Verebes; Students: Lindsay Bresser, Claudia Dorner, Sergio Reyes Rodr guez; Architectural Association, 2009)

complexity and reduced the potential for prescribed design results.[117] The intended effects of local, small-scale interactions and events create unexpected and unpredictable, yet legible, global effects.

Natural patterns, as observed by Frei Otto and countless others, are dynamic and formless, yet architects see the capture of shape through the articulation of geometric patterns as one of the essential attributes of space. The world provides a vast resource for design, yet Otto claims that the "field of occupations in the abiotic world is at least as large" as that of living nature.[118] Otto's experiments with soap bubbles, polystyrene chips, and magnetic shavings led him to conclude that these dynamic physical processes "create clusters, which assume forms closely resembling the outlines of organically developing colonies."[119] These simulations based on attractive and distancing forces in matter were seen as directly analogous to patterns of urban settlement. In addition, a biomimeticist reading of the city sees the connection of pathways as analogous to flows of nutrients in organisms on a microscopic scale, and to the collective behavior of large populations of fauna.

Although there are many points which can be tabled to confront, even contradict, Alexander's argument in the four books of *The Nature of Order*—principally regarding the valorization of traditional craft as the basis for an understanding of his elusive thesis on how to design "living processes"—he presents some pertinent and persistent beliefs about the ways in which geometric order emerges through steps of transformation.[120] Alexander excuses his reliance on "hard" geometrical form through default building elements (column grids, vertical walls, and so on), and identifies a need for a "balance of geometric hardness and terrain-induced or interior-induced softness." One can critique the implicit dichotomy—architecture is hard, nature is soft—but Alexander negotiates this paradox of the presence of humankind's creations, and argues that "it is from this moment of brutality, that real order must come."[121] The concept of designing "living structure" into the artefacts we make has even greater merit today than it did at the time *The Nature of Order* was written, and Alexander was limited to the formal repertoire of his time, which, it is argued, relied too much on an inherited, too-familiar, traditional, formal architectural syntax.

> It is inevitable that we cannot help working within an existing form-language—itself, of course, based on the available processes of our time—then even with the best will in the world, we shall only be able to reproduce versions and combinations of what can be "reached" by that formal language.
>
> Christopher Alexander[122]

Alexander excuses the default valorization of conventional, comprehensible order, yet he also expresses a degree of frustration with his own contemporary repertoire, and also with his inability to create the "kind of geometric order which is needed for living structure [and which] is not necessarily attainable within the combinations of today's form-language."[123] These statements indicate modernism's bankruptcy, and its inability to instigate a formal language appropriate to the desire for greater symbiosis with nature, as well as the limits, at the time, on coding life-generating procedures into design, hence the lifelessness

Diagram of land subdivisions and massing footprints informed by topographical and infrastructural conditions, Dan Zi Shi, Chongqing. (Studio Tutor: Tom Verebes; Students: Cai Hong Kui, Cheung Shiu Lun; MArch I Studio, The University of Hong Kong, 2012)

of architecture Alexander bemoans as lacking "harmonious feelings." Alexander searches for the words—in the absence of design methods, tools, and techniques which are animate, at least in their mimicry of nature—to describe the geometrical style of this new order, and hints at "unfolded geometries" in examples from history and his own projects, testimony to his insight into the limits of his tools and techniques. Breaking with conventions of any particular era is no guarantee of innovation, but embedding the rules of natural formation in artificial design processes remains a preoccupation among today's architects. In Alexander's words, this is the "enormous challenge of making such a language concrete, and culturally specific, while not hampering it with traditional or historic reference."[124] Calling for "simplicity" as it is found in "natural symmetries" that have "rough" or multiple local symmetries, Alexander argues against complexity, which in his terms "consists of distinctions which unnecessarily complicate a structure." Here again is evidence of his vision of bringing design processes closer to nature, but also of the inherent blindness of his methods to the inherent simplicity of complex systems. Asymmetry is a basis for differentiation in natural systems, as well as the underlying natural order in many artificial computational coding systems, which contemporary architects are working to unleash back into the world. Complexity is simple.

Nature provides endless evidence of iterative self-similar geometric patterns. For today's generation of architects, thinking and acting on scales of intervention never seen before on our planet, creating coherent order is a paramount concern. Recognizing complexity in our world is simple. Understanding and harnessing complex order so as to formulate design methodologies with the intelligence to create spatial differentiation and to embed the capacity for change and adaptation lies more in the realm of urbanism than of architecture. Architectural complexity has already been well demonstrated through two decades of research, experimental teaching studios and seminars, and increasingly in practice. Geometric intricacy on the scale of buildings and other artefacts or objects, though managing and delivering it requires skill, is not the only level of complexity at work in the city.

Benoît Mandelbrot, the mathematician who theorized fractal geometries, stated that "the existence of [complex] patterns challenges us to study those forms that Euclid leaves aside as being 'formless,' to investigate the morphology of the 'amorphous'."[125] Mandelbrot was searching for ways to represent the "amorphous," such as trees, coastlines, or clouds, which is "not easily represented in non-Euclidean geometry."[126] In less "natural" terms, the fractal order of the city is most simply explicated by the hierarchy of streets.[127] Fractal systems are characterized by coherent rules of spatial subdivision, along with principles of self-similarity, which guide their formation. New methodologies which connect "pattern and process, form and behaviour, with spatial and cultural parameters, [have] a symbiotic relationship with the natural world."[128] To frame an understanding of the city as the proliferation of a field, similar to fields "described by Einsteinian physics, is radically heterogeneous if viewed globally . . . yet the same laws unfailingly hold for every local instance."[129] Here lies a problem of urban form, as the outcome of the forces which continually shape it. Gases—clouds—are inherently unpredictable and chaotic. The information "cloud," as it has become known (in the sense of "cloud computing," for example), is a "new, always on, ubiquitous, and infinitely tap-able space." The cloud model "represents nothing less than a turn to evolutionary rule in our knowledge system and our conception about space, as full of pitfalls as it is rife with promise."[130]

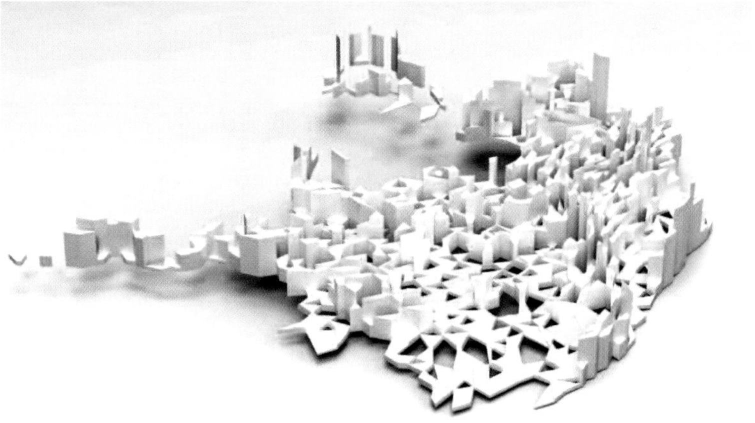

Abstract spatial pattern of a fused urban mat of plinths, tower extrusions, and open spaces. (Studio Tutor: Tom Verebes; Students: Cai Hong Kui, Cheung Shiu Lun; MArch I Studio, The University of Hong Kong, 2012)

Stan Allen's 1997 article, "From Object to Field," opened up a new area for architectural research, by shifting the emphasis for the objectives of design from the production of objects toward a new understanding of fields. In some sense it also shifted the architect's lens away from buildings to larger questions of urbanism. Through a series of analogies ranging from painting, natural sciences, electromagnetism, and landscapes, to selective architectural and urban references, Allen defined the ability of the "spatial matrix" of field conditions to "unify diverse elements while respecting the identity of each [to create] loosely bounded aggregates characterized by porosity and local interconnectivity."[131] Field conditions are inherently expandable, and can be grown or intensified incrementally without significant morphological transformation. In addition, Allen's theorization of fields denies that parts accumulate to form stable wholes, rather the idea of fields borrows from the complexity sciences the formulation that the whole is greater than the sum of the parts, and the valorization of bottom-up, rather than top-down, forms of control. Twenty years earlier, Alexander had articulated this principle as "the interaction among parts" or "organized wholes."[132]

> Architecture and planning, in a desperate attempt to survive, have simply opposed their idea of order to chaos; planning versus uncontrolled growth. But this is a kind of zero sum thinking, in which architecture can only be diminished in the measure to which it relinquishes control over the uncontrollable. We thrive in cities precisely because they are places of the unexpected, products of complex order emerging over time.
>
> Stan Allen[133]

Allen goes on to suggest the "need to recognize the limits of architecture's ability to order the city, and at the same time, to learn from the complex self-regulating orders already present in the city." Indeterminacy and order are simultaneously present in urbanism, while architecture "needs to learn to manage this complexity, which, paradoxically, it can only do by giving up some measure of control."[134]

> The form problem, from the time of pre-Socratics to the late twentieth century is, in fact, an almost unbroken concern with the mechanisms of formation, the process by which discernable patterns come to dissociate themselves from a less finely ordered field. Form, when seen from this perspective, is ordering action, a logic deployed, while the object is merely the latter's sectional image, a manifest variation on an always somewhat distant theme.
>
> Sanford Kwinter[135]

In his 1993 essay, "Toward a New Architecture," Jeffrey Kipnis made a case for a new spatial logic for heterogeneous space, positioning his argument for a new architecture as a fundamental critique of collage as "the pre-eminent design technique of the 20th century," and proposing two approaches to design techniques and spatial paradigms: information and deformation. Kipnis's argument against collage rests on the demonstration of collage effects, which juxtapose or superimpose contradictory spatial attributes, as being incoherent. In addition, Kipnis's essay is a response to Colin Rowe and Fred Koetter's *Collage*

City,[136] in which (European) urbanism is understood as the palimpsest of a multitude of layers of influence and sequential negotiation of new insertions into the preexisting fabric of the city. Influenced by the political theorist Roberto Mangabeira Unger, Kipnis positions his agenda as pursuing spatially coherent heterogeneous spaces, as opposed to collage's incoherent disjunctions, and rather than perpetuating the spatial homogeneity characterized by late modernism and the International Style.[137]

In their 2009 book *Space Reader*, Hensel, Hight, and Menges shift the focus of the discourse on heterogeneous space toward time rather than space. They see dynamic information as driving the formation of spatial qualities through the relation of plastic space to the forces which shape it, but instead of space being the measure or datum, "differentiation is produced via the imminent unfolding of spatial processes."[138] They recapitulate the identification of uniformity as modern space and collage as a postmodern paradigm, while reiterating Kipnis' insistence on coherence of differentiation, and also accepting discontinuities—presumably temporal discontinuities as well as spatial ones—as part of a coherent spatial agenda. More precisely, and with less quasi-scientific rhetoric, Reiser and Umemoto have employed Deleuze's analogy of the games of chess and go, as emblematic of "differences in kind" and "differences in degree," as potent contemporary models of heterogeneity.[139]

It seems an important assertion to make that spatial paradigms based on differentiation and heterogeneity are not speculations about a future for the city, but rather attributes of all cities. In this light, there is a distinction to be made between architectural paradigms and the reality of the city, as wildly evolutionary, with its spatial state shaped by dynamic, transitional conditions that unfold over time. Shunning the notion of an ideal form, and endorsing processes of formation in which properties are variable, De Landa argues that "the main source of variability in material form does not come from properties but from capacities," but that material entities can reach "critical points of a condition, which allow a change from one set of properties to another."[140] In this sense, properties can display a "repertoire of variabilities."[141] Without variability, the evolution of an organism would not be possible. In this lies the potential for the architecture of the city to be driven by information to achieve high degrees of local specificity. Whether designed or planned, grown or evolved, cities are undeniably variable over time, and this is not limited to a spatial model of differentiation. The challenges lie in employed visions without determinism.

The mechanisms of evolutionary patterns follow three principles: inheritance through reproduction; variation through mutation; and natural selection. These transformational processes take multiple generations to play out, and their sum is evolution. Form, which is the focus of interest here, "implies a surplus of direction in evolution, a proto-teleology that explains the forms of things," and which natural selection alone cannot explain.[142] In which ways can cities be said to evolve? Questions arise about the means by which designers can produce generated organizational structures, and, critically, why these kinds of patterns are so compelling. In the following chapters we will investigate the methodologies and projects which enable the phenomena involved in biological evolution analogically to drive tomorrow's architecture and urbanism.

NOTES

1 > F. Otto (2009) *Occupying and Connecting: Thoughts on Territories and Spheres of Influence with Particular Reference to Human Settlement* (Stuttgart: Edition Axel Menges), 111.

2 > M. Batty (2009) "A Digital Breeder for Designing Cities," *Architectural Design* 79, no. 4: 47.

3 > M. De Landa (2009) "The Limits of Urban Simulation," *Architectural Design* 53.

4 > D.G. Shane (2011) *Urban Design since 1945: A Global Perspective* (London: Wiley), 257–258.

5 > S. Hagan (2010) "Performalism: Environmental Metrics and Urban Design," in *Ecological Urbanism*, eds. M. Mostafavi and G. Doherty (Baden: Lars Müller), 466.

6 > Shane, *Urban Design since 1945*, 29.

7 > Shane, *Urban Design since 1945*, 67.

8 > G. Girard and I. Lambot (1993) *City of Darkness: Life in Kowloon Walled City* (Surrey: Watermark).

9 > Hagan, "Performalism," 458.

10 > De Landa, "The Limits of Urban Simulation," 53.

11 > S. Marshall (2009) *Cities, Design, Evolution* (New York: Routledge), 128.

12 > L. Mumford (1961) *The City in History* (London: Harvest/HBJ Book), 393–394.

13 > L. Mumford (1986) *The Lewis Mumford Reader*, ed. D.L. Miller (Athens, Georgia: University of Georgia Press), 112.

14 > M. Hensel and T. Verebes (1998) *Urbanisations* (London: Black Dog).

15 > S. Johnson (2001) *Emergence: The Connected Lives of Ants, Brains, Cities and Software* (London: Scribner), 24.

16 > J. Burry and M. Burry (2010) *The New Mathematics of Architecture* (New York: Thames & Hudson), 54.

17 > Mumford, *The City in History*, 453.

18 > C. Alexander (1980) *The Nature of Order, Book 2: The Process of Creating Life* (Berkley: CES), 51–85.

19 > A. Pope (1997) *Ladders* (Houston: Rice).

20 > Marshall, *Cities, Design, Evolution*, 243.

21 > R. Thom (1975) *Structural Stability and Morphogenesis* (Reading, MA: Addison-Wesley), 8.

22 > K. Kelly (1995) "Hive Mind," in *Out of Control: The New Biology of Machines* (New York: Perseus), 26.

23 > C. Jencks (2002) "Introduction," in *Informal*, C. Balmond (London: Pretzel Publishing), 7.

24 > J. Frazer (1995) *An Evolutionary Architecture* (London: Architectural Association), 67.

25 > Frazer, *An Evolutionary Architecture*, 67.

26 > M. Weinstock (2008) "Metabolism and Morphology," in *AD Versatility and Vicissitude* (London: Wiley-Academy), 233.

27 > M. De Landa (1997) *A Thousand Years of Nonlinear History* (New York: Zone), 118.

28 > M. Weinstock (2010) *The Architecture of Emergence*, (London: Wiley), 202.

29 > Alexander, *The Nature of Order, Book 2*, 13.

30 > Quoted in B. Mandelbrot (1977) *The Fractal Geometry of Nature* (New York), 7.

31 > Hensel and Verebes, *Urbanisations*.

32 > G. Lynn (1999) *Animate Form* (New York: Princeton Architectural Press), 13.

33 > G. Pask (2002) "The Architectural Relevance of Cybernetics," in *Cyber_Reader: Critical Writings for the Digital Era*, ed. Neil Spiller (London: Phaidon), 82.

34 > Pask, "The Architectural Relevance of Cybernetics."

35 > Pask, "The Architectural Relevance of Cybernetics."

36 > C. Hight (2012) "Manifest Variations," in *New Computational Paradigms in Architecture*, ed. Tom Verebes (Beijing: Tsinghua).

37 > Hight, "Manifest Variations."

38 > T. Kuhn (1991) "Scientific Revolutions," in *The Philosophy of Science*, eds. Richard Boyd, Philip Gasper, and J.D. Trout (Cambridge, MA: MIT Press), 78.

39 > W.J. Mitchell (1994) *City of Bits: Space, Place and the Infobahn* (Cambridge, MA: MIT), 107.

40 > Mitchell, *City of Bits*.

41 > B. Koralevic and K. Klinger (2008) "Manufacturing Material Effects," in *Manufacturing Material Effects: Rethinking Design and Making in Architecture*, ed. Branko Koralevic (New York: Routledge), 6.

42 > D. Mertins (2009) "Variability, Variety and Evolution in Early 20th Century

Bioconstructivism," in *The Architecture of Variation*, ed. Lars Spuybroek (London: Thames & Hudson), 55.

43 > Mertins, "Variability, Variety and Evolution."

44 > T. Verebes (2010) "Endurance and Obsolescence: Instant Cities, Disposable Buildings, and the Construction of Culture," in *Sustain and Develop: 306090, Vol. 13*, eds. Jonathan Solomon and Joshua Bolchover (New York: Princeton Architectural Press).

45 > N.T. Nassim (2007) *The Black Swan: The Impact of the Highly Improbable* (New York: Penguin), 128.

46 > Nassim, *The Black Swan*, 309.

47 > Nassim, *The Black Swan*, 149.

48 > S. Kwinter (2011) *Requiem for the City at the End of the Millennium* (Barcelona: Actar), 30.

49 > Kwinter, *Requiem for the City*, 93.

50 > Kwinter, *Requiem for the City*, 65.

51 > G. Soros (2008) *The Crash of 2008 and What It Means* (New York: Public Affairs), 6.

52 > Kwinter, *Requiem for the City*, 31.

53 > Marshall, *Cities, Design, Evolution*, 266.

54 > S. Kwinter and D. Fabricius (2001) "Generica," in *Mutations*, ed. R. Koolhaas, S. Boeri, S. Kwinter, N. Tazi, and H.U. Obrist (Barcelona: Actar), 525.

55 > M. Castells (1996) *The Rise of the Network Society* (Oxford: Blackwell), 147.

56 > De Landa, *A Thousand Years of Nonlinear History*, 20.

57 > H.A. Simon (1996) "The Science of Design: Creating the Artificial," in *The Sciences of the Artificial*, 3rd ed., (Cambridge, MA: MIT Press), 111–138.

58 > S. Johnson (2001) *Emergence: The Connected Lives of Ants, Brains, Cities and Software* (London: Scribner), 23.

59 > Weinstock, *The Architecture of Emergence*, 14.

60 > P. Ball (2009) *Flow* (London: Oxford), 124–163.

61 > Weinstock, *The Architecture of Emergence*, 10.

62 > Weinstock, *The Architecture of Emergence*, 18.

63 > C. Hight, M. Hensel, and A. Menges (2009) "En Route: Towards a Discourse on Heterogeneous Space beyond Modernist Space-Time and Post-Modernist Social Geography," in *Space Reader* (London: Wiley), 10.

64 > M. Batty (2005) *Urban Change* (Cambridge, MA: MIT Press), 7.

65 > De Landa, *A Thousand Years of Nonlinear History*, 15.

66 > M. Batty (2005) *Cities and Complexity* (Cambridge, MA: MIT Press), 30.

67 > S. Kwinter (2010) *Far From Equilibrium: Essays on Technology and Design Culture* (Barcelona: Actar), 16.

68 > J. Burry and M. Burry (2010) *The New Mathematics of Architecture* (New York: Thames & Hudson), 53.

69 > Batty, *Cities and Complexity*, 30.

70 > B.C. Goodwin (2008) 'Structuralist Research Program in Developmental Biology,' in *Greg Lynn Form,* ed. Mark Rappolt (New York: Rizzoli), 176–191.

71 > Johnson, *Emergence*, 17.

72 > Johnson, *Emergence*, 20.

73 > Johnson, *Emergence.*

74 > M. De Landa (1991) *War in the Age of Intelligent Machines* (New York: Zone), 2.

75 > Pask, "The Architectural Relevance of Cybernetics," 79.

76 > Pask, "The Architectural Relevance of Cybernetics."

77 > K. Kelly (1995) *Out of Control: The New Biology of Machines* (New York: Perseus), 7–36.

78 > J. Portugali (2000) *Self-Organisation and the City* (Berlin: Springer-Verlag), 3.

79 > Portugali, *Self-Organisation and the City*, 335.

80 > Burry and Burry, *The New Mathematics of Architecture*, 55.

81 > De Landa, *A Thousand Years of Nonlinear History*, 19.

82 > S. Allen (2010) "Landscape Infrastructures," in *Infrastructure as Architecture: Designing Composite Networks*, eds. K. Stoll and S. Lloyd (Berlin: Verlag), 43.

83 > E.O. Wilson (1998) *Consilience: The Unity of Knowledge* (New York: Alfred Knopf), 55, 226.

84 > Weinstock, *The Architecture of Emergence*, 31.

85 > Weinstock, *The Architecture of Emergence*.

86 > Marshall, *Cities, Design, Evolution*, 172.

87 > Weinstock, *The Architecture of Emergence*, 35.

88 > Weinstock, *The Architecture of Emergence*.

89 > Johnson, *Emergence*, 21.

90 > M. Weinstock (2008) "Metabolism and Morphology," in *AD Versatility and Vicissitude* (London: Wiley), 27.

91 > S. Kwinter (1993) "Soft Systems," in *Culture Lab 1*, ed. Brian Boigon (New York: Princeton), 208–227.

92 > Quoted in C. Alexander (1980) *The Nature of Order, Book 1: The Phenomenon of Life* (Berkeley: CES), 77.

93 > Alexander, *The Nature of Order, Book 1*, 231.

94 > Kelly, *Out of Control*, 7–36.

95 > Pask, "The Architectural Relevance of Cybernetics," 78.

96 > P. Ball (2009) *Shapes* (London: Oxford), 17.

97 > C. Alexander, S. Ishikawa, and M. Silverstein, with M. Jacobson, I. Fiksdahl-King, and S. Angel (1977) *A Pattern Language* (New York: Oxford University Press), X.

98 > C. Alexander (1965) "A City is Not a Tree: Part I," *Architectural Forum* 122, no. 1: 58–62.

99 > Marshall, *Cities, Design, Evolution*, 138.

100 > Burry and Burry, *The New Mathematics of Architecture*, 78.

101 > R. Woodbury (2010) *Elements of Parametric Design* (New York: Routledge), 185.

102 > C. Alexander et al., *A Pattern Language*.

103 > C. Alexander (1967) "The Question of Computers in Design," *Landscape* Autumn, 8–12.

104 > K. Terzidis (2006) *Algorithmic Architecture* (Oxford: Elsevier), 38.

105 > F. Scheurer (2009) "Architectural Algorithms and the Renaissance of the Design Pattern," in *Pattern: Ornament, Structure and Behaviour* (Berlin: Birkhäuser Verlag), 52–55.

106 > Johnson, *Emergence*, 104.

107 > Ball, *Shapes*, 17.

108 > Ball, *Shapes*.

109 > M. Garcia (2009) "Prologue for a History, Theory and Future of Patterns of Architecture and Spatial Design," *AD Patterns in Architecture* (London: Wiley-Academy), 8.

110 > Garcia, "Prologue."

111 > Garcia, "Prologue." 13.

112 > Koralevic and Klinger, "Manufacturing Material Effects," 13.

113 > Koralevic and Klinger, "Manufacturing Material Effects," 13.

114 > Batty, *Cities and Complexity*, 3.

115 > Batty, *Cities and Complexity*, 3.

116 > Alexander, *The Nature of Order, Book 1*, 9.

117 > Terzidis, *Algorithmic Architecture*, 51.

118 > Otto, *Occupying and Connecting*, 34.

119 > Otto, *Occupying and Connecting*, 45.

120 > Alexander, *The Nature of Order, Book 2*, 401.

121 > Alexander, *The Nature of Order, Book 2*, 407.

122 > Alexander, *The Nature of Order, Book 2*, 443.

123 > Alexander, *The Nature of Order, Book 2*, 443.

124 > Alexander, *The Nature of Order, Book 2*, 443.

125 > B. Mandelbrot (1977) *The Fractal Geometry of Nature* (New York), 1.

126 > Burry and Burry, *The New Mathematics of Architecture*, 56.

127 > Marshall, *Cities, Design, Evolution*, 74–76.

128 > Weinstock, "Metabolism and Morphology," 233.

129 > S. Kwinter (2002) *The Architecture of Time* (Cambridge, MA: MIT), 96.

130 > Kwinter, *Requiem for the City*, 71–75.

131 > S. Allen (1997) "From Object to Field," *Architectural Design* 67, no. 5–6: 24.

132 > C. Alexander (1968) "Systems Generating Systems" in *Systemat* (Berkley: Inland Steel Products Company).

133 > Allen, "From Object to Field," 30.

134 > Allen, "From Object to Field," 30.

135 > S. Kwinter (2010) "Who's Afraid of Formalism," in *Far From Equilibrium: Essays on Technology and Design Culture* (Barcelona: Actar), 146.

136 > C. Rowe and F. Koetter (1978) *Collage City* (Cambridge, MA: MIT Press).

137 > J. Kipnis (1993) "Toward a New Architecture," *Architecture Design* 102: 40–49.

138 > Hensel, Hight, Menges, "En Route," 9–39.

139 > J. Reiser and N. Umemoto (2006) *Atlas of Novel Tectonics* (New York: Princeton), 40–41.

140 > M. De Landa (2009) “Material Evolvability and Variability,” in *The Architecture of Variation*, ed. Lars Spuybroek (London: Thames & Hudson), 12.
141 > De Landa, “Material Evolvability and Variability,” 12.
142 > L. Spuybroek (2011) *The Sympathy of Things: Ruskin and the Ecology of Design* (Rotterdam: V2 Publishing), 285.

CHAPTER 11

PATRIK SCHUMACHER > FREE-MARKET URBANISM

URBANISM BEYOND PLANNING

Parametricism makes urbanism and urban order compatible with radically liberal market processes. Large-scale city planning receded during the 1970s, and since then urbanism as a discourse, discipline, and profession has all but disappeared. The disappearance of urbanism coincides with the crisis of modernism, which can be interpreted as the way in which the crisis of the Fordist planned economy manifested itself within architecture. The bankruptcy of modernist planning gave way everywhere to the same visual chaos of laissez-faire urban expansion under the auspices of stylistic pluralism and the antimethod of collage. However, in the last ten years innovative urbanism reemerged under the banner of "parametric urbanism," developing the conceptual, formal, and computational resources for forging a complex, variegated urban order on the basis of parametric logics that allow it to adapt to dynamic market forces. The global convergence and maturation of parametricist design research implies that this style of urbanism is ready to go mainstream and impact the global built environment by reestablishing strong urban orders and identities on the basis of its adaptive and evolutionary heuristics.

The fifty core years of architectural modernism (1925–1975) were also the golden era of urbanism. During this period the advanced industrial nations urbanized on a massive scale. This was also the era of Fordism; that is, the era of mechanical mass production and the era of the planned or mixed economy. The state dominated much of the city-building via big public investments in infrastructure, social housing, schools, hospitals, universities, and so on. This made large-scale, long-term physical planning possible. In Western Europe, energy, utilities, broadcasting, and railways, as well as many large-scale industries had been nationalized. This further enhanced the feasibility of large-scale, long-term urban planning. The most congenial societal context for modernist urbanism existed within the socialist block, with its centrally planned economies. Socialism delivered the logical conclusion of the tendencies of the era, rolling out the technological achievements of the period in a predictable, centrally planned manner, delivering the uniform consumption standard made possible by Fordist mass production to every member of society. Consequently, we find the fullest expression of modernist urbanism in the Eastern Block. Civilization evolved further. The crisis of Fordism, postfordist restructuring, the neoliberal turn in economic policy (privatization, deregulation), and the collapse of the Eastern Block system all coincided with the crisis of modernism in architecture and urbanism. The long-accumulated expertise of modern architecture was bankrupt. Postmodernism, deconstructivism and folding prepared the ground for parametricism but did not deliver viable, generalizable strategies for the reemergence of urbanism. The ongoing, global urban expansion had to proceed without the guidance of the discipline. In the meantime parametricism developed viable (yet barely tested) strategies under the banner of "parametric urbanism."

"Parametricism" is ready to be pushed into the mainstream, to finally allow the avant-garde design research of the last twenty years to impact the global built environment, just like modernism did in the twentieth century. A part of this broader mission is the task of pushing parametric urbanism forward as urbanism's chance to reemerge as a viable alternative to the prevailing, spontaneous "garbage-spill" mode of urban development. The computational, organizational, and compositional resources of parametric urbanism have matured to the point where urban visions that compel can be rendered by projecting the richness of contemporary life processes into a complex variegated urban order that produces urban identities. However, the question arises whether these urban visions are realistic. Can parametric urbanism go mainstream? The question might be posed whether the degree of order that parametric urbanism aspires to can be sustained within the contemporary dynamic and unpredictable societal environment.

This question can be generalized: Is urbanism at all possible in the face of free market dynamism? If we approach this question on the basis of the empirical evidence of the last thirty years—that is, since the neoliberal turn in the world economy—the answer is decisively negative. About thirty years ago modern urbanism vanished. The developmental focus switched to the revitalization and refurbishment of historical centres. When urban expansion returned it took the form of the above-mentioned "garbage-spill" mode of urban development. In the developing world—which has experienced a massive urbanization process in the last thirty years—we have witnessed a mixture of (retrograde) modernism and the same garbage-spill mode of urban development that was unleashed in the developed world since the neoliberal turn. This laissez faire mode of urban expansion produced everywhere a disorienting visual chaos, an isotropic "white noise" without the chance of creating urban identities. Although this result is dissatisfying, it makes no sense for architects to attack the neoliberal turn and call for state intervention to rescue urbanism. The unleashing of market forces cannot be reversed. The regime of Fordism/socialism that delivered the living standards of the 1970s cannot deliver twenty-first-century productivity and living standards. The task of architectural discourse is to reinvent and readapt architecture and urbanism under progressing societal (socioeconomic, technological, and political) conditions, rather than demanding the reversal of socioeconomic and political developments.

If urbanism was premised on top-down planning within a planned/mixed economy, can it continue to exist or reemerge in the absence of planning, within a society that allows for the free play of market forces? In short, the question is: Can there be a free-market urbanism, an urbanism without planning? We are moving here from the empirical domain into the domain of theoretical speculation: Can there be a bottom-up urbanism that produces urban order, coherence, and urban identity without planning? The thesis of this paper states that this is becoming possible today. What is required here is, first of all, a hegemonic style, and moreover a style that is able to deliver a legible order via local rules without imposing an overarching global order.

The discussion of this question might be structured along the lines of architecture's lead distinction of form versus function; that is, the question has both a functional and a formal dimension and ultimately concerns the establishment of systematic relations between forms and functions. The functional side of urban order concerns the efficient spatial distribution of society's divers programs—the spatial ordering of society's manifold activities. Modern planning handled this task via land-use plans adhering to the principle of monofunctional zoning. Postmodern planning—to the extent that planning still exists—prefers mixed-use zoning. In both cases it is the state authorities that impose the programmatic order of the city. The question arises here whether the state authorities have the relevant information and sufficient information-processing capacity to make rational, efficient decisions about the allocation of land resources. The same historical experience that casts doubt on the ability of central planning to deliver an efficient allocation of economic resources in general casts doubt in the particular case of the allocation of land resources. The increasing social complexity and dynamism of a Postfordist network society poses an insurmountable complexity barrier for all central planning efforts.[1] This complexity barrier cannot be conquered by ramping up demographic research, economic forecasting, and so on.[2] Instead the assumption promoted here is that the market—unencumbered by land-use constraints—effects a more efficient allocation, assigning each parcel of land to its most highly valued uses. Perhaps society should allow the market to discover the most productive mix and arrangement of land uses, a distribution that garners synergies[3] and maximizes overall value. The market process is an evolutionary one that operates via mutation (trial and error), selection, and reproduction. It is self-correcting and self-regulating, leading to a self-organized order. Thus we might presume that the land-use allocation and thus the programmatic dimension of the urban and architectural order is to be determined by architecture's private clients.[4]

The precise spatial organization and morphological articulation of the urban order is the task of architecture.

With the demise of modernism the architectural means of organization and articulation have proliferated and a pluralism of styles has replaced the coherence of modernism, including postmodernism, late (high-tech) modernism, neoclassicism, deconstructivism, and minimalism. This proliferation of architectural means of organization and articulation was initially a step forward in comparison to the relative poverty of the means of modernism. The relative monotony of the modernist city is no longer an adequate expression of the diversity, complexity, and dynamism of contemporary metropolitan society. However, the increase in versatility implies a loss of legible order. This proliferation of styles, together with the liberalization of planning rules, such as FAR and height limits, produced the garbage-spill mode of development described above.

To the extent that the current pluralism of styles contributes to a lack of urban order and identity, we might presume that a new hegemonic global style might alleviate this current condition of visual chaos. But this is not all. I would like to argue that neither a hegemonic postmodernism nor a hegemonic deconstructivism could overcome the visual chaos that allows the proliferation of differences to collapse into global sameness (white noise). Both postmodernism and deconstructivism operate via collage, via the unconstrained agglomeration of differences. Only parametricism has the capacity to combine an increase in complexity with a simultaneous increase in order, via the principles of lawful differentiation and systematic correlation. As indicated here, my theoretical assumption is that the free market in land resources produces a global programmatic order with meaningful/efficient distributions and adjacencies.

However, this programmatic order is invisible, hidden within the visual chaos generated by the unconstrained pluralism of styles and the collage process of architectural composition. Under the auspices of parametricism a spatiomorphological visual order that is able to reveal and articulate the underlying programmatic order emerges through the rigorous (computationally operationalized) application of parametric rules that systematically map positional and morphological differences and similitudes onto programmatic differences and similitudes.[5] Or, where morphological differentiation of the urban fabric is initially just a speculative (nonspecific) diversification of the urban offering (for example, the size differentiation of urban blocks in ZHA's One North masterplan in Singapore), its differential take up within the development market and finally its differential appropriation within the end-user market creates a post facto mapping of program to form. Whether prospectively or retrospectively programmed, the navigable formal law of differentiation will make the programmatic differentiation navigable, at least to the extent that the positional and morphological differences make a difference in systematically biasing the final programmatic designation/appropriation.

Masterplanning continues to exist on the level of large private land holdings that are gathered via market processes in order to realize or capitalize on the potential positional synergies that are inherent in urban renewal/development. The parametric setup of such private masterplans implies that any marketed product mix remains provisional and can be recalibrated during the design process that coincides with the presale and preletting process. As such developments are usually phased, this recalibration process can continue during construction. Moreover, it is most important to note that the order envisioned within the paradigm of parametricism does not rely on overarching figures of order that need to be completed in order to become effective, as was the case with baroque or Beaux Arts masterplans. Nor does parametricist order rely on the uniform repetition of patterns, as modernist urbanism does. In contrast to baroque or Beaux Arts masterplans, parametricist compositions are inherently open ended (incomplete) compositions. Their order is relational rather than geometric. They establish order and orientation via the lawful differentiation of fields, via vectors of transformation, as well as via contextual affiliations and subsystem correlations. This neither requires the completion of a figure, nor—in contrast to modernist masterplans—the uniform repetition of a pattern. There are always many (in principle infinitely many) creative ways to transform, to affiliate, to correlate. The paradigm delivers an unprecedented versatility. However, this does not imply that anything goes, as in the garbage-spill mode of agglomeration. The heuristic principles (taboos and dogmas) of parametricism are to be adhered to at any moment, with respect to any design move or design decision. The design process explores a radically constrained design world, the design world of parametricism. However, this design world is in itself already an infinitely rich universe of new possibilities. Thus we can afford to exclude some (already explored) regions of the totality of design possibilities, and yet remain superflexible and versatile in our responses to the dynamism of market forces. Only under this condition—under the condition of a hegemonic architectural paradigm/style—can the discipline ascertain that a flexible, dynamic, robust, and legible urban order (with many unique local identities) has a chance to emerge against the prevailing global default condition of the garbage-spill mode of urban development. Such a hegemonic style cannot be prescribed top down. It can only emerge bottom up within the autopoiesis (discourse) of architecture. The efforts of many creative hands and voices must converge to make this happen. Such a convergence of creative forces is already happening in the avant garde. The task is now to push parametricism into the mainstream, to allow the autopoiesis of architecture to once more impact the global built environment.

A first glimpse of this impact can be witnessed in Singapore, on account of the One North masterplan designed by Zaha Hadid Architects in 2001. This masterplan continues to evolve and adapt as execution proceeds. That a strong urban identity is being forged here should be evident. The scheme draws the diverse, preexisting urban contexts into a new, continuously differentiated order. All incoming roads are taken up into a soft grid that mediates the otherwise incongruent urban directionalities of the context. The contextual affiliations and continuities with the different adjacent urban patterns as well as the (initially nonspecific) internal differentiation of the urban fabric result in field logics that can be navigated along legible vectors of transformation. The correlation of block heights with plot sizes turns the urban elevation into a legible graph of the distribution of spatial depths. This complex, variegated order remains open to parametric recalibrations in response to shifting market demands, without corrupting its relational ordering logic. Its order is robust and inherently open ended, without ever losing its unmistakable identity. This is a masterplan without an ultimate end state. The particularities of its future states remain unpredictable. But as long as the participating architects adhere to its abstract relational principles and buy into its heuristics of forging continuities and correlations, a strong urban order/identity survives as it evolves.

NOTES

1 > It was F.A. Hayek who first understood the economic problem (the problem of efficient resource allocation) as a problem of knowledge utilization and information processing. Hayek writes: "In ordinary language we describe by the word 'planning' the complex of interrelated decisions about the allocation of our available resources. All economic activity is in this sense planning; and in any society in which many people collaborate, this planning, whoever does it, will in some measure have to be based on knowledge which, in the first instance, is not given to the planner but to somebody else, which somehow will have to be conveyed to the planner. The various ways in which the knowledge on which people base their plans is communicated to them is the crucial problem for any theory explaining the economic process, and the problem of what is the best way of utilizing knowledge initially dispersed among all the people." See: F.A. Hayek (1945) "The Use of Knowledge in Society," *American Economic Review* XXXV, no. 4: 519–530.

2 > Of course investors sometimes get it wrong too, but many more eyes are on the ball and mistakes are corrected quickly via the signalling of the profit and loss system.

3 > As an example, a hot-dog stand in front of a cinema entrance. The opposite of positive synergies—namely negative externalities—can also be solved via market processes, i.e. via a trading of externalities, as long as property rights are clearly defined. For example, if a hot-dog stand is considered a nuisance that distracts from the cinema experience then the cinema owner might buy the property of the hot-dog seller.

4 > These clients might give their architects a certain leeway in suggesting the microdistribution of the programmatic elements within a given project brief or masterplan, albeit usually in close collaboration with the client's marketing department.

5 The author has elaborated this in his theory of parametric semiology. See Patrik Schumacher (2012) *The Autopoiesis of Architecture, Volume 2: A New Agenda for Architecture* (London: John Wiley & Sons).

CHAPTER 12

CONVERSATION 4

TOM BARKER (TB) AND TOM VEREBES (TV)

TV The core thesis of this book raises questions concerning the evolutionary nature of cities, and the ways in which conceptual and technological apparatus can deal with the indeterminacies inherent to contexts that are rapidly urbanizing. I am thrilled to discuss these issues with you Tom, because your career has taken a unique path and your profile is that of a multidisciplinary technologist or even an inventor, working across design disciplines, from a background in structural and mechanical engineering, and industrial design engineering. Your research lies at the intersection of design and technology, from the scale of personal products, to building systems, to urban interfaces. Let's start by asking you to characterize the ways in which technology has historically changed cities, and more projectively, how do you see cities changing the evolution of technologies?

TB For me, the differences between disciplines are increasingly defined by the way in which a problematic is addressed, as opposed to the specific tool set of a discipline. When you talk to an engineer about city design they tend to think of cities as infrastructural systems. Economists think about cities in terms of commerce. Urban designers think about cities in terms of public space and quality of life within built spaces. Because cities are so complicated we tend to also see them in terms of all sorts of warm and fuzzy conditions. The hierarchy of urban evolution starts with commerce and trading as the driver, and in some cases theology in ancient civilizations, but those cities tended to get wiped out because they were built in the wrong places. Waterborne sewage has killed more people over the history of civilization than have been killed in war. It was during the industrial revolution that water and waste management became a coherent part of the city plan. Probably the next big technological leap was the advent of trains, trams, and vehicles, which had a massive impact on street patterns. When I was working on the One North masterplan in Singapore with Zaha Hadid Architects, the paradox of design you raised was evident in how a masterplan may be predictive. When designed with static tools, a masterplan can adequately work out linear phasing, but of course when a plan is handed over to the city authorities, the plan starts to get eroded by the dynamics of real life.

TV What still seems so relevant and compelling about the One North project is how it challenged a masterplan as an illustrative image of a final design, but instead sees the masterplan as an interface with which to manage dynamic data sets, related to the economy, urban densities, other policies such as setback and connections between buildings. It is a project which confronted the limitations of conventional masterplanning to operate as a mechanism to forecast the future, and rather set up a masterplan as a supple and reactive tool which can be updated in time. Conventional masterplans are defunct and useless at the moment they're delivered, because of the gap between the projection and the results. Through metrics and parametrics, what was developed in One North was a tool to manage the future, not a singular image of the future.

TB One of the biggest challenges of city design, when considered from a multidisciplinary perspective, is that you can't actually satisfy all criteria. The two directions are either tabular rasa or the design of a significant precinct component. Another is the notion of the instant city, and one example is Song Dao City in South Korea, which is due for completion in 2014. It is being built as a kind of benchmark of a superwired high-tech city. So although it is unproven, it is the most technologically advanced city to near completion. I find it interesting that even before completion, they're selling the blueprints as copies to delegations from China and India. It proposes a technical solution with no deference to context, no deference to even environmental conditions. The other extreme, I suppose, is a more intelligent, tool-based, generative or predictive model, such as One North. The component that I was researching was this notion of a masterplanning tool which would negotiate interrelated city criteria of design requirements which are all contradictory and divergent, and to use them as multilevel analysis that ignores conventional disciplinary segmentation. So the tool allowed disciplines to have specificity but in a holistic model that tried to join them together.

TV It's curious how we could be talking about the game environment of *SimCity*, as the management of a constrained number of criteria and parameters, in which the model is a simulation tool. If one simulates a monoparametric data set, it's very much possible to predict with accuracy how that one single parameter will behave. As soon as one begins to take multiple parameters and contingencies into consideration, the viability of any kind of simulation becomes muddled and difficult to ascertain. In many ways, cities have always played out the negotiation between associated disciplines and their criteria of performance. I don't think what we talking about is necessarily anything wholly new. Computational experts are the first to argue there's nothing new about parametric design, and that design has always been parametric. To what extent do you think advanced design and simulation tools can be applied to a series of specific prototypes designed for different contexts, rather than generic, repeated models?

TB That's a big question, related to the notion of top-down versus bottom-up. Most of the tools available currently for city design are generally not actually bottom-up. What is abundantly apparent is the need to get the overall city strategy right. The benefit of historical cities which evolved over time is that they often did not have a strategy. I was reading something the software developer of *SimCity* had written, and he sounds exactly like an urban designer. He says we can think of a city as a static structure, but when you look at it in time, fastforwarding a few hours or decades, you start seeing it as an organic living organism, rather than a static entity, adapting on a long time scale. *SimCity* is a simulation of variables, but the city is a more complex and interactive entity. Humans like patterns and we like cause and effect, but it's difficult to discern patterns from *SimCity*. It's fascinating seeing how computers have evolved in the last fifty years. Computers first emerged in the 1960s, followed by management and information systems in the 70s, which was deadly boring for people doing urban design. Forty years later we are in an incredible era of analytics, which followed visualization in the 80s, simulation in the 90s, and then from about 2000 we have procedural and generative methods, and finally, in the last few years, people have been researching time-based or evolutionary computational techniques. What we were interested in with One North was how tools can be harnessed in the early conceptual design stage to strategically point the project in multiple directions. Another area I think is really interesting in terms of managing a city once it's actually running is data analytics. Pathfinder technologies collate data from across the city, such as social and social–economic data. Of course there is the real-time component of cities, and these tools allow you to keep a live model of the city, and there is also the actual model of the real city, the data from the city itself, as a kind of shadow existence, which makes the city exist physically as well as digitally. Data analytics allows us to tie things together, and that's the really exciting aspect of contemporary technology.

TV I enjoyed your brief history of computational technologies and how we used them as designers over the decades. Of today's tools which address data analytics and management, there is the adaptiation of Building Information Modeling (BIM) toward City Informational Modeling (CIM), which aims to test divergent and related options, and update a model of the city. Perhaps unlike a BIM model, which may be seen as an ultimate, inclusive, totalizing model of a building in which every part is designed, and managerial and delivery issues are debugged, CIM is still very nascent, and there are few examples as yet. Unlike a BIM model which it seems is a process in which you produce the real thing, the building, it is unclear whether a City Information Model would have the same status of a design tool leading toward a design outcome. Will CIM tools be managerial, analytical, or a way of simulating potential further iterations and versions of changes to the city?

TB That's a great question. A lot of these issues have been bundled into the notion of the smartness of cities and buildings. I read a report in the *Economist* magazine in 2010, in which the most promising aspects of smart cities are mobile systems and physical infrastructure, which represents the area with the greatest capability for improvement. As for building management systems, you can design a fantastic building that is gloriously iconic and people love it, but it may be horrifically energy inefficient—the maintenance costs may be outrageous. There's a history of this with archetypal buildings and I think that is happening a little bit with cities. A really good example is Masdar in Abu Dhabi, which is a super-high-tech city for forty thousand people in the desert, but Masdar should never have been built in that location. The question is: What is a smart city? Smart buildings are about strategies for high-performance building cores and systems integration, and whether it operates well, and people use it effectively. We cannot scale this notion to an entire city, but you can find parallels of infrastructure and the notion of a smart grid, which is about being able to shift power between parts of the city without energy loss. Throughout history, smart energy power grids have always been problematic because they have never led to real-time responsiveness. IT infrastructure is where smartness is found today. Seoul has recently built the world's fastest broadband network and it has paid off, in terms of the growth of IT businesses and service industries. Of course in ten years' time the network could become redundant, so our notion of what's smart now may not necessarily be what will be smart later. For a city to be smart, the infrastructure should be there for a long time. Take the London Underground for example, which has been in place for over one hundred years. New cities don't have to deal with historically aging existing networks. So for me a big part of smartness is about how can you do small but influential interventions within the context of an existing city. About twenty-five years ago, Rothschilds bought the pneumatic air delivery system in London, which was used for many things: for delivering messages by compressed air tubes, and for powering elevators, but the system was closed long ago, and everybody thought Rothschilds was crazy. It was in fact genius, because it was the last available piece of network space in London when IT companies began to lay a fiber-optic cable network cross London. When you build infrastructure, a question to ask is how to upgrade it in the future.

TV Underscoring your fascinating take on intelligence is the endurance of infrastructure for different applications, whether purpose-built, or adapted over time in an existing city. Despite the real-time nature of smartness in cities, what is less predictable is the potential for infrastructure to adapt to future contingencies, what makes a system redundant, how systems decay. It is interesting how this discussion about technology is focussed on infrastructure, which has guided cities through the ages. In Vitruvius' *Ten Books on Architecture*, the first several chapters deal with various kinds of infrastructure needed to establish a city: firstly to make it healthy and liveable, then to make it connected, then defensible, and lastly, with all the other institutions and services to make it function through its commerce and its public spaces. The Romans built nearly six thousand cities in this systematized way, making the Roman system the first model of globalization. Every era of rapid urbanization was related to changes in industry. Can we shift our conversation toward the application of technology or infrastructure toward some of the current or future environmental problems of urbanization—what we call sustainable design, for lack of better terminology? To live up to the branding of eco-cities, how can we build cities that have greater ecological performance?

TB Again another interesting question. To me the notion of the environmentally sustainable city has to some extent been hijacked by the promotion that existing cities are doing to convince people they are attractive. Much of this is about greening cities and making them more livable, which is commendable but it is not necessarily making cities more sustainable. While I was in Australia I was working with Siemens on a definition of the sustainable city. Last year they decided to stop making nuclear power stations and they created a new division for city design, because they now believe integrated building services solutions have to do with citywide energy control. Siemens defines the sustainable city as about being holistically planned, environmentally friendly, and then they provide a set return-investment, among other criteria. The International Energy Agency describes sustainability as being the minimum adverse effect on the built and natural environment, in terms of the buildings, their immediate surroundings, and on a broader regional and the global setting, which again is quite foggy. If you want buildings to have minimum impact then don't build. The city is already a paradox in terms of sustainability, despite ongoing debates about whether cities are sustainable or not. On the one hand, there is the argument to concentrate people and activities rather than having people spread out. On the other hand, cities use huge amounts of energy. The visual approach to sustainability, such as urban farming or green roofs, has an almost negligible impact. If you are a vegan the amount of land you need to sustain yourself is about 280 square meters. If you are a red-meat-eating Texan you need 8,500 square meters. We are also still not sure how to minimize the carbon footprint of the city. On a precinct management level, for example, if we know which buildings at any one time are getting sunlight on them you can set up a variable air-conditioning system to shift excess cooling capability to another part of the building. It is these kinds of load-sharing elements which can happen across a city to form the basis of feeding energy from your building back to the grid. What's interesting is you suddenly quite quickly start moving to land initiatives, or ownership of energy grids and power, and there are still only a minority of countries which make it economic to actually sell energy back into the system, and the classic trick is retail versus wholesale prices, and that often is the difference whether solar installations make any sense at all. If you are taking a holistic approach, you consider not just the city but also where the power for that city is coming from, whether it is wind farms, or solar-thermal installations, or geothermal that will provide most of the city's energy requirements—then I think it's starting to make real progress. But if you don't do that, the city would be a net consumer of unsustainable energy.

TV You've cataloged some of the varied approaches to ecological urbanism, but I am still confused by your definition of "sustainability," which is a term I find so vague, because it usually entails listing through the definitions, which you've done so expertly. Allow me to propose another definition of sustainability, in a world rapidly urbanizing to such an extent, with so much poorly built, wasteful architecture. This may sound traditionalist, but if we build for longer durations wouldn't we be building in a way that would sustain the city to last and endure? In that sense, we wouldn't have to rebuild the city so often. This is one of the central paradoxes of this book: in the context of rapid urbanization how do we really build to last? This is potentially one of the definitions of sustainability that could overcome all of the ecological problems we are trying to solve, through all sorts of apparatus, to make the world either more efficient, or the world less energy consumptive. This echoes the traditional world, and whilst I'm not saying that traditional architecture or traditional cities are a solution, but rather, to build cities to endure. Now this is also caught in the paradox of how cities change. I don't have answers but I am raising a question.

TB Despite my commitment to technological progress, we still use materials that we used thousands of years ago—stone, bricks, timber, metals, and glass, and concrete and some composites now for structural design in buildings and bridges. I guess the reason is they are durable materials. Most new technology has a shorter lifespan, for example IT infrastructure, which will become redundant, or just because technology moves on. I was working with Rogers Stirk Harbor architects in Sydney, and they wanted to know about how to future-proof a commercial tower that they were designing. The reasons were commercially motivated, as the developer believed if they could tell potential tenants they had a future-proofed building, it would be an attractive proposition. They were a bit upset when I said to them that the only way to develop a future-proofed commercial building is not to put any IT infrastructure into it whatsoever, as it will go out of date. I actually think the strategy for me is unplugging, or removing technology for upgrading and refurbishment. How long a building lasts is interesting, but if you want a building to last then build a building without any windows. H.G. Wells wrote a novel which was turned into the UK's most expensive movie about a world that is taken over by technocrats. They were looking at old buildings with windows, and they thought it was ridiculous how people thought we had to have windows until we discovered an energy-efficient way of creating light within a space, and then buildings became much more efficient because there were no windows. When I was at Arup in the 90s we started specifying glazing systems which would be glued onto buildings, without physical structural components to hold the glass onto the building, rendering the design life quite short. We tend to think about building maintenance historically, in terms of something going wrong and we fix it. When we start to think about preventive maintenance we're moving to a city model which is more like the automotive industry where you buy a car with a five-year warranty. For example, building suppliers are starting to supply lighting systems for commercial buildings where you do not own the lighting, but you pay for a service contract which includes lighting, and when the lighting is out of date it's removed. I don't know if I really have answered your question, but did the Victorians or the Georgians think about durability? Or did they simply aim to make a great city and see what happens? Massive impermanence also has a role to play, which is counterintuitive. Alternatively, why not build as cheaply as possible and be prepared to rebuild it?

TV Another compelling aspect of sustainability is how culture is maintained and how social spaces thrive, and what makes a great city. So many cities are being built all over the developing world, especially in China, and I wonder whether we will have great regrets over the kinds of cities we are making. Many of these questions are centered on the value of making urbanism for the future which privileges quality of life and the cultural life of cities, not so much its efficiencies. Perhaps the Georgians, the Victorians, and the Romans didn't know they were messing up the world to the extent that we do. I don't think we have answers but what we're doing is raising questions to work through for years to come.

CASE STUDY

ZAHA HADID ARCHITECTS >ONE NORTH SINGAPORE SCIENCE HUB, SINGAPORE

2002

Design: Zaha Hadid with Patrik Schumacher
Project Director: Markus Dochantschi
Project architects (Masterplan Phase): David Gerber, Dillon Lin, Silvia Forlati,
Project team (Masterplan Phase): David Mah, Gunther Koppelhuber, Rodrigo O'Malley, Kim Thornton
Project architects (Rochester Detail Planning Phase): Gunther Koppelhuber
Project team (Rochester Detail Planning Phase): Kim Thornton, Hon Kong Chee, Yael Brosilovski, Fernando Perez
Competition team: David Gerber, Edgar Gonzalez, Chris Dopheide, David Salazar, Tiago Correia, Ken Bostock, Patrik Schumacher, Paola Cattarin, Dillon Lin, Barbara Kuit, Woody K.T. Yao
Urban strategy: Lawrence Barth, Architectural Association
Models: Riaan Steenkamp, Chris Dopheide, Ellen Haywood, Helena Feldman
Presentation models: Delicatessen Design—Ademir Volic
Infrastructural engineers: Ove Arup and Partners—Simon Hancock, Ian Carradice, David Johnson
Infrastructural audits: JTC Consultants Private Limited
Transport engineers: MVA—Paul Williams, Tim Booth
Landscape architects: Cicada Private Limited
Lighting planners: Lighting Planner Associates Incorporated—Karou Mende
Planning tool consultants: B consultants—Tom Barker, Graeme Jennings
Photographer: Ken Seet

This 190-hectare masterplan, a competition-winning entry in 2001, extends to pressing questions of adaptable urban strategies the office's many years of research and experimentation with dynamic form and spatial qualities. Cities present a kaleidoscope of spatial patterns, continuously evolving organically according to local circumstance and changing conditions, requiring designers to think adaptively and flexibly about the future of the built environment. The traditional two-dimensional land-use plan is therefore insufficient for managing the spatial complexity of such a project. To respond to this problem, numerous spatial scenarios were modeled in three dimensions and at a variety of scales, adapting the land-use planning process to the intensification of a complex urban environment. The proposed morphological system, the form of which is "free" and therefore malleable at any stage of its development, allows for infinite variation within the bounds of a strong formal coherence and lawfulness. The subtle differentiation of One North's seven urban districts supports fluid adaptation to changing conditions of investment and development, generating a masterplan that promotes both spatial control and adaptability under changing conditions, a richly conceived system of groundforms suited to the shaping of new relationships and intersections, and a forceful strategic response to a development of international significance.

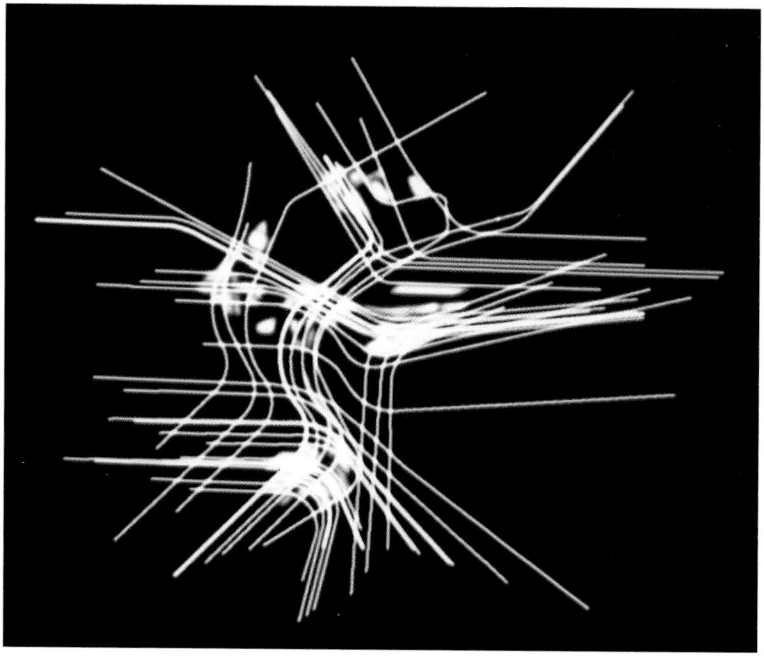

An early conceptual sketch of the relation of a transport vision of a road system patterned on a gently curved grid, effectively accommodating both topography and the high-intensity nodes, all of which are conceived as instruments of change and development

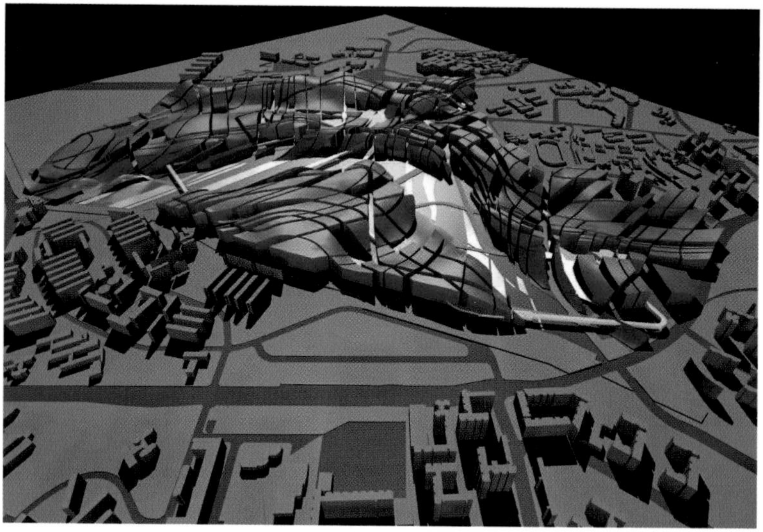

Aerial view of a proposed massing model, indicating the coherence of the overall massing topography, land subdivision, and infrastructural plan.

Photos of the completed buildings of the Biopolis Science Hub, indicating the interconnectivity and massing relations of discrete buildings, as well as the systemic integration of the urban order to topography.

CASE STUDY

OCEAN CN >URBAN CHINA RESEARCH

2009

Design team: Felix Robbins (Scripting), Gao Yan, Tom Verebes

Through code-based design, OCEAN CN developed a series of urban organizational models, generated as computational arrays of massing typologies and densities. This design exercise proliferates new hybrid urban massing prototypes, and varied species of architectural configurations associated with contemporary Chinese cities. The objective was to propose alternatives to stable, repetitive typologies, and to invent a range of specific, diverse forms of architectural organization with coherent global attributes. Population and density data were initially mined from several Chinese cities (Beijing, Shanghai, Guangzhou, Shenzhen, Dongguan), and were applied to the morphing of four dominant massing typologies (tier buildings, low-rise/deep-plan, high-rise towers, luxury detached villas). Computational operations targeting the variation of proximity of massing, as well as volumetric dimensions and formal attributes, were then applied to the arrays, which generated the emergence of new hybrid typologies of intensely connected forms of aggregate urbanism.The parametric logic of these prototypical spaces embodies dimensional constraints such as height limits, FAR, architectural footprint density, plot area, and the total buildable surface area.

Series of arrays of typological transformations from initial seed types.

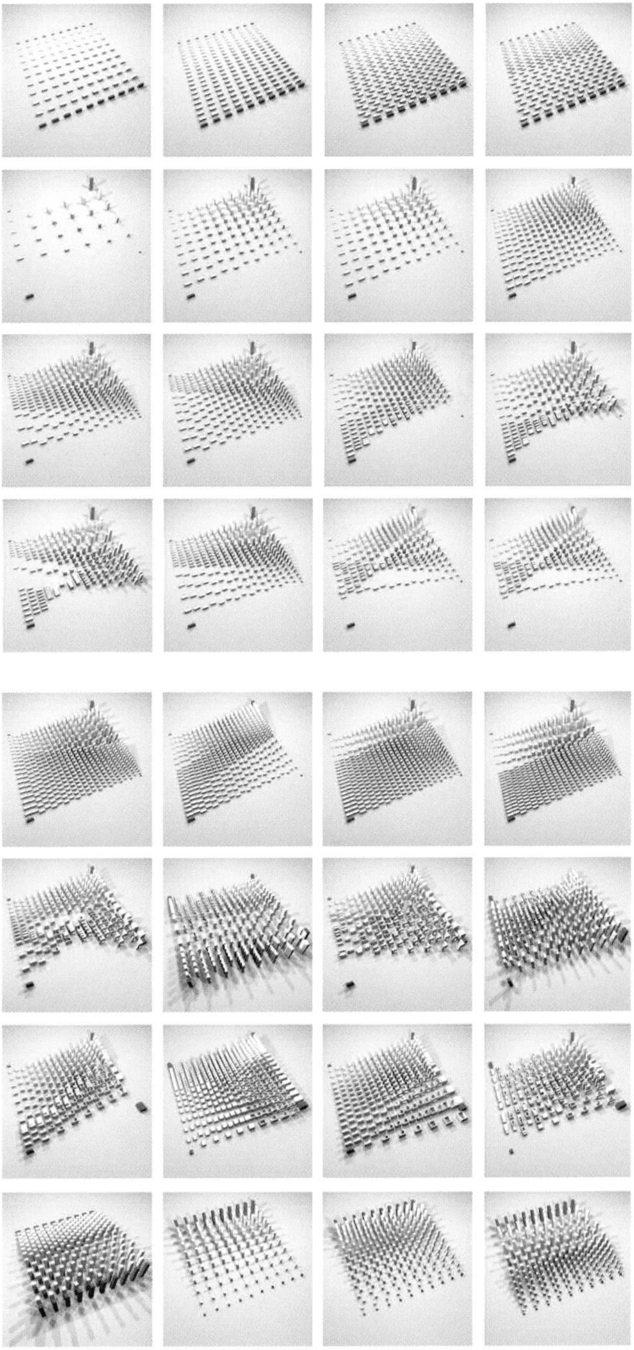

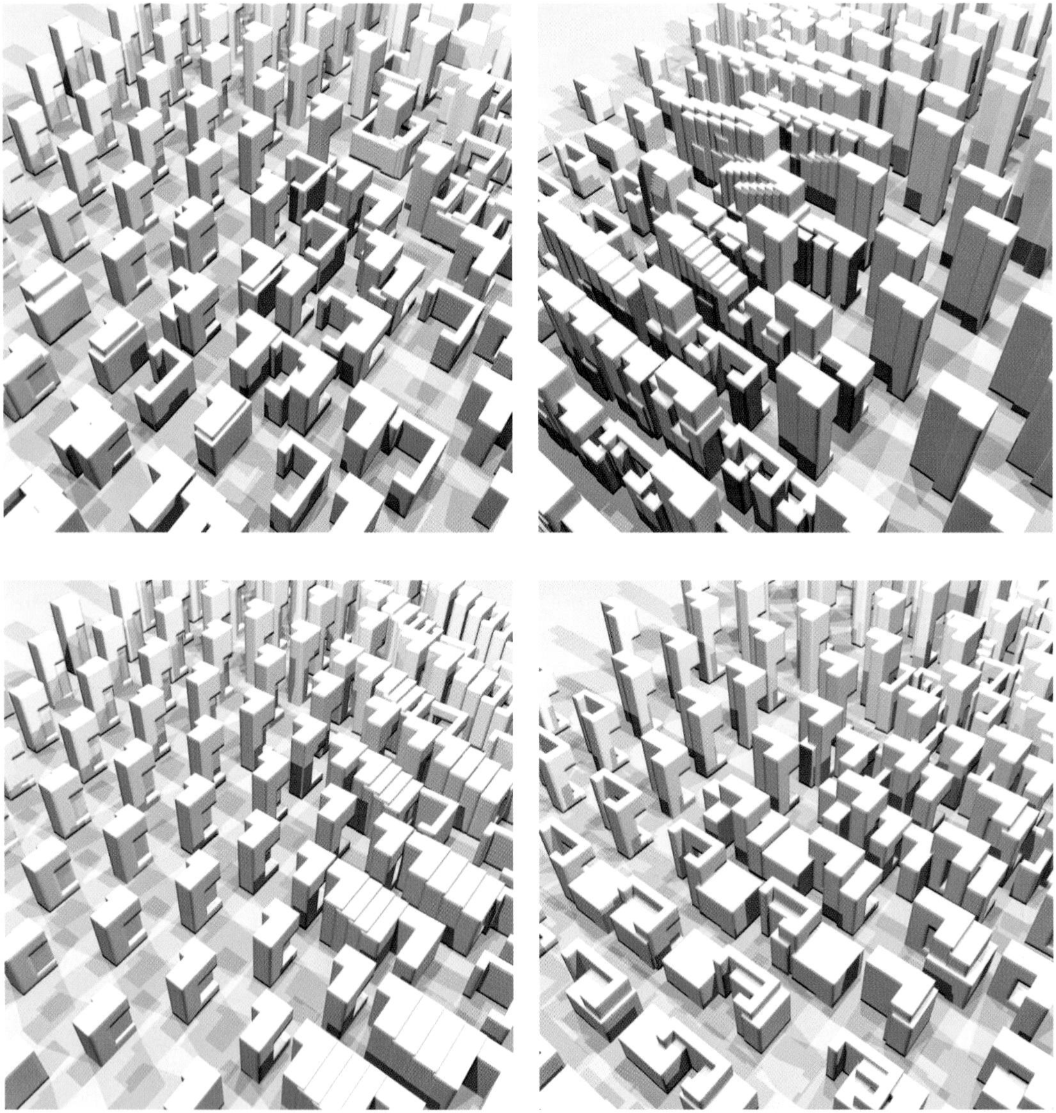

Details of scripted massing models indicating coherent morphological diversity and differentiation.

CASE STUDY

dotA AND SHANGHAI TONGJI URBAN PLANNING AND DESIGN INSTITUTE >KAILI ETHNIC CULTURAL COMPOUND, KAILI, GUIZHOU, CHINA

This project was a joint venture collaboration between dotA and Shanghai Tongji Urban Planning and Design Institute.

Shanghai Tongji Urban Planning and Design Institute Lead Planner: Su Yun Sheng
dotA Design Ltd. Lead Architects: Gao Yan, Duo Ning

The site, a green valley just outside Kaili City in Guizhou Province, is located between the old city center of Kaili and a newly planned city district triggered by its connection to the national high-speed railway. This ninety-five-hectare masterplan comprises a resort, commercial streets, a museum, leisure and sport facilities, and residential buildings. As an alternative to conventional masterplanning practices, this project transcends the inertia of two-dimensional planning with a new three-dimensional mode of planning. The main advancement is the computing of gradients of the site topography to generate the most beneficial position and size of architectural platforms, which then establish locations of individual buildings. The design team explored a set of techniques for

View of proposed massing, routing and terracing integrated into the topography of the site.

intelligent massing in relation to environmental information and local vernacular architectural morphologies. As a result, no single building is identical and all correspond to their topographical context. A series of evolutionary design strategies help to differentiate buildings and interstitial public spaces. These automated and customizing processes aim at a notion of collective architecture which has the capability to deliver coherent qualities of a genuine and diversified character, and which are also sustainable both culturally and economically.

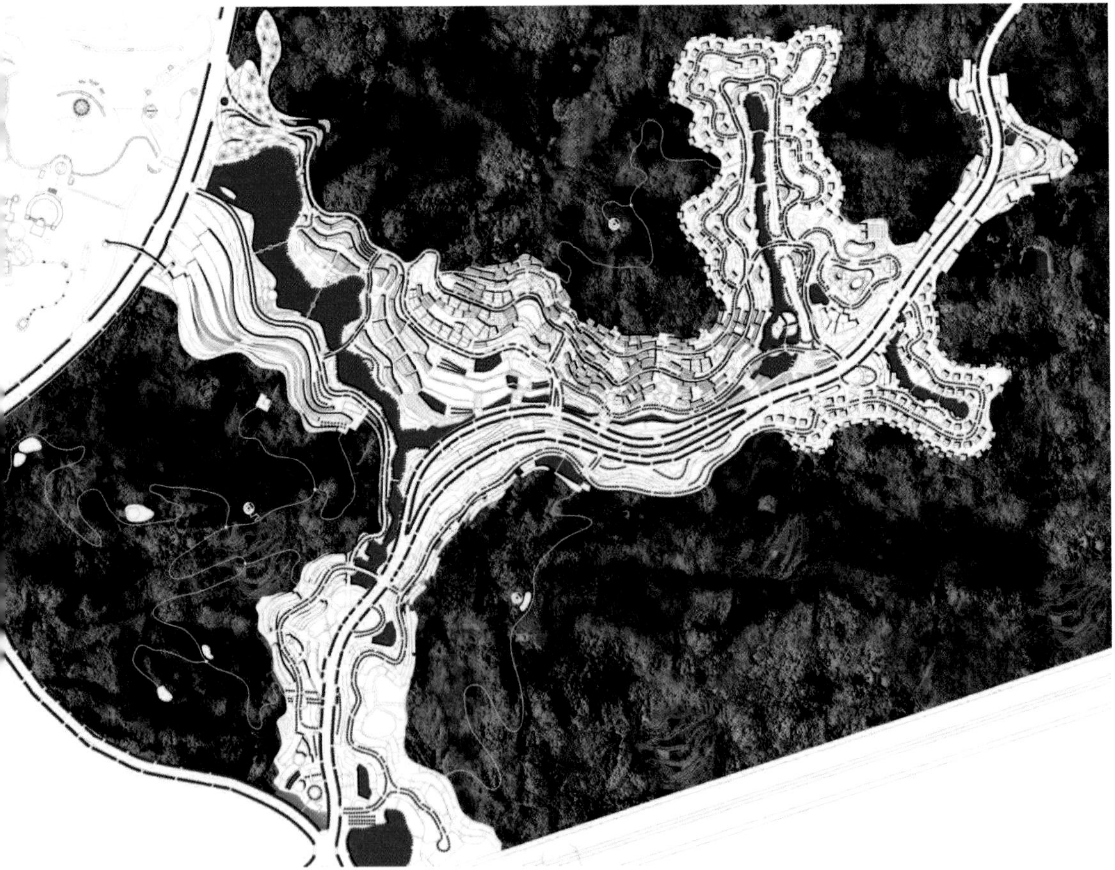

Masterplan proposal.

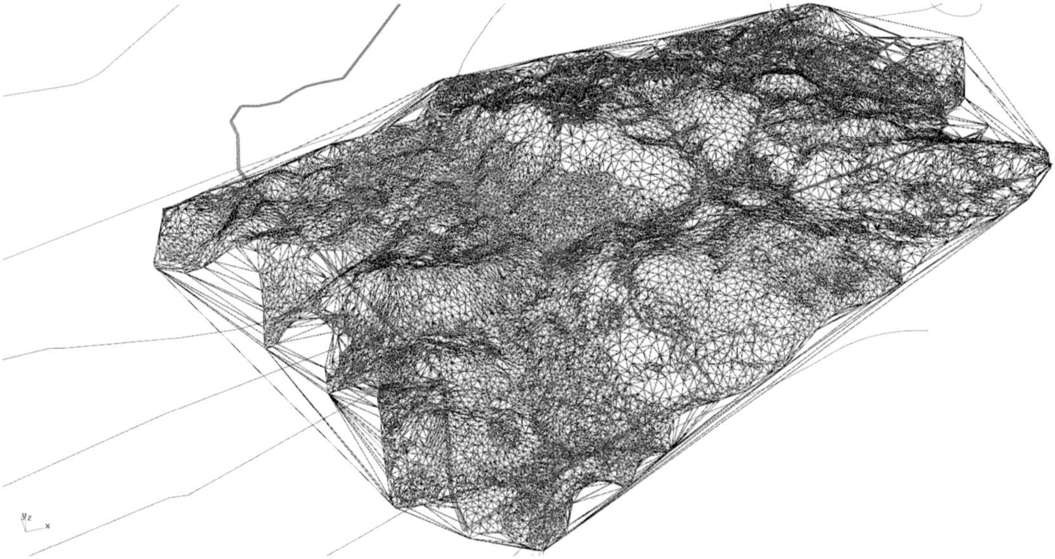

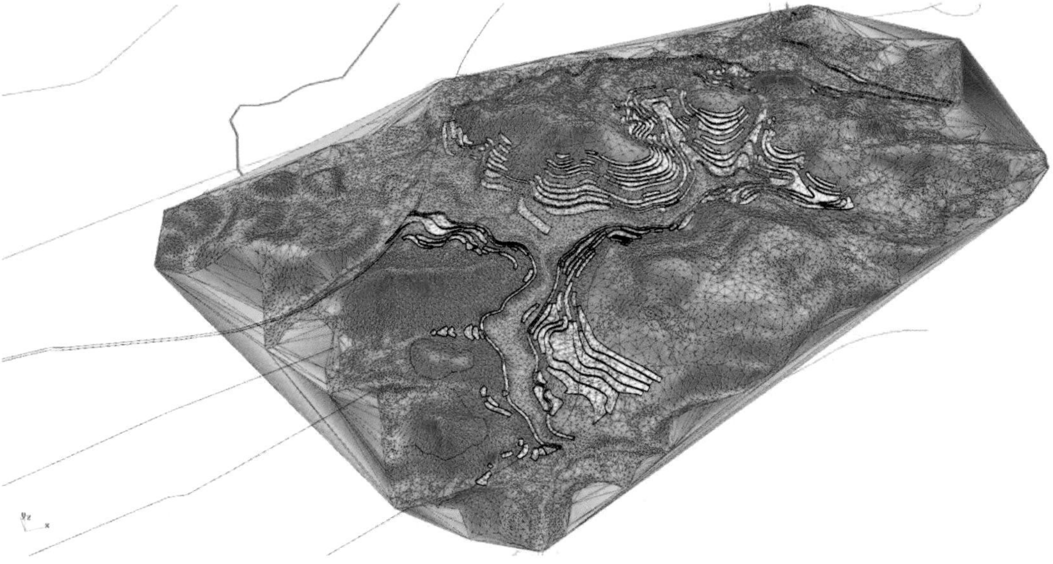

Generative computational model indicating metric data of topography and analysing fitness of data of topography to possible massing positions.

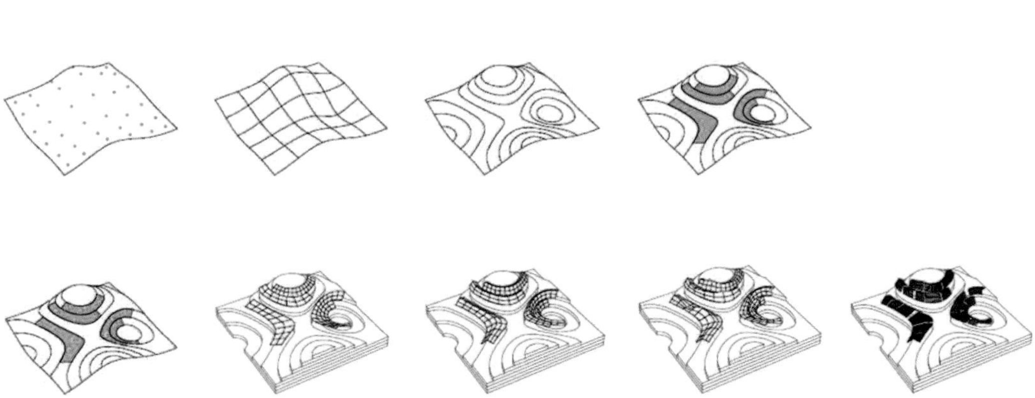

Description of relation of topography to massing.

III

METHODOLOGIES

TOOLS AND MOVING TARGETS

CHAPTER 13

TOM VEREBES >A NEW TOOLBOX FOR ADAPTABLE MASTERPLANNING

This chapter unpacks the new information-based toolbox of the contemporary architect and urbanist. Tracking innovations in computational design which now enable metric, data-driven methodologies, the potential for building associative logics in design models and for the city is explicated. Parametric and algorithmic methodologies are powerful tools for generating organizational heterogeneity and spatial variation and differentiation. It is the proliferation of interfaces and control systems which has led to the development of performance-oriented simulation and feedback systems. Today's lifelike and intelligent design environments have parallels with gaming interfaces and environments. Targeting, for the future, multiple design options with differentiated trajectories, we may in the twenty-first century develop greater capacity to adapt to and manage change.

13.1 MODELS AS INFORMATION

> Now I think that Form, properly so called, may be considered as a function or exponent of Growth or of Force, inherent or impressed; and that one of the steps to admiring it or understanding it must be a comprehension of the laws of formation and of the forces to be resisted; that all forms are thus either indicative of lines of energy, or pressure, or motion, variously impressed or resisted, and are therefore exquisitely abstract and precise.
>
> John Ruskin, 1903[1]

Information-based modes of design and production have arisen in the last two decades from the increasing prevalence of graphic notational systems. Such diagrammatic techniques address the principal task of design: to produce documents describing and communicating a design proposal. A prominent issue in architectural discourse since the mid-1990s, information structures can be distinguished from other forms of representation. In the toolbox of the contemporary designer, the drawing and the model are no longer products of manual labor, and are mediated, shared, and transferred between three-dimensional, virtual model spaces and material modes of description. Deleuze and Guattari's concept of the "abstract machine" in which a diagram is "a map of relations between forces" has driven architectural design discourse for over two decades, biasing the generative potential of information compressed into notation.[2] One of the significant developments in making this change from typology to topology is the shift from mapping (which is topographic) to diagramming (which is topological).[3] The immanence of matter in the diagram is what has drawn the avant garde to it; according to Robert Somol, "the emergence of another world, is precisely what the diagram diagrams."[4] Van Berkel and Bos's position on the diagram served to shift discourse from typological fixity toward more abstract topologies, in which information is made operational and instrumental through the generative tool of diagramming.[5] Concurrent with this increased interest in notational systems was the proliferation, in the 1990s, of graphics software.

> A Sahara, a rhinoceros skin, this is the diagram suddenly stretched out. It is like a catastrophe happening unexpectedly to the canvas, inside figurative or probabilistic data. It is like the emergence of another world . . . .The diagram is the possibility of fact—it is not the fact itself.
>
> Gilles Deleuze, 1993[6]

As the world becomes more complex, interfaces and notational systems help us to comprehend this increasing complexity. In this context, Thomas Daniell posits that the new task of the designer "is not to impose forms on the world but to coax them out of it."[7] Christopher Alexander argues that "the need to focus on non-living processes is new" since humans are the first creatures to have "managed to create non-living structure."[8]

Diagramming in urbanism is related to information and control systems, along with the foundation of "network theory," dating back to the Rand Corporation's "postwar military–industrial momentum" aimed at discovering a cross-disciplinary discourse and method.[9] John Frazer claims it was the *Cybernetics Serendipity* exhibition at the Institute of Contemporary Arts in London in 1968 which "set the agenda [of computation] for the next 50 years."[10] Today's modeling methods have the capacity to deal with large, varied, and complex datasets. At the confluence of information, models, maps, and diagrams the culture of the datascape, primitive as it was, became established. Discourse on the datascape in the 1990s conceived of space as being formed from informational forces and associations, and considered ways in which spatial and experiential effects could be recorded, analysed, and mapped. Jane and Mark Burry's coherent and redeeming definition of "datascape" looks to the etymology of "data" as "things that are given," while "scape" is shorthand for landscape. Information models capture data, and in doing so visualize and manage information. There is here an association with the roots of the term "landscape," as used by sixteenth-century Dutch and English painters, who aimed "to capture in paint their own rapidly changing countryside."[11]

> In order to understand, inhabit, and evaluate space it is crucial to recognize its temporal aspect.
>
> Olafur Eliasson, 2007[12]

Information related to urbanism is inherently dynamic. Time-based mapping techniques can capture and visualize motion, as well as operating as notational systems to capture changing phenomena as visual, aural, and haptic patterns. As we will see, data is not dry or even scientific, but fundamentally qualitative. In constrast to quantitative abstraction, which obscured the world's complexity, Kwinter has claimed that it is "only the qualitative—geometry, shape, form, behaviour" which can bring clarity.[13] Data is active and dynamic, even atmospheric.

Our new tools can simulate qualities through parametrically and algorithmically controlled machinic processes. Capturing the city as a dynamic set of forces can, according to Kwinter, be approached in two ways. First, there is a "bioptic" approach, in which a probe is sent "through the contemporary urban archive [to] yield a snapshot of something mobile but true." Here the organism is

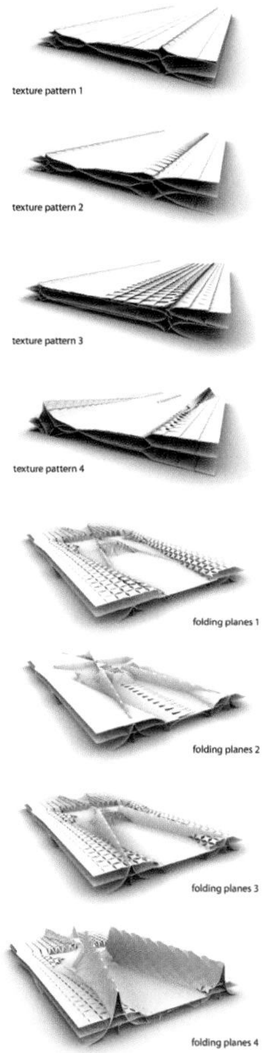

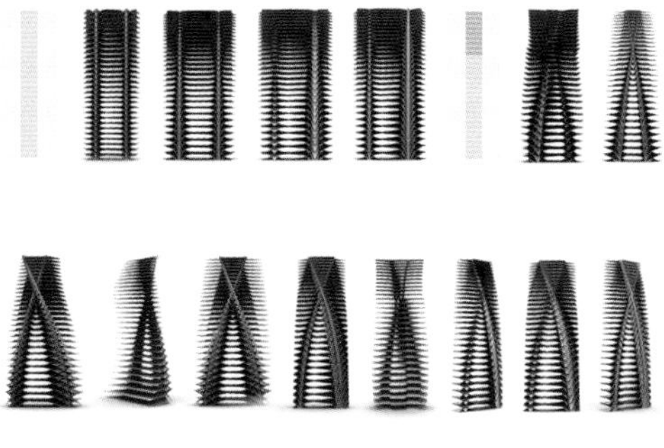

Tectonic and spatial systems, scripted in MEL and correlated to form a coherent yet complex organization logic. (Studio Tutor: Tom Verebes; Students: Aditya C. Chandra, Reza Esmaeeli, Galo Cazarez Fernandez; Architectural Association, 2008)

understood by extracting some cells for examination. The second approach "places scientific method and political action in the hands of everyone with a phone line and a hard drive."[14] In this chapter, our focus shifts to projects which seek to make demonstrable the ways in which designers can model changing conditions, as the outcome of information-driven dynamic environments.

Self-organization within architecture, engineering, and the material sciences has a history in contemporary practice. The interrelationship between material and digital methods follows from the premise that all matter has the capacity to compute its structural, geometrical, and topological organization, and gives rise to the possibility of exploring built space, structure, and organization as forms of material computation that define the performance of physical space.[15] Within material computational discourse, Lars Spuybroek has articulated the concept of self-organization with respect to materials: "materials are active agents that seek nothing but agency, that seek an order that is not transcendentally established but emerges from the bottom up."[16]

The tradition of experimental material practices as an engineering approach to architecture assumes matter has the potential to self-compute its state space, through the application of "form-finding" models, constructed to calculate and resolve forces in analog material models. At the turn of the twentieth century, Antoni Gaudí developed his weighted, tension-based, catenary models, which developed ideal parabolic curves for the configuration of load-bearing, compression-based stone arches in the Sagrada Família church in Barcelona. Frei Otto at the Institute for Lightweight Structures in Stuttgart worked on his networked minimal path wet-grid as well as other ruled surface tension roof structures, as a material methodology for computing the outcome of a final design configuration.[17]

> Architects might consider form as solid, but this is only a matter of scale and often also of time and temperature, because material form has two major properties: it is flexible and stable. It is flexible enough to be moved out of equilibrium and stable enough to be returned to equilibrium.
>
> Lars Spuybroek[18]

Here, Spuybroek describes machinic procedures which flow from a system, involving flexibility, rigidity, and morphology.

> In the representation of form and in the comparison of kindred forms, we see in the one case a diagram of forces in equilibrium, and in the other case we discern the magnitude and the direction of the forces which have sufficed to convert the one form into the other.
>
> D'Arcy Wentworth Thompson, 1917[19]

The wish to control a model space raises a paradox in contemporary design culture, between the increasing desire for regimes of control (of complexity, machinery, surveillance) and a simultaneous valorization of the accident as a basis for generating space. The outcome, in catastrophe theory, is the edge of chaos.

This serves to shift our attention from information embedded in the formation of space toward the methods, techniques and tools with which to manage differentiated datasets in design processes. Information shapes models, and models are of interest for their information structure.

13.2 PARAMETER SPACE, SOLUTION SPACE, URBAN SPACE

The demise of modernism in the twentieth century was paralleled by growing disillusion with principles of certainty. Abstraction and neutrality are no longer the backdrop for a generation of architects who imagine complexity as the script, in the filmic and literary sense of the term, and not the stage. If we accept the inherent complexity of urbanism, how do we model and map the variables of the city? This subchapter is concerned with the undeniably mathematical basis of computational design.

> The archetypal design medium is pencil and paper. More precisely: pencil, eraser and paper.
>
> Robert Woodbury, 2010[20]

Let us unpack the issues at stake in working with associative models. Woodbury claims that we can now "add, erase, relate and repair," whereas before parametric modeling we could only add and erase. Thus the significant reorientation of design methods occurring as a consequence of the introduction of computational constraint modeling, or parametric design, is that "parts of a design, relate and change together in a coordinated way."[21] Parametric design addresses the limitations of a copy-and-paste mode of design. Through the relationships between parts of a model, such design systems represent a paradigm shift, moving away from the preeminent set of design techniques of the last century—collage. Parametric models have nodes, some independent and others dependent. It is the "dependency chains" between nodes which propagate the flow of data through the "near hierarchies" of a model, locally, to enable it to perform globally. Elements and data structures are used to modify objects and their associations. Parametric design is not a new concept, as design is inherently the result of the association of varied contingencies, responsibilities, agents, and agencies. It is the role of the architect to organize and navigate "project dependencies and interdependencies with the complex formulation of a design problem and design solving strategy."[22]

As Jane and Mark Burry state, "the computer is used in a variety of ways to search a defined solution space," rather than to arrive at one ideal outcome.[23] Genetic algorithms, as we will explore in the next chapter, offer an evolutionary model which is "essentially a search process," and the "scale of the solution space makes the outcomes hard to predict and makes the process seem generative."[24] In this context, Mark Burry questions where "design freedom" lies, and whether it is "compromized by the inflexibility of almost all scripting languages."[25] Multiplicities and obsession with variation beg the question, when you can do so much—or so little if software is in fact limiting us—how does the contemporary designer select a single design scheme? Or, more simply, if a vast number of solutions to a problem are possible, how does a designer make judgments and selections?

Relating parametric design and the inherent solution spaces for given problems back to urbanism, planning policies can be conceived of and articulated as codes within which a soft form of regulation is formulated. Computational code-based design may not only result in the processing of simple procedures in less time, programming may also be "a way of conceiving and embracing the unknown."[26] A wonderful contrast thus arises between the strictures of planning and the generative potential of computational design. Although urbanism has always involved the negotiation of various contingent forces—social, economic, environmental, and so on—with the outcome being a negotiation of constraints and contingencies, we now have the power to harness complexity, differentiation, and difference as never before.

One of the first undertakings of the Institute for Lightweight Structures set up by Frei Otto in 1964 was a research project titled *Minimal Pathways*, which led to a series of sustained experiments in direct path systems, and geometric and generative path systems.[27] Research conducted at the Institute into relations of biological and physical systems to engineering structures and urban phenomena

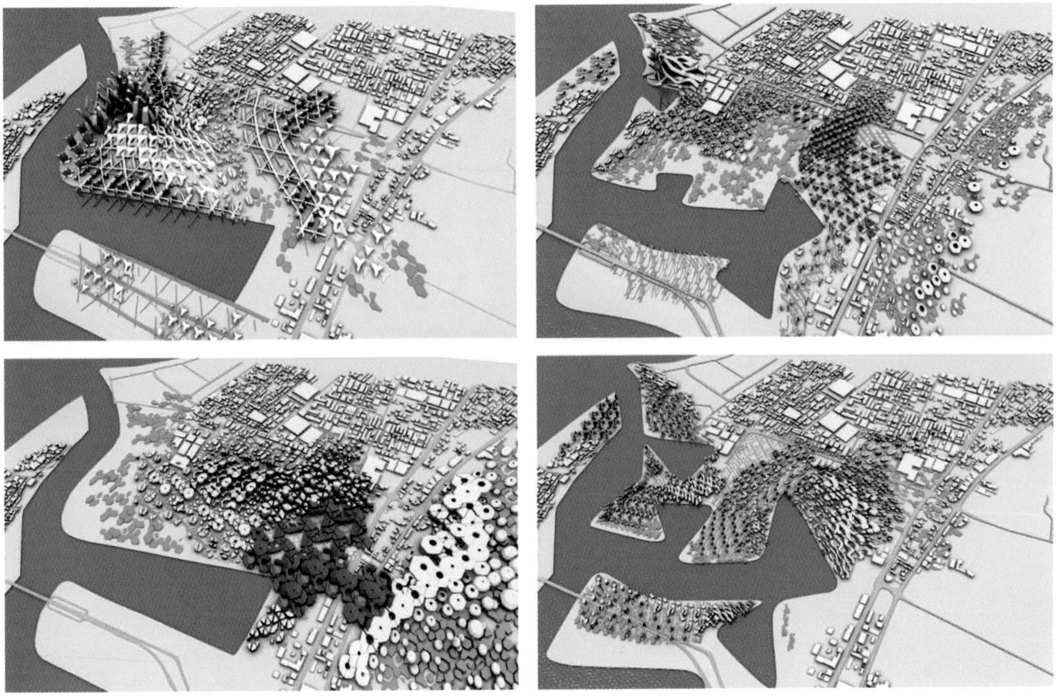

Four adaptable scenarios describing four possible organizational matrices of complex aggregate massing and open spaces; proposal for Ras Al-Khaima, UAE. (Studio Tutor: Tom Verebes; Students: Saif Ala'a Al-Masri, Suryansh Chandra, Peter Sovinc; Architectural Association, 2009)

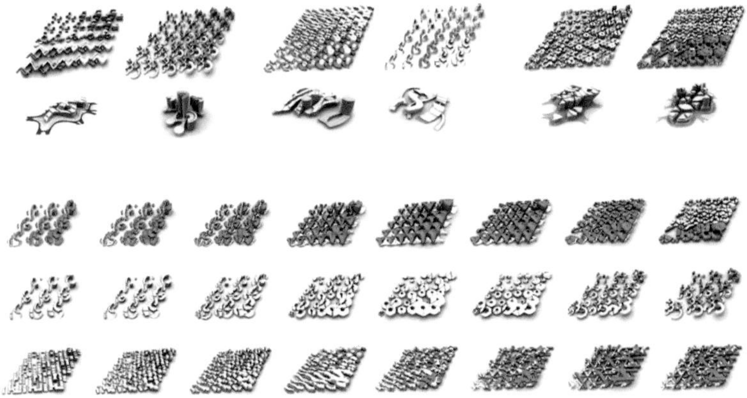

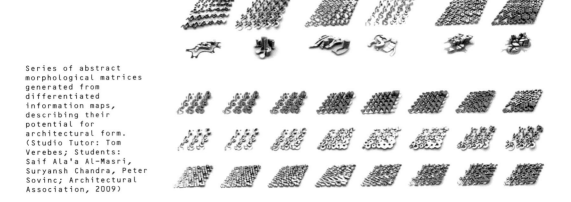

Series of abstract morphological matrices generated from differentiated information maps, describing their potential for architectural form. (Studio Tutor: Tom Verebes; Students: Saif Ala'a Al-Masri, Suryansh Chandra, Peter Sovinc; Architectural Association, 2009)

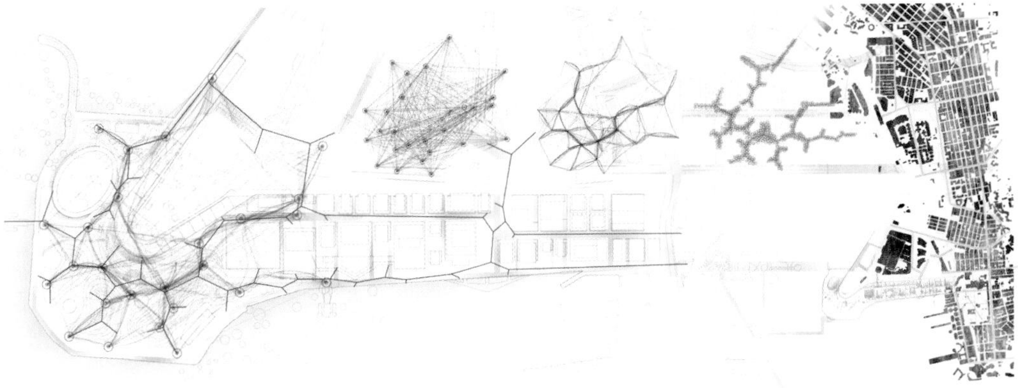

Computational form-finding techniques were developed to deploy a minimal path logic of connectivity and local subdivision for a series of pavilions and infrastructure for West Kowloon Cultural District, Hong Kong. (Studio Tutor: Tom Verebes; Thesis Student: Cheung Chun Chi; MArch Thesis, The University of Hong Kong, 2012)

was termed "analogy research," with the "raison d'être of analogy research [being] to research, compare and possibly thereby to explain identical or similar looking objects in relation to their genesis."[28] In material parametrics, a model takes shape from the stabilizing of dynamic forces, as a simulation.

Analytical and synthetic methods of design are widely accepted in the field of urbanism, as exemplified by one of the most notorious methods for assessing urban connectivity, space syntax. Bill Hillier's 1996 book, *Space is the Machine*, documented how pedestrian flow is channelled along the armature of a city, "creating networks between urban fragments."[29] Space syntax, the analytical theory as well as the commercial service developed by Hillier, is a method with which to analyze the relative connectivity, or integration and segregation, of particular streets, but has limitations. It is based on "breaking down complex building configurations into geometric spatial elements, such as corridors and city squares, [and] connections between these elements can be presented as a network of different navigation decision options," however it is limited to two-dimensional planar topographies.[30]

Such analytical and process-driven methods are akin to the "design thinking" of an engineer, and represent "not so much the design as . . . the design knowledge or intelligence that comes from analysis and testing."[31] As we will see, simulations assist in "deciphering the structure of possibility spaces" as a means by which to aid assurances of intentions.[32] Most computational design processes are not wholly predictable, and this is the result of the discrepancy between design intentions and the code put to work. Simple changes in the arrangement of rules can have repercussions for the relative predictability of the design outcome.[33] In this sense, probabilistic effects generate the likelihood of a particular pattern resulting from the local coding.[34] Parametric design and its solution spaces chart the probabilistic landscape of potential outcomes of form-generating procedures. The potentials of urbanism—which is always associative, as the interrelation of multiple systems, spaces, and agents with multiple possible trajectories—have led to the wholesale rethinking of the masterplan as a singular solution to a fixed problem.

13.3 SIMULATION AND GAMING ENVIRONMENTS AS MANAGEMENT SYSTEMS

Given the recognition of our diminished ability to control the complexity of the world, despite our increasing technical expertise, questions arise as to how to recreate the conditions of life, in general, and the specific dynamic conditions of the city. City design occurs as the result of the negotiation of top-down processes maintained by "the technocratic planning establishment," which shapes space prescriptively through "capital-intensive strategic actions," and more discrete "user-generated" models of space.[35]

Gordon Childe's fourth and current revolution is the information revolution, which is creating an intensely connected urban society. As information, communication, surveillance, sensing, data collection, and other technologies have permeated all aspects of contemporary urbanity, we increasingly live our lives online.[36] But is the internet the democratic forum heralded in the 1990s? Is it anything more than a vast shopping mall? Or a private or pornographic entertainment system? Have social networks created a new form of globalization, or do they simply intensify existing networks? Is the internet really democratic, as it was billed, or is it a tool for mining our personal data and tuning into our preferences through profiling so we will buy more stuff? Is the internet, as it is monitored in some parts of the world, a vehicle to control and suppress rather than to liberate and instigate?

> What becomes apparent is we are not designing the geometry of the artifact, but rather we are constructing a "control rig," some geometry that will never be built or seen, but which indirectly controls what will be constructed and experienced.
>
> Robert Aish, 2006[37]

Parametric design, though a new design methodology, is present in military security, transportation, hydrology and water management, and many other systemic aspects of contemporary urbanism. Parametric approaches to design establish "methods for interrelating particular behaviours of forms and forces, and how they might be represented as associative mathematical and geometric rules."[38] Design in general, according to the software developer Robert Aish, "necessarily has to be predictive in order to anticipate what the consequence of 'making' or 'doing' will be."[39] Parametric design maintains stable relationships between parts of a model space, while enabling interaction and change via "long-chain dependencies" linked to external decisions. Its association of systems, subsystems, and components needs external contingencies in order for parametric design to remain a set of tools and methods, and not an end in itself. In this context, is it still valid to see the designer as the controller of a design outcome? When space is understood to take shape from a field of forces, and when the contingencies are too many and too complex, what is the role of the designer?

A proliferation of interfaces and increasingly pervasive algorithmic simulation tools today run everything from the operation of search engines to the identification of our shopping preferences. For Deleuze and Guattari, virtuality is synonymous with simulation, which "designates the power of producing an effect," prior to, afterwards, or alongside the actual occurrence of a phenomenon.[40]

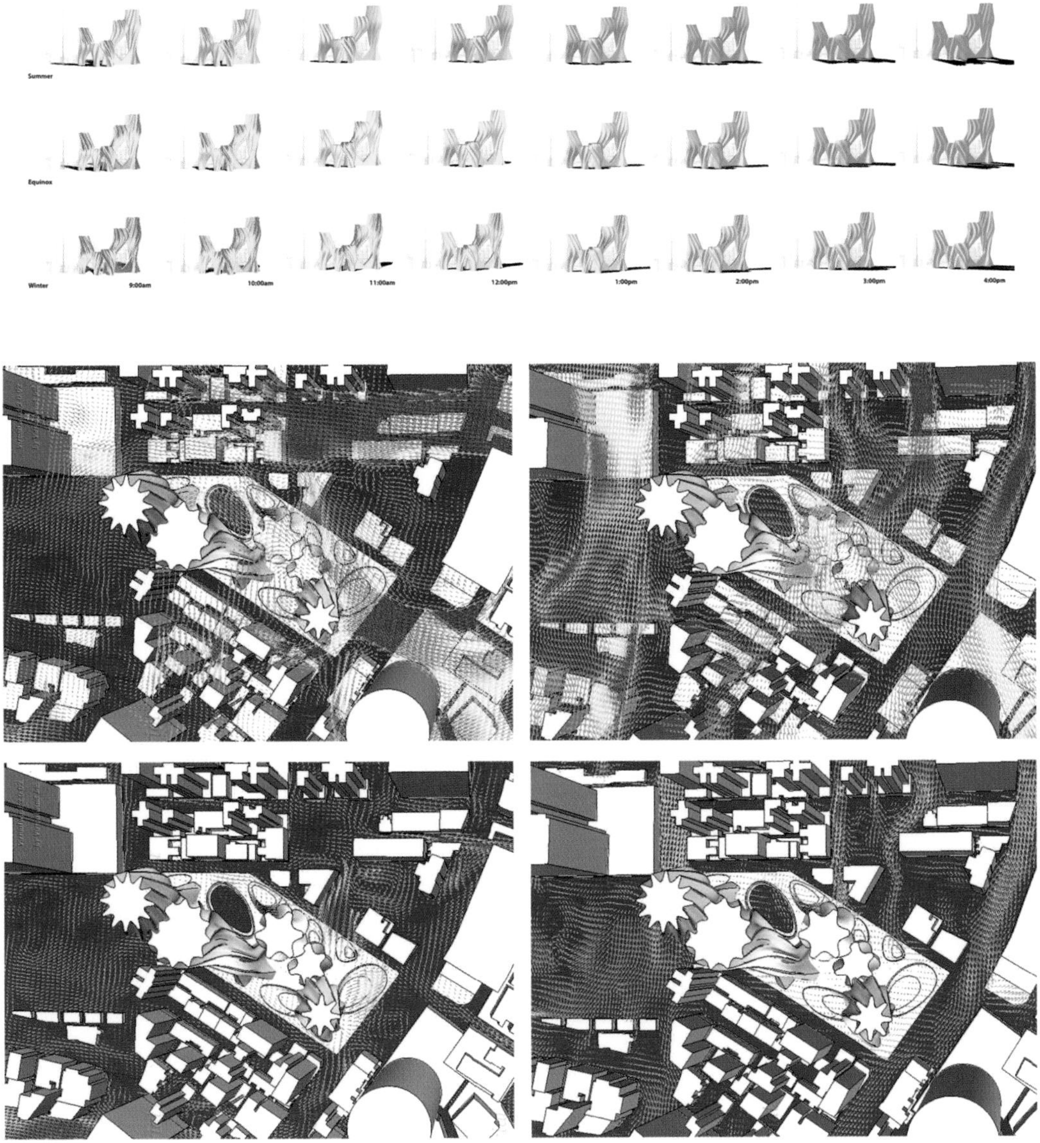

Performance simulations of sun exposure (above) and wind effects (below). (Studio Tutor: Tom Verebes; Thesis Student: Gordon Fu Kin Fai)

Calling a computer rendering a "simulation" is a misnomer. "Virtual reality," another misused term, provides a parallel bodily experience, in which "there is always an ambiguous overlap between what is real and what is not," between the engulfing virtual environment and actual space.[41] Kostas Terzidis claims that, while "simulation models are valuable tools for predicting and evaluating performance," their contribution is as yet limited to mainstream design processes.[42] In our era of fast computing, we have available design tools with "a new power with which to simulate the complex evolution of settlement patterns, even in the multifarious modern city."[43] It is the algorithmic basis of simulation, in which rules have a range of variance, which relates contemporary design to gaming environments and interfaces. It is through the "automatic generation of innovation by creative evolutionary systems" that designers can generate and evaluate a multitude of solutions, rather than a single outcome.[44]

> Simulations are partly responsible for the restoration of the legitimacy of the concept of emergence because they can stage interactions between virtual entities from which properties, tendencies, and capacities actually emerge.
>
> Manuel De Landa, 2011[45]

Games involve giving players combinations of possible decisions and actions to take with respect to rules and opponents. Game theory charts decision-making as a network of choices, mapped as branches over time, at the intersection of actions and probability. The development of interfaces, and gaming interfaces in particular, has led to a paradigm shift in how we think about designing. Evidence of this is the fundamental transformation from "passive to interactive" environmental design in recent years.[46] Some interfaces are used for data management, for example a Geographic Information System (GIS) provides associative mappings, avoiding the description of form and remaining at the level of "abstract relationships." While GIS has the ability to "organize vast quantities of data within a network structure," it is limited to diagrammatic operations.[47]

Using computational and gaming theories of "system dynamics," in which equilibrium, or at least dynamic equilibrium, is sought, Will Wright started working on the game *SimCity* in 1985, integrating recent research into system dynamics "applied to global problems of industrialization and overpopulation."[48] The objective of the game is to build and maintain a small city, and to achieve a balanced, thriving society in which public money is invested, taxes collected, infrastructures and services are adequate, crime rates and pollution are low, and so on. Although a simulacrum of a city, how different are the mechanisms, as well as the objectives, of this game environment to actual city planning? Equilibrium is achieved through mediating parameters—financial, environmental, demographic, programmatic, infrastructural—as a simulation of actual urban dynamics. The game is a model of the interaction of the forces which shape cities. Spontaneous or causal disasters are integrated into the game. How might this kind of interface provide an adaptive planning tool? The limitations of *SimCity* may be twofold: first, the city is constrained by modernist, gridded spatial land subdivisions and quite simple extrusions of buildings, making the game an a-formal model and perpetuating a generic modernist approach to city formation and expansion. Second, the game biases a modernist rationalism and hierarchy of decisions, in the sense that "organic [urban] growth will only pose insurmountable problems," yet its potential is to make the planner a "social engineer" of well-being.[49]

The architectural office MDRDV has produced some compelling work on interfaces and their relation to dynamic data. In 1999, they began work on a succession of three projects: the *RegionMaker*, *FunctionMixer*, and *Spacefighter*. These projects have emerged from "numerical and statistical diagram research into the preconditions and fundamental, systemic situations and principles of modern and possible future cities."[50] Combining modeling software and a parametric "back-end" control system linking to proprietary interfaces, these projects are compelling for their potential to modulate urbanism in a continual and gradual design process. Despite the a-formal, reductive and even ugly properties of the visualization, the significance of these interfaces is how they fuse "computer games, software design and programming, information design and visualization, and the predictive techniques, procedures and research methodologies of futurology."[51] Code-based design can also be "an antidote to standardization" and the repetitive effects of globalization, as described previously.[52] OCEAN CN's project *Parametric Pearl River Delta* develops this gaming paradigm and targets a parametric approach to urbanism.

It is through such methods that the designer can be positioned at the interface of ideas and implementation, and charged with the capacity to form a design scheme to climatic and topographic conditions, economic flows, and a range of institutional and regulatory regimes. Through the visual interfaces which have been developed in computing, designers of all kinds are learning to harness complex geometries "that are no longer based on proportions and algebraic relations, but on approximation through calculus."[53] These new tools do not so much replace social science methods as embed parameters from diverse contingencies and constituents, flows and forces.

NOTES

1 > J. Ruskin (1903–1912) *The Works of John Ruskin*, eds. E.T. Cook and A. Wedderburn, 39 vols. (London: George Allen.)

2 > G. Deleuze and F. Guattari (1988) *A Thousand Plateaus* (London: Althlone).

3 > H. Furján (2007) "Cities of Complexity," in *Models: 306090, Volume 11*, eds. E. Abruzzo, E. Ellingsen, and J. Solomon (New York: Princeton), 52.

4 > R.E. Somol (1999) "Introduction," in *Diagram Diaries*, P. Eisenman (New York: Rizzoli), 24.

5 > B. Van Berkel and C. Bos (1999) "The Diagrams of Architecture" in *Move* (Netherlands: Goose Press).

6 > G. Deleuze (1993) "The Diagram," in *The Deleuze Reader*, ed. Constantin V. Boundas (New York: Columbia University Press), 194.

7 > T. Daniell (2011) "Introduction," in *Requiem for the City at the End of the Millennium*, S. Kwinter (Barcelona: Actar), 11.

8 > C. Alexander (1980) *The Nature of Order, Book 2: The Process of Creating Life* (Berkeley: CES), 13.

9 > A. Burke and T. Tierney (2007) "Introduction," in *Network Practices: New Strategies in Architecture and Design* (New York: Princeton), 25.

10 > M. Burry (2011) *Scripting Cultures: Architectural Design and Programming* (Chichester: Wiley), 51.

11 > J. Burry and M. Burry (2010) *The New Mathematics of Architecture* (New York: Thames & Hudson), 209.

12 > O. Eliasson (2007) "Model as Real," in *Models: 306090, Volume 11*, eds. E. Abruzzo, E. Ellingsen, and J. Solomon (New York: Princeton), 19.

13 > S. Kwinter (2011) *Requiem for the City at the End of the Millennium* (Barcelona: Actar), 26.

14 > Kwinter, *Requiem for the City at the End of the Millennium*, 68.

15 > As exemplified in the work of Antoni Gaudí, Frei Otto, or NOX.
16 > L. Spuybroek (2004) *Machining Architecture* (London: Thames & Hudson), 7.
17 > T. Verebes (2010) "Computational Paradigms," in *New Computational Paradigms in Architecture*, ed. Tom Verebes (Beijing: Tsinghua).
18 > Lars Spuybroek (2004) *Machining Architecture* (London: Thames & Hudson), 9.
19 > D.W. Thompson (1917) "On the Theory of Transformations, or the Comparison of Related Forms," in *On Growth and Form* (New York: Dover), 1028.
20 > R. Woodbury (2010) *Elements of Parametric Design* (New York: Routledge), 11.
21 > Woodbury, *Elements of Parametric Design*, 11.
22 > D.J. Gerber (2009) *The Parametric Affect: Computation, Innovation and Models for Design Exploration in Contemporary Practice* (Cambridge, MA: Harvard), 2.
23 > Burry and Burry, *The New Mathematics of Architecture*, 13.
24 > A. Killian (2007) "The Question of the Underlying Model and Its Impact on Design," in *Models: 306090, Volume 11*, eds. E. Abruzzo, E. Ellingsen, and J. Solomon (New York: Princeton), 208.
25 > Burry, *Scripting Cultures*, 22.
26 > K. Terzidis (2006) *Algorithmic Architecture* (Oxford: Elsevier), 153.
27 > F. Otto (2009) *Occupying and Connecting: Thoughts on Territories and Spheres of Influence with Particular Reference to Human Settlement* (Stuttgart: Edition Axel Menges), 6.
28 > Otto, *Occupying and Connecting*, 83.
29 > D.G. Shane (2011) *Urban Design since 1945: A Global Perspective* (London: Wiley), 28.
30 > C. Holscher (2009) "Wayfinding Strategies and Behavioural Patterns in Built Space," in *Pattern: Ornament, Structure and Behaviour* (Berlin: Birkhäuser Verlag), 63.
31 > M. Speaks (2008) *Design Engineering AKT*, ed. H. Kara (Barcelona: Actar), 223.
32 > M. De Landa (2011) *Philosophy and Simulation* (London: Continuum), 6.
33 > Terzidis, *Algorithmic Architecture*, 21.
34 > S. Marshall (2009) *Cities, Design, Evolution* (New York: Routledge), 197.
35 > Rebar (2010) "User-Generated Urbanism," in *Ecological Urbanism*, eds. M. Mostafavi and G. Doherty (Baden: Lars Müller), 350.
36 > R.G. LeGates and F. Stout (1996) "Introduction to Part One: The Evolution of Cities," in *The City Reader*, eds. R.T. LeGates and F. Stout (London: Routledge), 31.
37 > R. Aish (2006) "Exploring the Analogy that Parametric Design is a Game," in *Game Set Match: On Computer Games, Advanced Geometries and Digital Technologies*, eds. K. Oosterhuis and L. Feireiss (Rotterdam: Episode), 203.
38 > R. Woodbury (2010) *Elements of Parametric Design* (Abingdon: Routledge), 24.
39 > Aish, "Exploring the Analogy," 202.
40 > G. Deleuze and F. Guattari (1988) *A Thousand Plateaus* (London: Althlone), 263.
41 > S. Shaviro (2003) *Connected, or What it Means to Live in the Network Society* (Minnesota: Regents), 109.
42 > Terzidis, *Algorithmic Architecture*, 47.
43 > Burry and Burry, *The New Mathematics of Architecture*, 54.
44 > P.J. Bentley and D.W. Corne (2011) "Creative Evolutionary Systems," in *Computational Design Thinking*, eds. A. Menges and S. Alquist (London: Wiley), 121.
45 > De Landa, *Philosophy and Simulation*, 6.
46 > Burry, *Scripting Cultures*, 226.
47 > J. Solomon (2007) "Seeing the City for the Trees," in *Models: 306090, Volume 11*, eds. E. Abruzzo, E. Ellingsen, and J. Solomon (New York: Princeton), 180.
48 > G. Vermeer (2006) "Games: Designing Cities and Civilisations," in *Game Set Match: On Computer Games, Advanced Geometries and Digital Technologies*, eds. K. Oosterhuis and L. Feireiss (Rotterdam: Episode), 90.
49 > Vermeer, "Games," 97.
50 > M. Garcia (2010) *The Diagrams of Architecture* (London: Wiley), 245.
51 > Garcia, *The Diagrams of Architecture*, 245.
52 > Burry, *Scripting Cultures*, 9.
53 > H. Kara (2008) *Design Engineering AKT* (Barcelona: Actar), 9.

CHAPTER 14

PETER TRUMMER > MORPHOGENETIC URBANISM

TOWARD A MATERIALIST APPROACH TO MASTERPLANNING

From a formalist position, urban planning can be understood as a figure/ground problem. This essay investigates two preeminent figure/ground diagrams within the history of urbanism. The first diagram, the Nolli plan, defines the ground of the city by its buildings seen as an anonymous mass, from which the figurative open spaces of circulation are carved. The second formalist diagram of the city, the Piranesi diagram, formulated for the Marte Campi project for Rome, sees the figure of the city as defined by all its architecture, and the ground is seen as the circulation spaces between buildings. It has been used to understand the modernist city, where the figure, defined as building mass, floats above a liberated ground. A materialist approach toward masterplanning views the city as an emergent effect of economic processes. Seeing all morphological formations driven by forces of money, the figure, as a building, can no longer stand as a unified entity or object. If from a materialist position the urban figure is defined as an aggregate, the ground of the city can then be seen as the matter in which these aggregations take their physical shape; the economic valuation of land is established. Two research projects will serve to exemplify this approach: a project for the former airport at Aspern in Vienna, and a project for a site in the San Fernando Valley in Los Angeles.

From a formalist position, urban planning is understood as a figure/ground problem. Within the history of urbanism, two preeminent figure/ground diagrams emerged: the Nolli plan and the Piranesi diagram. In the first of these two diagrams, the Nolli plan, buildings define the ground of the city and are seen as an anonymous solid mass from which spaces of circulation and open spaces are carved out as figures. This kind of figure/ground diagram helps to explain premodern cities, from the Greek polis until the postliberal European city of the nineteenth century. The second formalist diagram of the city can be called the Piranesi diagram, which was formulated for the Marte Campi project for Rome. Here, the figure of the city is defined by all its architecture and the ground is seen as the spaces between buildings. This figure/ground diagram stands especially for the modernist city, where the figure defines the building mass floating above a liberated ground. The value of these formalist approaches to urban design practices was their contribution to the postmodern reading of the city. Better known as contextualism, the formalist approach was used as an argument to repair the city after the failures of modern planning. Colin Rowe, seen as the father of a formalist approach to urban design, argued in his book *Collage City*[1] for architecture to be classified less as a figure or as pure ground than as a "poché" space, in which buildings should be used to negotiate the premodern and modern figure/ground relationships with the city.

From a materialist position, the city can be defined as an emerging effect of economic processes. While Jane Jacobs might have been the first thinker who saw the city, especially the metropolis, as an entity that should be treated as an environment of "organized complexity," her writing fell short of indicating what such a materialist position would mean for the form of the city. Rather, Jacobs made clear how the city, based on economic forces, is an environment which produces diversity.

In this essay, I aim to formulate a thesis on a materialist approach to urban form and its consequences for the practice of masterplanning. The implications of such an approach will be demonstrated by the effect it has on the definition of an urban figure and its urban ground. In order to visualize and exemplify this approach I will refer to two recent research projects: first, a project for the redevelopment of the former airport field in Aspern, Vienna, and second, a project for a site in the San Fernando Valley in Greater Los Angeles.

THE AGGREGATED FIGURE

Ludwig Hilberseimer defined the city from a materialist viewpoint. For him the city was a product of its economic development and it depended essentially

> on the solution given to two factors: the elementary cell and the urban organism as a whole. The single room as the constituent element of the habitation will determine the aspect of the habitation, and since the habitations in turn form blocks, the room will become a factor of urban configuration, which is architecture's true goal.[2]

Following Manfredo Tafuri's recapitulation of Hilberseimer's thesis, "the cell is not only the prime element of the continuous production of the city, but it is also the element that conditions the dynamics of the aggregation of building structures."[3] The figure is rather, as Hilberseimer describes in his book on the *Groszstadt*, a "place in which the elementary assemblage of single cells assumes physical form."[4] Tafuri therefore concludes that all morphological formations of urban buildings can no longer stand as a unified entity. "The single building is no longer an 'object.' It is only the place in which the elementary assemblage of single cells assumes physical form."[5]

The implication for any figural object in the city is that it be understood as an aggregated figure consisting of inhabitable cells. These cells might be loosely aggregated in suburban areas or define more densely packed aggregations in metropolitan contexts. If we see the aggregated figure as a disciplinary problem of how cells have been arranged to form an urban figure, we could start to view the production of the city as the evolution of problems of aggregation. For example, Le Corbusier proposed *Immeubles Villas* as an alternative to the garden city. The *Immeubles Villa* is an aggregation of two-story-high cells, whereby each of the cells consists of fifty percent inhabitable space and fifty percent outside space. Each villa is arranged around a common courtyard with leisure facilities, and the roof reproduces the lost ground as a running track. Altogether, Le Corbusier's scheme can be seen as an urban hotel, with common facilities on the ground floor. Another example of an aggregated figure might be Le Corbusier's designs for the *Unité d'Habitation* in Marseille, whereby pilotis elevate the aggregated cells in order to liberate the ground from individual ownership. In this context we can also mention Ivan Leonidow's prototypical design of two-story residences for communal living environments in his plan for a linear city in Magnitogorsk. Here, the sixteen individual living cells are arranged around a void, functioning as a collective

Scripted morphological patterns for generative urbanism.

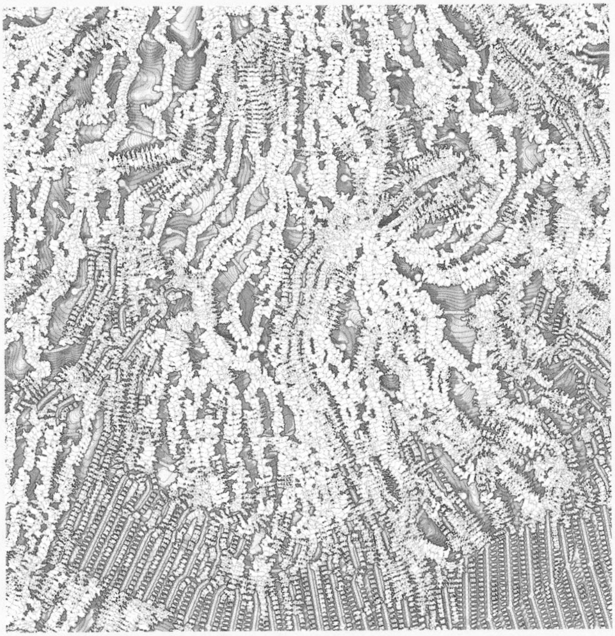

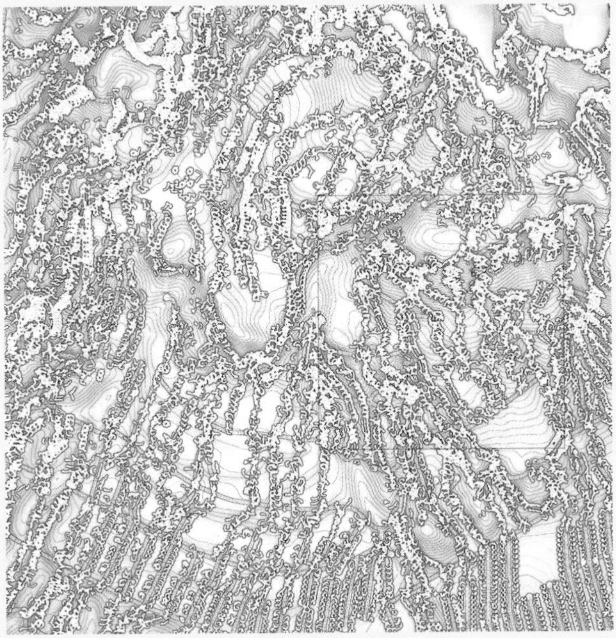

outdoor terrace, a winter garden, and sports facilities, all arranged within a nine-square grid. Two other examples of modernist aggregated figures are Gropius's *Wohnberg Project* from 1928—the *Wohnberg*, literally "living mountain," is an assemblage of inhabited units arranged around an inner collective void—and Hilberseimer's *Vertical City* (*Hochhausstadt*). Seen as a further development of Le Corbusier's contemporary city for three million inhabitants, Hilberseimer's project separates cells for living from those for working by staging mixes of both cell arrangements above each other. What appears is a multiplication of the existing ground as armature, separating various forms of movement.

After the Second World War, we can see the emergence of a radical new architectural form for the arrangement of individual cells, namely the "mat-building," a flat building assembled around figurative void spaces. Perhaps the first example of such a mat-building is Candilis/Josic/Woods's *Kasbah Project* in Casablanca, designed in 1952. In opposition to this idea of the habitat, which has been used to argue for mat-building structures, are the Smithson aggregated cells, similar to the Unité d'Habitation in Marseille, on elevated streets in the air. These streets formed a new cluster city by producing a new ground above the existing core of the destroyed city. As a precursor for the idea of megastructures, these multiple streets can be seen as an agglomeration of cells placed along lines of communication infrastructure. Examples of such aggregated figurations include Paul Rudolph's *Lower Manhattan Expressway* project and the *Plug-In City* by Archigram member Peter Cook. In opposition to the assemblage of cells along pure infrastructural arteries, the Italian rationalists, led by Aldo Rossi, developed an alternative to megastructures, namely urban megaforms. Such megaforms aggregated their cells around an urban historical form type, such as the arcades used for his *Gallaratese II* project in Milan. A further development of the idea of megaforms can be seen in the work of Oswald Mathias Ungers, in which an arrangement of cells formed an architectural object that can perform as a city within the city. This idea of a city within the city emerged again in OMA's projects for New York. In the *Sphinx Hotel* by Elia Zhengelis and in the *Welfare Hotel* by Rem Koolhaas, the hotel cells detach themselves from the Manhattan grid to form objects that have all the facilities of a city, without physically depending on the city itself. Perhaps the most economically successful contemporary application of these design approaches can be found in John Portman's hotels, in which cells are aggregated around a continuous void which defines a vertical lobby as an emergent effect of the negotiation between the assemblage of cells and the ground of the city.

THE GROUND AS MATTER

If from a materialist point of view the urban figure is defined as an aggregated figure, the ground of the city then can be seen as the matter through which these aggregations take their physical form. The matter of the ground is the economic value of its land. The model that is used throughout the world to define the value of land is the "hedonic prize model," based on databases and empirical knowledge. Every prize is the sum of its subdivided parts, with the parts covering all aspects of an urban entity. Most commonly considered in this respect is accessibility, such as distances to main infrastructural routes or to public transportation nodes. While physical objectives seem to be obvious aspects of the calculation of land values, the type of buyer, the type of seller, the year of purchase, the socioeconomic data for an area, the skill sets of inhabitants, their political interests, and so on, and subsequently all activities are measureable as factors on which to base the calculation urban land values.

Over recent years I have applied this materialist approach to a series of urban design research projects. The aim of this research has been to develop a morphogenetic design approach to generate urban aggregates according to the thesis defined here. The projects understand urban forms as an aggregation of habitable cells in which the ground is a territory of economic land values. Their aim is to find new forms of urban environment that are embedded within the forces of late capitalism.

NOTES

1 > C. Rowe and F. Koetter (1978) *Collage City* (Cambridge: MIT).

2 > L. Hilbersheimer (1927) *Groszstadt Architektur* (Stuttgart: Verlag Julius Hoffmann), 100. English translation from M. Tafuri (1976) *Architecture and Utopia: Design and Capitalist Development* (Cambridge, MA: MIT Press), 104.

3 > M. Tafuri (1976) "Radical Architecture and the City," in *Architecture and Utopia: Design and Capitalist Development*, Manfredo Tafuri (Cambridge, MA: MIT Press), 105.

4 > Tafuri, *Architecture and Utopia*, 104.

5 > Tafuri, "Radical Architecture and the City," 105.

CASE STUDY

OCEAN CN >PARAMETRIC PEARL RIVER DELTA

2009

OCEAN CN: Ercument Gorgul, Andrew Tirta Atmadjaja, Felix Robbins, Tom Verebes (Creative Director), Richard Wang, Stephen Wang; with assistance from Li Bin, Joyce Chan, Crystal Cheung, Kelvin Cheung, Kenneth Cheung, Man Ho Chu, Ariel Ip, John Tso, Chris Tsui, Middle Wong, Buzz Yip

Consultants
Crystal Design (Hong Kong, London): Gao Yan
Live Architecture Network, LaN: Luis Fraguada

Sponsors: Crystal Design (Hong Kong, London), E-Grow International Trading Shanghai Ltd (Shanghai)

The rapid urbanization of the Pearl River Delta has been shaped by top-down planning along with profit-driven architectural production, often resulting in cacophonous collages of homogenous and generic buildings. OCEAN CN's agenda challenges urbanism formed from featureless, nonspecific, bland, and—most worryingly—disposable architecture. For the Hong Kong-Shenzhen Biennale 2009, OCEAN CN documented sets of urban and architectural information related to one city from all nine prefectures of Guangdong province, as well as the two Special Administrative Regions (SARs) of Hong Kong and Macau. The spatial attributes of these eleven cities were embedded into a series of coded computational models, as well as an interface for visitors to this exhibition to "design their own city."

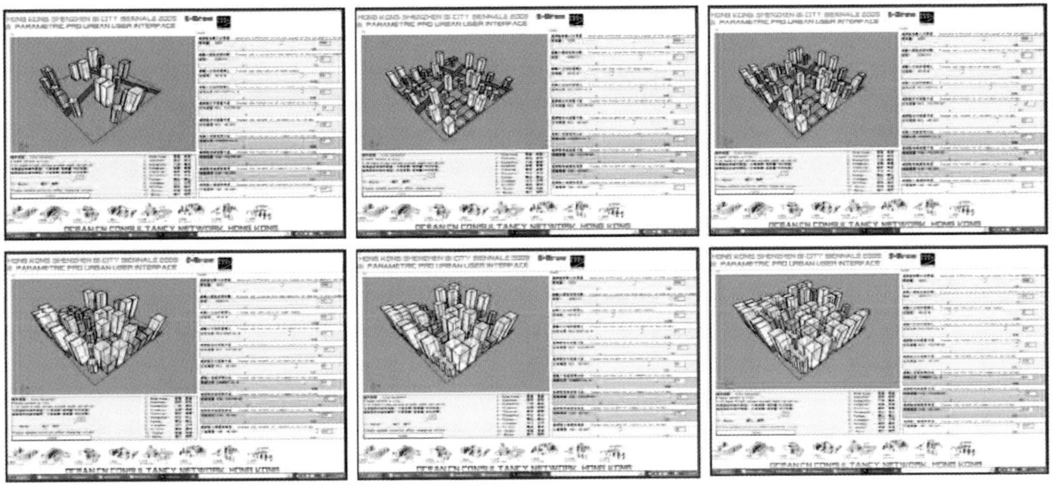

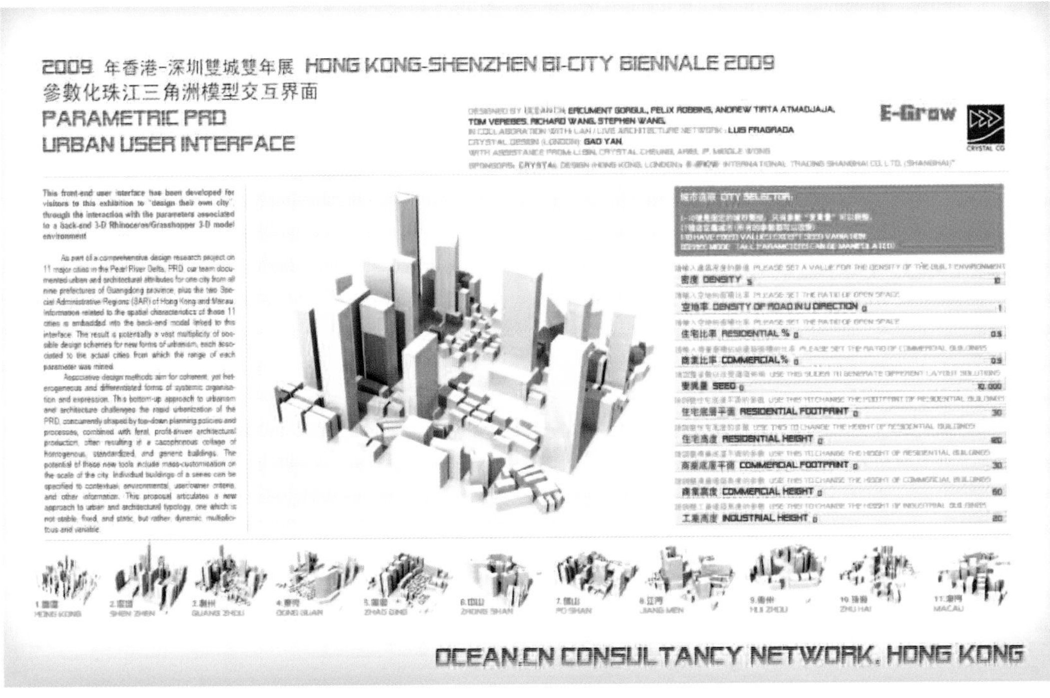

Interface models demonstrating variations of urban models, from initial seeds, typologies, program mixes, and density data.

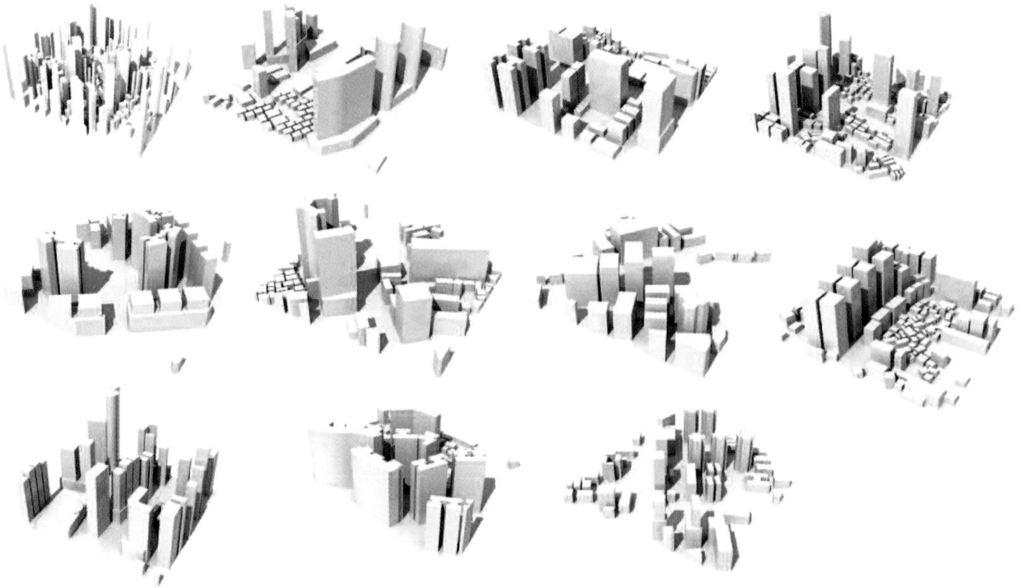

Models of 500-by-500-meter zones sampled from eleven cities in Guangdong province, Hong Kong and Macau.

Photo of exhibition installation of the user interface at the Hong Kong-Shenzhen Biennale 2009.

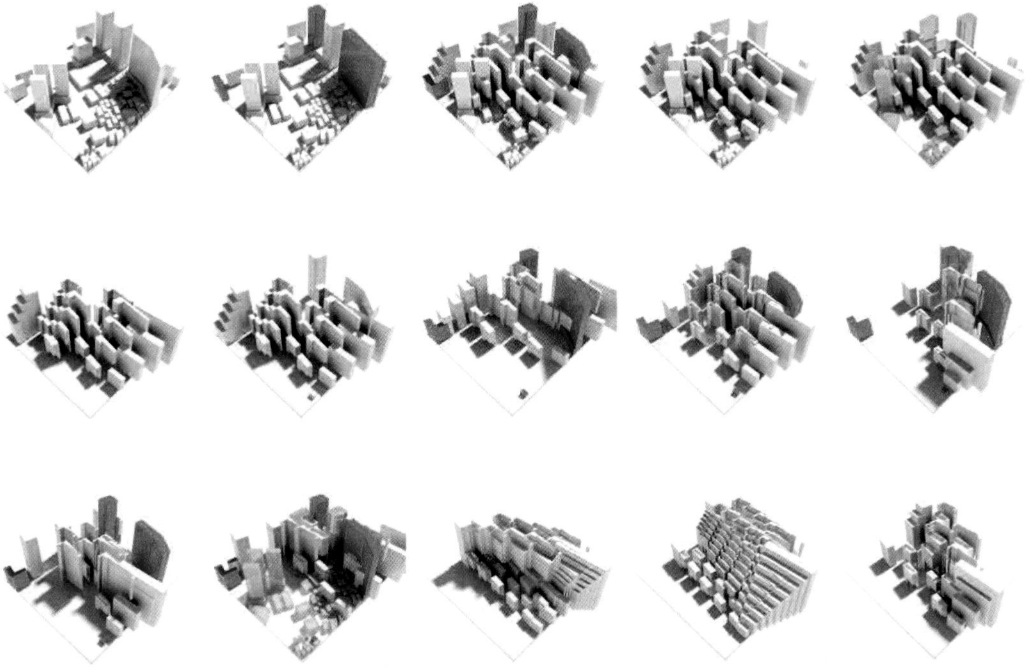

Series of scripted models, from four highly diverse initial massing topologies as seeds, playing out proximities, densities, and accumulations of massing.

CASE STUDY

OCEAN CN >SERIAL SYSTEMS: REMODELING HONG KONG HOUSING

VENICE BIENNALE 2010

OCEAN CN: Gao Yan, Tom Verebes, Felix Robbins (Scripting), Andrew Tirta Atmadjaja
In collaboration with: C:A+D Carlow Architecture + Design; Rocker-Lange Architects (Group Exhibition Installation)
Suppliers: Shenzhen JOM DIGI Icts (Shenzhen), holographic printing; Art Lab Ltd.
Carpentry (Installation): Ricci Wong Cheuk Kin

This project for the Venice Biennale 2010 challenges the perpetuation of homogenous, repetitive, reductive, and profit-driven approaches to conventional mass-produced housing in Hong Kong. The experience of urban life in Hong Kong is shaped by the pervasive legacy of its housing estates—vast, generic arrays of uniform, standardized, and repetitive buildings. Mass housing often reflects the constraints of contemporary modes of production, yet paradoxically housing continues to serve as a laboratory for experimentation with emerging technologies and their impact on the advancement and reformulation of existing production processes. This project proposes an alternative, variable, multiple, and adaptable model with which to address the customization of twenty-first-century living.
A series of standard housing plan types were transformed, generating a range of sectionally differentiated topological spaces, constrained by parameters of density, proximity, height, and the formal transformation of floor plates in section. Through coding these programmable models, the design team optioneered a vast multitude of possible design options at the scale of urban design and masterplanning, which led to a variety of successive, incremental outcomes demonstrating a range of complex urban conditions in a 500-meter by 500-meter zone of central Hong Kong.

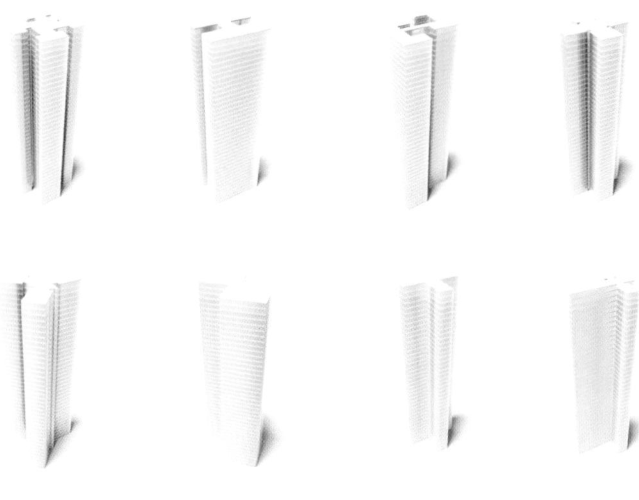

A series of standard housing typologies, prevalent in Hong Kong's repetitive housing, were taken as the basis for design operations to overturn the paradigm of repetitive, homogenous standardization.

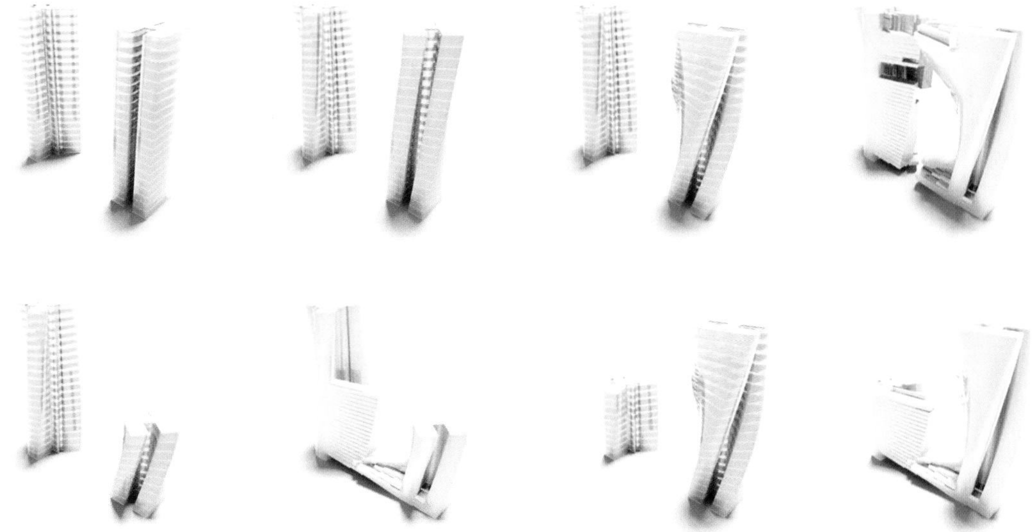

Moving away from single towers to investigate the correlation of two towers.

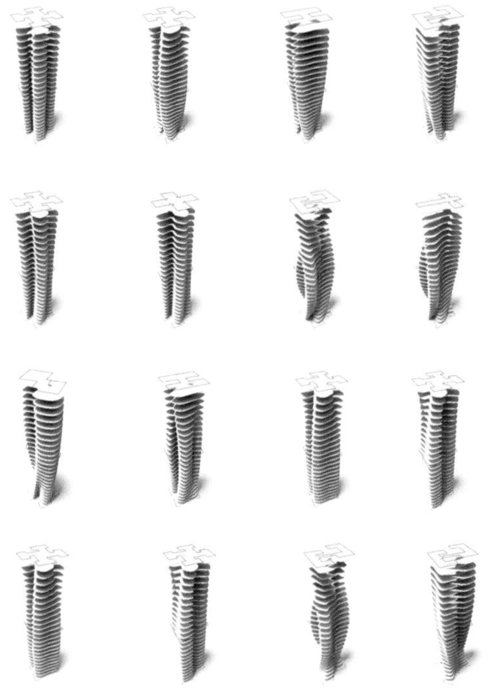

Further transformations of tower types, through the hybridization of housing plan types.

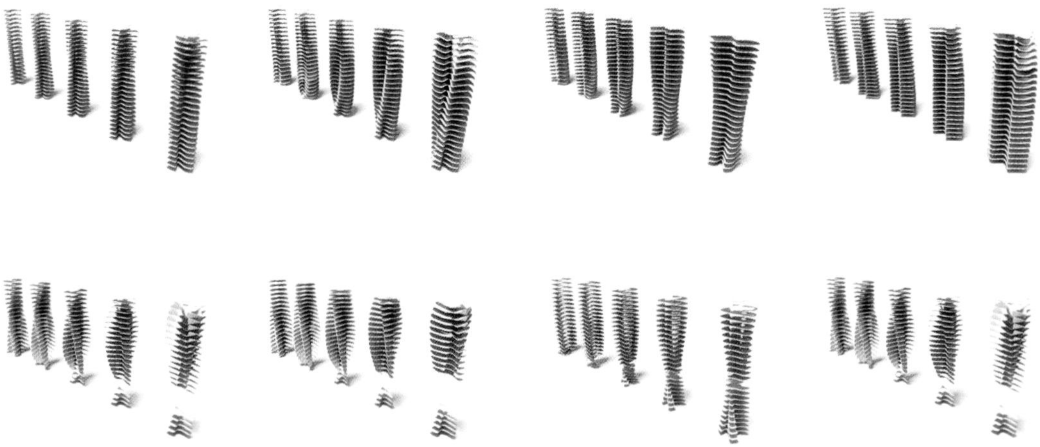

Series of related towers demonstrating diversity and coherence.

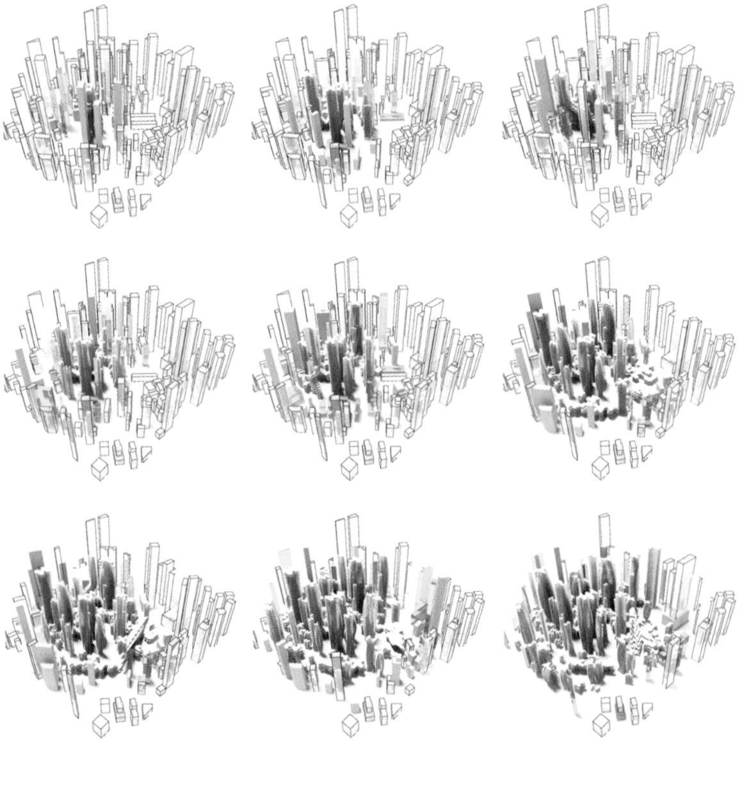

Urban intervention in Central in Hong Kong, describing the variations in context and the potential for time-based evolutionary growth in existing urban fabric.

CASE STUDY

ROCKER-LANGE ARCHITECTS >DENSITY AND OPENNESS REVISITED: RECODING BUILDING BULK IN HONG KONG 2012

Design team: Christian J. Lange and Ingeborg M. Rocker (Principals); with Matthew Waxman, Lauren Gerdeman, Patrick Hamon, Winnie Tang, Benny Leung, Vanessa Tse, Crystal Siu, Joe Qui, Alice Hui

Hong Kong's cityscape is primarily shaped by the typology of the tower, which functions as an extension of the urban programmatic user surface. The question of public space within this vertical urban fabric remains unaddressed. This research project for the Hong Kong-Shenzhen Biennale 2012 seeks an alternative approach to open and public spaces in the context of the city and the context of buildings. In Hong Kong, the building envelope usually expands to the maximum boundary of

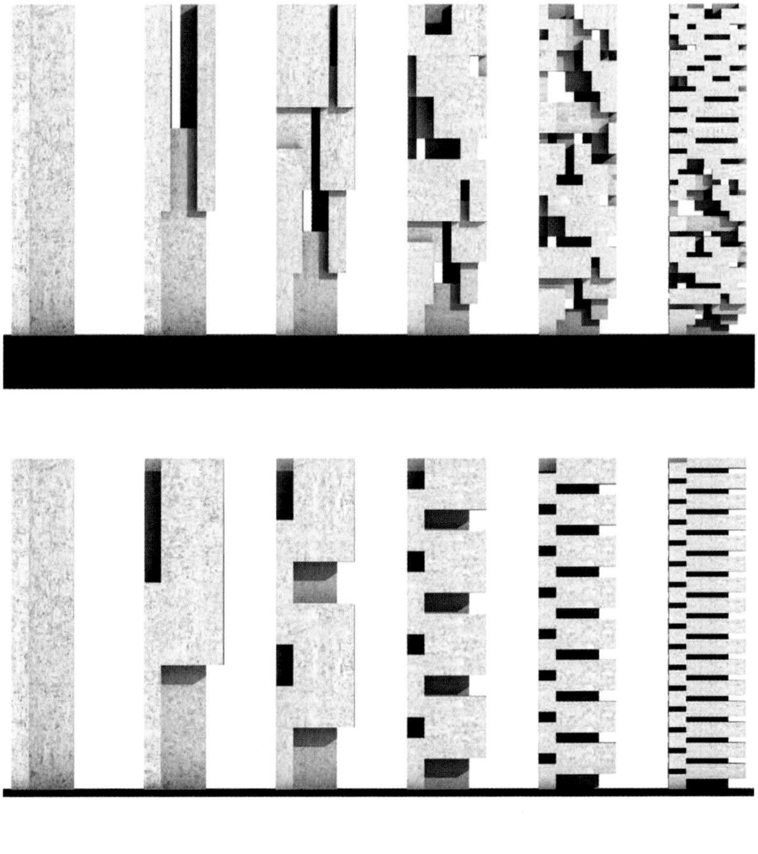

Elevations of two series of symmetrical and asymmetrical variations.

the site, defining the void space or possible exterior public space. It could be argued that the GFA (gross floor area) for building plots and the full extrusion of site boundaries is responsible for this dilemma. The building code is conceptually the genetic DNA for the life and success of cities. Hong Kong is shaped by its building code, but how can the building code be rethought in order to overcome the lack of public space in the city? This research project aims to establish an alternative system for defining building mass. As an alternative to extruding the maximum boundary condition of a given site to determine the building mass, this model incorporates a ratio of open space in the design process. At its core is a computational logic that calculates the amount of open space for each city plot. The rule-based model can adapt to different site and programmatic conditions, and the design outcomes may never be repeated. The intention of this set-up is to produce differentiated spaces and varying densities between solid and void patterns.

Planometrically asymmetrical and symmetrical series of models.

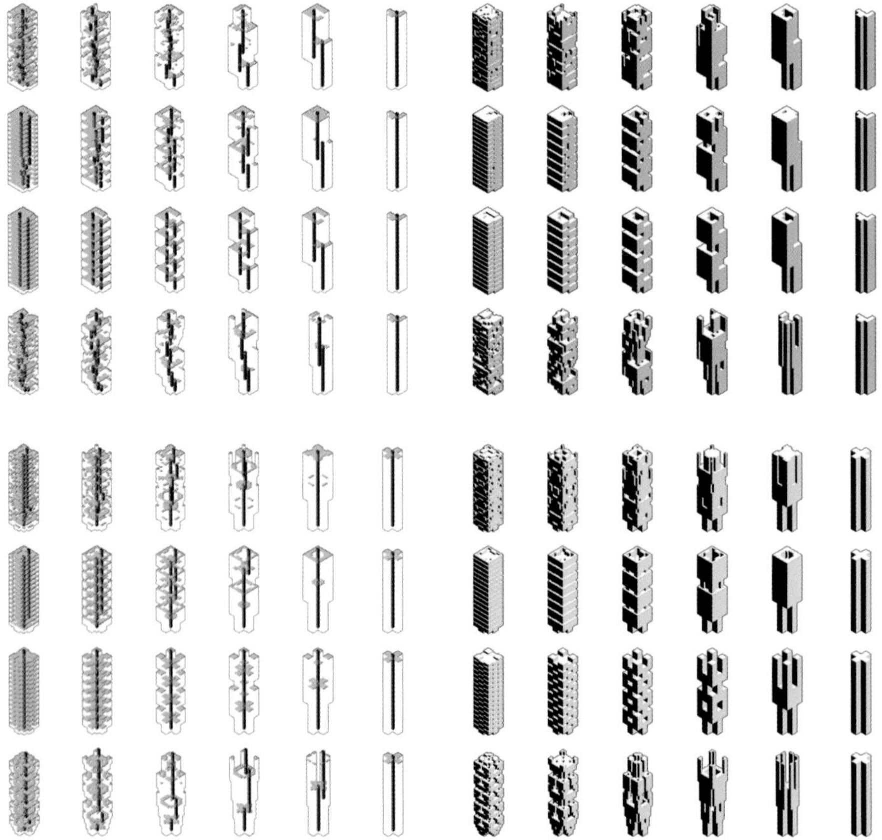

Photos of a series of laser-cut and 3D-printed tower models, indicating surface and volumetric conditions; and a series of solid 3D-printed tower models.

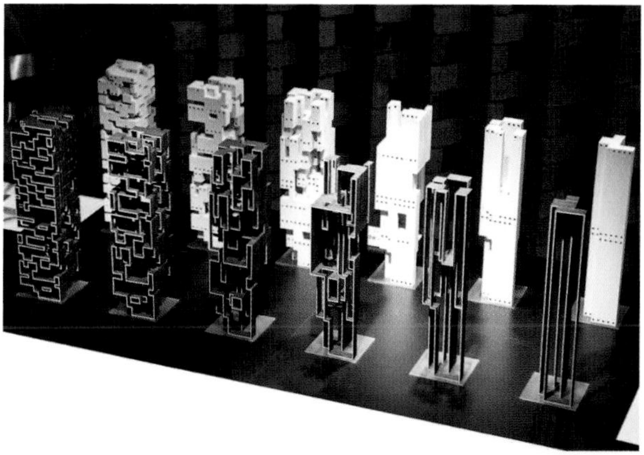

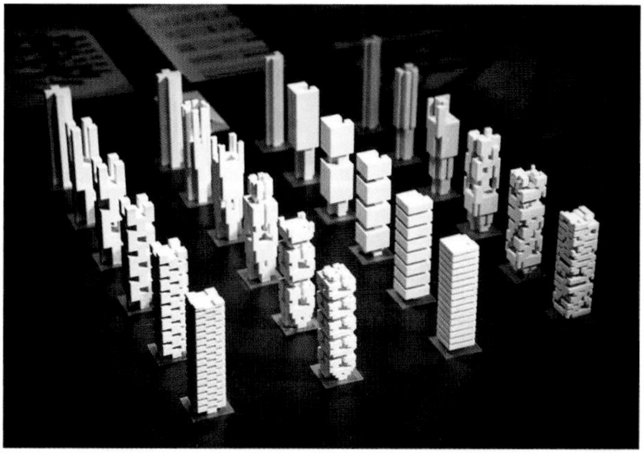

CHAPTER 15

TOM VEREBES > COMPUTATIONAL URBANISM

This chapter tracks a selective summary of the evolution of computational design methods, from the retooling of CAD, to code-based design. Shifting from top-down modeling to more generative, bottom-up systems, interest in biomorphics, biomimetics, and natural systems has brought about an intensified culture around morphogenetic design systems and evolutionary software in architecture and urbanism. From Building Information Modeling (BIM) and its potential to automate the design of options arises the potential for urban optioneering. This gives rise to the possibility of informing city design with dynamic, emergent processes, to help shape and regulate it. This chapter also presents the history and present status of parametric design for urbanism.

15.1 THE EVOLUTION OF COMPUTATIONAL METHODOLOGIES AND URBANISM

During the last two decades, a revolution has taken place across the global landscape of architectural culture—the digital revolution—which has irreversibly transformed nearly every office, institute, and school around the world. Digital technologies have not only re-formed contemporary notions of space, these new tools are also revolutionizing methodologies of manufacturing, delivery, assembly, and construction. Alongside this wholesale technological retooling of architectural practice and education there is the imminent intellectual challenge for our generation: to discover the theoretical, cultural, and social implications of these new computational practices.[1] Burry calls this the "cultures" of computation, intentionally pluralized to include varied groups and approaches to computational design.[2] In perhaps no arena is design more cultural than in addressing the city as the object of design.

This book is not a blueprint for successful management of urban growth, rather it is an operating manual for new, pertinent approaches to urbanization in this century.[3] It is through an architectural approach to the city that the disciplinary concepts and methodologies of conventional, top-down urban planning are implicitly critiqued, although not wholly discredited. If it were not for the consolidation of conventional practices, innovations could not arise to subvert the regimes of convention. What follows is not a history of computation but a reconsideration of the ways in which design computation can target problems in urbanism. More projective than historical, this chapter seeks to map out various possible methodological interests in the field today and for the future, yet the risk is also for these projections to be premature, or worse, wildly wrong.

We are witnessing a shift from the computerization of design intent, through Computer Aided Design (CAD), to the computation of more emergent, unexpected, and imaginative results;[4] from cheaper and faster to more exploratory work. Computational design started in the mainstream, then migrated to the fringe, and eventually returned to the mainstream. CAD was initially a mode of drafting, and, as the name suggests, the computer merely "aided" design—the original goal of CAD was to "free the designer from repetitive, tedious, or time-consuming tasks," and through this liberation it "sought to empower the designer with the means to explore beyond the traditional framework of manual design."[5] The two main operations of most early CAD software were "snapping and intersection"—linking a source object and a target object.[6] Good computing often suggests the misuse and customization of off-the-shelf software. The role of the designer in relation to the computer (and its software) and to the numeric data sent to production machines "requires architects essentially to learn a new language," made up in part of the syntax of these new ways of making, and in part of the finessing and mastery of these tools.[7] The use of computers in design, management, and construction has led to the systematization of manual, repetitive processes, yet these tools also have the capacity to organize, through coding, vast information sets approaching the complexity of the world outside the computer.

Geometry, according to Reyner Banham, has a double status, "as something both new and perennial." Not only is geometry "the thumb-print of modern technology, but it is also the manifestation of perennial laws governing art, justified by the past, not the present."[8] Geometry can be seen either as a residue of technological procedures or as the generator of spatial logics which require technology to design and produce their effects. Is the city beyond geometry? The city is already metrically organized through the application of Euclidian geometry. It is in the measurable and describable aspects of urbanism that computational methods gain their first entry into modeling and managing the city, but there is also a political dimension to innovation, difference, and novelty. Eighteenth-century calculus put to work, at long last!

"Computation" can be defined as "the processing of information and interactions between elements which constitute a specific environment."[9] Given the various methodologies being both played with and researched with seriousness today, it is possible to say that "there is something different, unprecedented, and extraordinary about the computer as it compares to traditional manual tools."[10] Also noteworthy is the shift, described in earlier chapters, from mechanical to biological explanations of systems. Embedded intelligence arises from matter of various kinds (material, electronic) and the forces acting upon it. Kwinter warns of the implicit routinization of computation as an extension of mechanization, claiming that "no computer on earth can match the processing power of even the most simple natural system."[11] Nevertheless, computation is increasingly enabling designers to capture dynamic material conditions and to transform them.

With its roots in the earliest computer programs written in the 1940s, code-based design is emerging as increasingly accessible and widespread. Shape grammar—whose pioneers include George Stiny and James Gips,[12] Bill Mitchell at MIT in the 1970s, and Paul Coates at the University of East London in the 1990s, among others—was a syntax (grammar) developed as a form-based design approach "to carry out spatial computations visually," and to generate combinations and patterns based on initial rules.[13] These methods linked advances in computation to their applications in architecture.

The goals of computation are meaningless to consider—the computer is only a tool with which to harness complexity, to seek provisional novelties with which to make substantive innovations. Open-source code is a new, non-authorial approach to design, in which information is shared on libraries and wikis on the internet

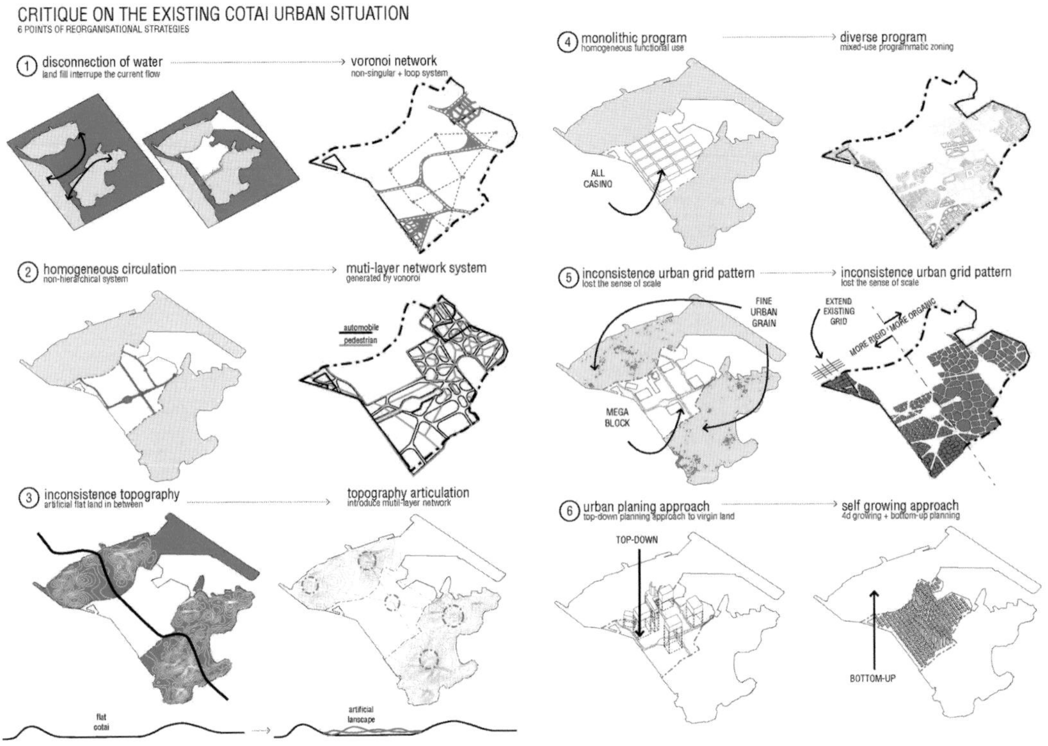

Diagrams correlating water, landscape and infrastructural networks, as a basis of associative logic for the proposal. (Studio Tutor: Tom Verebes; Students: Chan Shu-Kei Peter, Lai Wing Fung William, Yam Sai Tung Tony; MArch II Studio, *Forgetting Macau*, The University of Hong Kong, 2010)

within communities of code-writers and users. Rather than remaining constrained by off-the-shelf software applications, contemporary designers are building their own tools, linking plug-ins and libraries of code and hard-wiring new, unforeseen uses for tools.[14] This collaborative approach to coding marks a fundamental shift away from the cult of the individual hero architect, which dominated much of history.

> [Frazer's] fundamental thesis is that of architecture as a living, evolving thing.
> Gordon Pask, 1995[15]

John Frazer's work, described in his book *An Evolutionary Architecture*, was pioneering in its vision of how computation, nature, and architecture can be fused, although the body of work was preoccupied with the "back-end" of computation, and viewed design as a secondary and even residual outcome of processes. Often awkward, even crude, the spatial and visual repercussions of Frazer's teaching charted important new methods and concepts of morphogenesis.

Morphogenetic processes are informed by small-scale genetic information which is processed and transferred to develop larger living entities, and, in

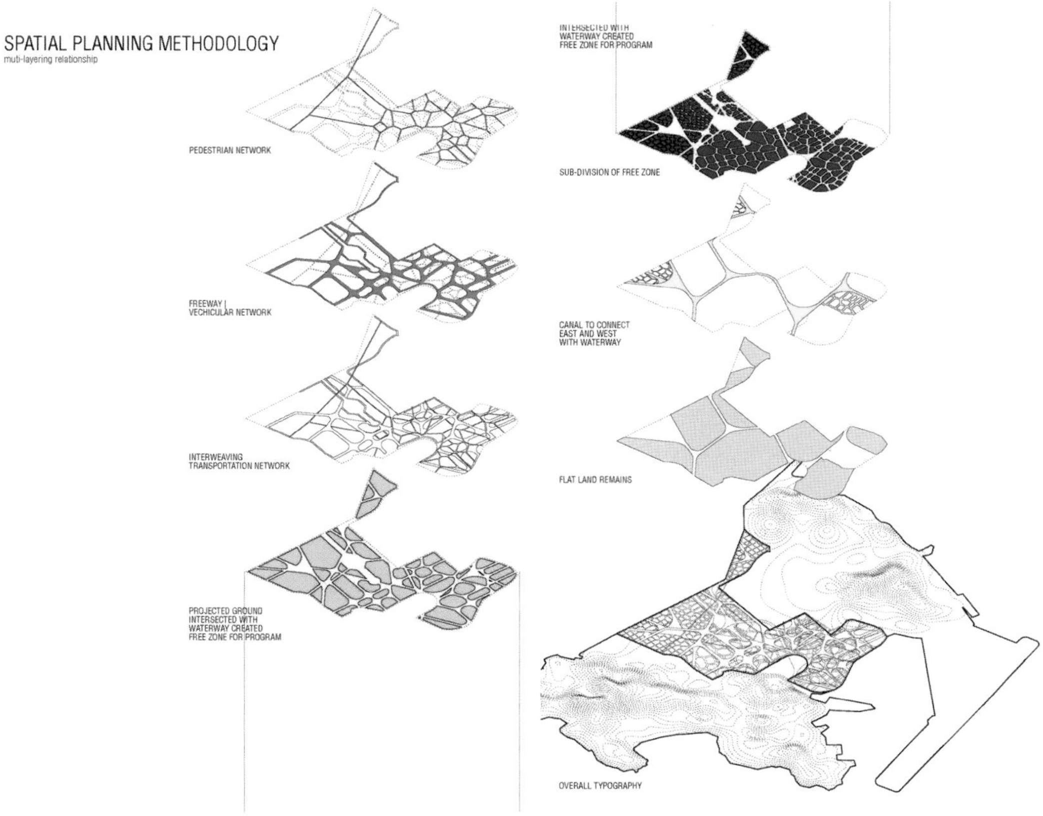

Diagrams projecting the hierarchies of vehicular and pedestrian networks, landscapes, and topographies. (Studio Tutor: Tom Verebes; Students: Chan Shu-Kei Peter, Lai Wing Fung William, Yam Sai Tung Tony; MArch II Studio, *Forgetting Macau*, The University of Hong Kong, 2010)

principle, to absorb external information, eventually evolving through processing and adaptation to stimuli. The rules which underlie these processes of formation share parallels, perhaps merely analogous, to design processes which embed computational coding as a basis upon which to generate, analyze, and provide feedback on an artefact, and hence build the capacity for intelligence into the resulting form.

> We increasingly refer to algorithms (instructions) as the agents that populate and produce modern space and no longer simply speak of a passive system of addresses, as in the classical three-dimensional world. Space today is no longer a backdrop or a foundation for events but a participant, an unstable and unpredictable process that both harvests and produces reality on the run. Space has never before so dramatically resembled a living organism.
>
> Sanford Kwinter[16]

Evolutionary computation is a nascent area for design to discover greater symbiosis with systems all around us, fusing what we classify as natural and artificial. Genetic algorithms "seek to model natural systems" by embedding the potential for complex, lifelike relationships in processes of formation through mimicry of "natural evolutionary processes."[17] Manuel De Landa has recapitulated Deleuze's notion of the genesis of form, described as "abstract diagrams," which breed form through variation, selection, adaptation, and evolution.[18] De Landa calls these morphogenetic processes "the emergence of novelty," and, related to computational design, they concern the relationship of constraints on organizational elements and the action of external forces upon those elements.[19] A genotype "defines the search space of the algorithm," and, in the process of mapping from genotype to phenotype, the genotype becomes "regarded as a set of 'growing instructions' known as an embryogeny."[20] There are three kinds of embryogenies: "external"—software is written for the process not to evolve; "explicit"—every step of the growth process evolves; and "implicit"—rules applied iteratively to "seeds" to build the growth, position, and type of components.[21]

What is the urban equivalent of an evolutionary architecture? An evolutionary urbanism? Models of growth and change are potentially key tools for urbanism in this century. The city is perhaps the most complex entity designed by mankind, and thus can be difficult to model. Through the application of computational fluid dynamics, urbanism gains a new capacity to unleash and control complex, mobile systems. Agent-based systems "simulate complex systems that develop over time, such as cities."[22] The contemporary paradigm for understanding—as well as modeling—higher-order complexity is the swarm. Flocking algorithms generate real-time models of change, with collective intelligence embedded through agency. An agent, as described by Burry, is "an autonomous unit of code with inbuilt behaviours" which operates as a collective yet distributed form of intelligence.[23]

Agent-based models follow simple rules but have the capacity to generate complex structures. The mathematicians Keller and Segal were the first to experiment with slime mold simulations, as lifelike time-based computational simulations. Within urban research, Michael Batty's work on cellular automata and agent-based systems has been applied to dynamic urban models which "generate both continuous and discontinuous change" and are essentially abstract, lacking contextual interference, feedback, or constraints.[24] Cellular automata are another simulation tool for generating complex organizational models from the growth of cells governed by local rules. As tools for generating urban organization, cellular automata have limits on their application to generating form. Their models rely on randomness, which Batty argues is "the source of novelty and change" in urbanism.[25] Batty has identified five drivers that are "critical to an understanding of how change takes place: randomness, historical accident, physical determinism, natural advantage, and comparative advantage."[26] In effect each of these conditions is causal—either directly through a sequence of decisions, or through geographical limits or advantages in resources, connections, or other facilitators of urban change. Batty's research is highly technical in its emphasis on computational systems. Despite the high level of technical sophistication in his methods of breeding urban organization, the research falls short of demonstrating a rigorous design methodology. The work relies on "bottom-up" generative algorithmic computational techniques, and it becomes questionable how much actual urban dynamics are driving the dynamic models, and how pertinent the outcomes are to actual urbanism. The limits of these methodologies as design tools is also never stated.

Casey Reas and Ben Fry developed the first version of the coding and dynamic modeling environment *Processing* in 2001.[27] Initially limited to a 2D scripted outcome, *Processing* has been developed as a 3D dynamic modeler, entirely code based and limited in its capacity to "manually" model form. As software, its function is to model growth and change through recursive sequences in a time-based environment. In the words of Reas, these kinds of codes "explore the themes of instability and plurality," in which "variations are never exhausted."[28] Evident in the outcomes of the coding are the emergence of often unanticipated graphic spaces.

Despite the risk of "formal parody" of natural processes and forms, we are now able, as demonstrated in this text, to conceive of designing in and with time. In today's design landscape, nature is a prominent and persistent theme. Bio-inspired metaphors permeate history; today's approaches relate design to nature. Through the correlation of nature and mathematics, designers can release authority, harness complexity, confident in the belief that nature can be designed if the compositional authority of the designer can be relinquished. In another approach, packaged calculus is used to translate the perceived conduct of natural systems."[29] It is the behavior of nature which fascinates and motivates the current generation.

We have seen, for decades now, the real possibilities for buildings to adapt to "changes in environmental circumstances," through a sensitive, responsive approach to design.[30] With or without the sensing and actuating technologies needed to literally respond to environmental changes, performance-driven design is a direct repercussion. In general, biomimetic approaches and methods in architecture share a default concern for the porosity of envelopes, as the spatial equivalent of the epidermis of an organism. The metaphor highlights the lifelike qualities of performance-based/driven design, in the literal adaptability of the tectonic and material systems to a set of multiple, differentiated, overlapping functional roles. Responsiveness, and the control systems which drive its behaviors, brings forth the elusive issue of intelligence in design systems. This entails not simply reaction but also anticipating, learning from feedback, and processing information. Scientistic narratives in contemporary architectural design research tend to obscure the underlying intention of achieving spatial differentiation, at which most "performance-oriented" methods are targeted. Those who champion systems engineering, bionics, and biomimetics tend to rely on arguments relating to smaller-scale spatial and material assemblages, and claims of their imminent ecological benefits.[31] These are relevant as ways of thinking about and designing small-scale architecture, but the reader is left wondering yet again what happened to urbanism, and all its complex auxiliary contingencies, in this bio-inspired (small) world.

A building, or for that matter a city, cannot literally be equated with the organization and function of a living organism, yet the metaphoric limits of biomorphism can be rejected in favor of a more robust model of adaptive urban growth, the criteria of which are related more to the dynamic nature of urban complexity than to the appearance of a biological similitude. If we can envision the

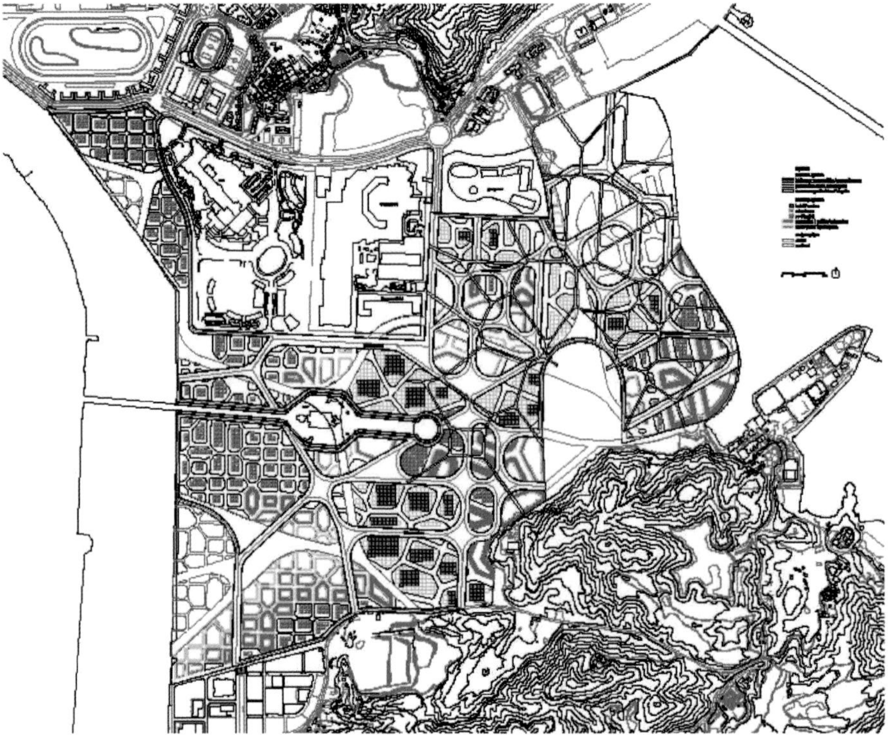

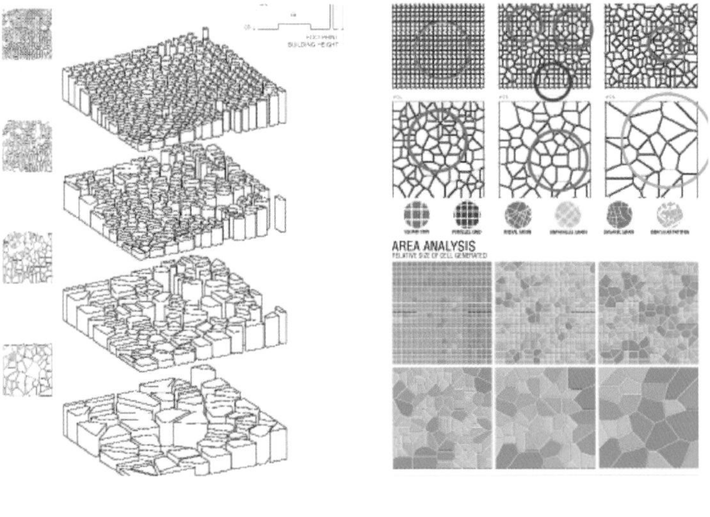

Diagram explaining the morphological patterning and the proposed masterplan for Cotai, Macau. (Studio Tutor: Tom Verebes; Students: Chan Shu-Kei Peter, Lai Wing Fung William, Yam Sai Tung Tony; MArch II Studio, *Forgetting Macau*, The University of Hong Kong, 2010)

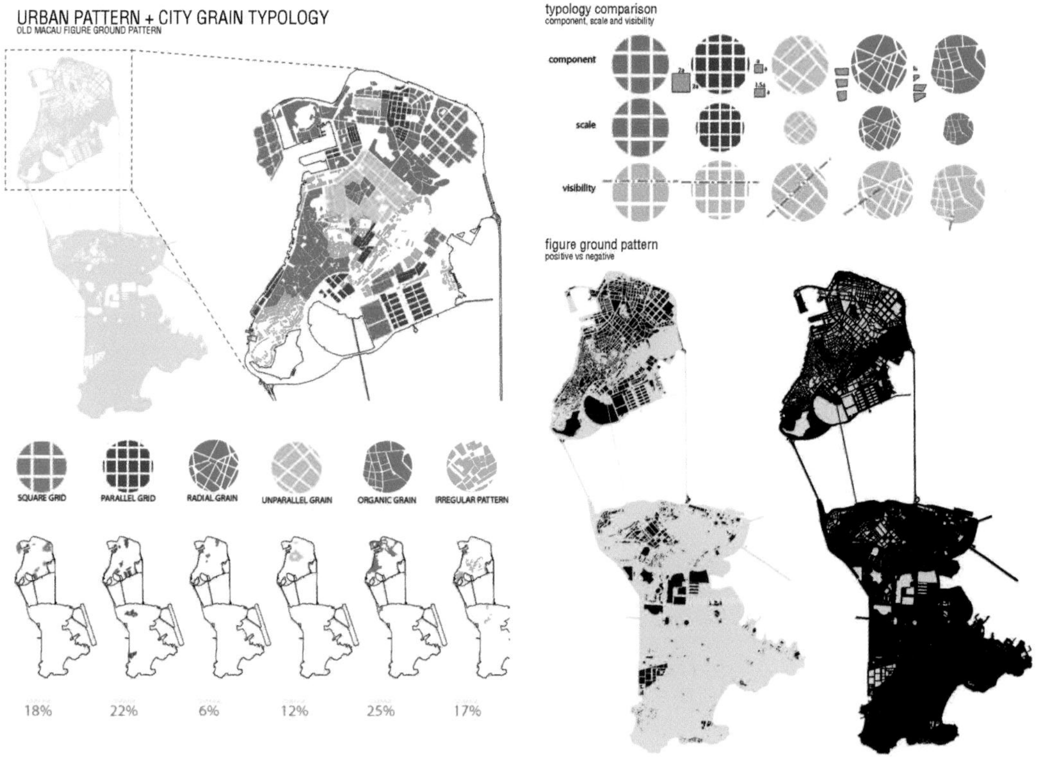

Diagrams extracting patterns, with particular features, scales, and grains, to deploy in a differentiated model of abstract contextualism. (Studio Tutor: Tom Verebes; Students: Chan Shu-Kei Peter, Lai Wing Fung William, Yam Sai Tung Tony; MArch II Studio, *Forgetting Macau*, The University of Hong Kong, 2010)

future of architecture to be one in which the design of buildings is augmented "to sense environmental cues and adapt their shape and function to continuously optimize energy efficiency, light transmission and thermal gain,"[32] then what possibilities lie ahead for designers to imagineer and deliver a new kind of intelligent, adaptable urbanism? The shift is such that cheap metaphors of organisms and ecologies do not scale up. What will the repercussions of architectural biomimetics be in the twenty-first century city? What are the mechanisms by which such intelligence can be embedded in the making and management of cities? As architecture desperately seeks to create the conditions for its embodiment of nature—or to become more natural in itself—what are the possibilities in the future for cities to exist in greater symbiosis with the environment?

15.2 AUTOMATION, OPTIONEERING, AND OPTIMIZATION

Technological evolution is the motor of innovation. Through successive variations, a technological construct can be optimized toward improved scope of performance, and adapted to changing environmental conditions. In this light, a design outcome falls within a solution space of possible orientations for a particular technological product or process.

As early as 1969, Nicholas Negroponte summarized three ways for "machines to assist the design process," comprising: automation to reduce costs; adapting then-current methods to become "machine compatible"; and working with evolutionary processes within evolutionary mechanisms.[33] He developed a theory of intelligence based on the interaction of man, machine, and feedback with the environment, later outlining the basis of a "soft architecture," involving a responsive, automated and evolutionary notion of space.

Contemporary automation is not wholly aligned to the capitalist regime, which enlisted standardization and rationalization as agents of automation. There is no doubt that there is great economic gain to be had from automation. According to Burry, the computer can be an aid to the practical delivery of projects within a "general framework of construction economics," however, as a "digital design agent," it can also achieve what would not otherwise be possible. Scripting is a tool of automated design. The simple definition of scripting, or code-based design, is that it "affords a significantly deeper engagement between the computer and user by automating routine aspects and repetitive activities, thus facilitating a far greater range of potential outcomes for the same investment in time."[34] Lisa Iwamoto highlights how computational control can "streamline production—effectively blending upstream and downstream processes that are typically compartmentalized, often eliminating intermediate steps between design and final production."[35] Compression of time, and inevitably of space, is achieved through a design's migration to factory and site—which can be anywhere—via communications infrastructure, giving rise to the potential for serial rather than singular design outcomes, and for the mass customization of products. Automation in today's most advanced architecture has a "newfound ability to generate construction information directly from design information." Branko Koralevic defines this workflow as "the most profound aspect of much of the contemporary architecture."[36] Those who argue on the basis of reduced time or cost are missing the point. Automation might make people more money in less time, but the cultural significance is the retooling of the world's production systems, the nascent implications of which include the reshaping of our cities.

The embedding of Building Information Modeling (BIM) as a standard method of production in architectural practices has been rapid. BIM systems facilitate nonstandard, mass-customized manufacturing systems and construction processes through the control of three-dimensional modeling environments, relating the fully detailed digital model to delivery and on-site time schedules, material mass and construction costs, and other real-world parameters of live projects. Both an "early adopter" and an "outlier," Frank Gehry is noteworthy for his ambitious efforts to build complex architectural surfaces since the late 1980s, having developed Gehry Technologies' proprietary *Digital Project* software by adapting *Catia*, originally an aerospace application for the design of fuselages. The implications of Building Information Modeling (BIM) for urbanism shift the relation of information and models in what is now called City Information Modeling (CIM), to be explored later in this chapter.

Optimization, which implies the identification of the best solution to a given problem, has always been a goal of all architectural methodologies—only in the

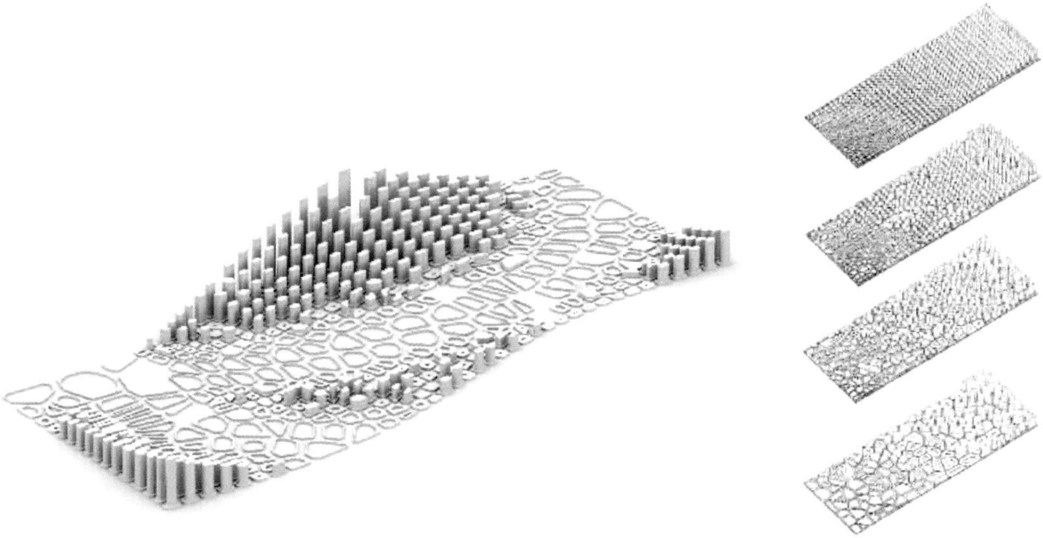

A set of differentiated urban massing diagrams. (Studio Tutor: Tom Verebes; Student: Lai Wing Fung William; MArch II Studio, *Forgetting Macau*, The University of Hong Kong, 2010)

past the tools available to investigate options, variants, and fitness were more crude and time-consuming than those we have today. An extreme example of form following function, optimization methods seek a "fitness for purpose" in which "a special state of equilibrium, performance, or best-achievable economy of means" is sought.[37] Optimization assumes a stable set of functional criteria, whereas deploying optimization toward an agenda of innovation shuns stable performance criteria for a mode in which feedback and selection in fact change the functional order initially sought after. The goal is the optimal state of a system.

John Frazer, who is "suspicious of tools without a purpose,"[38] summarizes three global trends in computational design: first, using BIM for optimization of design development, manufacturing, and construction delivery; second, applying this new technological power to meet heightened demand, in terms of time and quality, as parts of the world undergo unprecedentedly rapid urbanization; and third, responding to the "wake-up call" of ecological and energy issues through use of "virtual prototyping" to evaluate performance.[39]

In today's computational design landscape, optimization can focus on a range of modalities, including structural economies, minimal material use, and environmental performance.[40] Optimization models are not final representations. In the model space, "changes are made iteratively, and may or may not be recursive, looking for incremental improvement on the new temporary state of the model," thus the model is a tool for amelioration.[41] Several familiar goals of optimization in architecture include structural performance and economy, environmental performance (thermal properties, ventilation, light), and routing (distance, loading, integration or segregation), among others. There are two mathematical methods for optimization: stochastic and deterministic. Stochastic approaches deploy "a sequence that combines a random or probabilistic component with a selective process so that only certain outcomes of the random can prevail," in a recursive mode in which different outcomes emerge that are not necessarily related to the previous iteration. In a deterministic method of optimization, "there is no randomness" and "each state and operation exactly determines the next state."[42] Turing and von Neumann both sought to "duplicate not only the functions of mathematical machines but also the functions of nature."[43] John Holland's work on "problems of optimization and uncertainty" illustrates that the relation of optimization in synthetic design to biology is not a metaphorical but rather a methodological association.[44] As in biological organisms, the goal of optimization in design is to exhaust all possibility of amelioration and to arrive at a single "solution," yet the range of possibilities is, as we have seen, vast.

Design engineering taps into the historical line of architect-engineers who fail to fit with the conventional split between the architect, who is "the creator who makes designs[,] and the engineer[,] . . . who optimises and makes buildable those designs." Any discussion of automation and optimization cannot pretend these are strictly architectural preoccupations, and needs to hear the voice of engineers.[45] Unlike creative engineers of the past, who encroached on the projective and imaginative arenas in which architects believe they perform, designers of all kinds are today through diverse computational practices becoming more like engineers. Analysis and testing, once the domain of the engineer, are penetrating the processes of conception, development, and implementation of design work of all kinds. In such times of "revolution, or fast change in architecture," Charles Jencks writes, "professional barriers break down as specialists exchange roles."[46] The ways in which we engineer solutions no longer means an inferior or uncreative solution—in fact, design engineering plays out a multiplicity of options in relation to clear criteria.

Behavioral approaches to engineering design have parallels with architects who pursue optimal designs—meaning here a scheme's organizational elegance based on its organizational complexity, and not the best-functioning option selected according to specific criteria. Schumacher asserts that "elegant complexes" are akin to "highly integrated natural systems where all forms are the result of the lawful interaction of physical forces." He goes on to liken contemporary design methods to organic systems, in which form is the result of the "forces selected and integrated in adaptation to performance requirements."[47]

Shifting back to urbanism now, we probe the nascent implications of these new spatial relationships of parts to wholes, processes to products.

David Gerber outlines the paradigm and methods of "optioneering" in his essay "Parametric Urbanism Redux: Urban Design and Complexity in an Age of Infinite Computing," which immediately follows this chapter. Akin to a technique of optimization in computer science, "hill climbing" seeks increasingly optimal local solutions to a given function. If run in a recursive sequence, optimization becomes a way of engineering a design solution through vast, multiple options. Optioneering can be explained as an artificial mode of selecting variations for their fitness according to given criteria, echoing the mechanisms of evolution. This methodology, akin to engineering methods, challenges the traditional notion that "architecture and engineering [were] based upon a reversible, linear and hierarchical correspondence between the organization and the production process."[48] Today's advanced methods in architecture and engineering have great potential as tools of a new approach to adaptable yet highly specific urbanism. Advancements achieved through parametric design, automation, and optimization in architecture represent a shift away from modernism's determinism and standards and toward "sensitively variable accommodation."[49] These explorations undoubtedly bring economic benefits, yet the more significant impact of contemporary technology lies in its ability to be "interactive and performatively driven."[50] As we see throughout this book, urbanism should be flexible rather than fixed, varied rather than uniform, able to adapt rather than finite. City Information Modeling (CIM), as the basis for urban optioneering, is concerned with negotiating diverse inputs to discover design solutions through association of parts with wholes. Despite the potentials of BIM and parametric design, these design and management systems are often accused of being hierarchical, top-down in how the range of spatial potential is constrained to preconceived limits. These computational tools are no longer put to work simply to rationalize design projects, but rather "to conceive and generate them," thus exceeding the profession's original aims of realizing practical advances in design development and construction delivery.[51]

Urban optioneering may not be bounded by parametric design, but doubtless it can include a more generative, algorithmic basis for understanding the city as patterns which unfold in time. Different from evolution, optioneering aims for an intentional yet not necessarily preconceived performance-based optimization, through automated processes. Artificial evolution in nonbiological artefacts does not aim for one single ideal final condition; the same can be said about the evolution of species. The power of these tools lies in the possibility of simulating

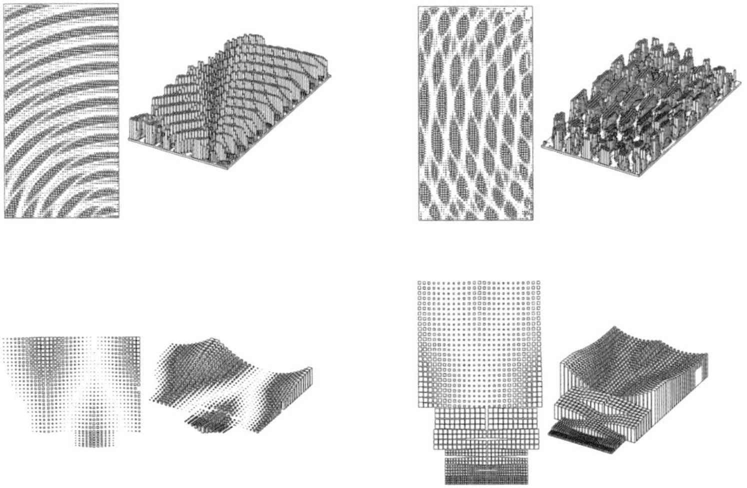

Spatial pattern exercises in Rhino/Grasshopper. (Studio Tutor: Tom Verebes; Students: LAI Sheng Ching, CHENG Chun; MArch I Studio, *Ground Control*, The University of Hong Kong, 2012)

patterns of proliferation toward the automation of multiplicities, rather than singular, prescribed design outcomes.

15.3 PARAMETRIC URBANISM

> After insuring on these principles of healthfulness of the future city, and selecting a neighborhood that can supply plenty of food stuffs to maintain the community, with good roads or else rivers or seaports affording means of transport to the city, the next thing to do is to lay the foundations for the towers and walls.
>
> Vitruvius, c. 20 BC[52]

Aerial view of proposal for Ras Al-Khaima, UAE, cohering the proposal with the existing urban pattern and topographical features. (Studio Tutor: Tom Verebes; Students: Lindsay Bresser, Claudia Dorner, Sergio Reyes Rodr guez; Architectural Association, 2009)

Parametric Urbanism was the title of a research agenda at the Design Research Lab at the Architectural Association, pursued with three cycles of March students between 2005 and 2008. Design teams of post-professional masters students were led by Patrik Schumacher, Yusuke Obuchi, Theodore Spyropoulos, and Tom Verebes, who co-directed the program. The belief was initially stated that urbanism has always been parametric, in that the city is comprised of complex associations and interactions of diverse and numerous agents, systems, and forces. This "deep relationality" between organizational components, or parts of a whole, is what makes the city dynamic, rather than static; adaptive rather than fixed and finite.

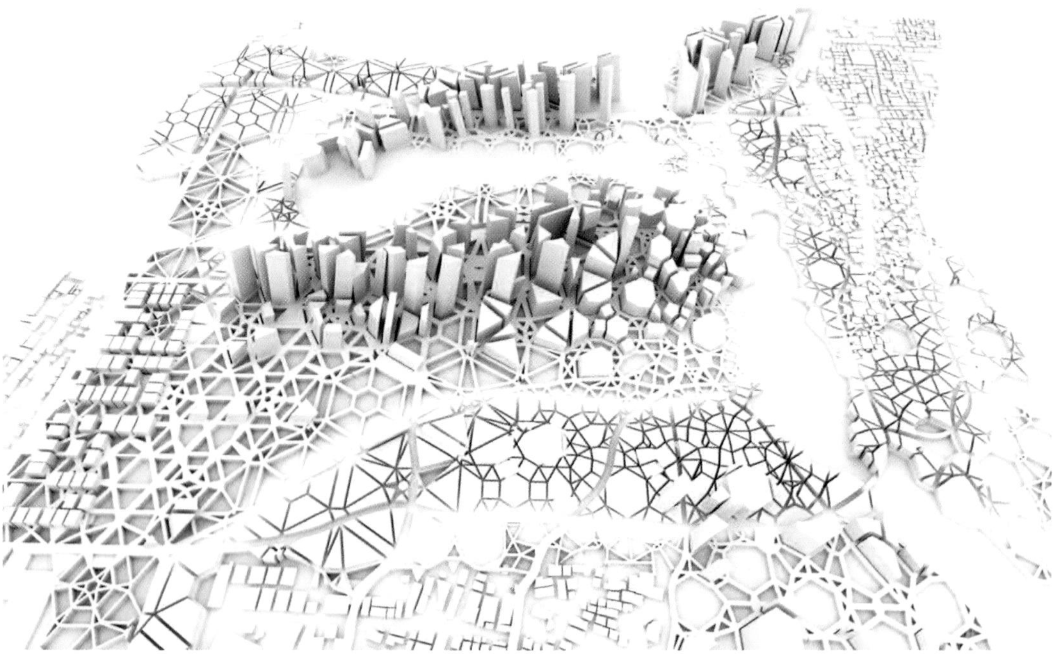

This associative approach to cities was coupled with a desire to explore the emerging toolbox of parametric and algorithmic design, to be applied to questions of urbanism rather than to be limited to architecture. Without making hard disciplinary distinctions, we recognized how much of the cutting-edge computational design research in the early 2000s was on small-scale architecture, and we were keen to investigate urbanism, led by architectural concepts and methodologies.

Lewis Mumford's term "cultural preparation" can be applied to the last two or three decades, during which computational design was focussed on architectural issues and not strictly on the city as a project. Computational tools were then being used by architects and engineers to harness complexity, at all scales from the smallest component to vast spatial conditions. Decomposition, as we have seen, of part-to-whole relations in complex systems is not possible for stable part-to-whole relations. Shifting scale from controlling details of complex wholes (buildings) to urbanism, where lies the problematic in this transition to an extreme design scale? In fact, a single building or product is the result of relationships, associated conditions, stimulated by interaction. These concepts are not new—parametric urbanism concerns the primary systems of land (topography, subdivision, etc.), routing of various systems and flows, massing morphology, programmatic and event structures, and so on.

A declaration of urbanism as associative does not, however, mean this approach is "parametricist." Modernism was a worldwide movement initially presented as singular and coherent, but its failure to endure was in part because of local and regional fragmentation and differentiation.[53] It is the same plurality of contemporary global architectural culture which raises questions over the quest for a single "unifying theory of architecture," as championed by Patrik Schumacher.[54] Parametric design need not settle into a singular, unified style. Any attempts toward this should be resisted. Rather, varied and diverse methodologies should be encouraged and celebrated. Despite the ubiquity of software and the apparent homogeneity of ways of using its interfaces, no doubt cultural identities and regional specificities will go far to create new kinds of spatial heterogeneities.

Modernist city planning was at once visionary, yet heavily reliant on the deployment of modern technologies of infrastructure, industry, and construction materials and techniques. Despite the similarity of arguments presented in this book concerning how contemporary technology is used to shape and regulate urbanism, the difference here is that technology is understood as generative and associative modeling, analysis and simulation of fundamentally dynamic behaviors, and management systems with which to harness complexity. Le Corbusier's seminal declaration in *Le poème de l'angle droite* (*Poem of the Right Angle*) was that *L'homme marche droît parce qu'il a un but*—people walk in straight lines because they have a goal; similarly, he distinguished *le chemin des ânes*—serpentine roads, literally roads for donkeys—from *le chemin des hommes*—straight roads, for people.[55] In contrast to Le Corbusier's defense of orthogonality, Schumacher claims "the work of Frei Otto is the only true precursor of Parametricism." Otto's "relational fields" serve as a paradigmatic analog of many of today's varied interests in computational urbanism.[56] Otto generated connective and aggregative fields in what were principally material processes of computation.

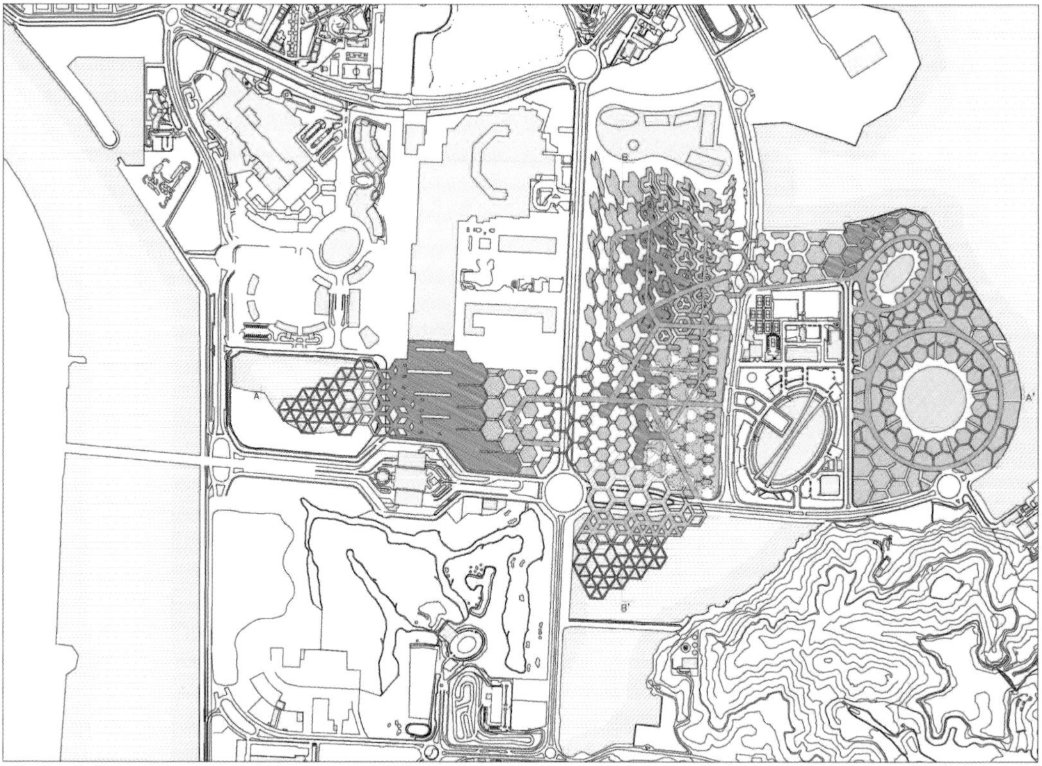

Masterplan for Cotai, Macau, integrating a dense, pedestrian order to the blank residual space between casino developments. (Studio Tutor: Tom Verebes; Students: Chan Chi Yin Stephen, Yeung Hiu Lei Samuel; MArch II Studio, *Forgetting Macau*, The University of Hong Kong, 2010)

The need for greater organization and control of the growth and functionality of cities sees the development of urban methodologies which embed emergent behaviors and self-organized systems, or simply complex organization, as a progression of cybernetics, as the management of "information flows through sorting and feedback mechanisms."[57]

The term "code" has several meanings, from a syntax of encrypted communication (as in Morse code), to a set of strictures or regulations (as in building code), to a set of instructions, often a computer program with which to execute and achieve a goal. The latter two compel us to probe for greater understanding of the potential to embed the regulatory mechanisms of cities within dynamic, interactive computational modeling and simulation environments. Generative codes produce unexpected and not wholly predictable outcomes. In this light, an emergent approach to coding in urbanism is not one which applies rules as limits of an acceptable, familiar design outcome, but one which enables correlation of multiple constraints to produce innovative solutions, which surpass expectations and normative cultural and professional practices. Coding can inform the patterns of streets, massing morphology, social order, activities, and so on.

Code-based design can lead to multiple hierarchies and emergent, unexpected patterns.

Codes—planning codes, social or cultural codes, computational programming languages, etc.—change over time; the natural evolution of cultural, social, political, and technological apparatus necessitates equally adaptable tools with which to design and manage complex urban order. Parametric design is increasingly understood to lead to a final outcome which is "a product of a construction process capable of incorporating a far more complex set of considerations" than conventional manual, representationally biased design approaches.[58] Conventional discourses and practices of architecture and urbanism presume form to be highly stable and permanent. In the short history of parametric approaches to urbanism, some of which is documented in this book, designers have developed systemic, scenario-based and time-based three-dimensional masterplans in which strategies for urban growth, change, and evolution over several years are established.

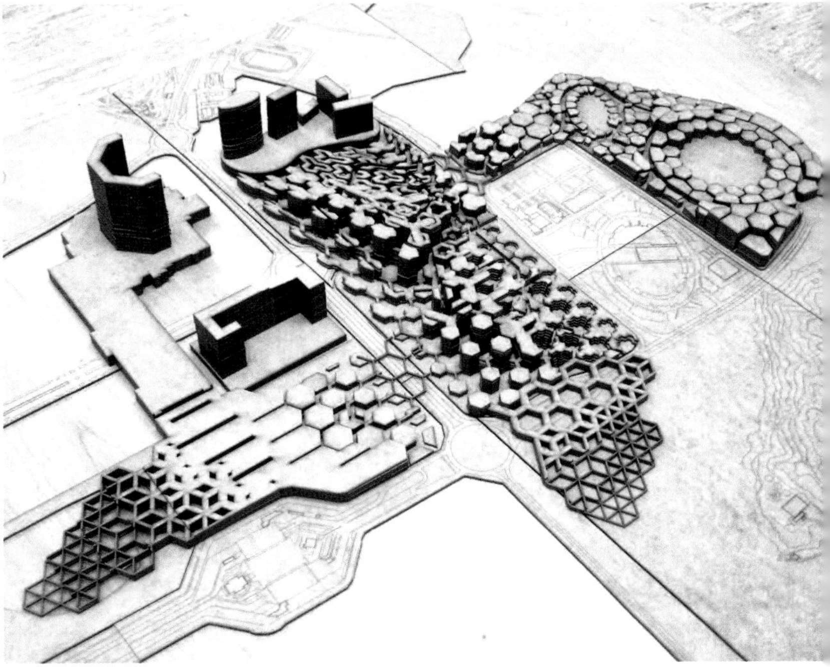

Urban prototype model of the proposed aggregate massing order for Cotai, Macau. (Studio Tutor: Tom Verebes; Students: Chan Chi Yin Stephen, Yeung Hiu Lei Samuel; MArch II Studio, *Forgetting Macau*, The University of Hong Kong, 2010)

NOTES

1 > T. Verebes (2012) *New Computational Paradigms in Architecture* (Beijing: Tsinghua).

2 > M. Burry (2011) *Scripting Cultures: Architectural Design and Programming* (Chichester: Wiley), 11.

3 > See C. Pasquero and M. Poletto (2012) *Systemic Architecture: Operating Manual for the Self-Organizing City* (New York: Routledge).

4 > K. Terzidis (2006) *Algorithmic Architecture* (Oxford: Elsevier), xi.

5 > Terzidis, *Algorithmic Architecture*, 54.

6 > R. Woodbury (2010) *Elements of Parametric Design* (New York: Routledge), 83.

7 > L. Iwamoto (2009) *Digital Fabrications: Architectural and Material Techniques* (New York: Princeton), 4.

8 > R. Banham (1960) *Theory and Design in the First Machine Age* (Oxford: Butterworth-Heinemann), 210.

9 > A. Menges and S. Ahlquist (2011) "Introduction," in *Computational Design Thinking*, eds. A. Menges and S. Ahlquist (Chichester: Wiley), 13.

10 > Terzidis, *Algorithmic Architecture*, 24.

11 > S. Kwinter (2003) "The Computational Fallacy" *Thresholds—Denatured* 26 (Cambridge: MIT), 90–91.

12 > See G. Stiny and J. Gips (1972) "Shape Grammars and the Generative Specification of Painting and Sculpture" *Information Processing* 71: 1460–1465.

13 > Terzidis, *Algorithmic Architecture*, 48.

14 > Burry, *Scripting Cultures*, 148.

15 > G. Pask (1995) "Foreword," in *An Evolutionary Architecture*, John Frazer (London: AA Publications), 6.

16 > S. Kwinter (2011) *Requiem for the City at the End of the Millennium* (Barcelona: Actar), 74.

17 > Burry, *Scripting Cultures*, 79.

18 > M. De Landa (2003) "Deleuze and the Use of the Genetic Algorithm in Architecture" in *Phylogenesis: FOA's Ark*, Foreign Office Architects (Barcelona: Actar), 520–529.

19 > P. Trummer (2011) "Associative Design," in *Computational Design Thinking*, eds. A. Menges and S. Ahlquist (London: Wiley), 18.

20 > P.J. Bentley and D.W. Corne (2011) "Creative Evolutionary Systems," in *Computational Design Thinking*, eds. A. Menges and S. Ahlquist (London: Wiley), 123–124.

21 > Bentley and Corne, "Creative Evolutionary Systems," 125.

22 > M. Felsen (2007) "Complex Populations," in *Models: 306090*, Volume 11, eds. E. Abruzzo, E. Ellingsen, J. Solomon (New York: Princeton), 166.

23 > Burry, *Scripting Cultures*, 86.

24 > M. Batty (2005) *Cities and Complexity*, Chapter 1, Urban Change (MIT Press, Cambridge, 2005), 7–8.

25 > Batty, *Cities and Complexity*, 21.

26 > Batty, *Cities and Complexity*.

27 > C. Reas (2007) *Processing: A Programming Handbook for Visual Designers and Artists* (Cambridge: MIT).

28 > C. Reas (2007) "Beyond Code," in *Network Practices: New Strategies in Architecture and Design*, eds. A. Burke, and T. Tierney (New York: Princeton), 166.

29 > P.S. Cohen (2010) "The Return of Nature," in *Ecological Urbanism*, eds. M. Mostafavi and G. Doherty (Baden: Lars Müller), 136.

30 > Burry, *Scripting Cultures*, 224.

31 > M. Hensel (2012) *Design Innovation for the Built Environment* (New York: Routledge), 126.

32 > D.E. Ingber (2010) "Bioinspired Adaptive Architecture and Sustainability," in *Ecological Urbanism*, eds. M. Mostafavi and G. Doherty (Baden: Lars Müller), 308.

33 > N. Negroponte (1969) "Towards a Humanism through Machines," in *Architectural Design* 7, no. 6: 511.

34 > Burry, *Scripting Cultures*, 8.

35 > L. Iwamoto (2009) *Digital Fabrications: Architectural and Material Techniques* (New York: Princeton), 4.

36 > B. Koralevic (2003) "Information and Master Builders," in *Architecture in the Digital Age*, ed. B. Koralevic (New York: Spon Press), 57.

37 > J. Burry and M. Burry (2010) *The New Mathematics of Architecture* (New York: Thames & Hudson), 117.

38 > J.H. Frazer (2006) "Exploring the Analogy that Parametric Design is a Game," in *Game Set Match: On Computer Games, Advanced Geometries and Digital Technologies*, eds. K. Oosterhuis and L. Feireiss (Rotterdam: Episode), 208–209.
39 > Frazer, "Exploring the Analogy that Parametric Design is a Game," 211.
40 > Burry and Burry, *The New Mathematics of Architecture*, 13.
41 > Burry and Burry, *The New Mathematics of Architecture*, 117.
42 > Burry and Burry, *The New Mathematics of Architecture*, 119.
43 > J. Frazer (1995) *An Evolutionary Architecture* (London: AA Publications), 14.
44 > Frazer, *An Evolutionary Architecture*, 14.
45 > M. Speaks (2008) *Design Engineering AKT*, ed. H. Kara (Barcelona: Actar), 218.
46 > C. Jencks (2002) "Introduction," in *Informal*, C. Balmond (London: Pretzel Publishing), 5.
47 > P. Schumacher (2008) *Design Engineering AKT*, ed. H. Kara (Barcelona: Actar), 69.
48 > H. Kara (2008) *Design Engineering AKT*, ed. H. Kara (Barcelona: Actar), 9.
49 > D.J. Gerber (2009) *The Parametric Affect: Computation, Innovation and Models for Design Exploration in Contemporary Architectural Practice* (Cambridge: Harvard GSD), 17.
50 > Gerber, *The Parametric Affect*, 17.
51 > Gerber, *The Parametric Affect*, 71.
52 > Vitruvius (1914) *The Ten Books on Architecture*, trans. M.H. Morgan, 21.
53 > Burry, *Scripting Cultures*, 19.
54 > P. Schumacher (2011) *The Autopoesis of Architecture, Vol. 1* (Chichester: Wiley).
55 > R. Banham (1960) *Theory and Design in the First Machine Age* (Oxford: Butterworth-Heinemann), 248.
56 > P. Schumacher (2012) *The Autopoesis of Architecture, Vol. 2* (Chichester: Wiley), 680–686.
57 > D.G. Shane (2011) *Urban Design Since 1945: A Global Perspective* (London: Wiley), 14.
58 > H. Kara (2008) *Design Engineering AKT* (Barcelona: Actar), 9.

CHAPTER 16

DAVID JASON GERBER > PARAMETRIC URBANISM REDUX

URBAN DESIGN AND COMPLEXITY IN AN AGE OF INFINITE COMPUTING

In the designing of urban infrastructure—its physical, economic, social, and biological systems and abstract geometric rule sets—one must consider the evolution of technology and its appropriations and applications. At issue is less the terminology or classification of, for example, explicit, top-down, parametric or algorithmic, and bottom-up, than an understanding of these as an amalgamation and paradigmatic shift in the practice of urban design (Kuhn 1996).[1] How to best "plan" for the present and near-term future of design in the age of infinite computing and the algorithm is the critical question. The position taken is simply that ostensibly we are just at the cusp of a paradigm shift which will finally enable the design and planning of large-scale urban infrastructure to embrace both top-down parametric design exploration and correlation with multi-agent systems and the exploration of emergent behaviors in highly complex and coupled dynamical systems. In short, as designers of the cities of the future we will be able to more accurately and with more formal ingenuity and confidence break down the monotony and homogeneity of twentieth-century planning tropes and begin to engender, harness, and enable urban vitality through an incorporation of emergent and intelligent intricacy, heterogeneity, and urban fluidity, as modeled and tested through both generative and parametric processes.

An issue for urban designers is the need to account for adaptation, evolution, uncertainty, and the influence of design technology and methods. At the core of a designer's agenda and goals for urbanism should be goals for urban identity and the enabling of productive emergence, and for the delivery of vitality and vibrancy in both the bottom-up and top-down fashions. All of these goals and opportunities are experiencing a newfound set of design exploration capabilities which are foundationally engendering complexity through an ever-more present, ubiquitous computing infrastructure. I use the term "design exploration" deliberately, as design implies the search of a solution space comprised of trade-offs and choice. In this way, contemporary digital design research has gained a new focus, on the informing of form through bottom-up approaches. One interest is understanding materiality at the cellular level to enhance the tectonic, affectual, and optimal sustainability in the use of material in the search for novel and informed form. Here and at the far end of the design scale spectrum similar approaches have been researched for over a decade, to achieve similar intrinsic intelligence to that of urbanism. Yet there is something inherently counterintuitive in the notion of the masterplan, in the use of both the term "master" and the term "plan." Evolution has no master nor does it have an explicit plan, beyond DNA and transcription rules.[2] This terminology suggests in itself a top-down concept, yet the desirable theory and practice of enabling the evolving city is more akin to bottom-up and emergent un-planning. In order for the cities of today, whether the wholly new in growing Asian economies or the regenerative in the west, to achieve a sustained growth in the capitalist model and with a sense of urgency for sustainability in the twenty-first century, a rethinking of the process for planning must be addressed. It is in the context of design processes, digital tools and techniques, and new computing paradigms that the argument for masterplanning in an age of infinite computing is manifest.

It is no longer adequate simply to provide the top-down plan and expect to see the city emerge as intended. Conversely, we cannot apply no rules at all to the growth of urban form. While it can be argued that a paradigm—both parametric and algorithmic—is happening with respect to the planning of the city, it has yet to be fully embraced or fully implemented. One of the recent emphases of the Rockefeller Foundation's research has been on the regenerative and adaptive city, on the city that will need to be designed and enabled in the face of crisis, whether climatic, economic, environmental, or more likely a coupled mixture of all of these. Their interest speaks to the issues we as designers must face, in simple terms complexity within dynamical systems. These issues are ever-more complex, multi-disciplinary, coupled, and consequently complexly correlated. While we can attest to our technological capability and an increase in our ability to manage complexity, what needs to be further theorized, experimented upon, validated, and tuned is in fact the mix of top-down and bottom-up design processes. At our fingertips or mouse clicks, in the background and in the participatory social network foreground, is the new paradigm of cloud computing, the economics and democratization of which need to be thought out in terms of their current, near-, and long-term impact on the development of existing and new urban conditions. Simplistically, infinite computing suggests the cost of the calculation is approaching zero, meaning that computing power itself is rapidly experiencing commodification. If this is the case then the designer, or more likely the interdisciplinary design team, must break down the barriers to including highly complex modeling and emergent behavior as part of the planning process.

While parametric urbanism has been a term and a project for over a decade now, with its origins in Singapore's Science Hub Development Group's One North project designed and delivered by the office of Zaha Hadid Architects, and further developed conceptually and practically in my own research, it remains a paradigm shift still in the making. Parametric urbanism has for some become a stylistic and formal endeavor, but it must be argued and understood more complexly as seeking to break down the top-down plan and infuse it with a highly correlative growth and synergy strategy which also intensifies the importance of intricacy and urban fluidity. Parametric urbanism would not have been possible without the use of digital tools and techniques that in the past involved lots of manual modeling and table-based accounting. While many of these tasks can now be in part automated (computerized) and/or more directly made relational (parameterized), there remains work to be done beyond even the most sophisticated parametric design definitions of today.[3]

One North, now ten years in progress, is a perfect opportunity for reflection on the evolution of architecture-driven masterplanning. In the context of Patrik Schumacher's parametricism[4] and the often-scrutinized urbanization of China, the processes and strategies of One North are bearing fruit in terms of furthering an advanced approach to the planning and design of dense urban infrastructure. At the core of this reflection is a discussion of the top-down versus the bottom-up

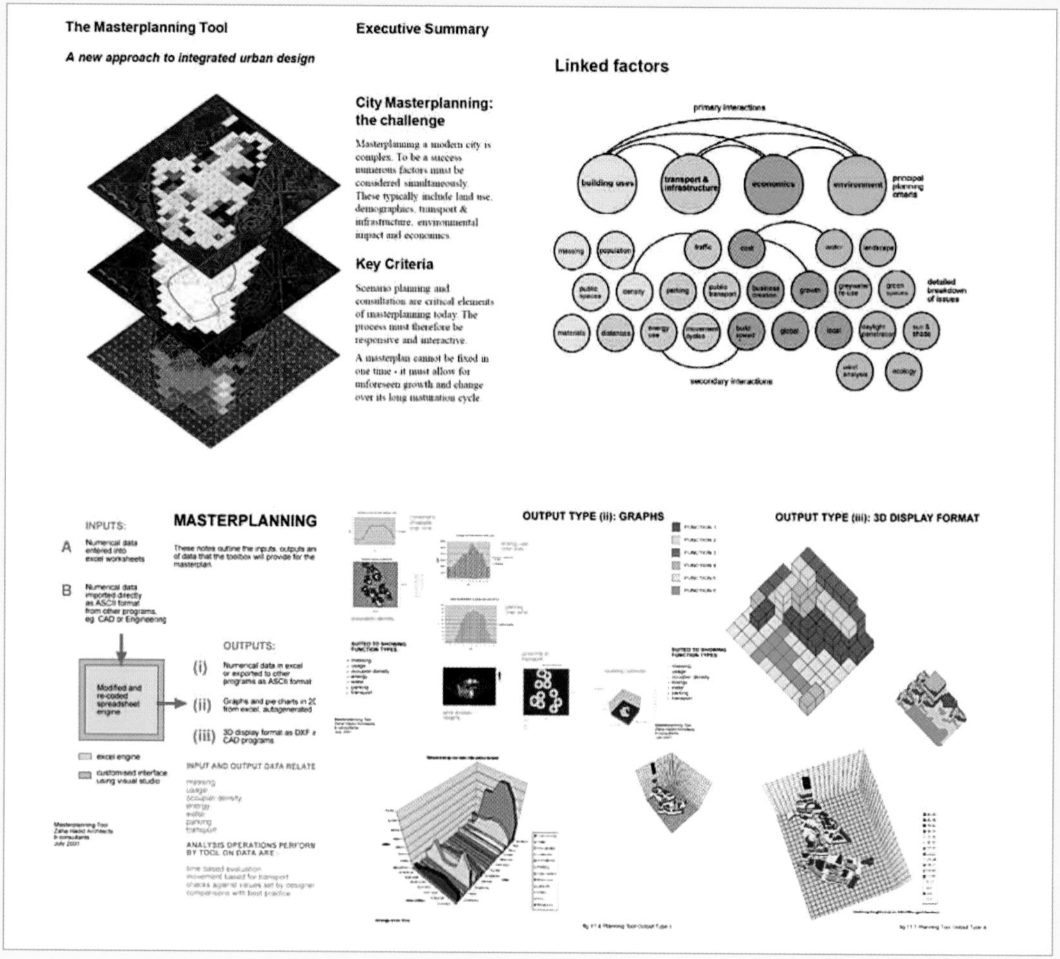

The Masterplanning Tool
A new approach to integrated urban design
Executive Summary
City Masterplanning: the challenge
Masterplanning a modern city is complex. To be a success numerous factors must be considered simultaneously. These typically include land use, demographics, transport & infrastructure, environmental impact and economics.
Key Criteria
Scenario planning and consultation are critical elements of masterplanning today. The process must therefore be responsive and interactive.
A masterplan cannot be fixed in one time - it must allow for unforeseen growth and change over its long maturation cycle.
Linked factors
primary interactions
building uses
transport & infrastructure
economics
environment
principal planning criteria
detailed breakdown of issues
secondary interactions
INPUTS:
MASTERPLANNING
A
B
OUTPUTS:
(i)
(ii)
(iii)
OUTPUT TYPE (ii): GRAPHS
OUTPUT TYPE (iii): 3D DISPLAY FORMAT

Demonstration of methodology and potential for the Masterplanning Tool.

within a dual push and pull. On one hand, the demands of the commercial and government client, and on the other the demands for exceptionalism and innovation of a now-Pritzker-prize-winning visionary Zaha Hadid.

In retrospect, much of what was proposed is, I would argue, still of relevance today. Much of the involvement of the client was appropriately directed toward a successful implementation of a commercially driven and strategic plan. The key drivers of the approach were a fluid landform approach influenced by the sketches of Zaha and Patrik Schumacher's sense for a topographically warped grid and void strategy. Though fluidity was intrinsic to our design sensibility it was not yet made explicit in the parameterizations. Another key driver was the notion of flexible growth and density through a radial and gradiated formal approach. Core to the top-down approach was establishing a minimum of common-sense loci for high-density and "anchor" tenants with which we expected to see increased mix and differentiated density in moving away from major epicenters and nodes of high-throughput transportation. Essential to the approach was a top-down establishment of voids, some understood as major park elements and others as pocket parks with a varied distribution and flexible in form. At the core of the void strategy was a new street form and approach for Singapore, one where an intentional proximity of façade to façade was incorporated to insure local climate shading and environmental advantage, as well as to enliven the street use and culture.

The One North project was the first to deploy the at-the-time unnamed parametric urbanism approach (on which I first published in *Interactive Cities* in 2007[5]). The project laid a foundation not only for the coining of the term but also for a multiyear brief undertaken at the AA DRL, as well as my own PhD work developed at Harvard's Graduate School of Design and MIT's Media Lab. The tools and technologies enabling the development of the approach included explicit modeling, both in geometric terms and through numeric tables and formulae. At issue was the dual problem of satisfying both the governmental strategic outcomes through some sense of metrics and the vision for a dynamic and contemporary and sustained urban culture desired by the office of Zaha Hadid Architects. At the inception of the invited competition I put forward the idea of developing a software toolkit—"the planning tool," as it was called then—that would enable the client and their design team to evolve scenarios and to adjust the plan as concretized decisions were made. The planning tool became a parallel

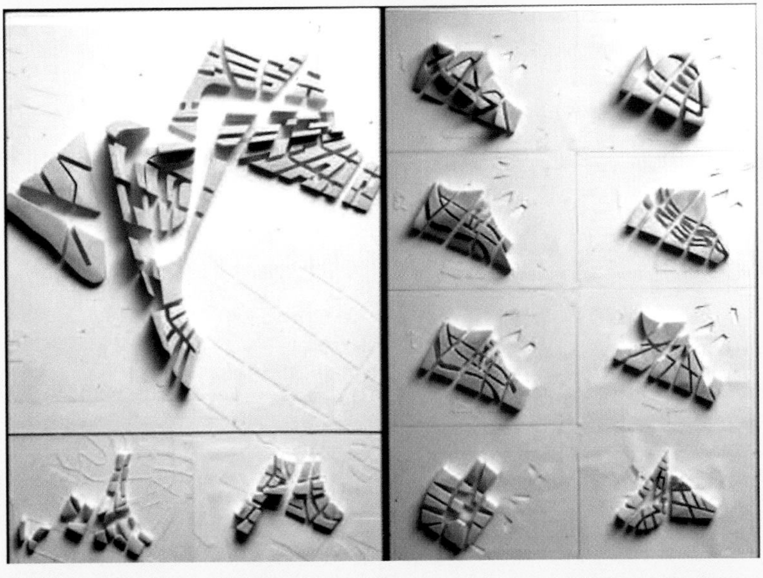

Models of variations of massing.

project, alongside the normal expected deliverables of the overall masterplan and detailed design guidelines. In our own vacuum we invented a prototypical approach that would engender much of what has become known as parametric urbanism. In its most simplified version, one can view it as a relational model of geometry driving planning tables and data sheets. More complexly, we could scenario-plan from geometry as a starting point and gain insight into the myriad civil engineering, resource utilization, transportation capture, and economic models and their results.

The strongest aspect of this paradigmatic project is in fact a core tenet of the parametricism theorized by Patrik Schumacher, namely the notion of integration and correlation in the design process. On one hand, the need for top-down decision making is unquestionable if one is to achieve a stylistic vision, yet on the other hand the project engendered a belief in flexible and self-generated growth patterns through complex networks of design relationships and multiple constituencies' goals. Aligning of these goals and understanding trade-offs, along with a need to manage rapid design exploration, was the impetus for the theorizing and protoytping of the parametric urbanism approach. It must be emphasized that the technology to pursue such an approach had not trickled down to architecture—we invented it from scratch. It must also be said that even the terminology had yet to become a de facto standard of the architectural lexicon; we were the first to use it. This work I later carried on into the development of a PhD entitled "Parametric Practices: Models for Design Exploration in Architecture," which in particular enumerated techniques for developing and deploying parametric design in architecture and for understanding the spectrum of pre- to post-rationalization purposes and approaches as they pertained to practice and pedagogy; in essence an initial questioning of the top-down versus bottom-up capabilities inherent in parametric design techniques and technologies and a categorization of to what end they can be used. What has since evolved is the prevalent use of the terminology, technology, and theorizing of the epoch, in the form of parametricism.

Despite a dependence on traditional modeling, explicit trial and error, and to some degree the use of our parametric design thinking, the core ideas in the One North masterplan included the idea of an armature to foster emergent growth and emergent mix. There was a belief in a multinodal and non–ring road or locked transportation infrastructure. The work fostered the ideas of protecting the void and of a modulated density. While the project was inherently top-down, through to the design guidelines of each parcel, it was conceived through a growth model akin to the biological; in some sense lichen-esque, yet not quite modeled and developed in that fashion. Underlying the team's agenda for a formalism that was beyond the norm, to say the least, was a belief in a tightly coupled experience of urbanism, of intricacy and fluidity amongst programs and populations and environments. Inbuilt in the strategy was self-regulation within the hostile environmental conditions and with respect to the constraints the project economics demanded. Intrinsic to the working methods was a correlative approach, or the integral approach of three- and and four-dimensional models to that of the planning economic tables. While the team had not operated with an understanding of the notion of parametric design common in mechanical engineering, we did build a planning tool incorporating these concepts, as independently invented. What we foresaw was a concept and project content defense and data management problem. Our solution was to link as much as possible the impact of one with the other. Fundamentally, once the project was out of our hands we wanted to enable the client to protect the vision they had chosen, and to do so in their terms as well as those of Zaha Hadid Architects. The net result of the process was a traditional top-down planning document. Yet our ambition was to enable growth and self-organization as much as possible under and within a top-down structure. At the core was the concept of the gradient plan. While the gradient is evident in the graphics, the work addressed much more complexly the problem of all or nothing, and the enabling of system dynamics.

Ten years post the delivery of the One North masterplan a problem for the future architecturally driven parametric urbanism is in part the need to understand the limitations of parametric design approaches, and, more conceptually, the need for a regenerative and more rapid-response approach to urbanism. In experiencing first hand the rapid development of China's first- and second-tier cities and the cause and effect of planning decisions in terms of quality of life, environment, and social upward mobility, the resourcing of these rapid developments, and a lack of reflection as to their long-term affects, clearly we can see a new set of challenges for the future. Of interest to the design community is the incorporation of novel biologically and computationally enhanced approaches which incorporate a more robust and richly complex set of approaches, those of the generative. While many criticize Patrik Schumacher's term "parametricism" as exclusive of the algorithmic approaches, I understand it to be inclusive of the notions of the correlative and the integrative, and inclusive of the importance of style and design quotient without which there are no projects. It is in this vein that we continue to evolve away from the "master," top-down approaches and move toward the mastery of the mix of both signature and the absence of signature.

Cities and places in order to thrive are requisite of design and in order to achieve a sustaining vitality of vision and identity the question is maybe: To what degree is signature necessary and to what degree is the architect's plan flexible and intelligent enough to enable a regenerative and responsive armature? If we are to "plan" and therefore implement some degree of the top down, at issue is how, where, and how much can we incorporate the notion of the complex, the biological, the self-organizing aspects of the complex socioeconomic design dynamic. For me, herein lies the problem opportunity for the future. Planning remains fraught with peril with respect to the design process itself and even more so with respect to the delivering of regenerative and responsive urban armatures. In essence, how do we provide enough body plan or DNA to enable a self-sustaining growth and one that also incorporates its own stops and switches? This peril is even more easy to see when we ourselves are not sure what it means when the music stops or when growth is no longer the sole driving force.

Much of my recent work has been on the development of multidomain design integration and optimization methods. Optimization in many respects can be undermined in architectural discourse, however the approach I have taken is one predicated on better-informed understanding of the trade-offs of dynamic and complex relationships. It is an approach inclusive of simple computerization, as Terzidis identifies, but more importantly one of the generative, as I have defined in my own work. I have sometimes called this integration and correlation approach "design optioneering" or, here, in the context of masterplanning, "optioneering urbanism." Given the nature of cities the prediction sciences acknowledge the uncertainty factors as being enormous, hence the continuing need for inventive human designers, however the value of the infinite computing paradigm is such that at the least we can evaluate more rapidly much more complex sets of correlated and competing design factors and agendas, and include scenarios of disaster, for example. It is here the position is most clearly manifested; simplistically, with the availability of infinite computing we as designers are far less restricted and therefore far more enabled to design with highly complex dynamic systems in mind. In other words, the reductionist approaches to much of how we design can in time be avoided, and the delight in ever more intricate design exploration can be fostered toward results which reflect stylistic top-down signature to some degree coupled with self-assembling intelligence contained within multiagent systems. Finally, if there is any lesson to be learned, it is that the masterplanning process is becoming both ever-more complex and ever-more enabled by infinite computing. Yet while we can model and design and correlate the expanding sets of objectives, constraints, and correlations, a wholesale review of the approach must be contextualized from a global to local scale. Similarly the idea of the totally emergent planning process must also be tempered by the reality that even within a multiagent system a set of rules are written—cohesion, avoidance, and attraction to name the basic few. My work going forward begins to account much more robustly for ever-more complex biologically inspired and driven phenomena within urban design, such as contagion, difference, habituation, and choice. From here we can expect to model, simulate, test, and deliver ever-more rich urban schemes built upon the notions of the evolutionary plan for urban design. It is upon reflecting on our parametric urbanism origins that we can benchmark our continued progress into the desirable unplanned future, one that we can only hope will promote the importance of stylistic endeavors and form, and one that will much more robustly incorporate the powers of agency, complexity, and the phenotypical proliferation, or in other words urbanism's potential for intricacy and superfluid generation and regeneration.

NOTES

1 > Thomas S. Kuhn (1996) *The Structure of Scientific Revolutions*, 3rd ed. (Chicago: University of Chicago Press).

2 > J.H. Frazer (1995) *An Evolutionary Architecture* (London: Architectural Association).

3 > Kostas Terzidis (2006) *Algorithmic Architecture* (Abingdon, UK: Taylor & Francis).

4 > Patrik Schumacher (2009) "Parametricism: A New Global Style for Architecture and Urban Design," *AD Architectural Design* 79, no. 4.

5 > D. Gerber (2007) "Towards a Parametric Urbanism," in *Interactive Cities*, ed. Valérie Châtelet (Paris: Editions Hyx). In English and French.

CHAPTER 17

CONVERSATION 5

SU YUNSHENG (SYS) WITH TOM VEREBES (TM)

TV Su Yunsheng, you have extensive experience of the urbanization of China, and your insights are highly valuable for this book. There have been great synergies in our professional and academic collaborations since 2005. I am keen to discuss with you the phenomenon of urbanization in terms of the achievements made, and also some of the problems associated to the largest, and fastest, urban project in the history of the world: the urbanization of modern China. I'd like to discuss the ten million units of housing per year which the central government intends to build for the foreseeable future, which will lead to three hundred to four hundred million additional rural people being urbanized in the coming decades. Different from cities which have long existed and expand, can you share your thoughts on the phenomenon of instant cities in twenty-first-century China?

SYS There are many reasons which contribute to why so many instant cities have sprouted in China, and this is a unique phenomenon that has never happened before in human history. During the ten years of the Cultural Revolution, urbanization stopped during the 1960s and 70s, and since then the pressure has been relieved. For thirty years since 1979, urbanization has been so rapid because it was suppressed and slowed down, just like when you relieve built up pressure, matter explodes out. This is the issue of speed. In addition, the government owns the land, they can easily move the population from one place to another. In countries where land is owned privately, Japan for example, to build infrastructure networks or larger urban developments land needs to be purchased from individuals, which can involve complicated negotiations over several years. China's efficiency comes from land being controlled at the national level. We also lack a robust bottom-up social system to enable all people to be involved in decision-making processes. We only have top-down decisions. When the mayors of cities are changed every two to five years, they often have a new plan and a new way of thinking, which allows urban planning to change. Sometimes this is good, as improvements can be made efficiently, but there is the risk of making mistakes from wrong decisions, very quickly. In the past, we lacked housing, food, and money. People are no longer hungry, and they have clothes to wear and houses to live in. It is now time to increase the quality of life in China, and it is better to slow down to make higher quality cities. We need long-term thinking. This cannot be solved only at a design level. Problems in the social, political, and economic systems need to be solved together, and this will be a big challenge for China in the next thirty years.

TV Given the speed of development and the changes which have occurred in Chinese society, in which ways do you think the social order of cities can be maintained, yet evolved, as the older material fabric of cities changes? Or is it inevitable that if one erases earlier urbanism and replaces it with a newer, more contemporary one, does this almost obliterate the social order that came with it?

SYS Actually these days there are great arguments about how to protect historic physical and social urban fabric of both high and low quality. Cities in China are so dynamic because developers' visions focus on profiting from land and construction, so existing fabric is erased to build anew. The social voice of existing urban fabric is very weak compared to that of developers, who are close with the government. Many experts are focussing on the value of traditional historic fabric, but their voice is weak because more density is needed to upgrade cities for the emerging middle class. A different way of thinking is to use policies in certain urban areas. For example, families, they can upgrade slowly, piece by piece, or they can do more simple alterations, rather than to tear down buildings and build new ones. Another argument, for example, is made in a public social housing project I am working on. We are challenging the idea of social housing as small units in a fixed structure, but rather making a structural skeleton with more long term flexibility, for a longer life cycle of a hundred years. Building interiors can be made more flexible to adapt to different functions and different family types. When a new city is proposed, debates often arise between short-term or long-term visions, and their economic arguments. There is little support on a social level or from business models for long-term value.

TV You're raising two very interesting issues. Firstly, the speed at which cities are built, and the societal implications of which result, possibly not directly, from poor quality construction, leading to architecture, and the city, being conceived and understood as disposable. The second, and longer-term issue, raises questions about how cities grow and change, whether because a precinct either may no longer be deemed functionally adequate, they might be so dilapidated that upgrading is not an option. The history of cities is about incremental change, albeit sometimes in quick, short increments. If the historic city is preserved without meeting the needs of either population growth, for urban densification, or meeting the profit demands of investors, there is a risk to freeze history, stripping it of its social and cultural space. Maybe a balanced middle ground can be found between complete erasure and total preservation, which are the two paradoxical strategies China currently is grappling with. Mixing these strategies would lead to less coherent mixes of older and newer buildings, higher and lower densities, mixes of typologies. I am suggesting a model of urbanization which is less top-down and driven by very short-term intentions and gains. Given the various models of urban expansion and densification in modern China, I would like to also know your opinion on the debate between concentrated urban density, versus low-density urban sprawl, and also strategies aiming to grow and evolve cities rather than to plan them wholly?

SYS I think we should focus on the city as an organic thing. Chinese urban planning theory in the last thirty years has been underpinned by a mix of the Russian system, and functionalist modernist urban planning theory from Europe and America. Chinese masterplans are based on two-dimensional programmatic color coding. There is not much mixing of functions vertically and the urban model is based on road grids built for cars which separate the functions of the city. There are pioneering theories heading in other directions, but we have already built a lot.

High-density Asian urbanism, for example Hong Kong and Singapore, is often referred to, as they have developed public transportation, vertically mixed use functions, open spaces, and pedestrian networks. Many Chinese cities are building subway lines, which is counter to the model of Pudong [developed on the east side of the Huang Pu River in Shanghai since 1987], which has already been reconsidered. One-hundred-metre-wide roads separate sectors of the city into islands. As for other urban models, I think Dubai is only focussed on style, and a low-density American model has also been rethought.

TV Through centralized top-down planning, the grid has been spread across China, but it's difficult to fix a sprawling low-density city built primarily for car transportation. In some ways, top-down, centralized planning processes and regulatory systems are at odds with bottom-up decision making and action.

Let's come back to the issue of the organic in urbanism. The city has been thought of as organic in terms of the way it grows and changes, or in the way that the city enables dynamic behavior of its citizens, and others have even argued for the city as analogous to a living organism. These formulations can be contrasted to modernism, in which the city was conceived and understood as a mechanized set of systems. I too am grappling with the complex paradox between biological and mechanical paradigms in urbanism.

SYS A mechanical city is about the space of buildings and its machine-like infrastructure, but an organic city is living, is about people. To think of a city as an organic thing, you cannot take out social exchange. Nowadays half to one-third of the Chinese government's income comes from the sale of land. They focus on making land more valuable, to sell more land. This orientation allows centralized, top-down decision making to commission big masterplans with little care for future development within their speculations. The government's income also comes from personal and corporate income tax, and property sales and income taxes, to build better cities, attract knowledge, and augment the economy. Long-term visions focus on the people, not only on land. There is a difference between cities based on tax from income from land sales and those based on income tax. The Chinese government is trying to switch from a land-orientated economy to a more property-orientated one. I believe the government will respect the opinions of citizens of a city, because by paying tax to the government they can have opinions and vote for their mayor. This is maybe a long-term vision for social agreement for not only one leader to have power to make urban development happen. Of course, there is much discussion about democratic systems in China, but because it's a big country with a huge population, with many uneducated people, so our system needs to be efficient, but we need to find balance. I think this is about value of people, about how they make the city organic. We are pushing toward a better direction, but the bottom line is still the income sources and structures of the government.

TV The scope of urbanism as always is interwoven with the political space of cities, but I am not a political scientist nor an economist. From an architect's point of view, the intense urbanization of China is resulting in countless uniform cities that are spatially homogenous and repetitive. Urbanism is still being conceived from outmoded planning mechanisms and organizational models aligned to a Fordist model of standardized production. Computational design and production systems may help to instill compelling differences in the countless cities across the nation. I am interested how Chinese cities in the future can be differentiated to local historic, cultural, geographic, and environmental specificities. Given China's trajectory toward globalization and internationalization, will China find a means with which to evolve more unique, heterogeneous attributes to cities? How do you foresee new modes of nonstandard production to influence Chinese cities to develop particular, identifiable features in the coming decades?

SYS These are important questions. Firstly, when development happens without urban planning, different regions develop different social and material culture, food, language, building typologies, and technologies, as a model of diversity. China had a clear hierarchical structure in empire times, which brought about many local and regional differences in architecture, towns, and cities, but by now much local culture has become extinct. We need to protect traditional values and culture. Secondly, cities are identical because of the technologies used to design them. When we had hand-made cities, made from bricks and wood, we used to cut our own symbols on houses, to literally draw your own stories on your house. Now everything has become machine made and mass produced. I see this only as infrastructure. In the housing prototype I was describing earlier, we are conceiving architecture made from four systems: skin, skeleton, infill, and the MEP systems. The skeleton of the city can be more like infrastructure, and separated from the infill system. The skin can integrate the diversities of the climate, culture, community, and individuals. The infill part adapts to users' requirements, and could have a life cycle of ten to twenty years, but the skeleton can have a life cycle of one hundred to two hundred years, and the skin thirty to fifty years.

TV I recall the influence of *Plug-In City* by Archigram in the mid-1960s, which developed a model of a structural frame and infrastructure of the city within which people can customize space, or move it elsewhere. It seems, though, you are proposing this building prototype on an even larger scale of urban infrastructure.

SYS I am suggesting cities can behave in a more soft and supple mode. It has become very difficult these days to define cultural character. Looking back to history, contemporary Italian architecture has changed from ancient times. We should not misuse historical forms. We should make the city more able to adapt to change.

TV Through working on an intelligent approach to the design life of buildings, your aim in this project is to develop the ability for the city, through your prototype, to absorb change over long durations, to avoid obsolescence, wasteful demolition and constantly new construction. The intention is also to prevent architecture from being overly generic or disposable by extending a network approach to the city, because network topologies adapt well to changing conditions.

SYS These issues are at the core of why cities have become so similar. In China, we are having serious discussions about who has the right to make decisions. In traditional cities, each family follows regulations when they build their house. These regulations include the color of roofs, the numbers of south-facing rooms, while there are other freedoms, such as the dimensions of buildings and the numbers of courtyards. If you let people make decisions, they will follow each other, and new languages will emerge. Localities create character, although they might not be beautiful, but they are at least features.

TV It's interesting to contrast the traditional and contemporary worlds, globalization to local conditions, uniformity to uniqueness. I think the only risk is to say that in the past when the world was not globalized there was more cultural difference, and we now have too much uninformed nostalgia for looking back. What is needed is to find local articulations of difference with our contemporary industrial paradigms, without relying upon references such as traditional roofs to establish a cultural identity in the architecture of the city. In this vast country it will be fascinating to see how Chinese urbanism will be differentiated in the future, and how future cities might avoid the homogenizing tendencies of today's urbanism. Despite the force of globalization, it is the vitality of the differences between cities which remains compelling.

SYS As a last point, I am interested in how parametric design can make housing different, as we tried to demonstrate in our project for the Shenzhen Biennale.

TV One of the ways in which computational design, broadly speaking, and parametric design especially, can address these issues is spatial differentiation, based on local information informing universal systems.

SYS Still, I think we come back to the question of who makes decisions, the users or the single designer or commissioner. Diversity comes from bottom-up systems. This is what we're trying to do.

TV We're both trying!

CASE STUDY

dotA AND OCEAN CN >YAN JIAO HUA RUN 4D CITY, HEBEI PROVINCE, CHINA

This project was a joint venture collaboration between dotA and OCEAN CN.

Design Team:
dotA: Gao Yan, Duo Ning, Chang Qiang, Wang Xin, Yui Shuk Yin
OCEAN CN: Tom Verebes, Nathan Melenbrink (Coding)
Engineer: Chang Qiang (dotA)

Commissioned to design the layout of a block structure, road layout, and a broad and varied set of programs for a twenty-five-square-kilometer brownfield site fifty kilometers south of Beijing, our team developed a methodology for defining a masterplan as multiple, not singular, indeterminate rather than fixed. The masterplan still defines a specific set of articulated massing and ground coverage diagrams, as the outcome of a method of defining varied densities and architectural typologies. The parameters included heights, type and program as seeds, footprint, and landscape distribution. The riverfront, a canal, and some existing roads modulate the megablock infrastructural grid and differentiate its orientations and dimensions. Program mixes and a height diagram help to differentiate the massing and ground coverage of the proposal. As a method, the computational logic and interface developed in this project can be applied as a tool to manage the masterplan over years, while still aiming for a coherent identity to the city.

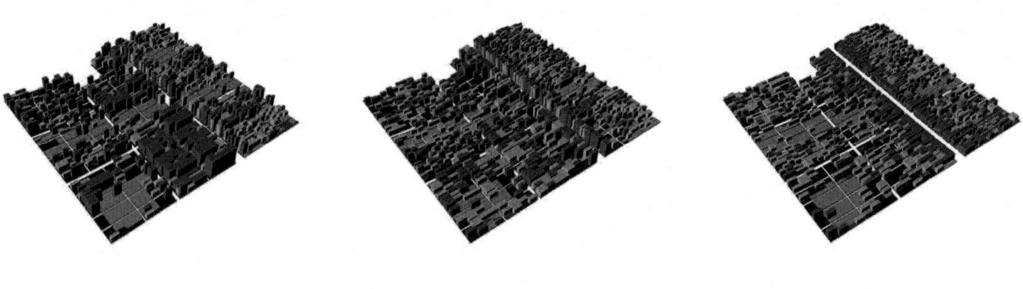

Three variations of a detailed 1-square-kilometer block, demonstrating varied programming and massing.

Exploded diagrams of systems, including block structures and massing organisation.

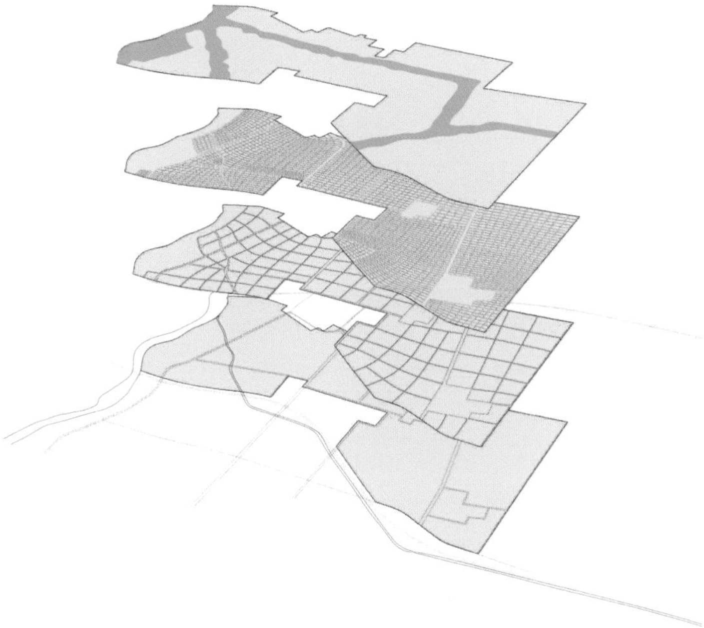

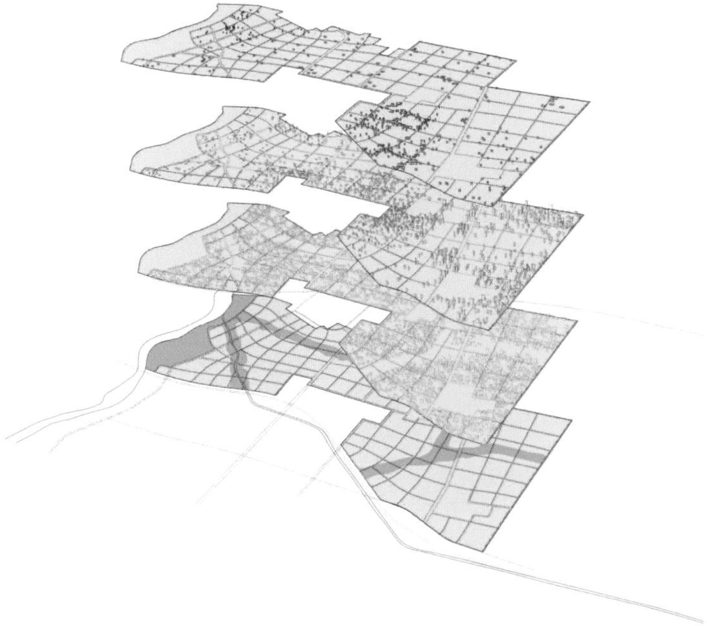

Final overall masterplanning options, based on different programmatic mixes and their associated typologies.

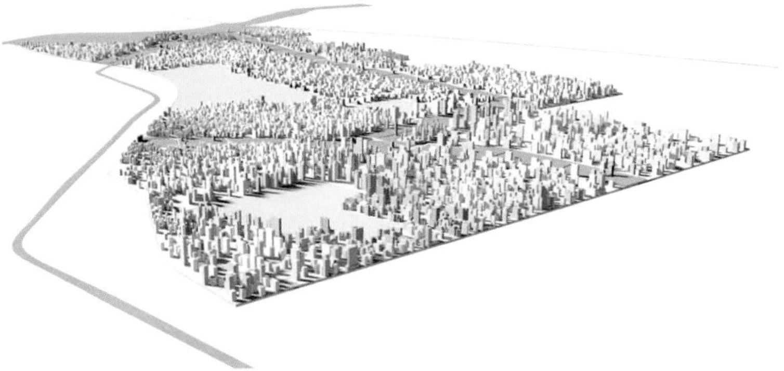

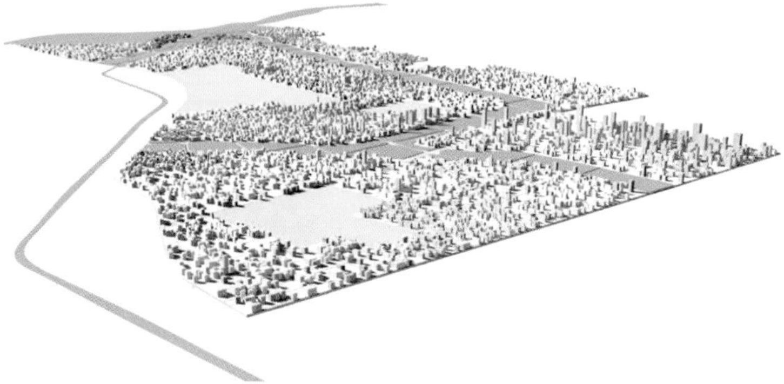

201
YAN JIAO HUA RUN 4D CITY

Series of density studies of a 500-by-500-meter block, demonstrating differential height, footprint, and typology mixes, based on variations of landscape patterns.

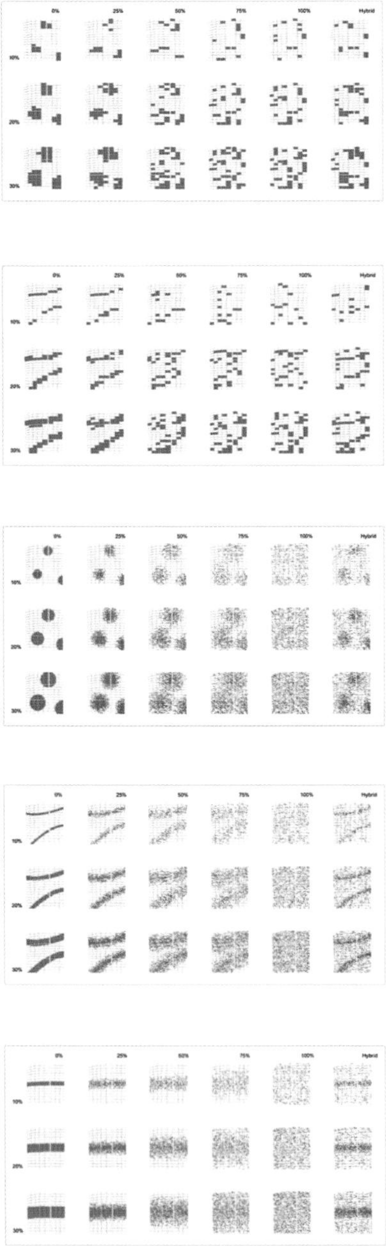

Graphic data for differential landscape patterns applied to density studies.

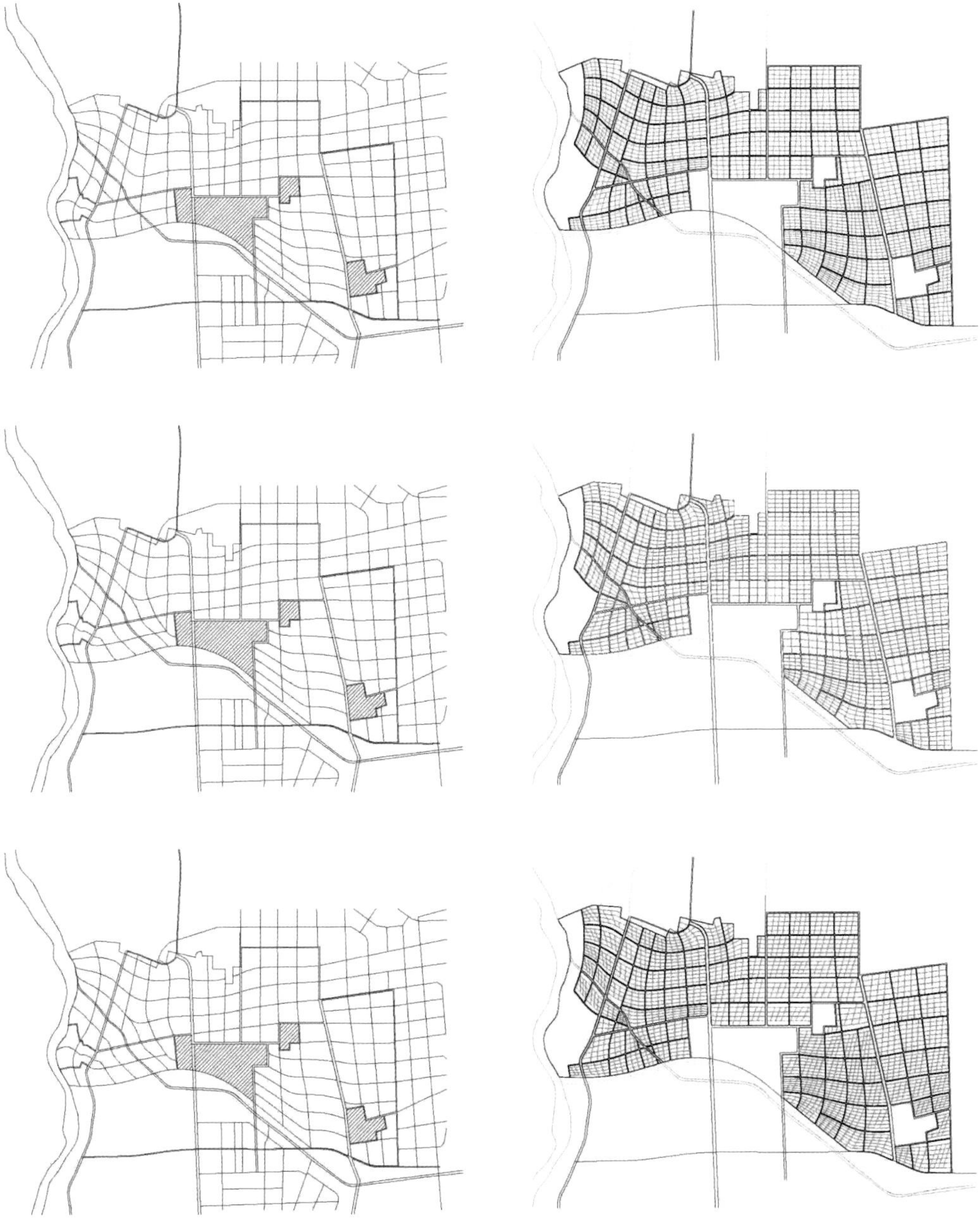

Three options for block patterns and subdivisions.

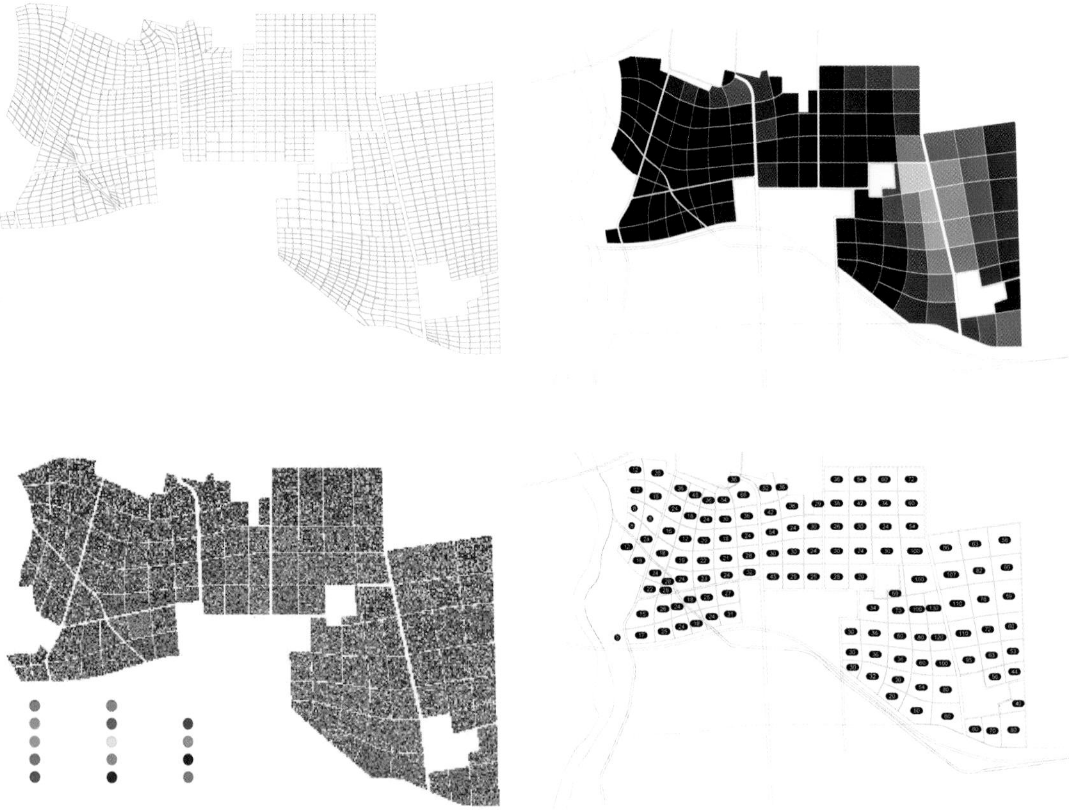

Block structure, subdivisions; urban envelope based on programmatic mixing diagram using a pointillist graphic notation.

CASE STUDY

GROUP8 ARCHITECTS AND KAISERSROT >MICA URBAN PICTURESQUE, GENEVA, SWITZERLAND

2008

This project was carried out as a joint venture with Kaisersrot supporting Group8 Architects, Geneva in an invited competition.

Partner: Group8 Architects, Geneva, Switzerland
Design Team: Kaisersrot (Markus Braach, Benjamin Dillenburger, Oliver Fritz, Alexander Lehnerer)

The topic of the competition was to define an urban enclave in the rural suburbs of Geneva. The program consists mainly of housing (ca. 400 flats with 40,000 square meters total area) and also commercial buildings and other activities (ca. 10,000 square meters). The concept was neither to start the design process with a formal system, for example a grid, nor to adapt existing typologies. Instead, Kaisersrot

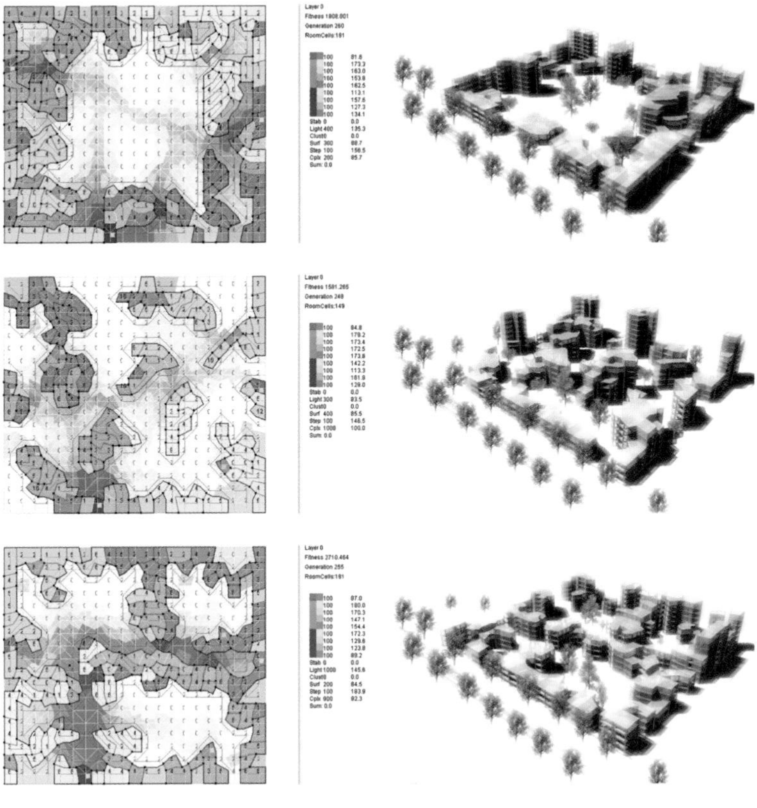

A software interface demonstrating visualizations of three variations of courtyard dimensions and the same mixture of apartments.

developed an informal, bottom-up approach, in which the form itself is not defined but rather only the global and local design goals. The solution is found through an evolutionary strategy within an open search space. As a result, new urban morphologies emerge that are grown rather than designed. No straight axis or repetitive, geometrical order dominates the layout, instead the buildings appear in a complex configuration: a new digital picturesque. With the software developed by Kaisersrot, it was possible to organize the 400 flats with optimized infrastructure, light exposure, and view, while maintaining the organic quality of the urban arrangement.

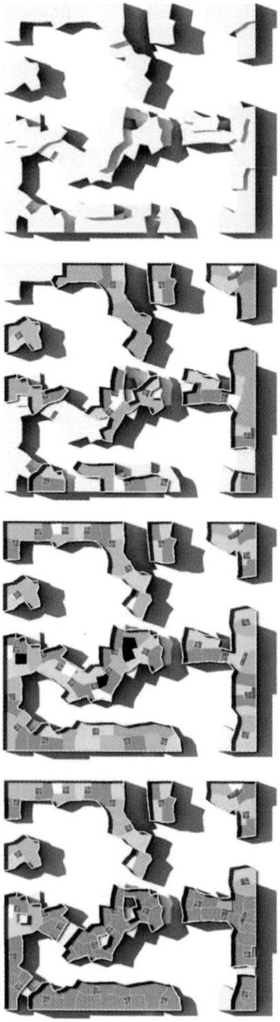

Top view and horizontal sections of the selected proposal, with each color representing a different apartment type.

Aerial view and plan of research work by Benjamin Dillenberger on agent-based evolutionary design systems.

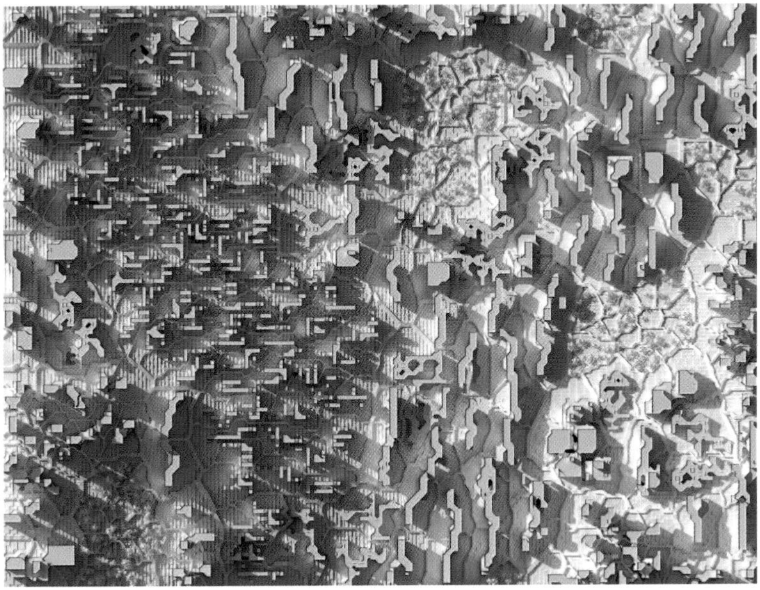

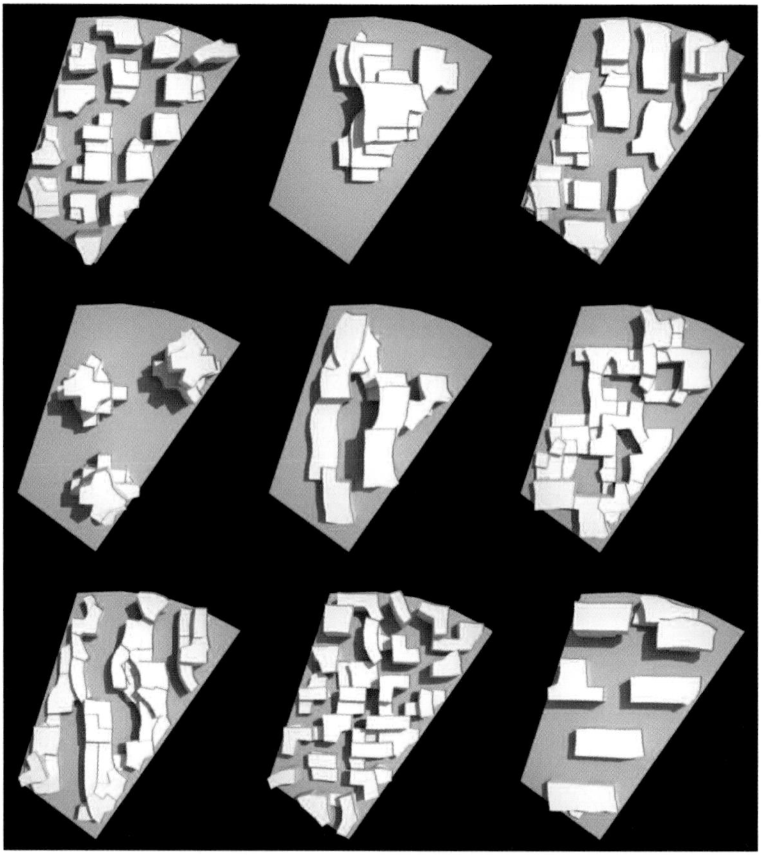

Research work by Benjamin Dillenberger demonstrating a series of varations in greater detail.

CASE STUDY

PETER TRUMMER, ASSOCIATIVE DESIGN PROGRAM, BERLAGE INSTITUTE >THE MEGABLOCK AND ITS POPULATED FIELD, AND THE AGGREGATION OF STREETS

2010

These projects were conceived and carried out within the Associative Design Program directed by Peter Trummer at the Berlage Institute, in 2010.

The Megablock and Its Populated Field: Peter Trummer with Janki Shah, Xiaodi Yang, and Marc Hoppermann (scripting support)
The Aggregation of Streets: Peter Trummer with Wei-Jung Hsu, Joune Ho Kim

These two related projects develop models and methods for the megablock and the street. Blocks have been used as architectural morphologies throughout the history of urbanization. In opposition to the famous plan of Barcelona, where the block was formed on the basis of the subdivision of land ownership, or to how blocks were used in postwar Vienna as megaforms for social housing, the megablock designed for this project, in Aspern, Vienna, is a block that contains various typologies. These typologies range from single-family houses to big urban block figures, on 500 individual plots driven by land values.

The Aggregation of Streets is based on Vienna's baroque avenues, used historically in the city to connect the city center with the hinterland. These roads continuously changed in character along their path between built and non-built areas. The project proposes a street–avenue hybrid which negotiates various architectural diagrams. The modernist diagram, whereby the buildings are detached from the street, is used in low-density areas, coupled with a premodern diagram where the houses are adjacent to the road for high-density areas. Also driven by economics, the street transforms into a sequential line of differentiated densities, as an urban mesh or an urban rhizome, without particular hierarchies, but rather singular moments of intensity.

The site for this project is the former Aspern airfield, located in the suburbs of Vienna. The intention is for a population of 20,000 to live and work there.

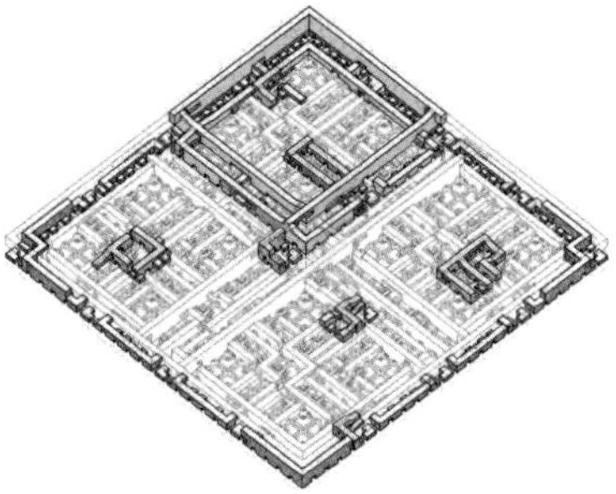

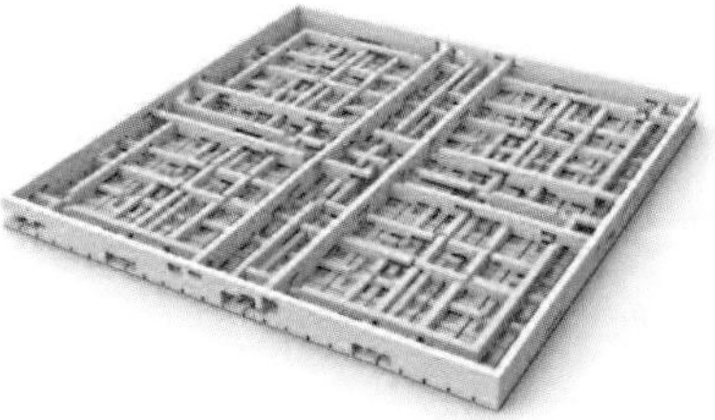

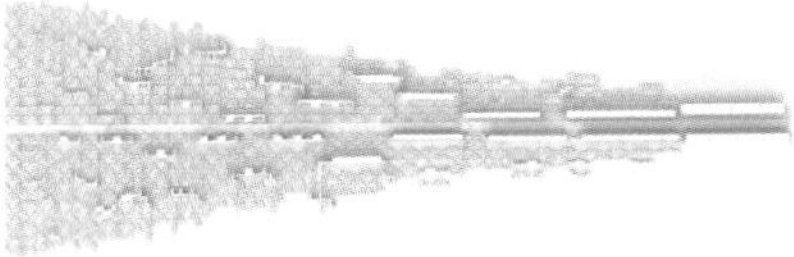

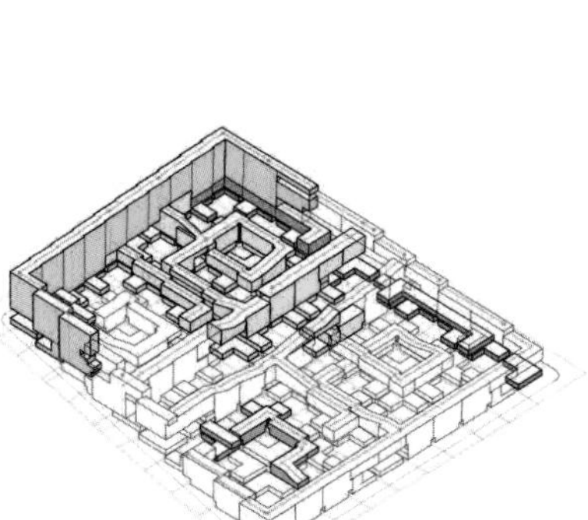

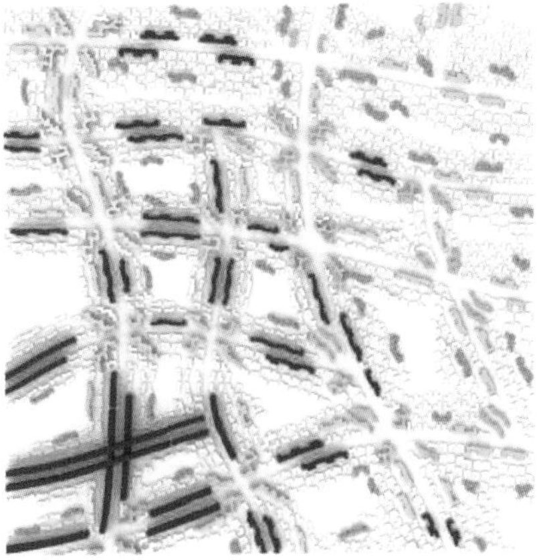

Architectural prototypes of the mega-block and the street.

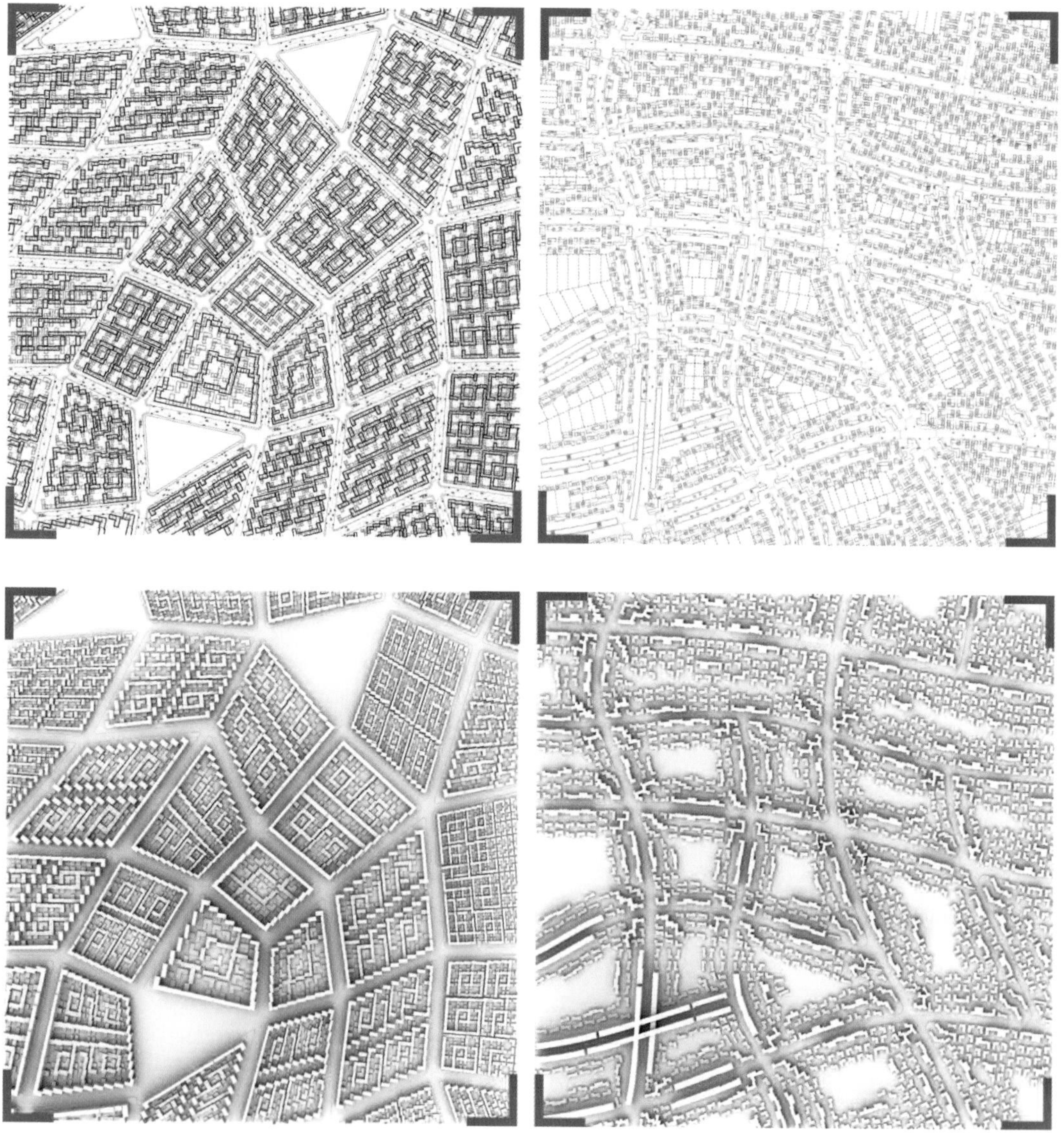

The process of actualization of the mega-block and the streets on the site. Due to the gradient land value of the site, the mega-block transforms its internal organization, its size, and the number of different typological units. Correspondingly, the street transforms its sequential character of densities, typologies, and morphology.

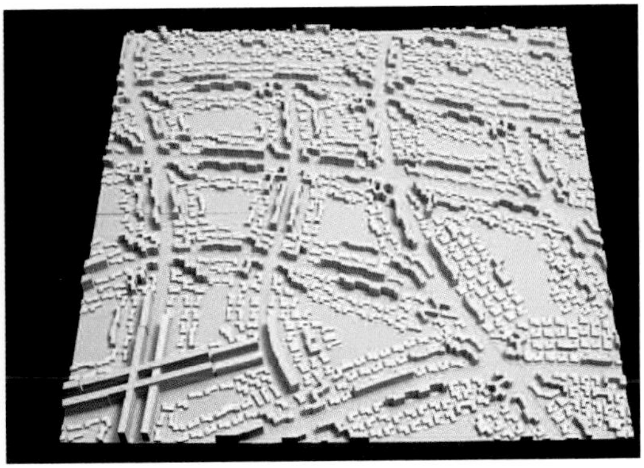

Models demonstrating the intensive field of mega-blocks and the aggregation of streets.

CASE STUDY

THE UNIVERSITY OF HONG KONG >ENDURANCE AND OBSOLESCENCE TOOLBOX: STUDIES OF ADAPTABLE MASTERPLANNING

2009–2011

Principal Investigator: Tom Verebes
Research Assistants: Nathan Melenbrink, Li Bin, Kenneth Sit Hoi Chang

This University Grants Council-funded research project, conducted over a two-year period, was led by Tom Verebes at the University of Hong Kong. The team of Research Assistants were central to the development of this project, especially Nathan Melenbrink, who helped propel the design research work in Rhino/Grasshopper. It is at once a design research project concerning advanced technology, and a project which seeks to rethink the conceptual and intellectual arena of contemporary design methodologies within the disciplines of architecture, urban design, and masterplanning. As an alternative approach to conventional design processes, the focus of this project is the development of computational design technologies for the design of urban systems, within an intellectually disciplined academic context. Computational approaches to urbanism engage with a complexity of factors, contingencies, and responsibilities related to the design of large-scale architectural projects, urban design, and masterplanning. As a challenge to the static nature of masterplanning, this provides an information-driven understanding of urban growth, change, densification, and time-based long-term development.

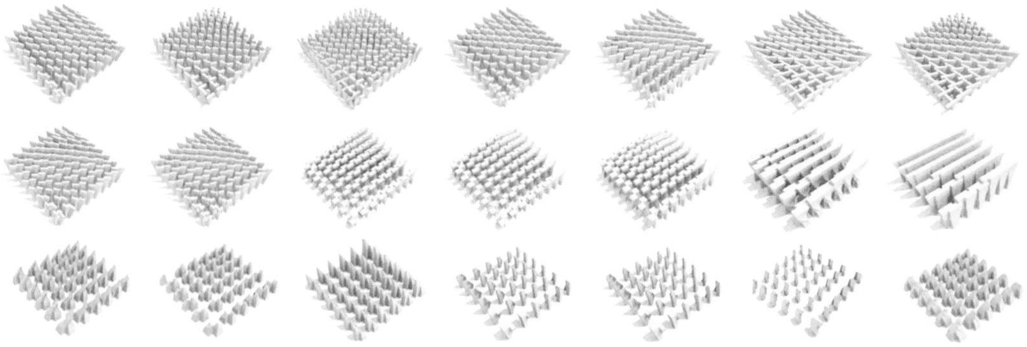

Arrays differentiating massing volumes, their proximity and orientation.

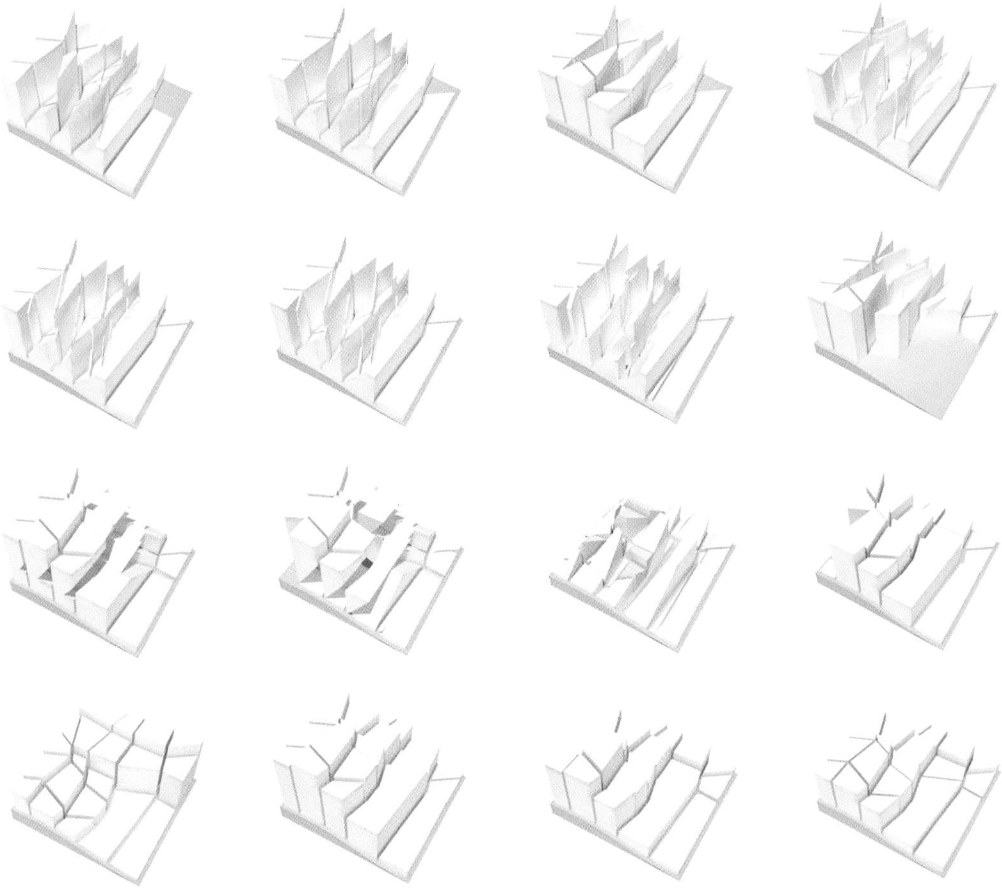

Array of a 500-meter by 500-meter swatch of massing carved away by solar angles as a generator for a dense urbanism into which daylight can penetrate.

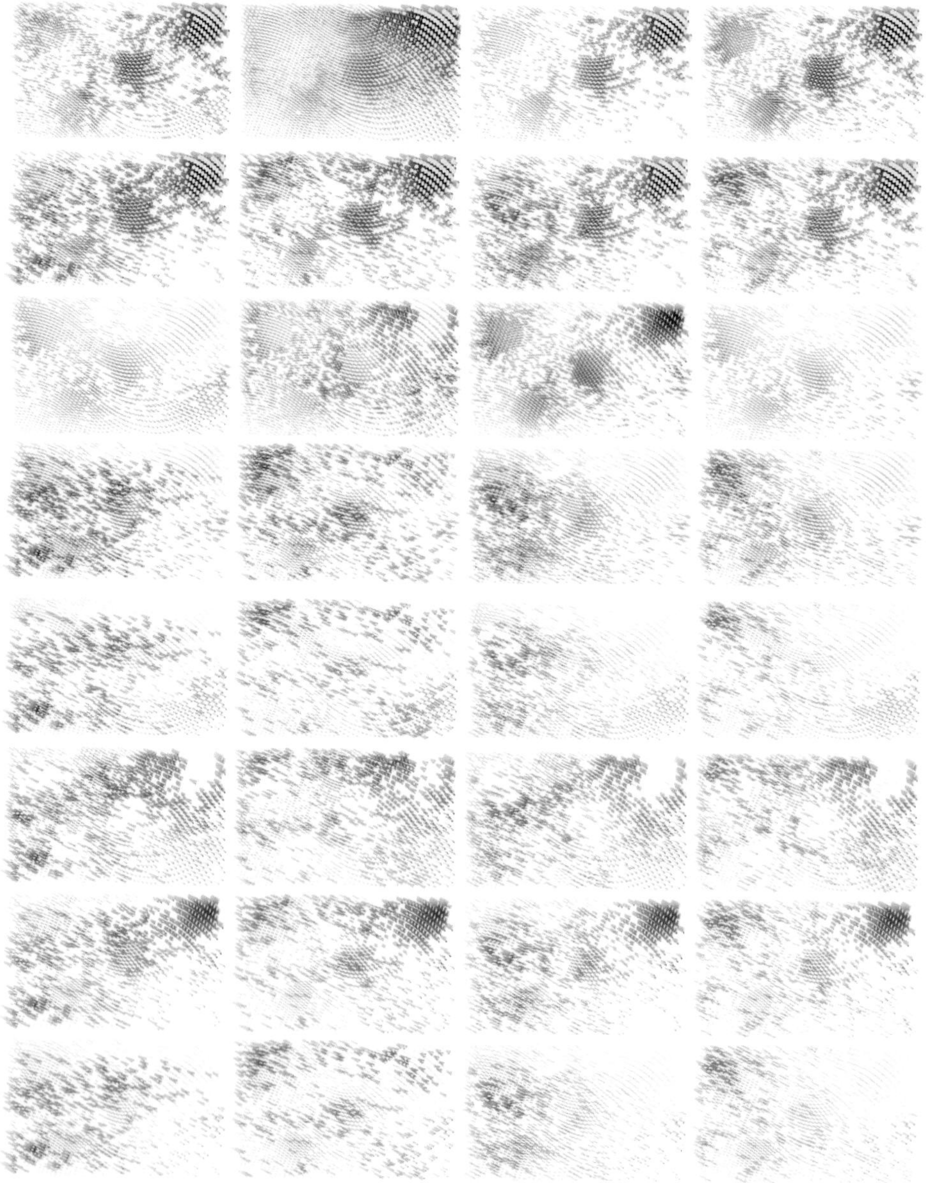

Plan and views of arrays of three-dimensional differentiated fields of building massing, reading a two-dimensional graphic field to generate distributed abstract urban patterns.

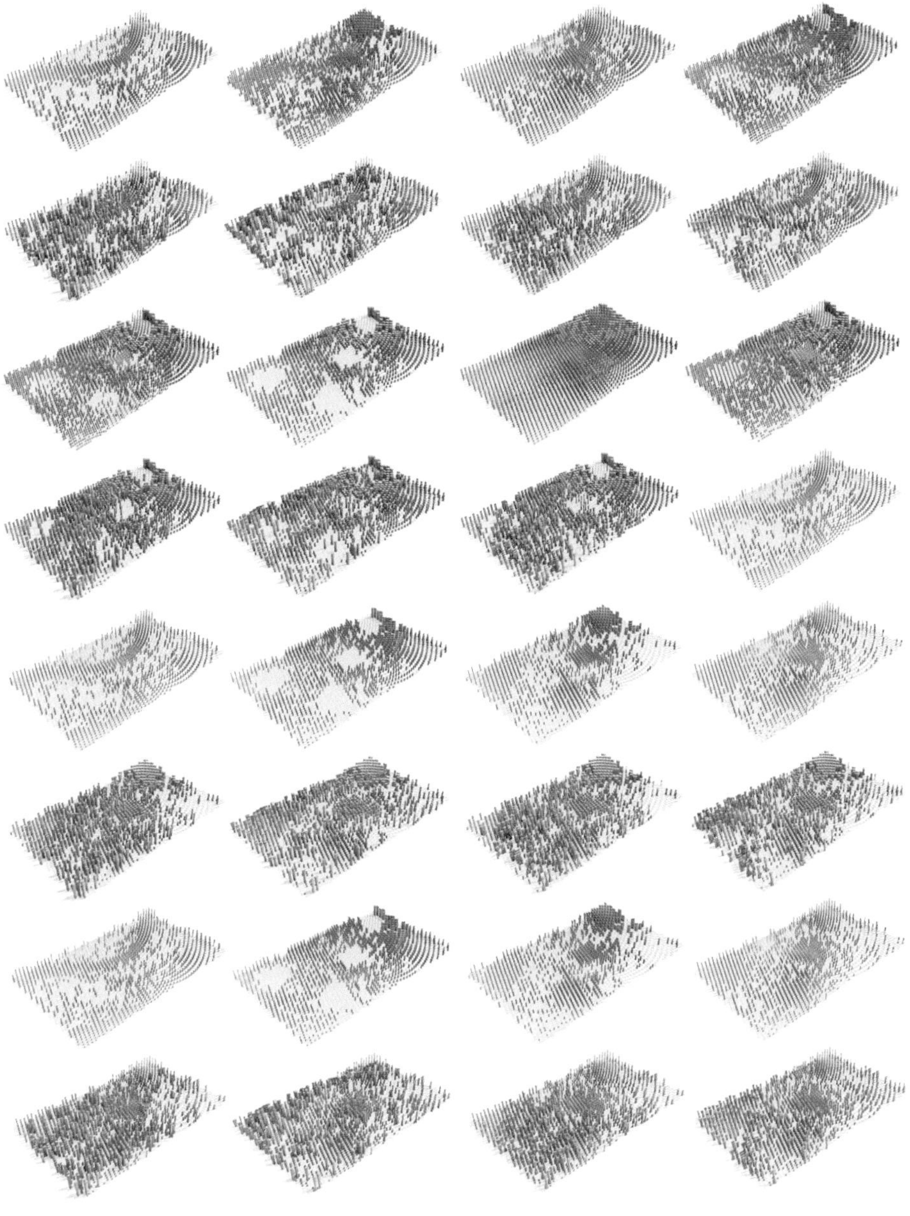

Arrays of urban road patterns on a steep topography.

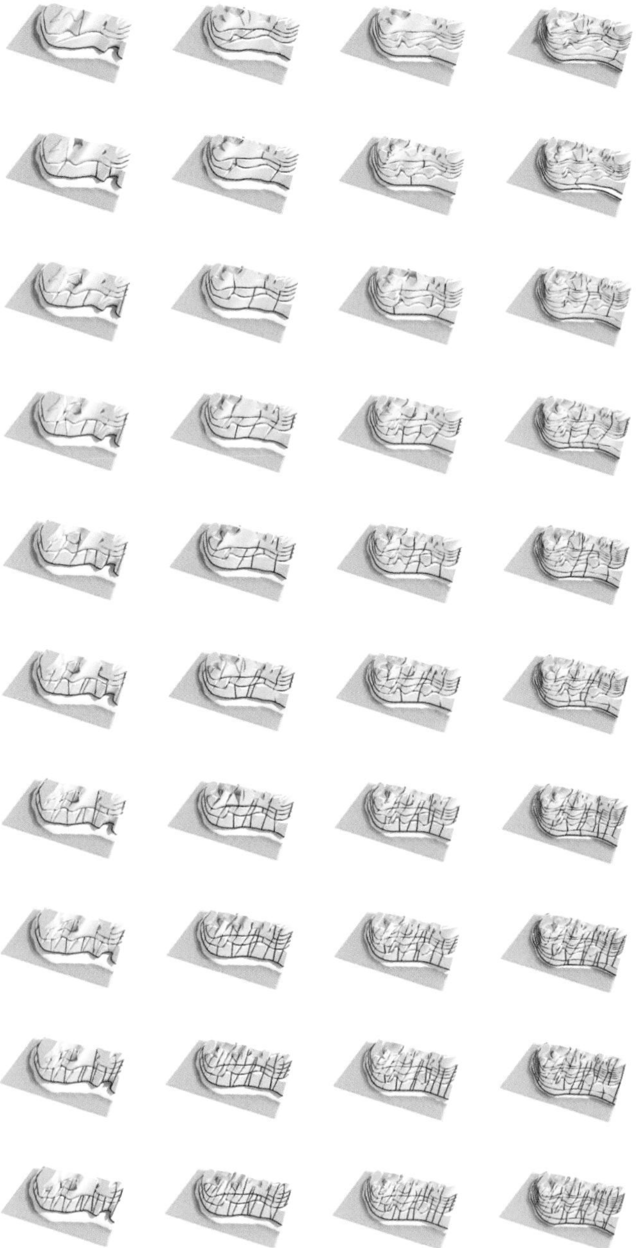

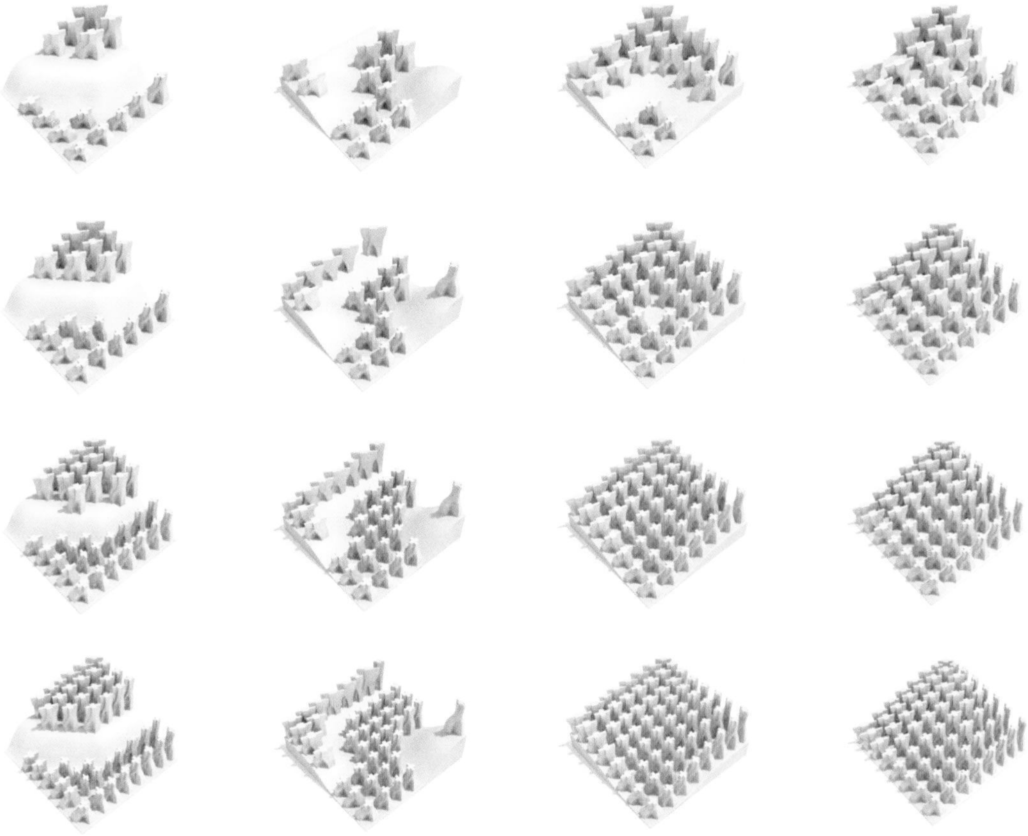

Arrays of building massing deployed in relation to topography.

IV

PROJECTIONS

PROTOTYPING MULTIPLE FUTURES

CHAPTER 18

TOM VEREBES > ENDURANCE, OBSOLESCENCE, AND THE ADAPTIVE CITY

This chapter critiques the legacy of standardization of material practices, shifting from repetitive production toward increasing customization of spaces, systems, and experiences. Prototyping technologies, now commonplace as recursive methods in the design of small-scale objects and building, are investigated as the basis for harnessing complexity at the scale of the city. Control is understood neither as a constraining regime nor as standardization, but rather as an experimental mode of testing multiple urban futures. Architectural typology is not viewed as stable and fixed but open to transformation and repositioning. Promoting innovation and experimentation, this final chapter elaborates an argument for heterogeneous and high-quality architecture, which balances endurance and change, longevity and adaptability.

18.1 NEW PROTOTYPICAL PRACTICES

From the standpoint of the second decade of the twenty-first century, it now seems clear that in the twentieth century standardized production methods and materials, coupled with a throwaway culture in construction, led to a decrease in the lifespan of buildings.[1] Such standardized production has in the past two decades been challenged by a small, experimental, globally distributed culture of computational designers who have shifted their attention to materialization. An implication of this project to actualize the virtual is a high degree of control and precision. Unlike the twentieth century paradigm of control as being the mastery of standards and efficiencies, our current industrial paradigm is one of computational control, put to work to harness and manage complexity, and to deliver it. The practice of urbanism in this century will forge a critical link between architecture, landscape architecture, infrastructure, and the city.

> The fact that, for architects, the discovery of their decline as ideologists, the awareness of the enormous technological possibilities available for rationalizing cities and territories, coupled with the daily spectacle of their waste, and the fact that specific design methods become outdated even before it is possible to verify their underlying hypotheses in reality, all create an atmosphere of anxiety.
>
> Manfredo Tafuri, 1976[2]

Monotony has been, for much of the last century, the default effect of standardization, while variety was rare. Consider the main innovation of Henry Ford, that of the assembly line for making Ford's Model T cars, and its ensuing impact on twentieth-century production. This single innovation contributed substantively to a new model of standardized production. In which ways can computational methods of material production "narrow the gap between representation and building," or from file to factory production?[3] Interestingly, contemporary prototyping tools come from the automotive industry and industrial design, but the question here is one of scale—we are concerned with extra-large

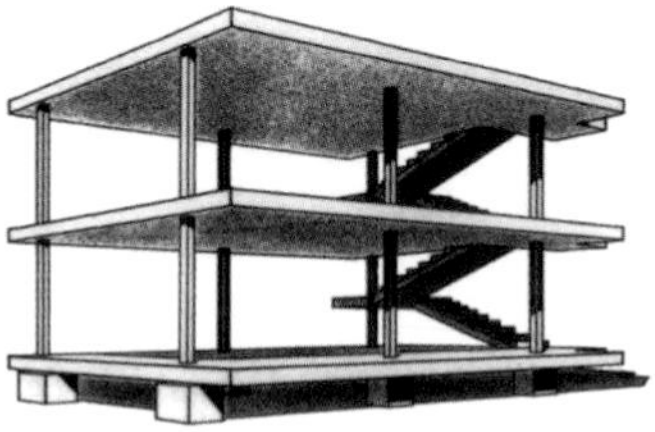

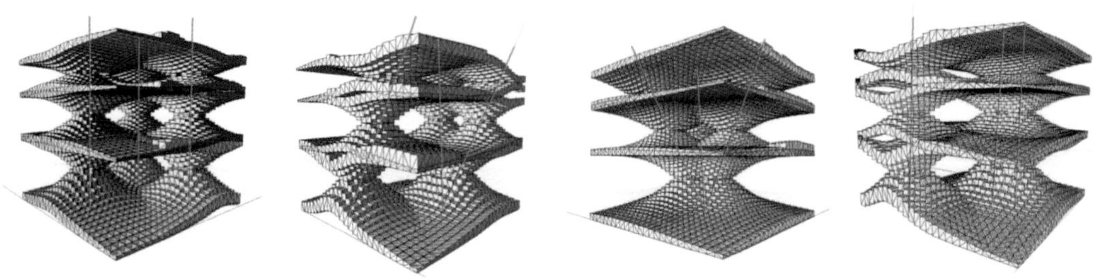

Computational models presented as an alternative to Le Corbusier's *Domino House* model, which drove architectural production throughout the twentieth century. (Studio Tutor: Tom Verebes; Students: Kwong Yan Kit Kyle, Sit Hoi Chang Kenneth, Yang Hui Bella, Yu Hun Yan Krist; MArch I Studio, *Go West Chongqing*, The University of Hong Kong, 2011)

architecture, urban design, and vast urban areas, rather than car parts or consumer goods.

Prototyping methodologies have a long history in industrial and product design, robotics and interaction design, and the automotive, naval, aerospace, and other industries, and this approach to developing viable products is quickly becoming firmly embedded in the contemporary design arena, in both avant-garde and mainstream architectural practice. Contemporary prototyping tools arrived as imports from these parallel design disciplines, and their value within all design disciplines today lies in their ability to test computational systems through a series of "hard" physical prototypes. Prototyping in any field aims for progressive updating and optimization via feedback from demonstrations of performance, evaluated in relation to predefined project criteria. These evolutionary design methods, in which the prototype is a design instrument, differ from the notion of a model as an ultimate representation of a final design proposal. Prototyping enables recursive and iterative workflows, rather than linear design methods focussed on singular outcomes, of which facsimiles can easily be reproduced.

> The shift from an empirical, tradition-bound technics to an experimental mode has opened up such new realms as those of nuclear energy, supersonic transportation, cybernetic intelligence, and instantaneous distant communication.
>
> Lewis Mumford, 1944[4]

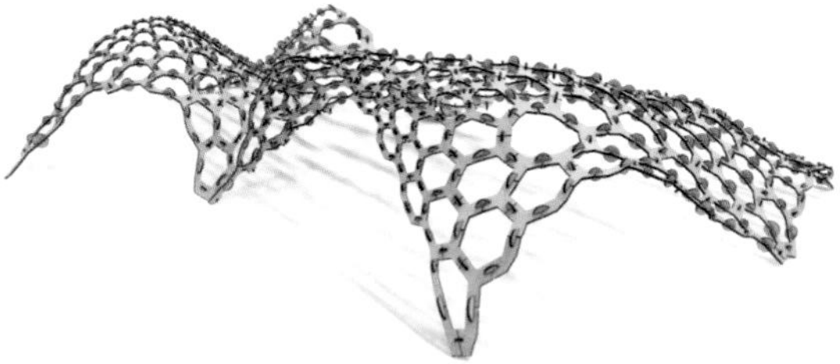

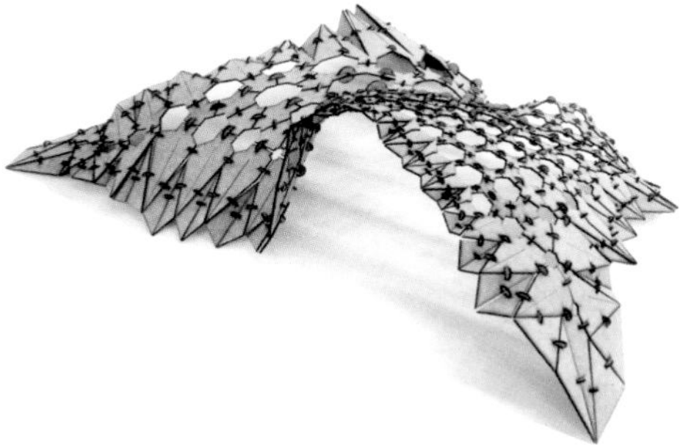

Two 1:10 scale material prototypes, in laser-cut MDF, for a series of urban pavilions, West Kowloon Cultural District, Hong Kong. (Studio Tutor: Tom Verebes; Thesis Student: Cheung Chun Chi; MArch Thesis, The University of Hong Kong, 2012)

The second machine age, which Reyner Banham claims flowered briefly in the "Fabulous Sixties," vaunted "miniaturisation, transistorisation, jet and rocket travel, wonder drugs and new domestic chemistries, television and the computer."[5] More of the same for machine enthusiasts, or the foundation of things to come? Fuller's notions of technology transfer, as seen in the airplane fuselage techniques applied to his *Dymaxion House* and developed over a lifetime of geodesic prototypes, were paralleled by innovations pursued by Jean Prouvé in his transfer of steel aeronautical structures to airplane hangars and furniture, and later by Ray and Charles Eames's bentwood furniture produced using their "Kazam" machine to bend plywood on molds which had been adapted from military technology for producing leg splints. Gilbert Simondon, the French philosopher of technology, theorized processes of molding, often associated with repetitive, uniform products, as "continuous temporal modulation."[6] Modulation, for Simendon, was achieved through the electrification of material in the molding process. As Spuybroek highlights, "when seen from a broader perspective . . . variable modulation liberates the mould from the doom of identical copies, in which design work is done and the execution is purely atemporal."[7] Here we see the potential for variability, or customization, in the fabrication process, yielding a differentiated series of results rather than the uniformity of the standardized production which began in the nineteenth century and continued throughout the twentieth century. In effect, it is the coding of difference, which allows any production process to provide for modulation. This is not mere replication with a predetermined degree of variation, rather quantitatively differentiated coding gives rise to products which are *qualitatively* different.

As a methodology, today's prototyping practices may also lead to more than a new material paradigm. The repercussions extend to the globalized city, and the networks which enable the flow of knowledge and material resources within a new model of production. Prototypes help to create "design intelligence," enabling designers to call upon the flow of new, aggregated knowledge for future projects.[8] They allow designers to learn, from successes and especially from mistakes. Simulation, testing, analysis, and feedback using ubiquitous digital and material media requires learning new codes, protocols, and procedures. Innovation therefore involves striving for insight in the present, and change in the future. Innovation can come about serendipitously, accidentally, through error, or through the consolidation of groups which share knowledge, and thus gain intelligence.

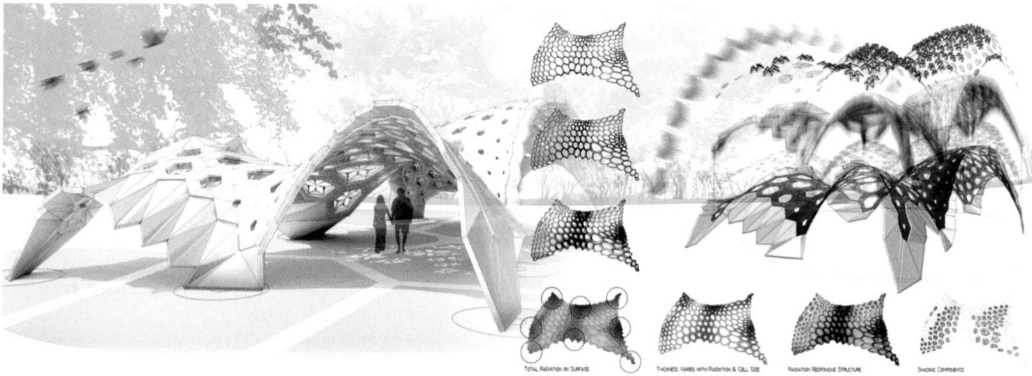

The porosity of the pavilion is generated from simulations of solar radiation, in a design process which charges decisions with evaluation and feedback. (Studio Tutor: Tom Verebes; Thesis Student: Cheung Chun Chi; MArch Thesis, The University of Hong Kong, 2012)

Long before computational urbanism could be theorized, Frei Otto proposed "the art of urban development" as a new kind of "non-living nature" requiring expertise in the "present state and the possibilities of technology."[9] John Fraser, who conducted research into "predictive planning models" with his Architectural Association (AA) students in the early 1990s, focussed on an adaptive and responsive set of behaviors with which to forecast future urban conditions, and, importantly, how they are differentiated and how they evolve.[10] Around the same time, Jeffrey Kipnis and Bahram Shirdel, together with the AA graduate design program, launched the basis for an inclusive, heterogeneous, and adaptive urbanism.

What are the consequences of prototypical practices for urbanism? Given the inevitable paradigm shift from a model of standardized production, in which uniformity and repetition are by-products of globalization, prototyping at the scale and complexity of the city raises some compelling questions for models of planning. The notion of the urban project as a prototype of the future charges urbanism, as a discipline, with scheming multiple futures, testing their performance, evaluating, de-bugging, and adapting them to new, changing criteria. What, then, is the potential of computational prototyping methods for creating diverse and differentiated cities?

18.2 TYPOLOGICAL VARIANTS AND TOPOLOGICAL TRANSFORMATIONS

> The word type presents less the image of a thing to copy or imitate completely than the idea of an element which ought itself to serve as a rule for the model.
>
> Quatremère de Quincy, 1825[11]

Quatremère de Quincy, whose theories on type were set out in his *Encyclopédie méthodique* in the late eighteenth century, made a distinction between an idea and a model. This can also be understood as the difference between a "copy" and an "imitation," where the model "is not to be misinterpreted as an exact copy, but is constituted by formal resemblance, [and] type is a product of moral imitation."[12] Julien Guadet's *Éléments et théories* of 1894 set out to describe the functional elementalism of proto-modern architecture, aligning modern functional hierarchies with classical typological organization. This was a way of breaking down the parts of a building into their elemental characteristics, rather than viewing architecture as rooted in compositional strategies.[13] Here, the relation of function and a given type is static and does not evolve. Aldo Rossi and the Italian rationalists, nearly half a century ago, made associations between this notion of the model and material history in the city, using the historic artefacts present in the city—which Rossi called "permanences," and which call on the collective memory of citizens—as a means of understanding and defining urbanism, rather than the functionalism of the modernists. Christopher Lee warns against the use of type with "an overreliance on precedents [which lead] to repetition and imitation," and rather highlights how "if type is an idea, its material manifestation and expression can take on many forms."[14]

> When we study forms, the organic ones in particular, nowhere do we find permanence, repose or termination.
>
> Johann Wolfgang von Goethe, 1806[15]

Topology is a branch of mathematics concerned with the qualitative spatial attributes of geometry, and how spatial properties are invariant under continuous deformation or transformation. All topologies are geometries, but not all geometric figures are topological. Topological spaces undergo transformation such that they "lose all metric and projective characteristics, but retain their topological identity" through transitions from one state to another. It was Leibniz, in the seventeenth century, who first studied problems of spatial analysis, which formed the roots of modern topology; Henri Poincaré is often credited as founder of the field. Leonhard Euler's often-cited solution to the Seven Bridges of Königsberg problem—which was to identify a route through the city that involved traversing each bridge only once—is a topological solution, and possibly the first conception of an urban network diagram.[16] In fact, Euler's "solution" of 1735 is not a solution but rather the presentation of a new problem or paradigm, establishing "a new geometry of position" which represents a "distinction from metrical Euclidean or Cartesian geometry" through nodes in a scale-free network.[17]

The relation of typology to topology, the study of transformation, is key to re-defining type as a plastic, morphologically adaptable condition where information contained in the model or diagram is not stable but in transition, and is also re-formed each time it is deployed. Topology does not replace the functional–performative contingencies of typology as a form of classification; it is not stable and absolute, rather it is in transitional, in-between states.[18] A hylomorphic model, according to Peter Trummer, "has clear directionality of how matter moves into form."[19] Trummer counters the essentialism of the hylomorph, as instructions for a facsimile, with the Deleuzian idea of multiplicity. The biological notion of speciation in breeding was employed by Foreign Office Architects as a system of classification for the diagramming of their projects as an evolutionary, phylogenic tree. In this system of taxonomy, "projects are not something designed but a breed of a particular species," in opposition to the notion of type as "eternal and static."[20] Here, organizational attributes come from rules which form types and their variants.

Contemporary computational design approaches aid speculations on culturally specific spatial paradigms, patterns, and topologies, and have given rise to innovations on default typological models, in the form of recent architectural experimentation involving differentiated volumetric and surface conditions. Mathematical models provide the basis for understanding architectural objects as the result of the interaction of information and forces on "rubber sheet geometries," involving "transformational events" and discontinuities. Various topological themes continue to be explored by computational designers, including embedding, homology, topological equivalence, immersion, minimal surfaces, multidimensional spaces, and non-orientable surfaces, among others. Numerous architects in the 1990s played out topological fetishes involving objects such as the Möbius strip, the Klein bottle, knots, and holes, which provided the basis for computational modeling of architectural spaces. Typological modeling need not be a fixed, formulaic mode of perpetuating normative spatial conditions, rather it can be the diagrammatic basis for innovations borne from a topological or transformational approach, as a generator of complex yet legible differentiated morphologies. Form, then, is a mathematical notion which emerges through transformational dynamics.

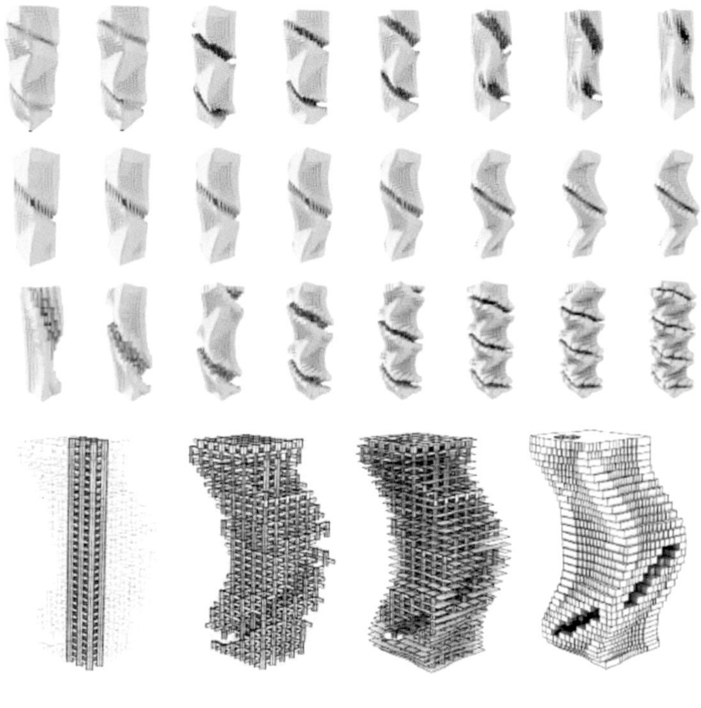

Diagrams of an evolutionary series of solid models with void, and a set of tectonic systems explaining their architectural potential. (Studio Tutor: Tom Verebes; Students: Mak Wing Sze, Li Ho Chun, Li Tsz Man; MArch I Studio, *Go West Chongqing*, The University of Hong Kong, 2011)

Series of differentiated spatial models generated from torsion and topological holes in three dimensions. (Studio Tutor: Tom Verebes; Students: Rochana Chaugule, Yevgeniya Pozigun, Ujjal Roy, Praneet Verma; Architectural Association, 2009)

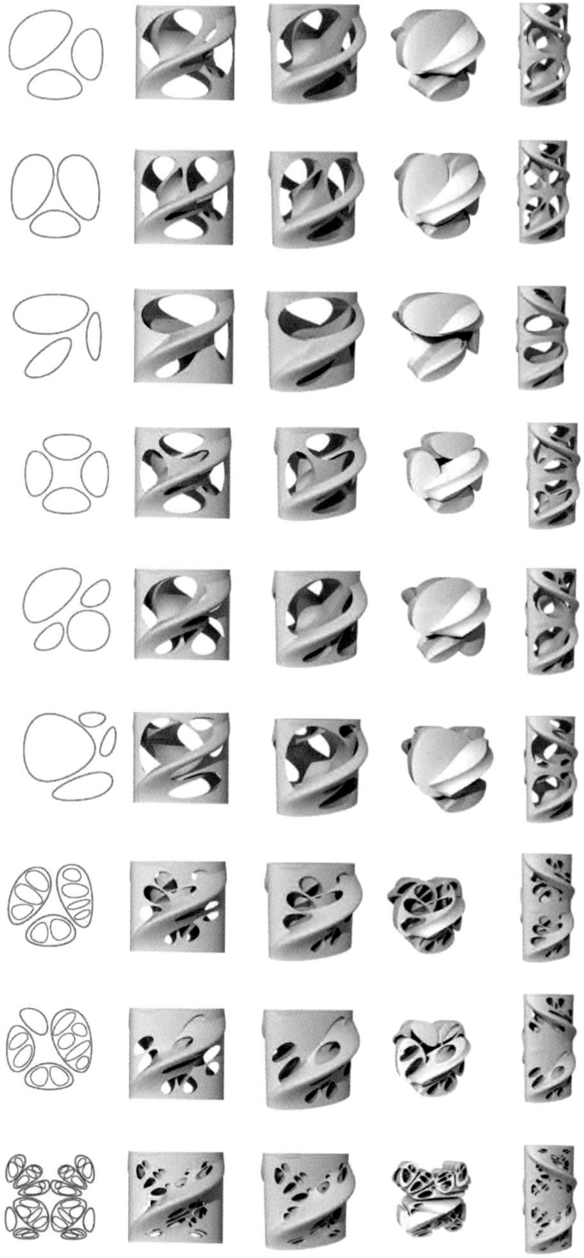

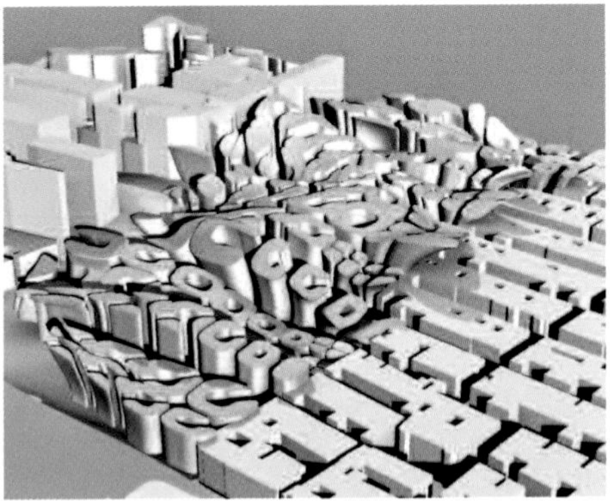

Morphological model of proposed fabric inserted into the historic fabric of the Old Town of Shanghai. (Studio Tutor: Tom Verebes; Student: Claire Yuen; MArch II Studio, HKU-Harvard GSD Joint Studio, *Types, Prototypes and Systems,* The University of Hong Kong, 2009)

Informational diagrams have become the basis for most of the preeminent contemporary design approaches in architecture and urbanism. Termed by the Burrys "nongeometric diagrams," these notational systems chart relationships between spaces, activities, and events, some of which are not wholly predictable. As a shift from a "critique of the power of the plane and gravitational vector in mainstream Modernism," today's interest in topology leads us to consider distributed networks. This, the Burrys argue, "is a fundamentally different space in which to live."[21] The emphasis here is on the relevance of topology to the study as well as the making of the city—the ultimate transformational space. Topology is therefore a way of understanding, and modeling, urban change. As we have seen, cities exist within global networks, local and internal relationships, and are essentially always in transition. In this light, topology turns out to be a fertile arena for researching approaches to understanding existing urban conditions, and projecting ideas of urbanism into the future.

Over two decades, design culture has developed an enduring fascination with surface complexities. Architectural discourse continues to grapple with the theoretical consequences. Many of the projects presented in this book interrogate aspects of the use of topological instruments for urbanism. At stake here is the possibility of a noncompositional approach to urbanism which embeds change in the formation and transformation of urban organization.

18.3 ICONS AND INNOVATION

Despite the global financial crisis unfolding over the last five years, architects and urbanists, whether avant garde or "rear garde," are still aiming to satisfy the "market driven appetite for more and ever more complex and formally exotic buildings."[22] Iconic architecture, as it has become known, challenges conventions, and enables experimentation and innovation. To deny the world its icons renders it grayscale, strips it of color. "Background buildings" are always in the plural (though the notion of a background and foreground is one of emphasis), but the transformative building that "fully transcends its specialized context—that is, that challenges and intervenes within developments taking place across an entire society"—remains rare.[23] The history of architecture has been a history of iconic, seminal moments, and in order to maintain a meaningful history cities need to invest in cultural production, even if some of that culture stands out.

Many architects have outlined the terms upon which architecture should be redefined, and hence arrived at a description of the "new" role of the architect. In order to chart the future and to innovate, designers need to be in "literal and continual modulation of, and communication with, social and historical process."[24] Innovation has cultural dimensions which go beyond an understanding of design as finding solutions to given problems. As Speaks claims, problem-solving approaches to design provide "answers without questioning the problem given, and therefore [add] nothing new," whereas innovation "interrogates and reforms the problem given and adds value by creating new knowledge and new products not anticipated in the problem."[25] Unlike the modernist masters, today's "experimental architecture practices [are] compelled by the need to innovate, to create solutions to problems the larger implications of which have not yet been formulated."[26]

The important advances being made in computational design in architecture, and their "affordances and efficiencies," are leading global urbanism to valorize the icon. Innovations in our ability to model and manage complexity represent a paradigm shift, in that we are now able "to generate design variants which break from Fordism," and inevitably can "more rapidly conceive, explore, describe and construct non-standard projects within the real world constraints of economy, materiality and function."[27] Schumacher describes elegance in design work as that which "achieves a reduction of visual complexity, thereby preserving an underlying organizational complexity."[28] Elegance is therefore not simplicity but rather differentiation, qualified and ordered. Organizational complexity is comprised of the modulation of quantities related to component parts in continuously iterative spatial logics.

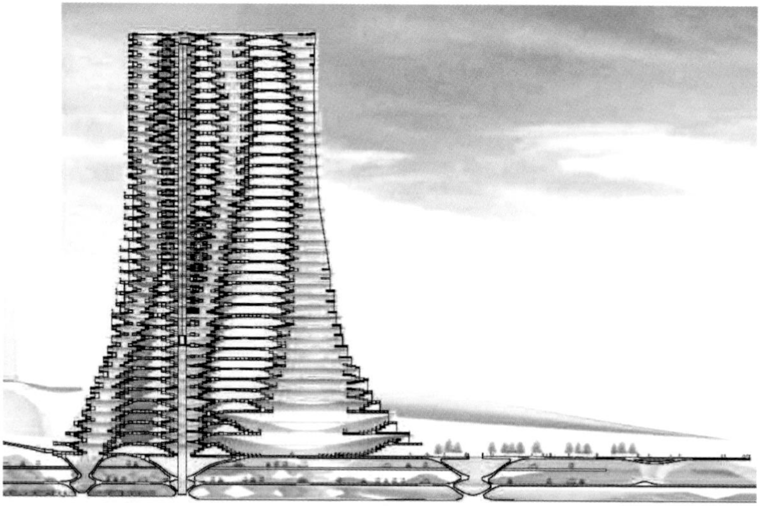

Section of proposed urbanism within a thick ground and deep tower. (Studio Tutor: Tom Verebes; Students: Kwong Yan Kit Kyle, Sit Hoi Chang Kenneth, Yang Hui Bella, Yu Hun Yan Krist; MArch I Studio, *Go West Chongqing*, The University of Hong Kong, 2011)

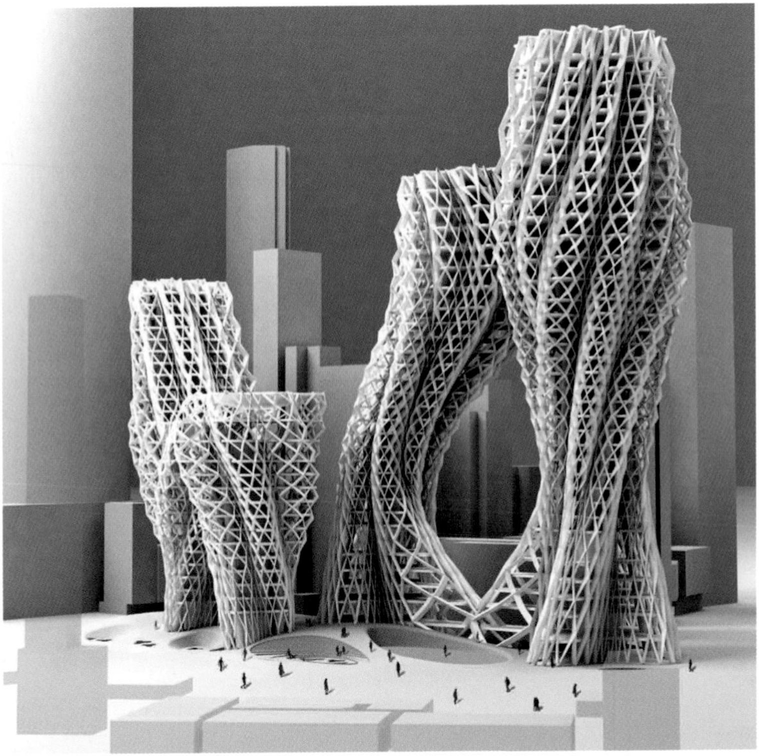

View of proposed interconnected towers in Wan Chai, Hong Kong. (Studio Tutor: Tom Verebes; Thesis Student: Gordon Fu Kin Fai; Thesis Student: Cheung Chun Chi; MArch Thesis, The University of Hong Kong, 2010)

The city, according to Steven Johnson, is an environment which "squelches new ideas . . . effortlessly," and which, for historical reasons, is "powerfully suited for the creation, diffusion and adoption of good ideas."[29] Johnson identifies numerous modes in which innovations are generally made, often relying on platforms of collaboration, and on serendipity, error, or misappropriation. Urbanity is a motor for new ideas, technologies, practices, and spaces. If the world is changing quickly, it seems designers need to ride these transitions and to learn better how to adapt to an evolving world. One thing is sure: ignorance is the enemy of insight—it creates complacency instead of proactivity, and gives space to conservatives who lobby against innovation without a clue that they are doing it.

18.4 CONTROL, RESILIENCE, AND CHANGE

> In organic planning, one thing leads to another, and what began as the seizure of an accidental advantage may prompt a strong element in a design, which an a-priori plan could not anticipate, and in all probability would overlook or rule out . . . . Organic planning does not begin with a preconceived goal: it moves from need to need, from opportunity to

> opportunity, in a series of adaptations that themselves become interestingly coherent and purposeful.
>
> Lewis Mumford, 1961[30]

Goethe's definition of morphology distinguishes between form and formation, or in German *bildung*:"to designate what has been brought forth and what is in the process of being brought forth."[31] This distinction "marks a turning away from the simple structure of end-products and toward the active, ever-changing processes that bring them into being."[32]

Urbanism and architecture are more than services to investors; they are at their best cultural practices. However, "periods of cumulative avant-garde work" are hard to sustain and fall victim to obsolescence as changes in society "ensure that premises, procedures and model solutions become maladapted and thus dysfunctional,"[33] recalling Thomas Khun's distinction between eras of "normal science" and "revolutionary science."

> The technology of the natural world is already all around us and within us—and it is vastly superior to our technology.
>
> Peter J. Bentley and David W. Corne, 2002[34]

Given the precariousness of ecological conditions and the global economic system how can urban earth sustain itself? Asking new questions brings new answers to challenging problems. To confront the challenges of extreme urbanization facing us in this century, it is necessary to relearn, even unlearn, our biases. What, then, are our options? Do we build for the short term and maximize recycling? Should we shift to high-endurance, resilient architecture and infrastructure? The paradoxes of endurance and decay, permanence and ephemerality, fixity and adaptability have been persistent themes throughout this book, and while no direct solution has here been sought to the problem of change in what we still call the city, there seems to be little material justification for giving up on endurance as a model of sustainability—as vague as that term "sustainability" is—given environmental performance, material resilience, energy consumption, cultural heritage, and other vital parameters.

Architecture is a material practice, and the city has become increasingly mineralized over the course of its history, from its origins as temporary dwellings to now, when more than half the world's population is living in cities. As a material paradigm, matter has a capacity to change over time, and the opportunity presented by the mutability of materials "was something to be avoided in much twentieth-century architecture, and was rarely embraced as a design opportunity. Decay is seen as the enemy in buildings, and a great deal of technical effort is aimed at combating and arresting it."[35] Henri Bergson, however, described matter as comprised of "modifications, perturbations, changes of tension or energy and nothing else,"[36] reflecting an understanding of matter as alive and in transition, rather than dead and inert. An argument for urban endurance must not be confused with nostalgia for architectural "weathering," understood as the valorization of the "patina" of desired, even designed deterioration, highlighting light and coloration effects on the surface of so-called natural materials.[37] But what, if any, are the urban alternatives to whitewashing all surfaces, in the manner

Proposed differentiated massing systems for Dan Zi Shi, Chongqing, China. (Studio Tutor: Tom Verebes; Students: Lai Sheng Ching, Cheng Chun; MArch I Studio, *Ground Control*, The University of Hong Kong, 2012)

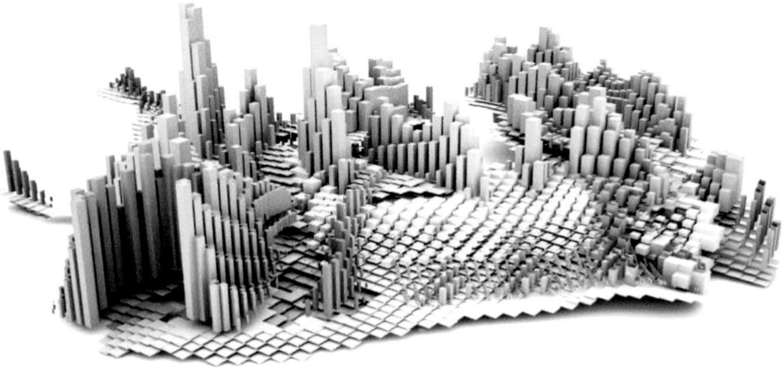

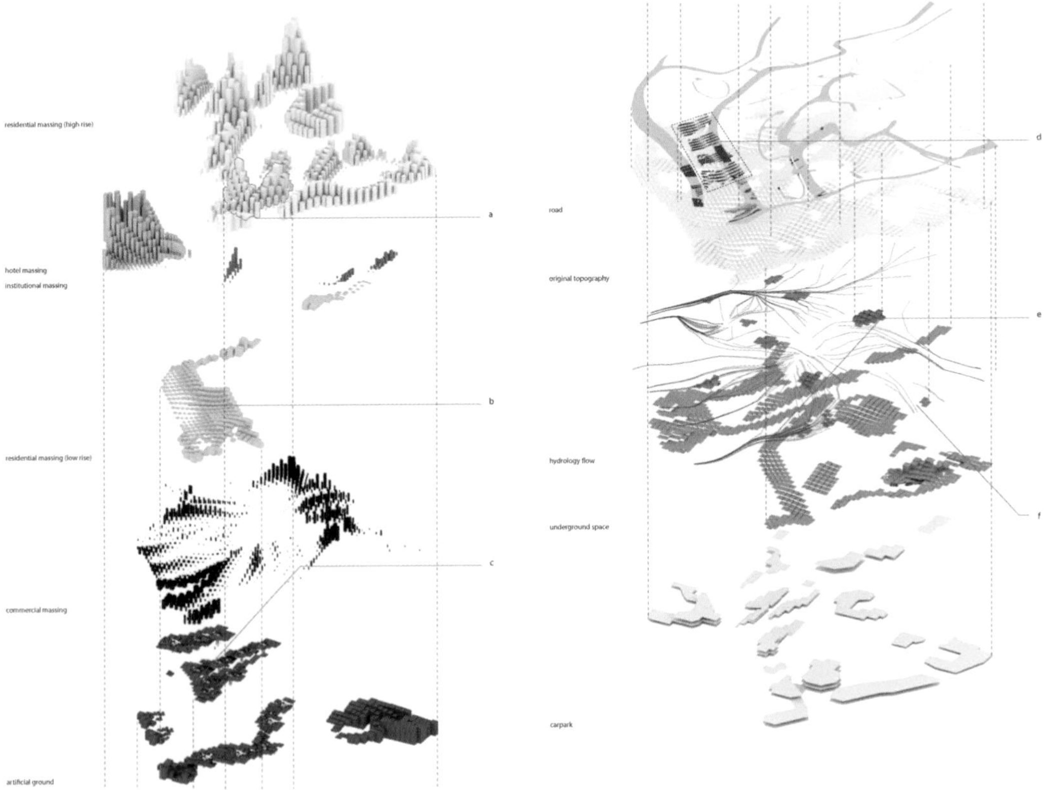

Diagrams of urban massing, infrastructural, landscape, hydrological, and topographical systems. (Studio Tutor: Tom Verebes; Students: Lai Sheng Ching, Cheng Chun; MArch I Studio, *Ground Control*, The University of Hong Kong, 2012)

of Le Corbusier's Law of Ripolin, which was aimed at dematerializing surfaces? What alternatives might be found to the design of short-term, disposable or recyclable cities? Old cannot simply be equated to good, and new to bad. As highlighted, the ecological footprint of short-term design implies that longer design life can be equated with a "sustainable" approach to design. Cities should not be pickled and preserved, however.

Cities grow, are transformed, fall into decline, and sometimes they are abandoned and disappear. Despite these risks, there is now nowhere to go but cities. In the context of a global culture of short termism, the future lies between planning and emergence, top-down control and self-organization.[38] A sea change in urbanism based on implementation of the concepts and methodologies here proposed may give rise to new approaches to city design, "the aim of which is not to control, but to participate."[39] Since change is the only constant in urbanity, change should occur through adaptation rather than by erasure. Permanence resists change, hence the paradoxical interaction between a wished-for permanence and the inescapable temporality of urbanism. Letting go does not entail giving up all control.

NOTES

1 > M. Mostafavi and D. Leatherbarrow (1993) *On Weathering: The Life of Buildings in Time* (Cambridge: MIT), 17.

2 > M. Tafuri (1976) *Architecture and Utopia: Design and Capitalist Development* (Cambridge: MIT), 176.

3 > L. Iwamoto (2009) *Digital Fabrications: Architectural and Material Techniques* (New York: Princeton), 4.

4 > Reprinted in L. Mumford (1986) *The Lewis Mumford Reader*, ed. D.L. Miller (Athens, Georgia: University of Georgia Press), 304.

5 > R. Banham (1960) *Theory and Design in the First Machine Age* (Oxford: Butterworth-Heinemann), 10.

6 > G. Deleuze (2003) *Francis Bacon: The Logic of Sensation* (London: Continuum), 140.

7 > L. Spuybroek (2011) *The Sympathy of Things: Ruskin and the Ecology of Design* (Rotterdam: V2 Publishing), 56.

8 > M. Speaks (2007) "Intelligence after Theory," in *Network Practices: New Strategies in Architecture and Design*, eds. A. Burke and T. Tierney (New York: Princeton), 214.

9 > F. Otto (2009) *Occupying and Connecting: Thoughts on Territories and Spheres of Influence with Particular Reference to Human Settlement* (Stuttgart: Edition Axel Menges), 111.

10 > J.H. Frazer (2006) "Exploring the Analogy that Parametric Design is a Game," in *Game Set Match: On Computer Games, Advanced Geometries and Digital Technologies*, eds. K. Oosterhuis and L. Feireiss (Rotterdam: Episode), 211.

11 > Quatremère de Quincy (2000, first published 1825) "Type," in *The Historic Dictionary of Architecture of Quatremère de Quincy*.

12 > S. Jacoby (2008) "What's Your Type?" in *Typological Formations: Renewable Building Types and the City* (London: AA Publications), 149–150.

13 > R. Banham, *Theory and Design in the First Machine Age*, 21–22.

14 > C.M. Lee (2008) "Projective Series," in *Typological Formations: Renewable Building Types and the City* (London: AA Publications), 137.

15 > J.W. von Goethe (1806) "Form and Transformation," in *Goethe's Botanical Writings* (Woodbridge, CT:OX Bow), 24.

16 > Otto, *Occupying and Connecting*, 7.

17 > J. Burry and M. Burry (2010) *The New Mathematics of Architecture* (New York: Thames & Hudson), 157.

18 > P. Schumacher (2012) *The Autopoesis of Architecture: A New Framework for Architecture, Vol. 2* (London: Wiley), 28–30.

19 > P. Trummer (2011) "Associative Design," in *Computational Design Thinking*, eds. A. Menges and S. Alquist (London: Wiley), 180.

20 > F. Moussavi and A. Zaera-Polo (2003) "Phylogenesis: FOA's Ark," in *Phylogenesis: FOA's Ark*, Foreign Office Architects (Barcelona: Actar), 10–11.
21 > Burry and Burry, *The New Mathematics of Architecture*, 10.
22 > M. Speaks (2008) *Design Engineering AKT*, ed. H. Kara (Barcelona: Actar), 218.
23 > S. Kwinter (2011) *Requiem for the City at the End of the Millennium* (Barcelona: Actar), 19.
24 > Kwinter, *Requiem for the City at the End of the Millennium*, 20.
25 > Speaks, *Design Engineering AKT*, 219.
26 > M. Speaks, "Intelligence after Theory," 216.
27 > D.J. Gerber (2009) *The Parametric Affect: Computation, Innovation and Models for Design Exploration in Contemporary Architectural Practice* (Cambridge: Harvard GSD), 70.
28 > P. Schumacher (2008) *Design Engineering AKT*, ed. H. Kara (Barcelona: Actar), 68.
29 > S. Johnson (2010) *Where Good Ideas Come From: The Natural History of Innovation* (New York: Penguin), 16.
30 > L. Mumford (1961) *The City in History* (London: Harcourt Brace Jovanovitch), 302.
31 > J.W. von Goethe (1806) "Form and Transformation," in *Goethe's Botanical Writings* (Woodbridge, CT: OX Bow), 24.
32 > S. Kwinter (2008) *Far from Equilibrium: Essays on Technology and Design Culture* (Barcelona: Actar), 147.
33 > P. Schumacher (2011) *The Autopoesis of Architecture: A New Framework for Architecture, Vol. 1* (London: Wiley), 113.
34 > P.J. Bentley and D.W. Corne (2011) "Creative Evolutionary Systems," in *Computational Design Thinking*, eds. A. Menges and S. Alquist (London: Wiley), 121.
35 > B. Koralevic and K.R. Klinger (2008) "Manufacturing Material Effects," in *Manufacturing Material Effects: Rethinking Design and Making in Architecture*, ed. Branko Koralevic (New York: Routledge), 8.
36 > H. Bergson (1988) *Matter and Memory*, trans. Nancy Margaret Paul and W. Scott Palmer (New York: Zone), 201.
37 > Mostafavi and Leatherbarrow, *On Weathering*, 47.
38 > S. Hagan (2010) "Performalism: Environmental Metrics and Urban Design," in *Ecological Urbanism*, eds. M. Mostafavi and G. Doherty (Baden: Lars Müller), 463.
39 > J. Portugali (2000) *Self-Organisation and the City* (Berlin: Springer Verlag), 336.

CASE STUDY

GROUNDLAB >DEEP GROUND: REGENERATION MASTERPLAN FOR LONGGANG CENTER AND LONGCHENG SQUARE, SHENZHEN, CHINA

2008

Client: Shenzhen Planning Institute
Design Team: Eva Castro, Alfredo Ramirez, Eduardo Rico, Holger Kehne, (Groundlab Directors), Alejandra Bosch, Clara Oloriz, Maria Paez, Brendon Carlin

Deep Ground is a winning competition entry for an international design competition for Longgang Centre and Longcheng Square, northeast of Shenzhen, involving an estimated population of 350,000 and 9,000,000 square meters of proposed new development on 11.8 square kilometers of mixed urban fabric in the centre of Longgang. The project radically expands the scope of urbanism to deal with the contemporary challenges of modern China. Through this project and the workshops that took place with the local authorities and other organizations in Shenzhen, a significant understanding of both the local and global conditions in China enabled the development of a series of concepts that condensed the different issues and agents involved into a set of operative design tools that shaped three main strategies. These design strategies are specific to the local requirements in Shenzhen and can be understood also as responses with a certain degree of typicality, addressing conditions that are symptomatic of the top-down, centrally controlled urbanization process found today throughout China. Through the concept of a "thickened ground," multiple ground datums are fused to foster intuitive orientation and connectivity. Via a second strategy, of an "infrastrucutural landscape," the polluted and neglected river is projected to become an ecological corridor, while the existing urban villages are retained to form nucleuses to lend identity, vitality, and human scale to the new development. Lastly, the project develops a strategy of spatial, typological, and programmatic differentiation from a parametric modeling methodology.

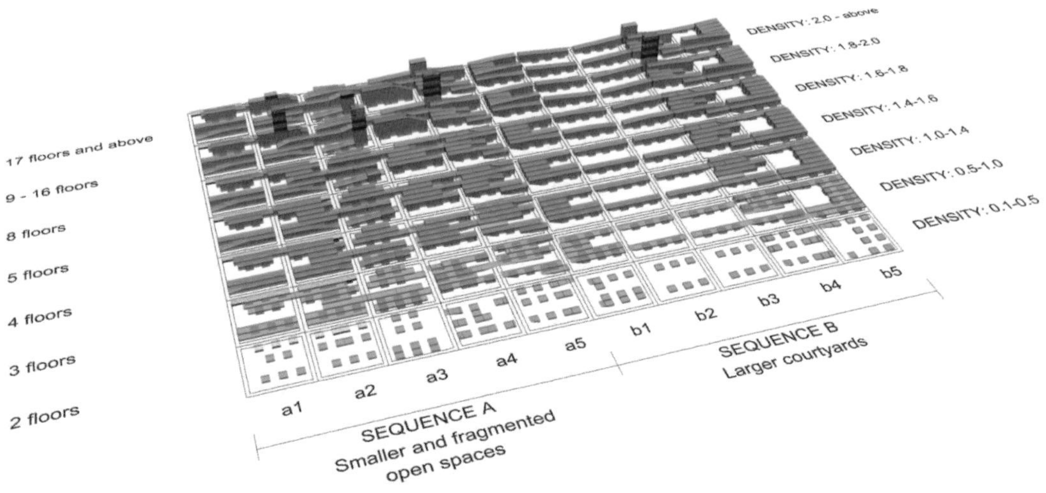

A computational method of varying the typology, density, height, and footprint of massing is demonstrated in these two instances.

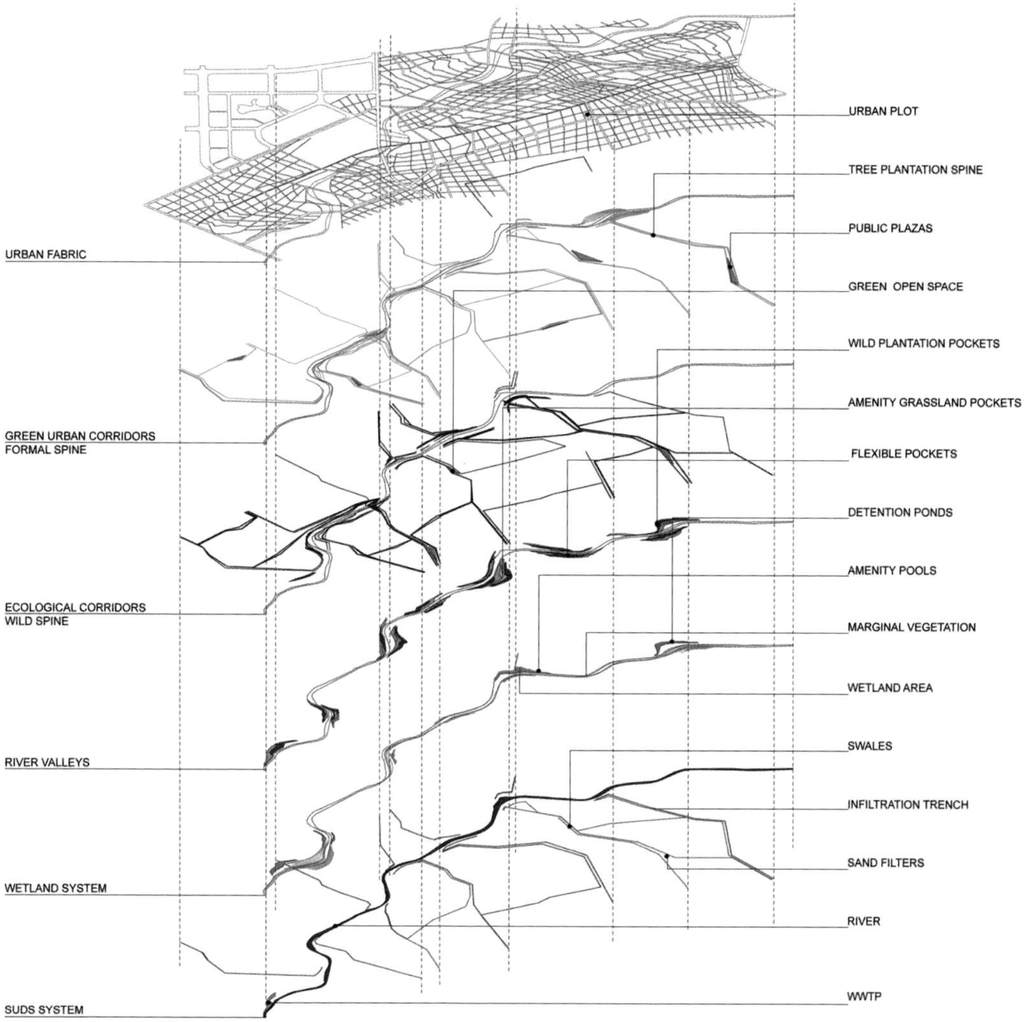

LANDSCAPE NETWORK STRATEGY

Demonstration of environmental systems deployed in the masterplan.

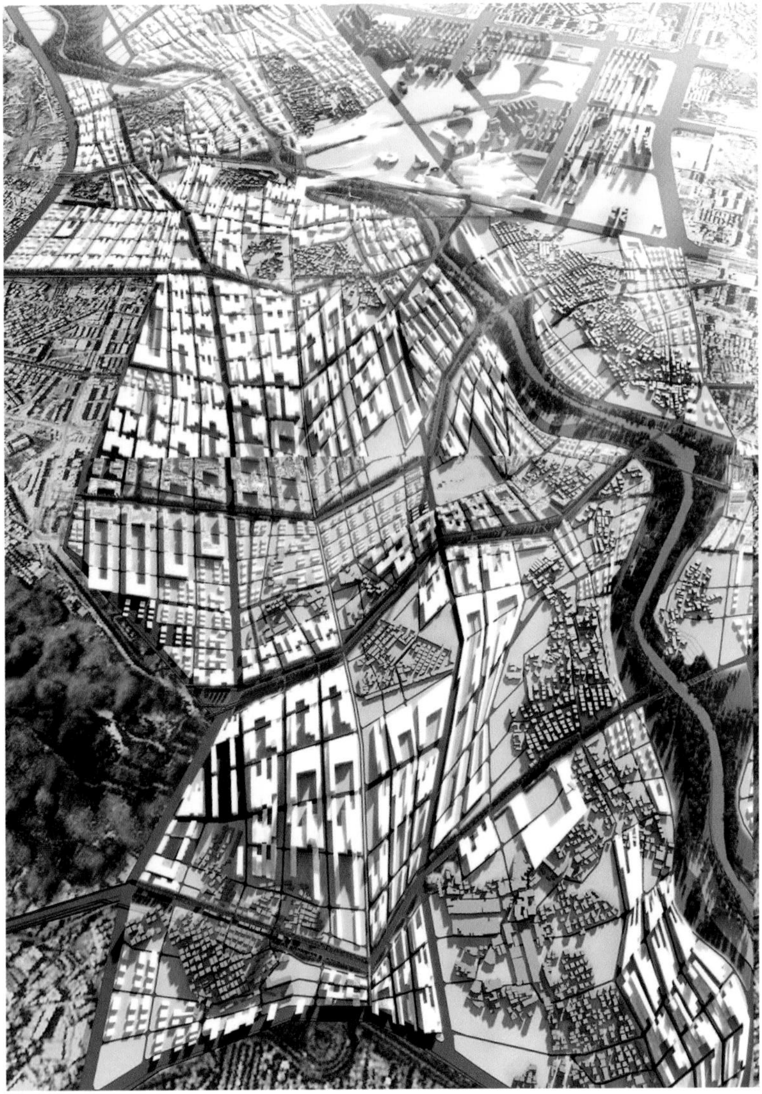

Aerial view of the proposed masterplan, indicating the variety of massing and its adaptability to local contextual conditions.

CASE STUDY

SERIE ARCHITECTS >XIN TIAN DI FACTORY H, HANGZHOU, CHINA

2010

Design Team: Christopher Lee, Bolam Lee, Martin Jameson, Kapil Gupta, Suril Patel, Stephie Sun, Charlotte Sue
Models: Joseph Halligan, Michelle Young, Fung Tsui

Serie Architects, alongside Grimshaw of London and Pysall Ruge Arkitekten of Berlin, was selected to renovate and design four large disused factories in Hangzhou, with Serie and Pysall Ruge designing one of the four factories each, and Grimshaw the remaining two. The 7,680-square-meter project for the adaptive reuse of factory to commercial and offices faced several conflicting demands. For the project to be economically viable, an insertion of floor areas totalling four times its original footprint would have to be accommodated. On the other hand, to fill up the factory would completely diminish its most unique feature—its sixteen-meter-high volume. Thus the main concern was to preserve the main hall of the factory as a spectacular internal volume and to accentuate the industrial drama of this massive void. The supporting programs—shops, restaurants, bars and creative offices—are placed in a surrounding plinth. This plinth acts as a device to emphasize the main factory building: in one sense it frames the factory, in another sense it serves as a pedestal above which we come face to face with the factory. The top surface of the plinth gently undulates and is punctured with green patios and water bodies, constituting an abstraction and re-reading of the natural landscape of Hangzhou.

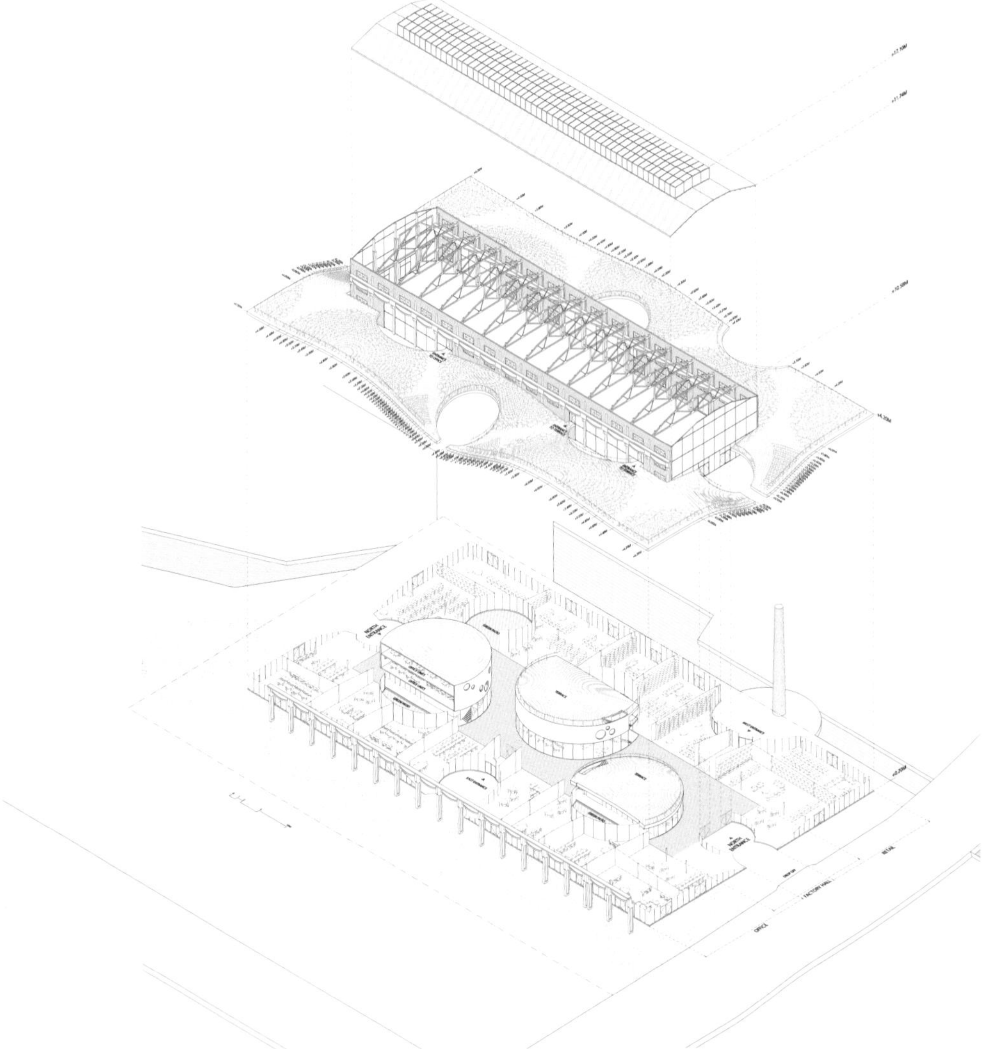

Axonometric drawing showing relation of existing building transformed with a programmatic plinth.

Elevation of proposal.

Model photo of proposed building regeneration.

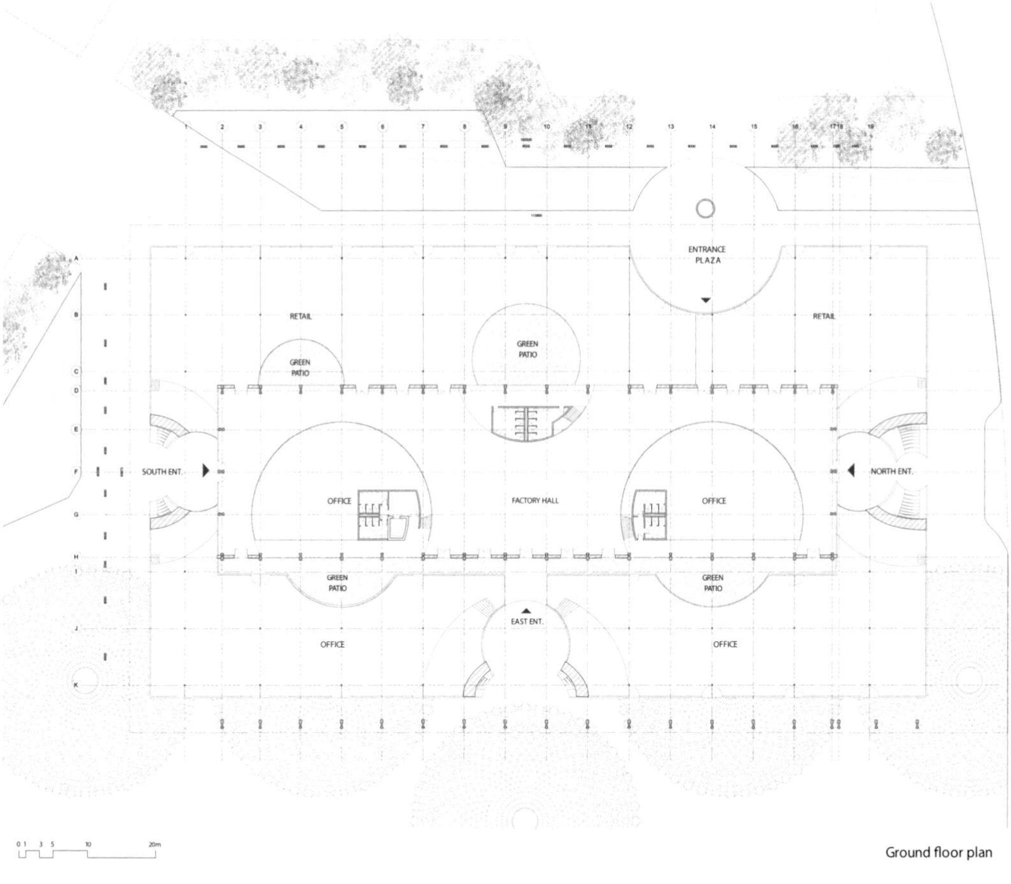

Ground floor plan

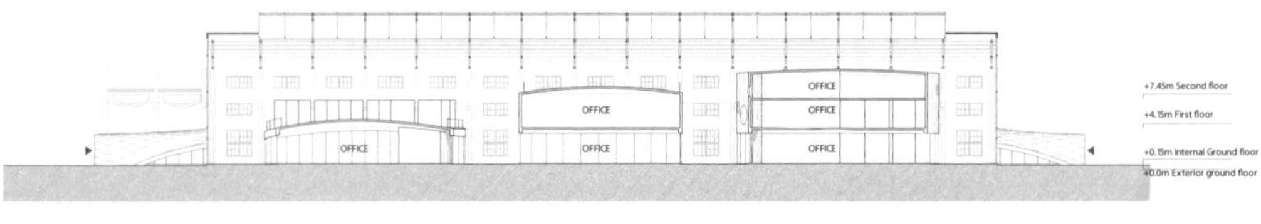

Section

Plan and section.

CASE STUDY

XWG STUDIO >REGENERATION OF PHOENIX SHOPPING STREET, BEIJING, CHINA

2010

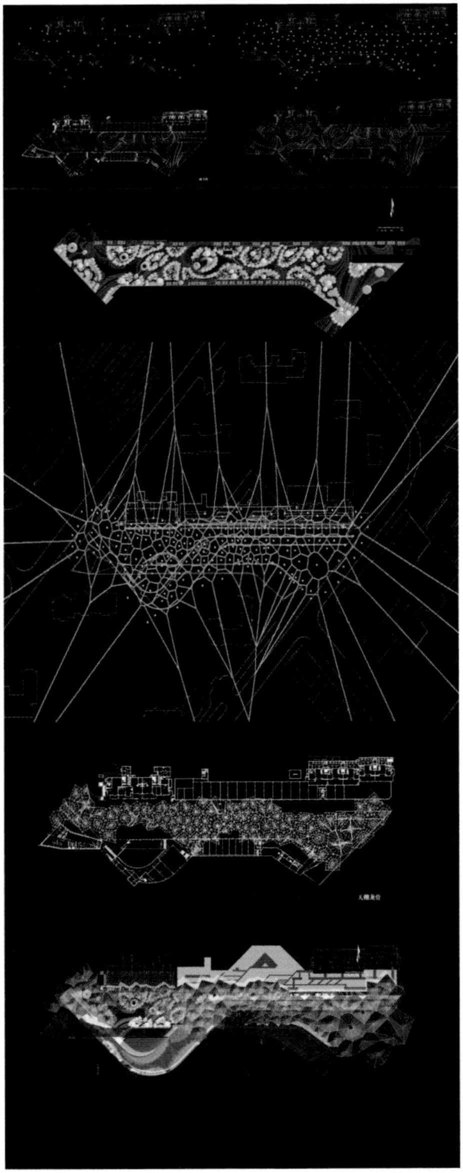

Client: CRLand Group Ltd., Beijing
Architects: XWG Studio
Design: Xu Weiguo and Xu Feng
Team: Yin Zhiwei, Guo Liang, Ma Lan, Xu Yujie

In this project for the regeneration of the 500-meter long, 15,000-square-meter Phoenix commercial street, the design team conducted some initial field investigations and statistical analysis, then set up an attractor system to break the isolated and static function of the existing shops. The existing linearity of the shopping street is thus broken to install greater communication between stores through the association of crowd movement and activities. A lightweight cellular structure is created and aggregated to form a canopy which responds to the specific conditions of programming on the ground level. The canopy transforms a disused urban zone, and creates a new, environment-friendly shopping experience. By adjusting the parameters of size, height, density, and transparency, the design team generated a gradated sense of differentiation through the entire site.

Process diagrams indicating points relating shopping programs to the distributed occupation of the vacant exterior, and their lines of flow generated from the points in the existing landscape and furnishing. An abstract Voronio diagram of cellular structure is generated and edited, leading to the final canopy design.

Diagrams in Ecotech software analysing environmental performance for heat gain.

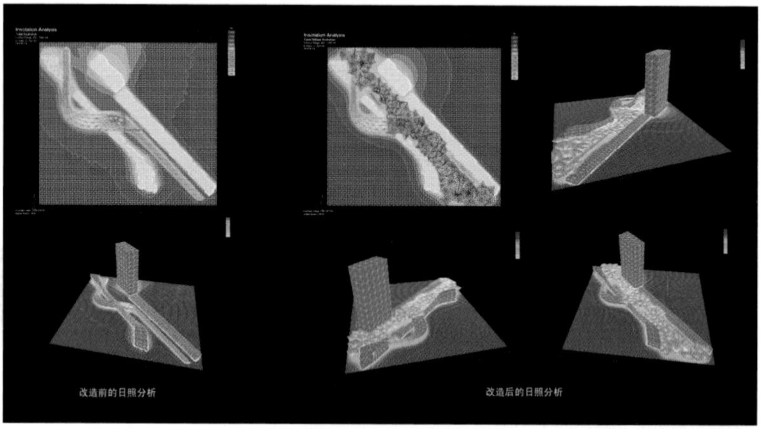

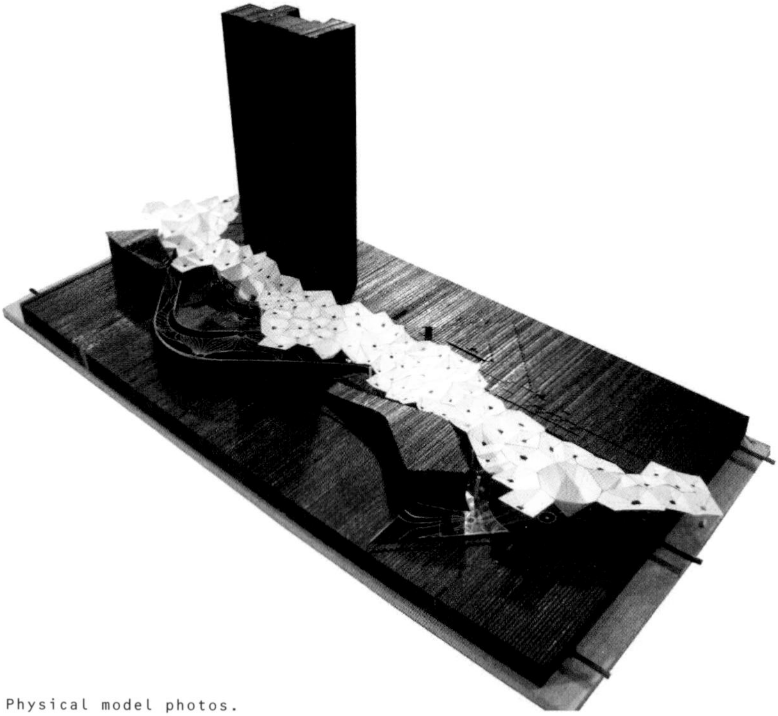

Physical model photos.

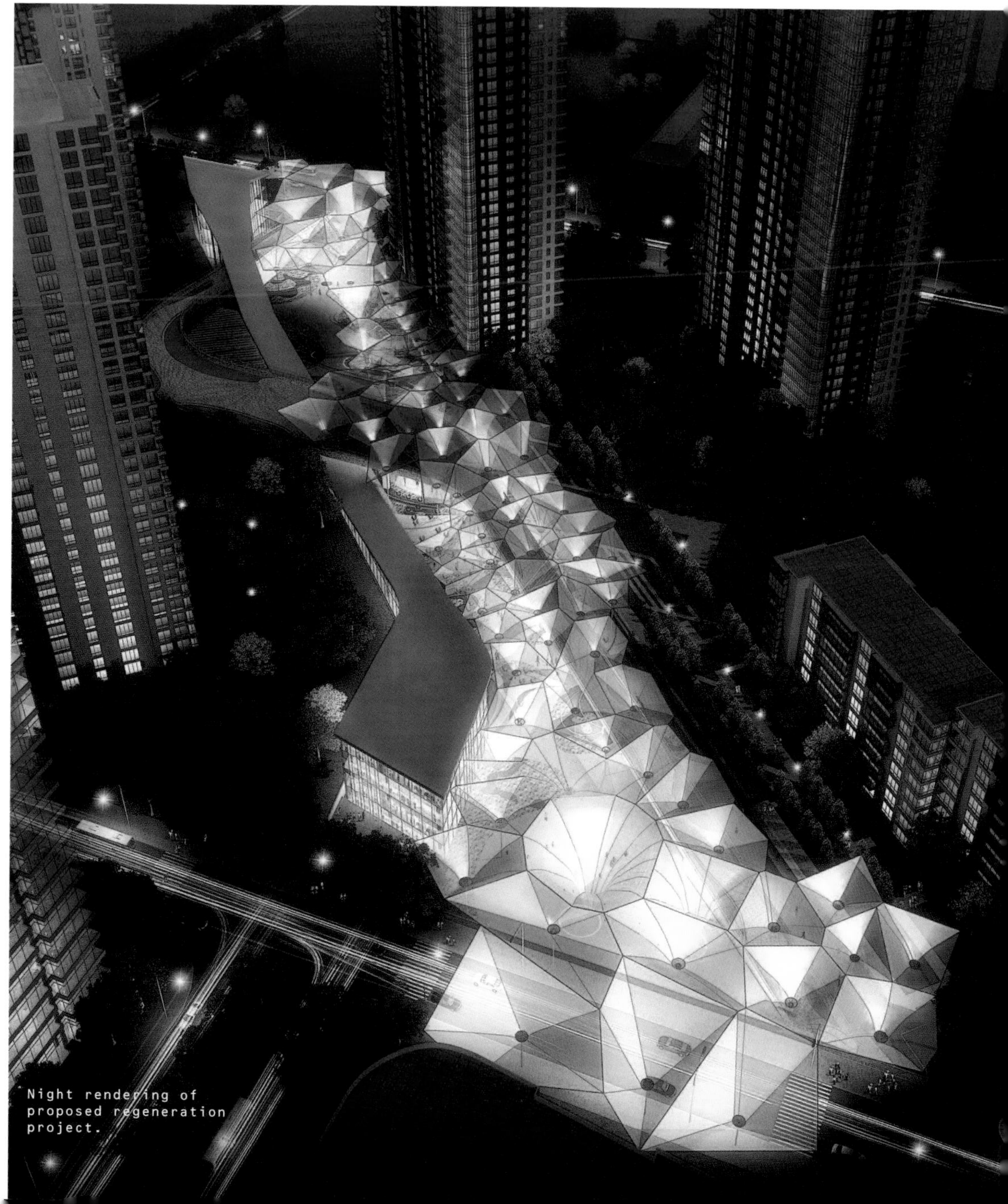

Night rendering of proposed regeneration project.

CASE STUDY

MAD >ORDOS MUSEUM, ORDOS, INNER MONGOLIA, CHINA

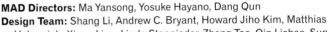

MAD Directors: Ma Yansong, Yosuke Hayano, Dang Qun
Design Team: Shang Li, Andrew C. Bryant, Howard Jiho Kim, Matthias Helmreich, Xiang Ling, Linda Stannieder, Zheng Tao, Qin Lichao, Sun Jieming, Yin Zhao, Du Zhijian, Yuan Zhongwei, Yuan Ta, Xie Xinyu, Liu Weiwei, Felipe Escudero, Sophia Tang, Diego Perez, Art Terry, Jtravis B. Russett, Dustin Harris
Associate Engineers: China Institute of Building Standard Design and Research
Mechanical Engineer: Institute of Shanxi Architectural Design and Research
Façade/Cladding Consultants: SuP Ingenieure GmbH, Melendez and Dickinson Architects
Construction Contractor: Huhehaote Construction Co., Ltd.
Façade Contractor: Zhuhai King Glass Engineering Co., Ltd.
Photographer: Iwan Baan

Six years ago, Ordos was part of the majestic Gobi desert. Today, it represents the common controversy of modern Chinese civilization: the conflict between the people's longstanding traditions and their dreams of the future. MAD was commissioned in 2005 to conceive a museum to be a centerpiece of the masterplan for a new great city. The 41,227-square-meter museum is a mysterious abstract form capable of fostering an alternate, timeless development of Chinese traditions and the future. The museum appears to float over an undulating artificial sand dune, a gesture saluting the landscapes which have now been supplanted by the streets and buildings of the new cityscape. Local citizens meet organically in the landscapes of the museum, at the intersection of nature and urban development. The interior presents a strong contrast to the exterior: an airy, monumental, cave-like space flushed with natural light through skylights, linking to a canyon between the galleries and exhibition hall.

Photographs documenting the transformation of Ordos, from 2004, when it was a patch of the Gobi Desert, to an urban center by 2009.

Views of the museum from the undulating plaza, and approaching the entrance of the museum.
Photos: Iwan Baan.

Interior of the museum.
Photo: Iwan Baan.

Aerial view of the relation of the museum massing and the undulating plaza.

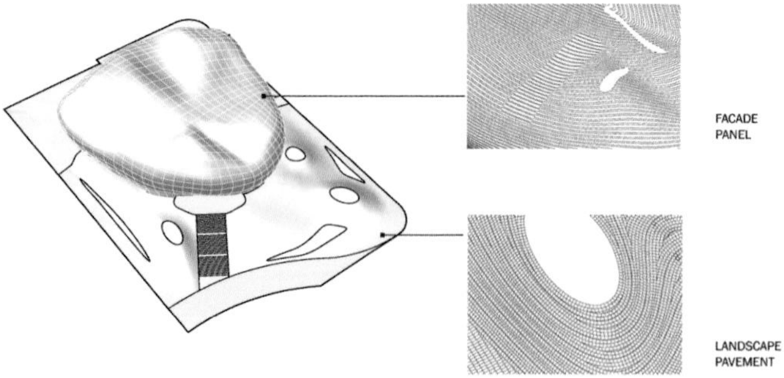

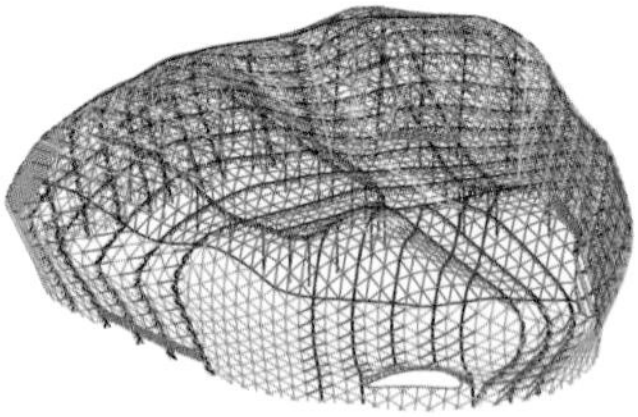

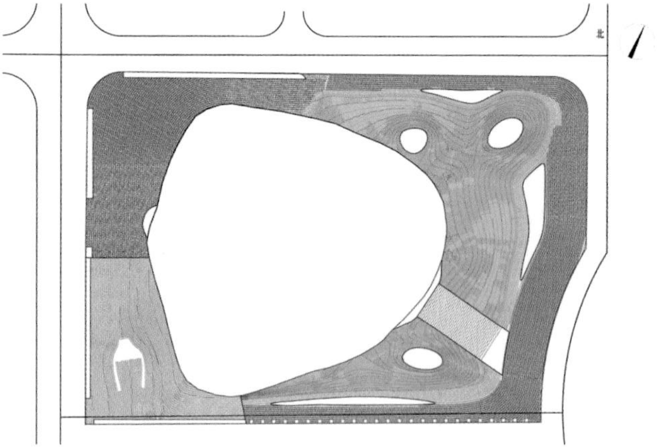

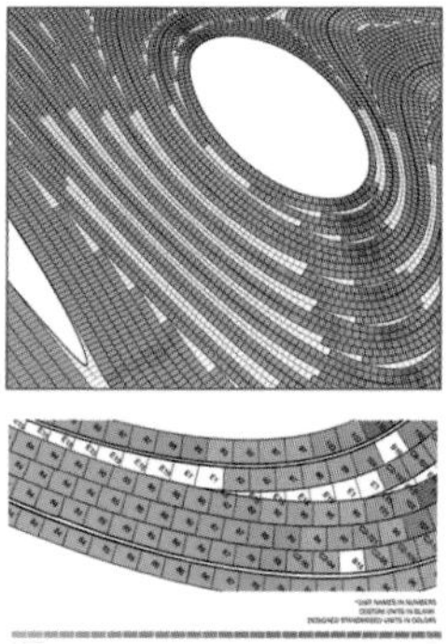

Diagrams indicating the pavement pattern of the undulating plaza, the organization of structural elements, and cladding.

CASE STUDY

HONG KONG PARAMETRIC DESIGN ASSOCIATION, DOTA, AND OCEAN CN >LIANTANG/ HEUNG YUEN WAI BOUNDARY CONTROL POINT PASSENGER TERMINAL BUILDING, HONG KONG SAR/SHENZHEN, CHINA

2011

This project was conceived and executed through the collaboration between three organizations, Hong Kong Parametric Design Association (HKPDA), dotA and OCEAN CN.

Design Team:
HKPDA: Sam Cho, Yang Wang, Ben Dai, Jaenes Bong
dotA: Gao Yan, Duo Ning, Chang Qiang
OCEAN CN: Tom Verebes, Eric Liu
Engineer: Chang Qiang (dotA)

This proposal for a border crossing facility between Hong Kong and Shenzhen inscribes an explicit, fluid connection between two disjoined territories while maintaining the discrete identities of both. The graphic qualities of traditional Chinese calligraphy, in which the movement of brushstrokes is frozen in space and time, helps to express the connection between these two cities, two geographies, two systems, as a fluid transitional space in which the identifiable characteristics of each side are concurrently associated yet distinguished through the peeling away of a series of tectonic roof bands, flanked by two strokes of office volumes which hover above on either side of the passenger crossing. Given the two parallel yet divergent ecological, planning, and political histories, the Hong Kong side is characterized primarily by wild protected landscapes and topographies, while the Shenzhen side is overwhelmingly artificial and urban. This proposal aims to synthesize the categories of the artificial and the natural through an emergent ecological paradigm, in which man-made, "mineral" urbanism is no longer conceived of as being in opposition with the natural, "biological" environment, but rather as fused in a symbiotic association of mobile dynamic forces and interactions. Gradient fields of computationally coded graphics become more dense and pronounced in slow zones, and more porous and ephemeral in the fast zones. Space is no longer fixed and static, but rather fluid as time.

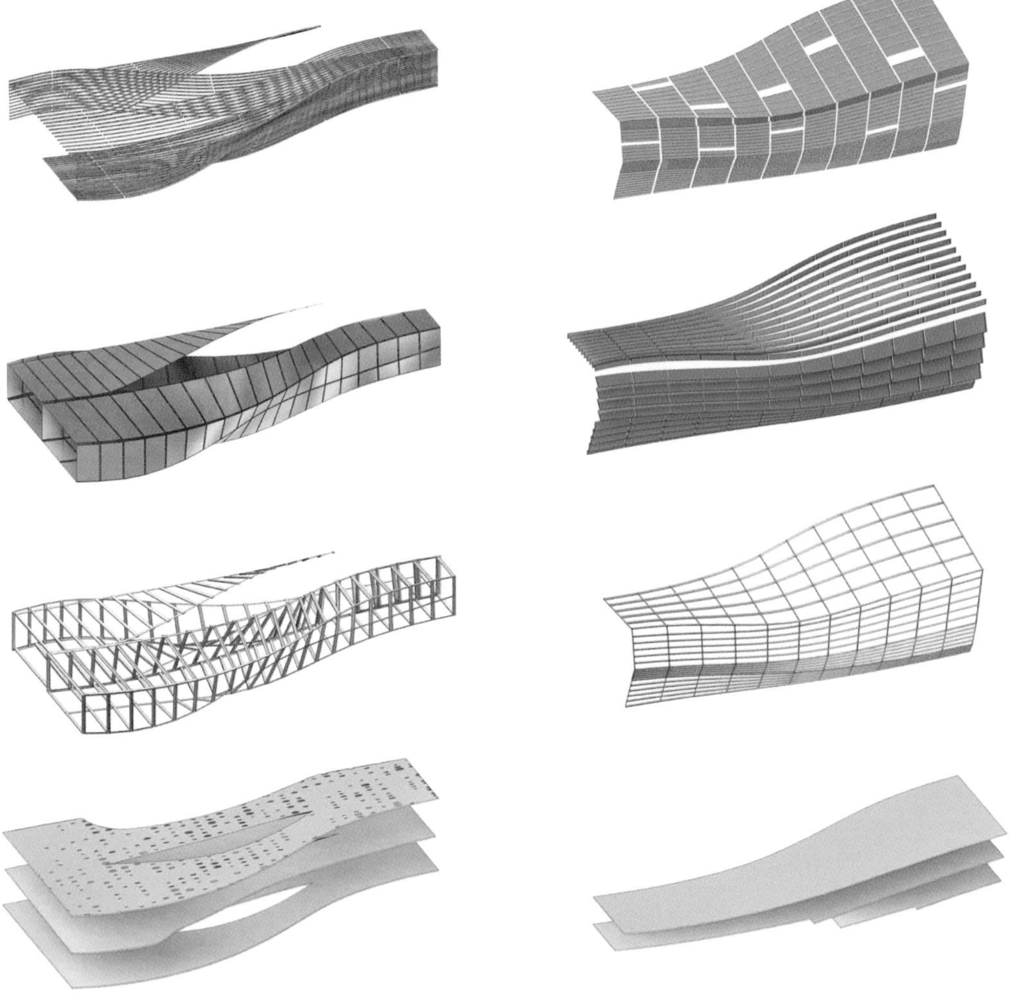

Diagrams indicating the correlation of surface, envelope, and structural systems.

Masterplan of the border crossing facility across both sides of the boundary.

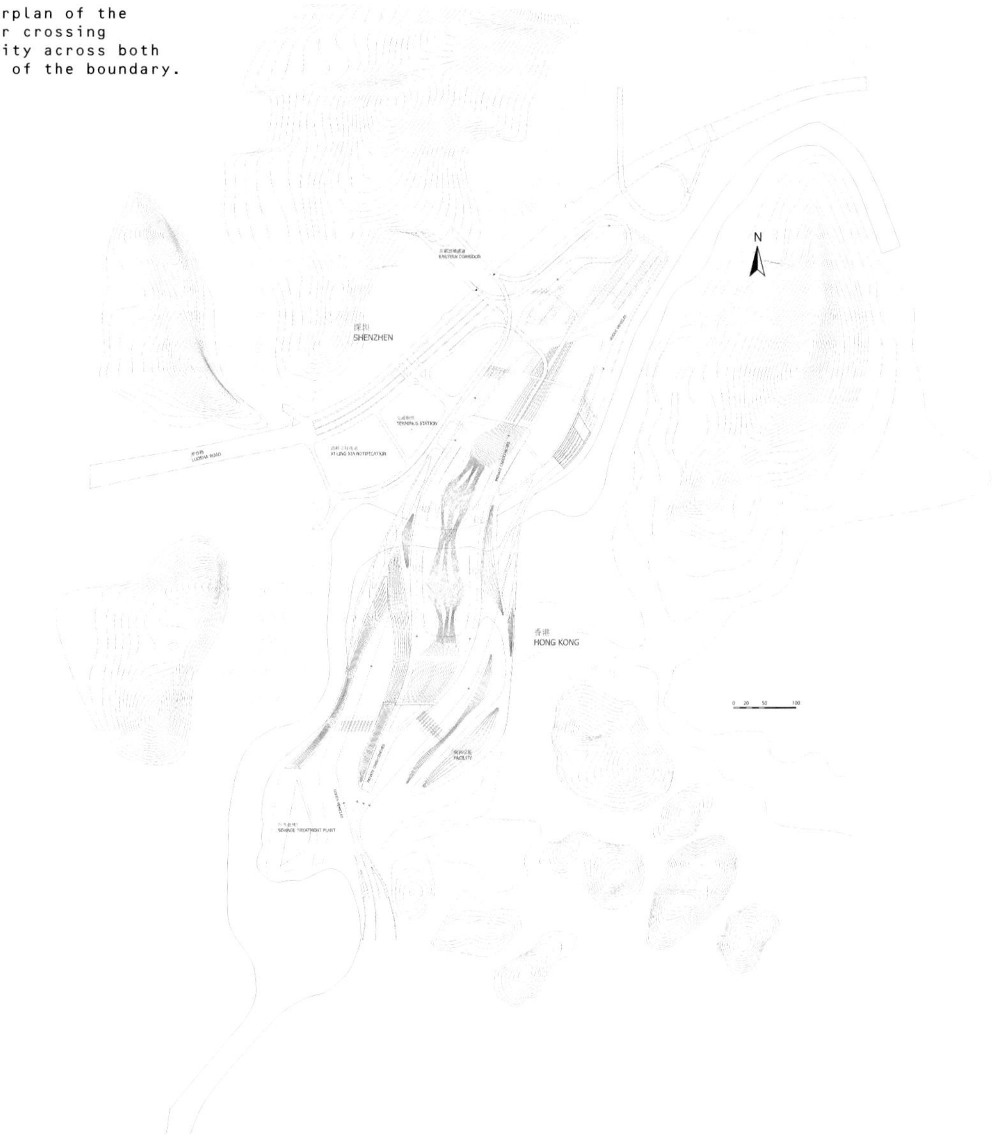

剖面 1:800
E - E SECTION

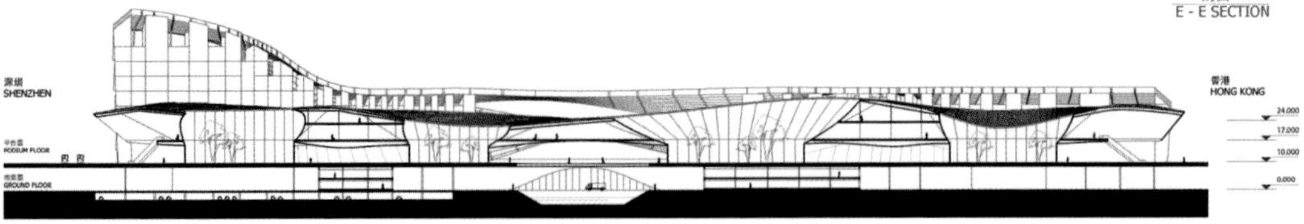

I - I 剖面
Section 1:1000

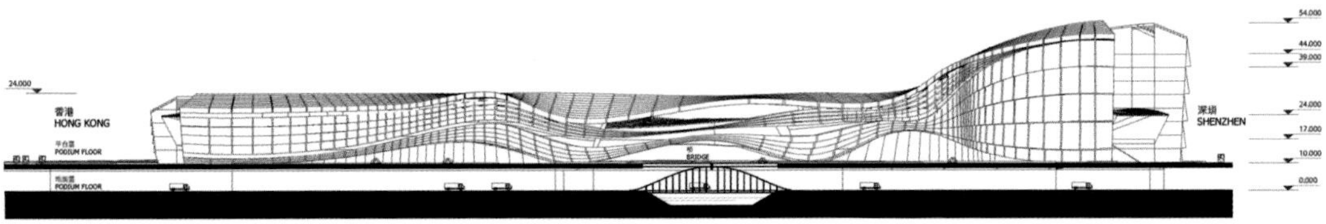

东立面
EAST ELEVATION 1:1000

Section and elevation of proposal, indicating the route across the boundary.

Aerial view of proposal, demonstrating fluid spatial effects across the boundary.

Night aerial view of proposal, demonstrating lighting effects.

CASE STUDY

THE UNIVERSITY OF HONG KONG RESEARCH TEAM, LED BY TOM VEREBES >COUNTERPART CITIES: FUTUREPORT, HONG KONG SAR, SHENZHEN, CHINA

2011

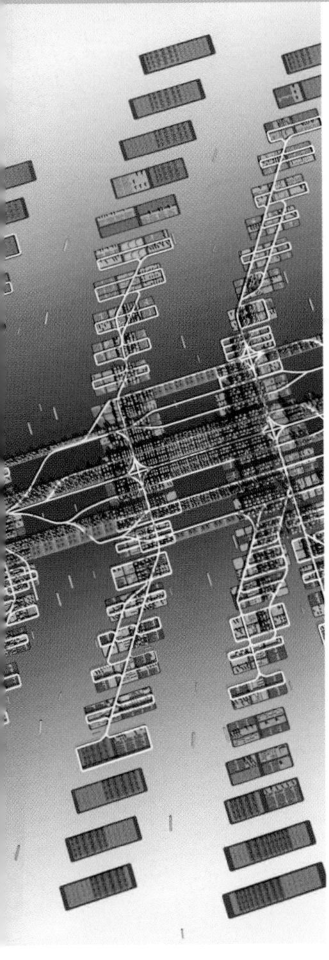

Funded Research Project (Tom Verebes, Principal Investigator)

HKU Team: Tom Verebes (Team Leader), Kristof Crolla, Gao Yan, Christian Lange, Praneet Verma (Research Assistant)
Arup Hong Kong: Ander Chow (Transportation); Iris Hwang, Ricky Tsui (Research)
Counterpart Cities Curators: Jonathan Solomon, Dorothy Tang

The *FUTUREPort* project is a design research project which speculates on the future of shipping, land management, manufacturing, environmental sustainability, and future urbanization in the Pearl River Delta (PRD). From an examination of thirteen ports in the PRD region, there is evidence of an acute limit on the available land for expansion, while older ports have crowded waterways and cannot cater to the largest vessels. As a visionary strategy for the development of a postindustrial economy in the PRD in relation to the future of the SZ-HK ports, a dynamic network of offshore cargo ports is proposed with a new high-density urban corridor in the mouth of the Pearl River, along the future Hong Kong–Macau–Zhuhai Bridge. Projected as a series of differentiated scenarios documented at instances from 2011 to 2111, the aim is to link the PRD region as a continuous city with a population of fifty million by the year 2111. The direct proximity of offshore ports to industrial production is the primary driver of this new model of the symbiosis of Shenzhen and Hong Kong. In addition, sources of clean energy harvesting are proposed as integrated wind and solar farms on offshore islands.

Detail plan of one sequence of islands of the maximum extent of proposal, one hundred years in the future.

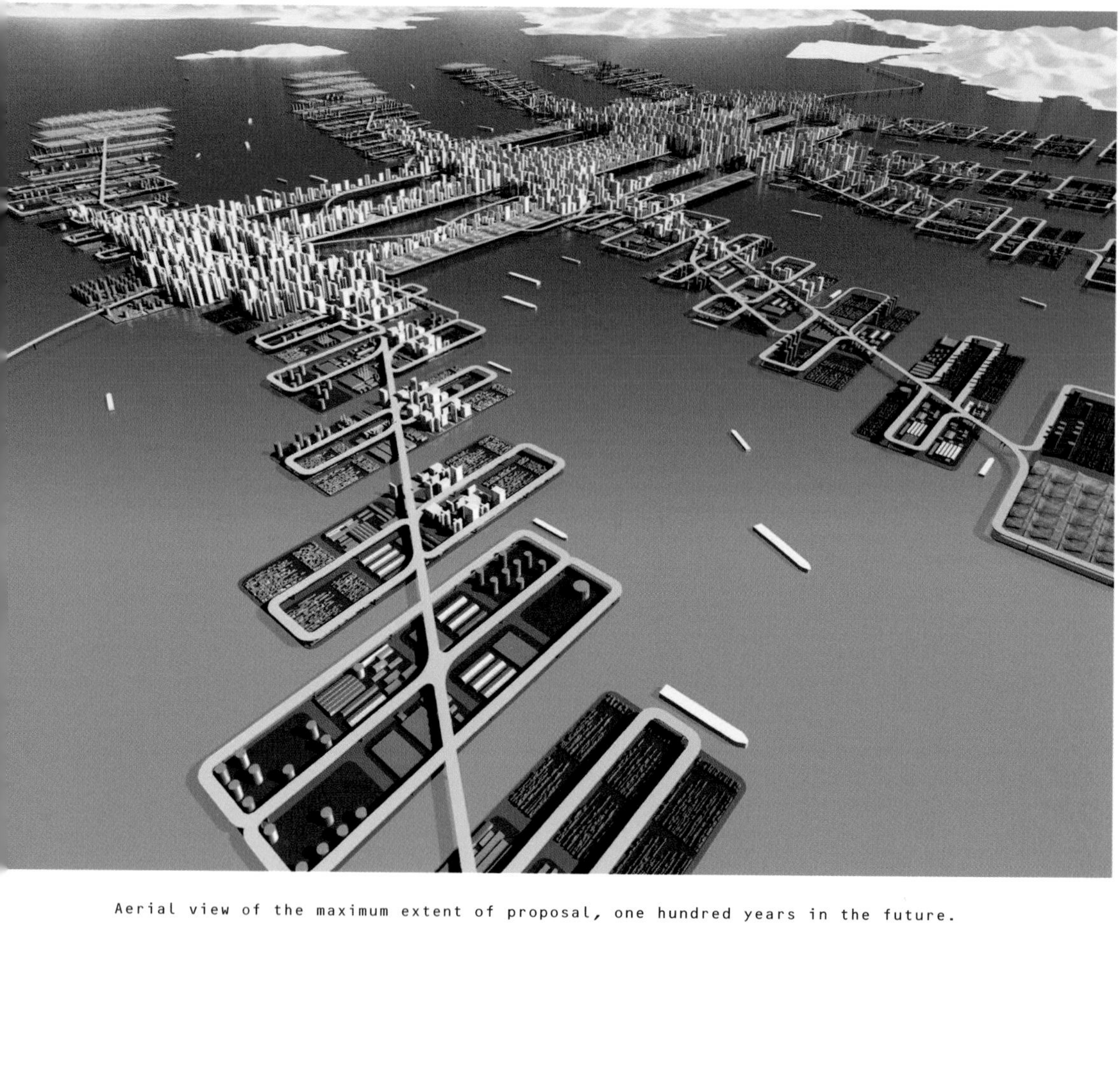

Aerial view of the maximum extent of proposal, one hundred years in the future.

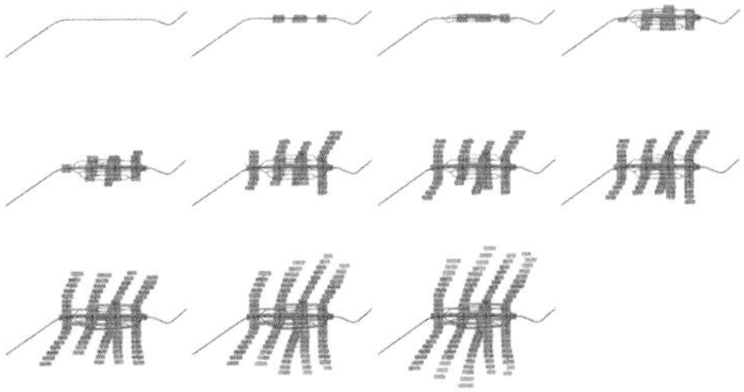

Projected growth of the Futureport over one hundred years.

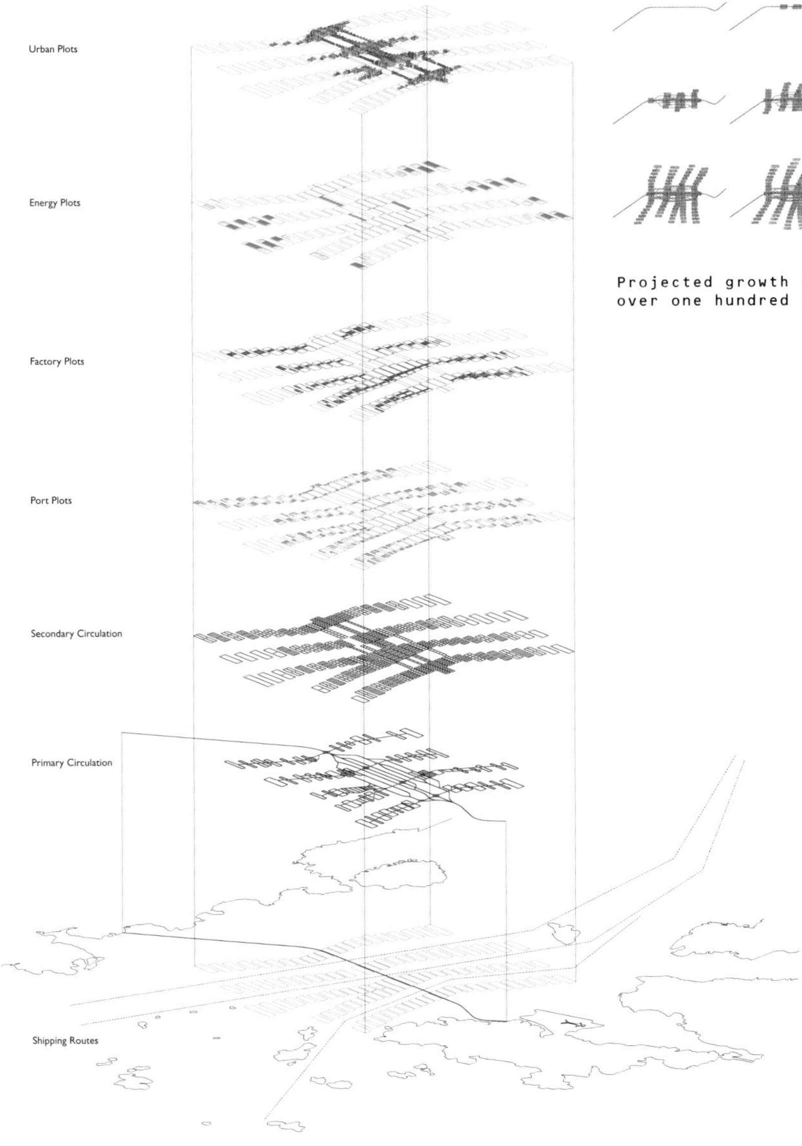

Axonometric drawing of four systems: urban, port, industry, and energy harvesting.

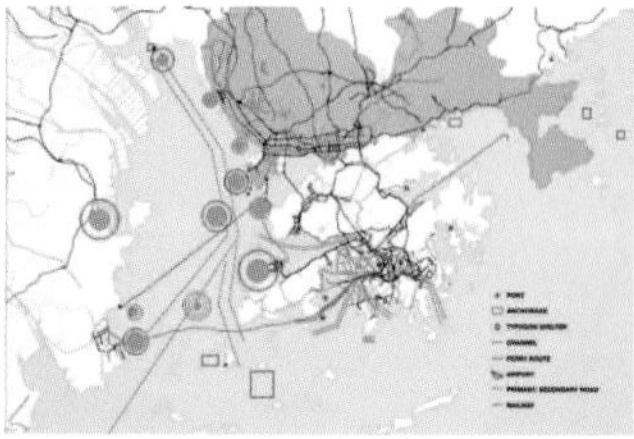

2055

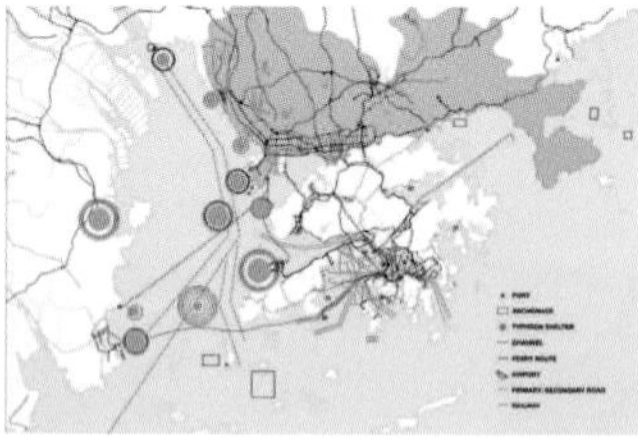

2070

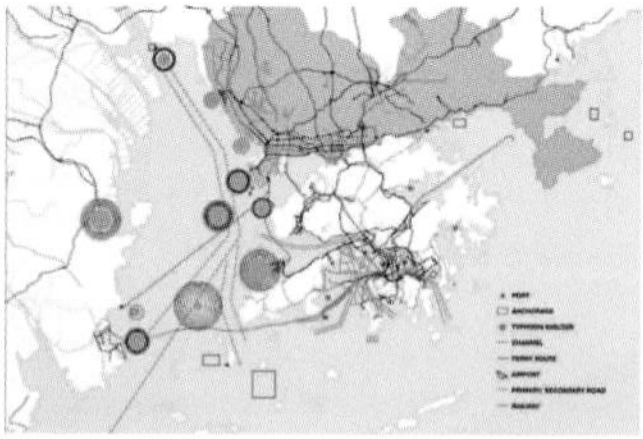

2085

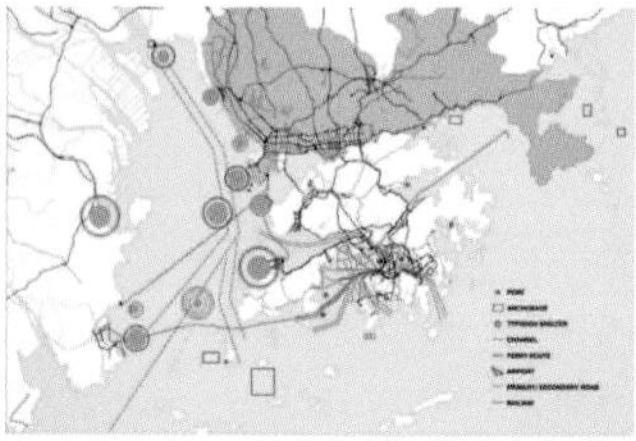

2060

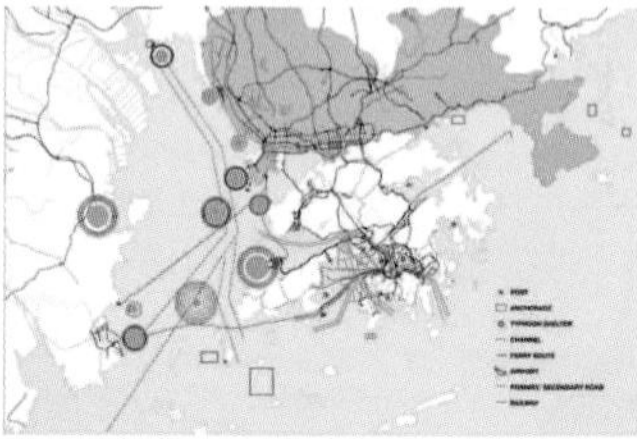

2075

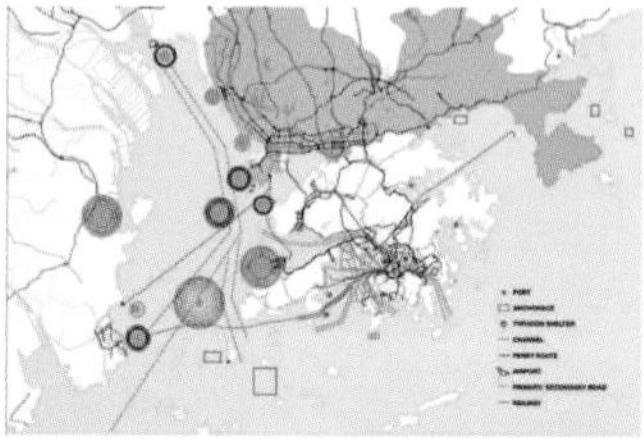

2090

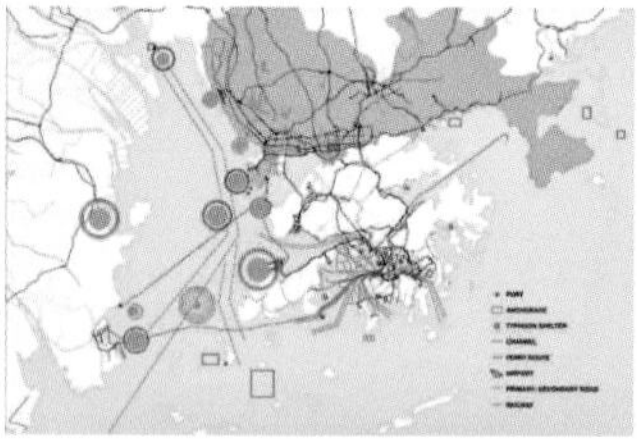

2065

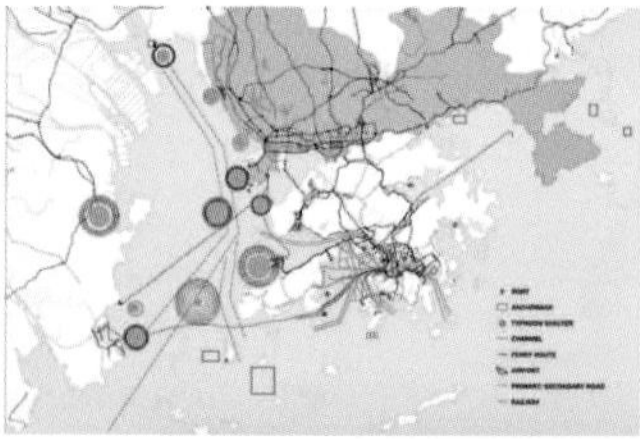

2080

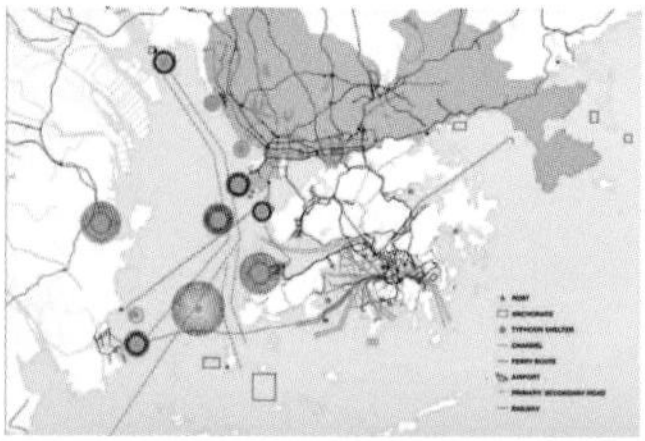

2095

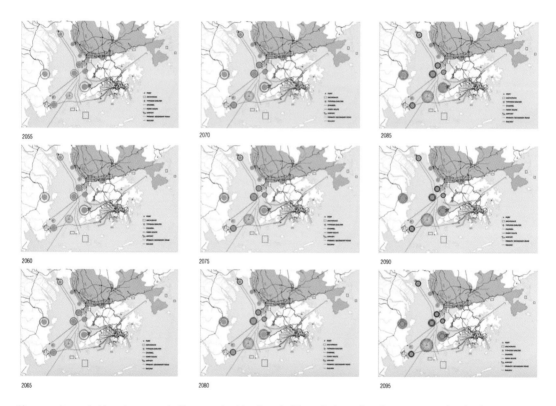

Changes to existing transport diagram in the Pearl River Delta, in the next one hundred years.

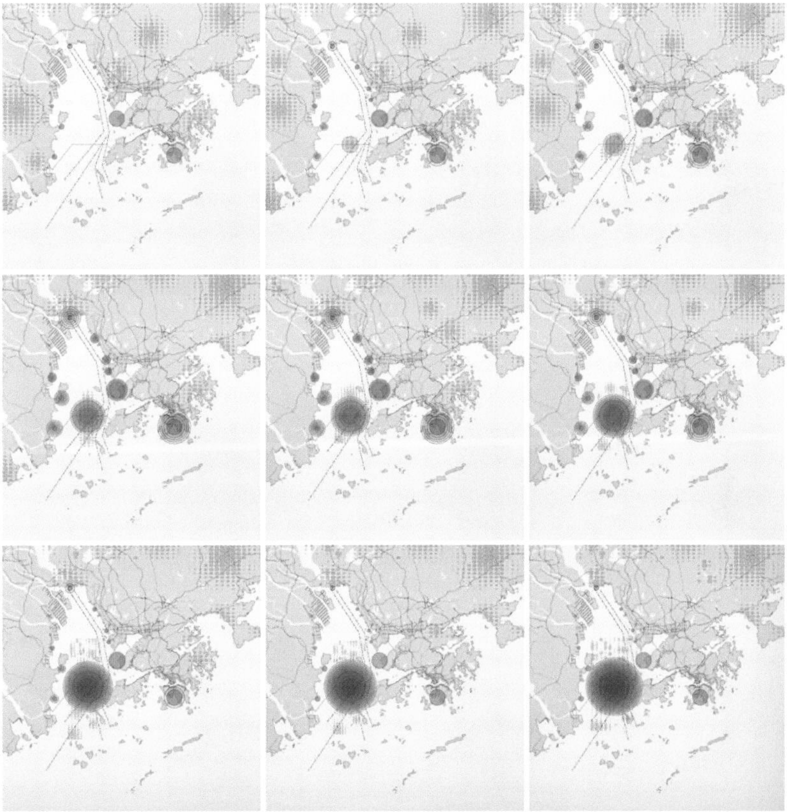

Projected growth of the ports of Hong Kong and Shenzhen, in the next one hundred years, towards the Hong Kong Macau Zhuhai Bridge.

Detailed axonometric drawing of one island indicating four systems: urban, port, industry, and energy harvesting.

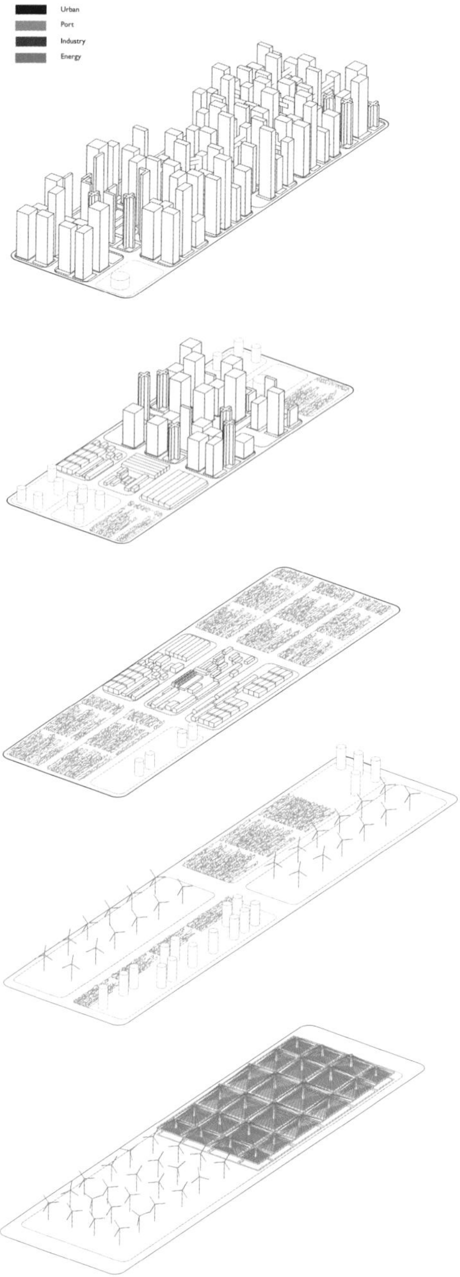

Physical model of the proposed scheme, demonstrating the integration of the urban, port, industry, and energy harvesting fields.

CHAPTER 19

CONVERSATION 6

BRETT STEELE (BS) WITH TOM VEREBES (TV)

TV This book aims to challenge the pervasive urban planning masterplanning concepts and methodologies which aim to project the final state of the city. In a context in which never before has so much urbanization occurred as in the last twenty years in China, cities are growing and changing so quickly, I am championing an evolutionary approach to urbanization. What is interesting at this stage is we have computational tools to not only design formal differentiations and specificities, but also to develop the capacity to manage and to control change without determining its final state. This thesis assumes all cities are not finite but rather that they are always in transition. The city offers a whole new level of complexity to harness and manage, but not to overdetermine.

BS I understand the thesis and the argument. Firstly, the city is a different category of problem than a structure, and also that the tools of the computational project might be aimed at new problems that architecture in its traditional scale cannot confront.

TV As the background from which to confront the reality of the extent of urbanization that has never before occurred, let's discuss and evaluate the pervasive models of urbanization of the twentieth century, and their relative successes, ongoing relevance, or even their pitfalls and possible mistakes that might be recurring within the extreme urbanization of Asia.

BS I sense a need to distinguish between what we think of as the city and the topic of urbanization. Urbanization is the history of how to modernize the city. The city itself is a concept and a reality that exists in a historical and contemporary form. What we think of the Asian urbanization today—it's very fast, it's very big, it's very unpredictable—is an iteration of phenomena that in the twentieth century could be found in Europe. In fact, I'm fascinated by the fact that Asia is Europe Version 2.0. It's not something that's wholly new, it's happening at a different scale, which brings an increasing complexity, but I think we need to reflect upon the European experience in the twentieth century. Problems of genericization, of universalization, were played out at a smaller scale when industrialization swept across cities beginning in the middle of the nineteenth century, and continued throughout the twentieth century to the rebuilding after the war. I don't find the condition of the early twenty-first-century in Asia new at all in terms of anything but quantities. The question that it raises has to do with our continuing expectation that a new condition demands new tools, which is what our generation has grown up on. Now what's most interesting about urbanization now, especially in Asia, is how old fashioned the models and the tools are. In this latest wave of urbanization, of which China is just an extreme end of something that started in Europe 150 years ago, built into architectural urban culture during this period is an expectation which many of us share, that new tools must be found to recognize new complex conditions. China is a record of bad urban strategies and histories being played out in real time. For me, when I come to the question of what are the new tools, techniques, ways of working, where I try and intersect it right now is at the level of saying: How do we take what's already out there and transform those rather than to invent a whole new category of how to think and act? The reality is China is a horrible record of this right now; nineteenth century stuff works. However bad those cities are, that's exactly what's driving the greatest wave of urbanization in human history. They are working on stuff Semper developed in the nineteenth century. I'm interested in, as a discipline, how those strategies and techniques can be reinvented, rather than just to ignore them and develop alternative universes. I feel like in the DRL world we created together, all that stuff didn't exist and we would start each year, on an October morning, developing a whole new way of thinking and working. In terms of our long-term conversation, that's where things for me have changed in the last couple of years. I'm oddly attracted to the old fashionedness of Chinese urbanization today, because it's not something to replace with a completely different world, it's actually something to work with in some ways.

TV It would be an impossibility to entirely supplant the current modes of production in China. One of the features of contemporary Asian urbanization, which I find problematic, is the spatial homogeneity of Chinese cities, which results from Fordist standardization of architectural production, brought toward urban planning. Increasingly nearly all Chinese cities look alike and they are ruthlessly repetitive and monotonous. In some ways there are opportunities to enable specificities to topographies, climates, local policies, cultural histories, and such. It may seem like I am harping on the legacy of Kenneth Frampton's critical regionalism, but in some ways he recognized some of the limitations of modernist ideologies and methodologies, which had failed as a universal model. A Brazilian city looks different than an Indian city, which looks different than Switzerland. So, in effect, what are the potentials for the kinds of tools that can create and amplify specificities? To what extent can computational design and production methods usher in large-scale nonstandardization as a means to confront the generic nature of contemporary cities?

BS For me the striking thing about Chinese cities is not how much they look alike, one to the other, but how much they look like Le Corbusier's urban visions a hundred years ago. The legacy of modern principles has persisted to an almost unbelievable degree. The differentiation I'm looking for is a disciplinary or discursive one, which is that cities ought to look like something other than last century's modernism. That's where I think Asia is crushing the world by validating Le Corbusier's primacy on infrastructure and his relationship of figure–ground. The consultants building those cities are trained with the legacy of modernism, and this needs to be combated in some way. In how you frame your question, I don't know if the specificity should be that of the specific differences of one city to another. For me personally, I don't need local differentiation the way Kenneth Frampton does. Computation does not necessarily deal with specificity because the computer is a machine designed for universalization. When Turing invented the computer, he called it the "universal machine." There are other technologies and ways of working that can introduce specificity, but I'm not so worried about making cities different from one another.

TV I think one of the features of European modernism that all architects and urbanists had to deal with in the last century was the persistence of the historical legacy of the city upon which they superposed their modern world. Recapitulating Colin Rowe and Fred Koetter, the city is a field for negotiating its history and modernization. Asian urbanization has confidence to build and finalize the city in one go, which seems not only shortsighted, but incredibly wasteful. The history of Hong Kong as a model should raise alarm for what China should not do: build the city once, tear it down; do it again, tear it down; keep tearing it down until it seems right and mature. All cities grow and change and eventually go through a feverish state of redefinition, and then they settle to be mature cities.

BS Don't you find that interesting how cities can be built, torn down, and rebuilt?

TV I think it's more interesting that cities are built in ways to enable urban culture to mature and endure.

BS Well, that's good European sentiment. I think that you need to defend your belief against a billion people today who think otherwise.

TV Here are some paradoxes. Between flexibility and inflexibility of a design; the wish for permanent, long-lasting, and enduring architecture versus the adaptability of the city and its ability to change; fitness for purpose versus indeterminacy. On the one hand the city should be long-lasting, which albeit is a European bias. On the other hand, the city needs to have the capacity to be able to absorb all kinds of dynamics and change.

BS It's a very clear point of view, but I think you have to then defend the argument that that form of change and transformation cannot be accommodated in any other ways. The Asian solution seems not to adapt the city but simply build a new, different city, which is a countermodel to the argument you are making, that cities themselves don't need to adapt. You and I would expect that cities inherently have that structural and cultural capacity to do that. Clearly the Asian experience is suggesting a countermodel, which is that the city is actually the latest extension of a functionalist form of adaptation which modernist architecture was willing to live with at the scale of building, but not at the scale of a precinct or city. When you think of the ways in which buildings themselves outlive their purposes, in say Cedric Price's argument, you just tear the building down and refigure it. Cedric's other extreme, which is to say when I need a university I'll adapt a disused postindustrial landscape, as Potteries Thinkbelt, and turn that into a university. The Asian phenomenon demonstrates how that argument can be scaled up so that it happens at the scale of the city and that seems to be the thing you are resisting in your argument. You're saying that there can actually be a considerably malleable urban settlement strategy or pattern that can carry on in time. Asia seems to be saying the opposite, and they just keep building new cities.

TV Also demonstrated over the last twenty years is how such bad architecture has been built as a result of ongoing rapid urbanization, leaving little choice but to tear it down and rebuild it again, but better. So I agree with Cedric Price's second category of adaptive reuse. Reprogramming is a model which is still materially, economically, and environmentally more sustainable than a tabula rasa model, which is what is happening all over Asia. It is increasingly a bankrupt ideology on economic, social, environmental grounds to build only for the short term.

Let's discuss the extent to which computation isn't just a tool for spatial heterogeneity or geometric complexity, but to build in capabilities to manage and interact in real time with change in cities.

BS As a kind of design operation?

TV Yes, but also as a management tool, as an interface, or a way of interacting with the ongoing changes which differs from the overspecificity and determination of the masterplan to be describing a fixed, teleological endpoint.

BS Although you could say that's a quality that is increasingly hard to find. Perhaps the functionality that a plan played in the past is now being performed in other ways through real-time sensing, or more malleable planning regulations or something that allows for change of some other form. It's almost the loss of teleology today that I guess I'm wondering about. The one thing that the discipline had was the ability to project a future, which our generation seems to have surrendered that will. It's another century now—we are not going to do the big plan, rather, we are going to expect that the future is unknowable, unpredictable and we are going to set up infrastructure for many different scenarios to play out. On the other hand you can say if that entirely surrendered free-market altitude to the future is really in place, you know what's going to happen is the most valuable people in the world are those who claim the ability to plan the future. I've been thinking a lot about this lately, not at an urban scale but at the scale of architectural knowledge, that the idea of investing in a vision of the future has almost universally been unloaded. No one our age has a vision of the city in twenty years. Fifty years ago everyone was doing a city of the future. Your project is aiming for a vision of the future too.

TV I'm keen to confront the seeming crisis of a distinct lack of capability to conceive, with great certainty, multiple ways in which the future can play out. Over the last five years, we've discovered the world is incredibly unpredictable. A masterplan from early 2008 would soon have become an almost useless document as a result of the GFC [Global Financial Crisis]. Alternatively, we can develop methodologies to project the future but knowing that the future can change and adapt. We might get it entirely wrong, as the city is wild and not fully controllable. I am trying once again to make claims that we can project the future but admit that it's not a future that we'll be able to say that there's an absolute end to it. How, then, can we harness and embed complexity through computational tools and interfaces, rather than trying to eliminate complexity?

BS It can sound very quickly like the purpose of that project is to avoid failure. In fact, one of architecture's great capacities is its consistent failure. Every version of the future that architects have ever drawn up has been categorically wrong, and yet we look back on the history over centuries and it still defines the form of knowledge we think of as architecture. Palladio's cities, Ledoux's cities, Le Corbusier's cities were never realized in their time. In each case it was its failure that makes it still so compelling today as a form of knowledge. What you are making an argument for is the urgency for architects to get things right, not by prescribing it but by setting up a model that recognizes a form of reality that will align with that. As architects, we cannot avoid glimpsing into the future, and in fact we spend most of our time doing projects that don't come close to fruition. The thing you and I would share is the vision that these cities being created at lightning speed are wrong precisely because their models are from several decades ago, instead of somebody's new model today that we know will never be proliferated or even built.

TV Maybe there is a shift from an understanding of the vision of the future being fixed and attainable, toward the notion of an interface that engages with the complexities that shape the model, or the parameters that need to be recognized and accommodated in the model. If we accept the inevitable failure of all models, we can redeem the model if it becomes more plastic and interactive. Can this also address the urgent need for architecture or architects not to be become redundant, that our discipline remains relevant and capable of projecting futures? I am saying we need to provide tools, or interfaces, rather than images, which can be informed by a range of constituents and contingencies, from the abstract economy, planners and policy makers, individual investors and clients. For a masterplan to avoid failure, I believe this will entail the development of adaptive capabilities, to absorb difference and change without its model, or masterplan, becoming defunct and useless, or deemed a failure.

BS Surely that could be accomplished. I could imagine a team in Google achieving this, if they would throw enough resources, intelligence, computational wherewithal, specialization, etc. If you scan the discipline today for visions of the future of cities, one of the striking features is the lack of its imagery. Zaha [Hadid] had no problem in 1983 to draw the future of Hong Kong. The Peak was one little building that was used as an excuse for drawing a vision of the city. For that generation, images of the future were a way to organize a kind of research project that careers eventually grew out of. At some point the model you are describing will need to be consolidated into images people can understand. If you think of a global economy now dominated by the circulation of images, I feel like architects especially are put in a privileged position to play a key role in imaging the future. Most of Corb's images highlight the difference between reality and the model, and he was able to collapse into literally an image which then much of twentieth-century architectural culture gets organized around. What you're looking for is an equivalent to the *Domino House*, to scale it from architecture to the city.

TV It may not be the image of computational architecture, which generally involves spatial, mathematical, and geometric operations, because these kinds of models cannot be simply scaled up, despite their topology. So I think there are potentials to use Building Information Modeling (BIM) for what is notionally being called City Information Modeling (CIM), a way of conceiving the model as something plastic and interactive which can take many different states. The city model is then informational and it produces ranges of options that potentially house a degree of automation, not for the goal of the efficiency and construction delivery like the Building Information Modeling paradigm, but rather to model the city as unfinished, to be contaminated, polluted, and still maintain its coherence. We have game environments that do that, for instance *SimCity*. In which ways can these new tools help to reshape models of the city as interactive processes rather than as representations of static images?

BS Then urbanism, as a practice, becomes a form of interactivity with which to reshape the thing you refer to as the masterplan. You want it to be malleable, elastic, undoubtedly adaptable in time, to take in different kinds of information that might not be predictable, and with that remain a living, viable model to unfold the city. I think that's very interesting, because clearly Asia disagrees. Asia simply wants to make it happen and they are quite happy to work with nineteenth- and twentieth-century models, and they have proven in fact they can house 300 million people with old models. Their models don't need to be interactive. It can be entirely top-down. A billion people in China are saying the opposite: that twentieth-century models can be scaled up, but with more resources, more centralized control, less questioning. I agree we should proliferate new models and new ways of working, but how we do that should acknowledge the fact that we're an extreme minority who would like to overcome old models.

TV Perhaps there is a parallel of the scale of architecture to the city, which can piggyback how computational design was sold to developers by convincing them the buildings can be produced cheaper and faster, and they will last longer, i.e. they will make more money. This is where the City Information Model analogy can be understood as a new piece of software that's able to manage the city better. It will not result in its infrastructure and its architecture being defunct and obsolete so quickly, which defines its selling point.

BS That's exactly right. I was going to get to the same point. If we look at my bad analogy, what Le Corbusier did was to create an argument around his *Domino* model that people could access and understand. But you're right to say that's the task for today, as these forces are already at play in the informational city, and there's a way in which you can convey that reality legitimates the tools you want to bring to it.

TV But will this thesis succeed? Shall we predict that everything in this book will be proven wrong toward the end of our careers?

BS Much faster than that! The world is moving fast. The leapfrogging is staggering. When they learn to grow buildings next week, all of this becomes irrelevant.

TV I still believe we need to combat the recurring history of sequential failed projections which mars the history of twentieth-century urbanization.

BS It's funny, we are talking about the Asian experience a lot at the AA right now for a number of reasons. The difference between European cities and Asian cities is increasingly interesting. Are you really making an argument, then, for models that are geographically differentiated in their logics, expectations, and understandings? This oddly fits with Kenneth Frampton for it ought to be differentiation in the geographic sense; he was arguing for cultural difference, but in the end it was geography which drove the differences of Northern Europe versus Southern Europe, for instance. I think you are actually progressing Frampton's critical regionalism and the universal assumptions of the twentieth century. There are ways to defend the Asian bias, but I have to confess complete innocence to the whole thing, since I don't get Asian cities at all. I'm completely baffled as well by European cities because I come from America.

TV There are parallels between American and Asian urbanization. Contemporary Asian urbanism has a propensity toward a tabula rasa model, generally incapable of negotiating and including preexisting historic urban conditions.

BS You see, you're Colin Rowe in the end!

TV The conflict arises recognizing that ancient cities, towns, or villages are incapable of meeting current demands of urbanization, so this exceeds juxtaposition, as in Rowe's incoherent assemblages, it is really the inadequacy of history to remain relevant and for current models to make it relevant. So history is pickled and left unable to negotiate, accommodate, and fulfill contemporary demands. Yet erasing Asia's material history is an incredible mistake.

BS It's hard to not agree with that position. China locked into the notion that heritage drives global economies much too late. Travel and tourism is the largest segment in the global market today, without which they're left with all the factories.

TV The problem with heritage in mainland China is that it is equated only with tourism. This is really a kind of different problem than the one that Colin Rowe and Fred Koetter faced when trying to reconcile the failures of modernization in Europe through layering the contemporary world onto the historical world, which meshed neatly, even if incoherently. The historic fabric in Asia, tragically, due to its total dysfunctionality, is unmeshable with the new.

BS We're publishing a series of Mao essays in the Words series. He does not see urbanization as two conditions with an onus to negotiate a historical condition. Mao sees only one condition. The failure of all previous models is the justification of his singular model. That's what makes it a political project. He's barking mad. This is a guy who thought he was the center of the universe.

Thanks, Tom, this has been super-interesting and I'll be thinking about it all day.

TV Thanks Brett, for an inspirational conversation this afternoon and for helping to shape the discourse emanating from this book.

TOM VEREBES >CONCLUSION

In the months of working through the writing and editing of this book, the cumulative mission has been to challenge the static nature of conventional masterplanning practices. The line of questioning has focussed on the relevance of pursuing conclusive, determinable projections of the future. In this light, it may be somewhat fitting that the reader now be presented with a conclusion arguing, in effect, against conclusions.

In considering an information-driven approach to urban growth, change, densification, and time-based long-term development, this book has probed the complex implications of advanced computational design technologies for the design and management of dynamic urban systems. These new approaches to urbanism engage with a multiplicity of factors, contingencies, and responsibilities involved in the design of large scale architectural projects, urban design, and masterplanning. It is against such projects, and their behavior as temporal constructs, that this thesis will be measured in the future.

A series of oppositions characterizing the evolutionary mechanisms of urbanism have arisen, including history and the future, convention and innovation, endurance and ephemerality, permanence and change—all of these help to explicate the concept of evolution in cities, society, and culture. These are complex issues, and we have sought to negotiate these seeming dichotomies, rather than to present them as polarizing. The ways in which oppositions such as planned versus informal urbanization, top-down versus bottom-up growth, or control versus deregulation can be discredited perhaps provide this book with its underlying motive—finding a balance between mechanisms and processes, man and nature. These negotiations encapsulate the urgent issues facing contemporary urbanization.

Although aspects of computational approaches to design are increasingly prevalent in architectural research, education, and practice, these methodologies remain largely untheorized. Despite the disciplinary and professional transformations which have occurred as a result of the progressive embedding of digital design, analysis, simulation, management, and production systems, there is an absence of theory underpinning contemporary design work. There is a need for research and intellectual formulation to catch up with the proliferation of emergent technologies, which has been driven primarily by the technical interests of avant-garde design technologists. This technological retooling in practice and education presents one of the most profound intellectual challenges for our generation: to discover the theoretical, cultural, political, social—and urban—implications of these new computational practices. In this light, this book elaborates the intellectual formulation of the rich, and relatively undiscovered, conceptual arena inherent in designers' new ways of working.

The thesis of this book represents a unique opportunity to overcome some of the familiar criticisms of western dominance in architectural culture, and to articulate a new, evolutionary approach to urbanism with immediate pertinence for professionals, academics, and students worldwide. Within the rapidly growing community of computational designers, the repertoire of computational design at the scale of architecture is already well rehearsed, yet computational urbanism is still largely untheorized, with only a few examples of built projects. This lack of concrete, grounded examples of evolutionary urbanism has been a challenge as well as an opportunity and a central motivation for this research initiative. It has involved a quest which is far from new, but one which may provide a vital set of correspondences, conduits for the transfer of knowledge, and areas for further investigation into this fertile arena for years to come.

This book is less about teaching than it is about learning; less about dissemination than it is about discovery; less about answers than it is about questions. Rather than confirming teleological solutions, new problems have been outlined. "Time," as the saying goes, "will tell."

BIBLIOGRAPHY

Aish, R. (2006) "Exploring the Analogy that Parametric Design is a Game," in *Game Set Match: On Computer Games, Advanced Geometries and Digital Technologies*, eds. K. Oosterhuis and L. Feireiss (Rotterdam: Episode).

Alexander, C. (1967) "The Question of Computers in Design," *Landscape*, Autumn.

Alexander, C. (1968) "Systems Generating Systems," in *Systemat* (Berkley: Inland Steel Products Company).

Alexander, C. (1977) *A Pattern Language* (New York: Oxford University Press).

Alexander, C. (1980) *The Nature of Order, Book 1: The Phenomenon of Life* (Berkeley: CES).

Alexander, C. (1980) *The Nature of Order, Book 2: The Process of Creating Life* (Berkley: CES).

Allen, S. (1995) "From Object to Field," in *Architectural Design* 67, no. 5–6: 24.

Andraos, A., El-Samahy, R., Heyda P., et al. (2001) "How to Build a City: Roman Operating System," in *Mutations*, ed. R. Koolhaas, S. Boeri, S. Kwinter, N. Tazi, and H.U. Obrist (Barcelona: Actar).

Attali, J. (2001) "The Roman System, or the Generic in All Times and Tenses," in *Mutations*, ed. R. Koolhaas, S. Boeri, S. Kwinter, N. Tazi, and H.U. Obrist (Barcelona: Actar).

Ball, P. (1999) *Pattern Formation in Nature* (Oxford: Oxford University Press).

Ball, P. (2004) *Critical Mass: How One Thing Leads to Another* (London: Arrow).

Ball, P. (2009) "The Shape of Things," in *Shapes* (London: Oxford).

Balmond, C. (2002) *Informal* (Munich: Prestel).

Banham, R. (1960) *Theory and Design in the First Machine Age* (Oxford: Butterworth-Heinemann).

Banham, R. (1969) *The Architecture of the Well-Tempered Environment* (Chicago: University of Chicago).

Banham, R. (1973) *Los Angeles: The Architecture of Four Ecologies* (London: Pelican).

Barabasi, A.L. (2002) *Linked: The New Sciences of Networks* (Cambridge: Perseus).

Batty, M. (2005) *Cities and Complexity* (Cambridge: MIT Press).

Batty, M. (2009) "A Digital Breeder for Designing Cities," *Architectural Design* 79, no. 4.

Bentley, P.J. and Corne, D.W. (2002) "Creative Evolutionary Systems," in *Computational Design Thinking*, ed. A. Menges and S. Alquist (London: Wiley).

Bergson, H. (1988) *Matter and Memory*, trans. Nancy Margaret Paul and W. Scott Palmer (New York: Zone).

Berlinsky, D. (1996) *A Tour of the Calculus: The Philosophy of Mathematics* (London: Heinemann).

Boeri, S. (2010) "Five Ecological Challenges for the Contemporary City," in *Ecological Urbanism*, ed. M. Mostafavi and G. Doherty (Baden: Lars Müller).

Bouman, O. (2011) *Volume 23: Al Manakh Gulf Continued*, ed. T. Reisz (The Netherlands: Archis).

Brazier, J.C. and Lam, T. (2009) "Go West, Go Big, Go Green? A Journey through China's 'Great Opening of the West'," *Sustain and Develop* 13.

Brenner, N. and Kiel, R. (2011) "From Global Cities to Globalised Urbanisation," in *The City Reader*, ed. R.T. LeGates and F. Stout (London: Routledge).

Burke, A. (2007) "Redefining Network Paradigms," in Network Practices: New Strategies in Architecture and Design, ed. A. Burke and T. Tierney (New York: Princeton).

Burke, A. and Tierney, T. (2007) "Preface," in *Network Practices: New Strategies in Architecture and Design*, ed. A. Burke and T. Tierney (New York: Princeton).

Burry, M. (2011) *Scripting Cultures: Architectural Design and Programming* (Chichester: Wiley).

Burry, J. and Burry, M. (2010) *The New Mathematics of Architecture* (New York: Thames & Hudson).

Cache, B. (1995) *Earth Moves: The Furnishing of Territories*, ed. Michael Speaks (Cambridge, MA: MIT).

Campanella, T.J. (2008) *The Concrete Dragon: China's Urban Revolution and What It Means to the World* (New York: Princeton Architectural Press).

Castells, M. (1996) *The Rise of the Network Society* (Oxford: Blackwell).

Chung, C.J., Inaba, J. Koolhaas, R. and Sze, T.L. (2001) *Great Leap Forward* (Köln: Taschen).

Cohen, P.S. (2010) "The Return of Nature," in *Ecological Urbanism*, ed. M. Mostafavi and G. Doherty (Baden: Lars Müller).

Daniell, T. (2011) "Introduction," in *Requiem for the City at the End of the Millennium*, S. Kwinter (Barcelona: Actar).

Davis, K. (1965) "The Urbanisation of the Human Population," in *The City Reader*, ed. R.T. LeGates and F. Stout (London: Routledge).

De Landa, M. (1991) *War in the Age of Intelligent Machines* (New York: Zone).

Deleuze, G. (1993) "The Diagram," in *The Deleuze Reader*, ed. Constantin V. Boundas (New York: Columbia University Press).

De Landa, M. (1997) *A Thousand Years of Nonlinear History* (New York: Zone).

De Landa, M. (2002) *Intensive Science and Virtual Philosophy* (New York: Continuum).

De Landa, M. (2003) "Deleuze and the Use of the Genetic Algorithm in Architecture," in *Phylogenesis: FOA's Ark* (Barcelona: Actar).

De Landa, M. (2009) "Material Evolvability and Variability," in *The Architecture of Variation*, ed. Lars Spuybroek (London: Thames & Hudson)

De Landa, M. (2011) *Philosophy and Simulation* (London: Continuum).

Deleuze, G. (2003) *Francis Bacon: The Logic of Sensation* (London: Continuum).

Deleuze, G. and Guattari, F. (1988) *A Thousand Plateaus* (London: Althlone).

Eliasson, O. (2007) "Model as Real," in *Models: 306090, Volume 11*, eds. E. Abruzzo, E. Ellingsen, and J. Solomon (New York: Princeton).

Felsen, M. (2007) "Complex Populations," in *Models: 306090, Volume 11*, eds. E. Abruzzo, E. Ellingsen, and J. Solomon (New York: Princeton).

Frazer, J. (1995) *An Evolutionary Architecture* (London: Architectural Association).

Frazer, J.H. (2006) "Exploring the Analogy that Parametric Design is a Game," in *Game Set Match: On Computer Games, Advanced Geometries and Digital Technologies*, ed. K. Oosterhuis and L. Feireiss (Rotterdam: Episode).

Frazer, J. (2011) *Scripting Cultures: Architectural Design and Programming*, M. Burry (Chichester: Wiley).

Furján, H. (2007) "Cities of Complexity," in *Models: 306090, Volume 11*, eds. E. Abruzzo, E. Ellingsen, and J. Solomon (New York: Princeton).

Garcia, M. (2009) "Prologue for a History, Theory and Future of Patterns of Architecture and Spatial Design," in *AD Patterns in Architecture* (London: Wiley-Academy).

Garcia, M. (2010) *The Diagrams of Architecture* (London: Wiley).

Gerber, D.J. (2009) *The Parametric Affect: Computation, Innovation and Models for Design Exploration in Contemporary Architectural Practice* (Cambridge, MA: Harvard GSD).

Girard, G. and Lambot, I. (1993) *City of Darkness: Life in Kowloon Walled City* (Surrey: Watermark).

Gleick, J. (1999) *Faster: The Acceleration of Just About Everything* (New York: Random House).

Goethe, J.W. von (1989) "Form and Transformation," in Goethe's Botanical Writings, J.W. von Goethe (Woodbridge, CT: OX Bow).

Goodwin, B.C. (2008) "Structuralist Research Program in Developmental Biology," in *Greg Lynn Form*, ed. Mark Rappolt (New York: Rizzoli).

Grasso, J., Corrin J., and Kort, M. (1991) *Modernization and Revolution in China* (New York: M.E. Sharpe).

Hadid, Z. and Schumacher, P. (2003) *Latent Utopias: Experiments with Contemporary Architecture* (New York: Princeton Architectural Press).

Hagan, S. (2010) "Performalism: Environmental Metrics and Urban Design," in *Ecological Urbanism*, ed. M. Mostafavi and G. Doherty (Baden: Lars Müller).

Haken, H. (2000) "Foreword," in *Self-Organisation and the City*, J. Portugali (Berlin: Springer Verlag).

Hensel, M. (2012) *Design Innovation for the Built Environment* (New York: Routledge).

Hensel, M. and Verebes, T. (1998) *Urbanisations* (London: Blackdog).

Hight, C (2012) "Manifest Variations," in *New Computational Paradigms in Architecture*, ed. Tom Verebes (Beijing: Tsinghua).

Hight, C., Hensel, M., and Menges, A. (2009) "En route: Towards a Discourse on Heterogeneous Space beyond Modernist Space-Time and Post-Modernist Social Geography," in *Space Reader*, eds. M. Hensel, C. Hight, and A. Menges (London: Wiley).

Holscher, C. (2009) "Wayfinding Strategies and Behavioural Patterns in Built Space," in *Pattern: Ornament, Structure and Behavior*, eds. Andrea Gleiniger and Georg Vrachliotis (Berlin: Birkhäuser Verlag).

Hornsby, A. (2008) "Hey Fuck! Where'd the City Go?" in *The Chinese Dream*, ed. N. Mars and A. Hornsby (Rotterdam: 010).

Hulshof, M. and Roggeveen, D. (2011) *How the City Moved to Mr. Sun* (Amsterdam: SUN).

Ingber, D.E. (2010) "Bioinspired Adaptive Architecture and Sustainability," in *Ecological Urbanism*, ed. M. Mostafavi and G. Doherty (Baden: Lars Müller).

Isozaki, A. (2011) "Introduction," in *Project Japan*, eds. R. Koolhaas and H.U. Obrist (Köln: Taschen).

Iwamoto, L. (2009) *Digital Fabrications: Architectural and Material Techniques* (New York: Princeton).

Jacoby, S. (2008) "What's Your Type?" in *Typological Formations: Renewable Building Types and the City* (London: AA Publications).
Jencks, C. (1997) *The Architecture of the Jumping Universe* (London: Academy Editions).
Jencks, C. (2002) "Introduction," in Informal, C. Balmond (London: Pretzel Publishing).
Jiang, J. (2009) "Go China's Sustainability: Asynchronous Revolutions," in *Sustain and Develop: 306090, Volume 13*, eds. J. Bolchover and J. Solomon (New York: Princeton).
Jiang, J. (2011) *Volume 23: Al Manakh Gulf Continued*, ed. T. Reisz (The Netherlands: Archis)
Johnson, S. (2001) *Emergence: The Connected Lives of Ants, Brains, Cities and Software* (London: Penguin).
Johnson, S. (2010) *Where Good Ideas Come From: The Natural History of Innovation* (New York: Penguin).
Kara, H. (2008) *Design Engineering AKT* (Barcelona: Actar).
Kelly, K. (1995) "Hive Mind," in *Out of Control: The New Biology of Machines* (New York: Perseus).
Killian, A. (2007) "The Question of the Underlying Model and Its Impact on Design," in *Models: 306090, Volume 11*, eds. E. Abruzzo, E. Ellingsen, and J. Solomon (New York: Princeton).
Kipnis, J. (1993) "Towards a New Architecture," in *Architecture Design Profile No. 102: Folding in Architecture*, ed. Greg Lynn (London: Wiley-Academy).
Koolhaas, R. (1995) "Bigness, or the Problem of Large," in *S, M, L, XL,* OMA, R. Koolhaas, and B. Mau (Rotterdam: 010).
Koolhaas, R. (1995) "The Generic City," in *S, M, L, XL,* OMA, R. Koolhaas, and B. Mau (Rotterdam: 010).
Koolhaas, R. (1995) "Whatever Happened to Urbanism?" in *S, M, L, XL,* OMA, R. Koolhaas, and B. Mau (Rotterdam: 010).
Koolhaas, R. (1996) "Architecture Against Urbanism," in *Managing Urban Change*, ed. Y. Verwijnen and P. Lehtovuori (Helsinki: UIAH).
Koolhaas, R. and Obrist, H.U. (2011) *Project Japan* (Köln: Taschen).
Koolhaas, R. (2012) Interview with Paul Fraioli, *Journal of International Affairs* (April 2012).
Koralevic, B. (2003) *Architecture in the Digital Age* (New York: Spon Press).
Koralevic, B. and Klinger, K. (2008) "Manufacturing Material Effects," in *Manufacturing Material Effects: Rethinking Design and Making in Architecture*, ed. Branko Koralevic (New York: Routledge).
Kryza, F.T. (2006) *The Race for Timbuktu: In Search of Africa's City of Gold* (New York: HarperCollins).
Kuhn, T. (1991) "Scientific Revolutions," in *The Philosophy of Science*, ed. Richard Boyd, Philip Gasper, and J.D. Trout (Cambridge, MA: MIT).
Kwinter, S. (2002) *The Architecture of Time* (Cambridge: MIT).
Kwinter, S. (2003) "The Computational Fallacy," *Thresholds – Denatured* 26 (Cambridge: MIT).
Kwinter, S. (2010) "Notes on the Third Ecology," in *Ecological Urbanism*, ed. M. Mostafavi and G. Doherty (Baden: Lars Müller).
Kwinter, S. (2010) "Who's Afraid of Formalism," *Far From Equilibrium: Essays on Technology and Design Culture* (Barcelona: Actar).

Kwinter, S. (2011) *Requiem for the City at the End of the Millennium* (Barcelona: Actar).

Kwinter, S. and Fabricius, D. (2001) "Houston," in *Mutations*, ed. R. Koolhaas, S. Boeri, S. Kwinter, N. Tazi, and H.U. Obrist (Barcelona: Actar).

Le Corbusier (1929) *The City of Tomorrow and its Planning* (London: Dover).

Leach, N., ed. (2009) *Digital Cities, Architectural Design AD* (London: Wiley-Academy).

Lee, C.M. (2008) "Projective Series," in *Typological Formations: Renewable Building Types and the City* (London: AA Publications).

LeGates, R.T. and Stout, F. (1996) "Introduction to Part One: The Evolution of Cities," in *The City Reader*, ed. R.T. LeGates and F. Stout (London: Routledge).

Lévy, P. (1997) *Collective Intelligence: Man's Emerging World in Cyberspace* (New York: Perseus Books).

Liauw, L. (ed.) (2008) *New Urban China, Architectural Design AD* (London: Wiley-Academy) 2008.

Lynn, G. (1999) *Animate Form* (New York: Princeton Architectural Press).

McHarg, I. (1995) *Designing with Nature* (London: Wiley).

Malé-Alemany, M. (2007) "Parametric Constructions: An Exploration on Virtual Standardisation," in *Models: 306090, Volume 11*, ed. J. Solomon (New York: Princeton).

Mandelbrot, B. (1977) "Theme," "The Irregular and Fragmented in Nature," in *The Fractal Geometry of Nature* (New York).

Mars, N. (2008) "Cities Without History," in *The Chinese Dream*, ed. N. Mars and A. Hornsby (Rotterdam: 010).

Mars, N. and Schienke, E.W. (2008) "The Green Edge," in *The Chinese Dream*, ed. N. Mars and A. Hornsby (Rotterdam: 010).

Marshall, S. (2009) *Cities, Design, Evolution* (New York: Routledge).

Menges, A. and Ahlquist, S. (2011) "Introduction," in *Computational Design Thinking*, ed. A. Menges and S. Ahlquist (Chichester: Wiley).

Mertins, D. (2009) "Variability, Variety and Evolution in Early 20th Century Bioconstructivism," in *The Architecture of Variation*, ed. Lars Spuybroek (London: Thames & Hudson).

Mostafavi, M. and Leatherbarrow, D. (1993) *On Weathering: The Life of Buildings in Time* (Cambridge: MIT).

Moussavi, M. and Kubo, M. (2008) *The Function of Ornament* (Barcelona: Actar).

Moussavi, F. and Zaera-Polo, A. (2003) "Phylogenesis: FOA's Ark," in *Phylogenesis: FOA's Ark* (Barcelona: Actar).

Mitchell, W.J. (1994) "Soft Cities," in *City of Bits: Space, Place and the Infobahn* (Cambridge: MIT).

Mumford, L. (1934) *Technics and Civilisation* (New York: Harvest).

Mumford, L. (1961) *The City in History* (New York: Harvest/HBJ Book).

Mumford, L. (1986) *The Lewis Mumford Reader*, ed. D.L. Miller (Athens, GA: University of Georgia Press).

Nassim N.T. (2007) *The Black Swan: The Impact of the Highly Improbable* (New York: Penguin).

Negroponte, N. (1969) "Towards a Humanism through Machines," *Architectural Design* 6, no. 6.

Obrist, H.U. (2011) "Introduction," in *Project Japan*, ed. R. Koolhaas and H.U. Obrist (Köln: Taschen).

Obuchi, Y., Schumacher, P., Spyropoulos, T. and Verebes, T. (2008) *DRLTEN: A Design Research Compendium* (London: AA Publications).

Otto, F. (2009) *Occupying and Connecting: Thoughts on Territories and Spheres of Influence with Particular Reference to Human Settlement* (Stuttgart: Edition Axel Menges).

Pan, W. (2008) "Utopian Cities: Or How the Author Solves the Problems of Rural China," in *The Chinese Dream*, ed. N. Mars and A. Hornsby (Rotterdam: 010).

Park, R.E., Burgess, E.W. and McKenzie, R.D. (1925) "The Growth of a City: An Introduction to a Research Project," in *The City Reader* (London: Routledge).

Perez-Gomez, A. (1986) *The Origins of Modern Science* (Cambridge: MIT Press).

Pask, G. (1995) "Foreword," in *An Evolutionary Architecture*, John Frazer (London: AA Publications).

Pask, G. (2002) "The Architectural Relevance of Cybernetics," in *Cyber_Reader: Critical Writings for the Digital Era*, ed. Neil Spiller (London: Phaidon).

Pasquero, C. and Poletto, M. (2012) *Systemic Architecture: Operating Manual for the Self-Organizing City* (New York: Routledge).

Picon, A. (2010) "Nature, Infrastructures, and the Urban Condition," in *Ecological Urbanism*, ed. M. Mostafavi and G. Doherty (Baden: Lars Müller).

Pope, A. (1997) *Ladders* (Houston: Rice).

Portugali, J. (2000) *Self-Organisation and the City* (Berlin: Springer-Verlag).

Quatremère de Quincy (2000, first published 1825) "Type," in The Historic Dictionary of Architecture of Quatremère de Quincy.

Rahim, A., ed. (2002) "Contemporary Techniques in Architecture," *AD* 72, no. 1.

Reas, C. (2007) "Beyond Code," in *Network Practices: New Strategies in Architecture and Design*, ed. A. Burke and T. Tierney (New York: Princeton).

Reas, C. (2007) *Processing: A Programming Handbook for Visual Designers and Artists* (Cambridge: MIT).

Rebar (2010) "User-Generated Urbanism," in *Ecological Urbanism*, ed. M. Mostafavi and G. Doherty (Baden: Lars Müller).

Reiser, J. and Umemoto, N. (2006) *Atlas of Novel Tectonics* (New York: Princeton).

Rowe, P.G. (2008) "Urbanising China," in *Shanghai Transforming*, ed. I. Gil (Barcelona: Actar).

Rowe, C. and Koetter, F. (1978) *Collage City* (Cambridge: MIT).

Rudofsky, B. (1964) *Architecture without Architects: A Short Introduction to Non-Pedigreed Architecture* (New York: MOMA).

Ruskin, J. (1903–1912) *The Works of John Ruskin*, eds. E.T. Cook and A. Wedderburn, 39 vols. (London: George Allen).

Rykwert, J. (1976) *The Idea of a Town: The Anthropology of Urban Form in Rome, Italy and the Ancient World* (Cambridge: MIT).

Sassen, S. (2001) "The Global City: Introducing a Concept and its History," in *Mutations*, ed. R. Koolhaas, S. Boeri, S. Kwinter, N. Tazi, and H.U. Obrist (Barcelona: Actar).

Sassen, S. (2001) "The Impact of the New Technologies and Globalisation on Cities," in *The City Reader*, eds. R.T. LeGates and F. Stout (London: Routledge).

Sassen, S. (2008) "Disaggregating the Global Economy," in *Shanghai Transforming*, ed. I. Gil (Barcelona: Actar).

Scheurer, F. (2009) "Architectural Algorithms and the Renaissance of the Design Pattern," in *Pattern: Ornament, Structure and Behaviour* (Berlin: Birkhäuser Verlag).
Schoenauer, N. (1982) *6000 Years of Housing* (New York: Norton & Co.).
Schumacher, P. (2008) *Design Engineering AKT*, ed. H. Kara (Barcelona: Actar).
Schumacher, P. (2011) *The Autopoesis of Architecture, Vol. 1* (Chichester: Wiley).
Schumacher, P. (2012) *The Autopoesis of Architecture, Vol. 2* (Chichester: Wiley).
Shane, D.G. (2011) *Urban Design Since 1945: A Global Perspective* (London: Wiley).
Shaviro, S. (2003) *Connected, or What it Means to Live in the Network Society* (Minnesota: Regents).
Silver, M. and Balmori, D., ed. (2003) *Mapping in the Age of Digital Machines* (London: Wiley).
Simon, H.A. (1996) "The Science of Design: Creating the Artificial," in *The Sciences of the Artificial*, 3rd ed. (Cambridge, MA: MIT Press).
Skinner, W. (1977) *The City in Late Imperial China* (Stanford, CA: Stanford Press).
Solomon, J. (2007) "Seeing the City for the Trees," in *Models: 306090, Volume 11*, eds. E. Abruzzo, E. Ellingsen, and J. Solomon (New York: Princeton).
Somol, R.E. (1999) "Introduction," in *Diagram Diaries*, P. Eisenman (New York: Rizzoli).
Soros, G. (2008) *The Crash of 2008 and What It Means* (New York: Public Affairs).
Speaks, M. (2007) "Intelligence After Theory," in *Network Practices: New Strategies in Architecture and Design*, ed. A. Burke and T. Tierney (New York: Princeton).
Speaks, M. (2008) *Design Engineering AKT*, ed. H. Kara (Barcelona: Actar).
Spuybroek, L. (2004) *Machining Architecture* (London: Thames & Hudson).
Spuybroek, L. (2009) *Architecture and Variation* (London: Thames & Hudson).
Spuybroek, L. (2011) *The Sympathy of Things: Ruskin and the Ecology of Design* (Rotterdam: V2 Publishing).
Stiny, G. and Gips, J. (1972) "Shape Grammars and the Generative Specification of Painting and Sculpture," *Information Processing* 71.
Tafuri, M. (1976) *Architecture and Utopia: Design and Capitalist Development* (Cambridge: MIT).
Terzidis, K. (2006) *Algorithmic Architecture* (Oxford: Elsevier).
Thom, R. (1975) "Introduction," "Form and Structural Stability," in *Structural Stability and Morphogenesis* (Reading, MA: Addison-Wesley).
Thompson, D.W. (1917) "On the Theory of Transformations, or the Comparison of Related Forms," in *On Growth and Form* (New York: Dover).
Trummer, P. (2011) "Associative Design" in *Computational Design Thinking*, eds. A. Menges and S. Alquist (London: Wiley).
Tschumi, B. (2004) *Event Cities* (Cambridge: MIT).
Valeur, H. (2006) *Co-Evolution: Danish/Chinese Collaboration on Sustainable Urban Development in China* (Strandgade: DAC).
Van Berkel, B. and Bos, C. (1999) "The Diagrams of Architecture," in *Move* (Netherlands: Goose Press).
Venturi, R., Scott-Brown, D. and Eisenauer, S. (1965) *Learning from Las Vegas* (New Haven: Yale).
Venturi, R. (1966) *Complexity and Contradiction in Architecture* (New York: MOMA).
Verebes, T. (2007) "Architectural Computation: Reasons and/or Experiments," *Esempi di Architecttura Eda, Info-Architecture* issue, vol. 3.

Verebes, T. (2009) "Experiments in Associative Urbanism," in *Digital Cities*, ed. Neil Leach (London: Wiley).

Verebes, T. (2010) "Endurance and Obsolescence: Instant Cities, Disposable Buildings, and the Construction of Culture," in *Sustain and Develop: 306090*, Vol. 13, eds. Jonathan Solomon and Joshua Bolchover (New York: Princeton Architectural Press).

Verebes, T. (2012) *New Computational Paradigms in Architecture* (Beijing: Tsinghua).

Vermeer, G. (2006) "Games: Designing Cities and Civilisations," in *Game Set Match: On Computer Games, Advanced Geometries and Digital Technologies*, ed. K. Oosterhuis and L. Feireiss (Rotterdam: Episode).

Verwijnen, Y. and Lehtovuori, P., ed. (1996) *Managing Urban Change* (Helsinki: UIAH)

Vitruvius (1914) *The Ten Books on Architecture*, trans. M.H. Morgan (Cambridge, MA: Harvard).

Waldheim, C. (2010) "Weak Work," in *Ecological Urbanism*, ed. M. Mostafavi and G. Doherty (Baden: Lars Müller).

Waldheim, C. and Berger, A. (2008) "Logistics Landscape," *Landscape Journal* 27, no. 2.

Warner, S.B. (1996) "The American Industrial Metropolis, 1840–1940," in *The City Reader*, eds. R.T. LeGates and F. Stout (London: Routledge).

Weiner, N. (2002) "Organisation of the Message," in *Cyber_Reader: Critical Writings for the Digital Era*, ed. Neil Spiller (London: Phaidon).

Weinstock, M. (2008) "Metabolism and Morphology," in *AD Versatility and Vicissitude* (London: Wiley-Academy).

Weinstock, W. (2010) *The Architecture of Emergence* (London: Wiley).

Wheeler, S. (2011) "Urban Planning and Global Climate Change," in *The City Reader*, ed. R.T. LeGates and F. Stout (London: Routledge).

Wigley, M. (2007) "The Architectural Brain," in *Network Practices: New Strategies in Architecture and Design*, ed. A. Burke and T. Tierney (New York: Princeton).

Wilson, E.O. (1998) *Consilience: The Unity of Knowledge* (New York: Alfred Knopf).

Woodbury, R. (2010) *Elements of Parametric Design* (New York: Routledge).

Zhang, T. (2011) "Chinese Cities in a Global Society," in *The City Reader*, ed. R.T. LeGates and F. Stout (London: Routledge).

CONTRIBUTORS

ESSAYS

Jorge Fiori
Jorge Fiori is a sociologist and urban planner. He is Director of the Housing and Urbanism Programme and Chairman at the Architectural Association Graduate School. He is also Senior Lecturer in the Development Planning Unit of University College London, and Visiting Lecturer at several European and Latin American universities. His teaching, research, and publications focus mainly on the interface of urban social policies and spatial strategies, with particular emphasis on issues of housing, irregular settlements, and scaling up in slum upgrading and poverty alleviation. He is also a consultant to several international and national agencies on issues of urban development planning and housing.

David Jason Gerber
Dr. David Jason Gerber researches the intersection of design with computation and technology, and his team is funded by industry and the National Science Foundation. He is Assistant Professor of Architecture and Engineering at the University of Southern California. From 2006 to 2010, he was Vice President at Gehry Technologies Inc., and he has also worked as an architect at Zaha Hadid Architects, Moshe Safdie, and Steinberg Group. He holds degrees from UC Berkley (BArch, 1996), AADRL (MArch, 2000), Harvard GSD (MDS, 2003; DDes, 2007). Previous academic positions include Harvard University, MIT's Media Lab, SCIArc, the Architectural Association, UCLA, Stanford University, Innsbruck University, and EPFL.

Marina Lathouri
Marina Lathouri is an architect and critic whose research interests lie between urban theory and political philosophy, focussing on emerging forms of urban dwelling and public spaces, and the role of writing, production, and communication in architecture. Lathouri is Director of the History and Critical Thinking program at the Architectural Association. She is Visiting Lecturer at the University of Cambridge, and previous positions include the University of Pennsylvania, the University of Navarra, Spain, and Universidad Catolica in Santiago, Chile. Her architectural projects and urban studies include consultancy to the Urban Planning Department in Geneva. Her publications include *Intimate Metropolis: Urban Subjects in the Modern City* (with Di Palma and Periton; Routledge, 2009).

Patrik Schumacher
Patrik Schumacher is partner at Zaha Hadid Architects and founding director of the Design Research Lab at the Architectural Association in London, together with Brett Steele, where he continues to teach in the program. Schumacher joined Zaha Hadid Architects in 1988 and has since been a co-author of numerous key projects. He studied philosophy, mathematics, and architecture in Bonn, London, and Stuttgart (Diploma, 1990), and at the Institute for Cultural Science, Klagenfurt University (PhD, 1999). He is also Tenured Professor at the Institute for Experimental Architecture, Innsbruck University and Guest Professor at the University of Applied Arts in Vienna. In 2012 he published the second volume of *The Autopoesis of Architecture* (John Wiley & Sons).

Jonathan D. Solomon

Jonathan D. Solomon is Associate Dean at the School of Architecture at Syracuse University. His work explores public space and the contemporary city, through design projects such as Ooi Botos Gallery in Hong Kong; research projects such as his 2004 book *13 Projects for the Sheridan Expressway* (Princeton Architectural Press); curatorial projects such as *Workshopping* in the U.S. Pavilion at the Venice Architecture Biennale 2010; and publication projects through 306090 books, of which he is a founding editor and where he has served since 2001. His latest book, *Cities without Ground* (with Adam Frampton and Clara Wong), explores the relationship between climate and public space in the unique three-dimensional urbanism of Hong Kong.

Peter Trummer

Peter Trummer is Professor for Urban Design and Head of ioud, the Institute for Urban Design and Urban Planning, at the University of Innsbruck. He is a former Head of the Associative Design Program at the Berlage Institute, Rotterdam (2004–2010). Trummer studied at TU Graz (Masters), the Berlage Institute, Amsterdam, and is currently working on his PhD. He was project architect at UN Studio before establishing his practice in 2001. He has taught at Sci-Arc, University of Pennsylvania, TU Munich, and the Academy of Fine Arts in Vienna, and he has lectured at the AA, IAAC, and Rice University. His recent publications can be found in: *AD Reader: Computational Design Thinking*, *AD Digital Cities*, volume 18, *Arch+189*, *Morpho-Ecologies*, and *Manifold*.

Tom Verebes

Tom Verebes is Associate Dean (Teaching and Learning) in the Faculty of Architecture and Associate Professor in the Department of Architecture at the University of Hong Kong. Formerly Co-Director of the Architectural Association Design Research Lab (DRL) in London, where he taught from 1997–2009, he has been the Director of the AA Shanghai Visiting School since 2007, and is a former Guest/Visiting Professor at ABK Stuttgart. Tom is the founder and Creative Director of OCEAN CN, a network of specialist design consultants based in Hong Kong, with links to Beijing, Shanghai, and London. He has written, published, exhibited, and lectured extensively in Europe, North America, Asia and the Middle East, and serves on several editorial and advisory boards.

INTERVIEWS

Tom Barker

Tom Barker is the Chair of the Digital Futures Initiative at OCAD University in Toronto. Formerly Professor of Architecture, Design and Innovation at the University of Technology, Sydney and Head of the Industrial Design Engineering department at the Royal College of Art, London, Barker invented SmartSlab, a multimedia large-scale digital LED display panel system, in 1999, in collaboration with Zaha Hadid Architects. Barker also collaborated to develop V/SpaceLAB, a virtual reality system for architecture in 2003. From 1997 to 2005, he ran DCA-b (later b Consultants Ltd.), a multidisciplinary design practice.

Dana Cuff
Dana Cuff is Professor of Architecture and Urban Design at the University of California, Los Angeles, where she is the founding Director of cityLAB, a think tank that explores design innovations for the emerging metropolis. Her research endeavors include infill housing prototypes, embedded spatial computing, the role of transit in new city form, and infrastructure as urban design. Cuff has published and lectured internationally, and her recent books include *The Provisional City* (2000), a collection of Robert Gutman's writings, *Architecture from the Outside In* (with J. Wreidt; 2010), and *Fast-Forward Urbanism* (with R. Sherman; 2011).

Gao Yan
Gao Yan is currently a Consulting Creative Director of dotA Architectural Design Ltd. in Beijing, and also Design Director at OCEAN CN in Hong Kong. Formerly Gao was Architectural Director of the Department of Research and Development at Crystal CG, London. He is Assistant Professor of architecture and the Program Director for the Digital Practice CPD program at the University of Hong Kong, and Director of the AA Beijing Visiting School (2010–2013), hosted at Tsinghua University. He has previously taught at the AA Design Research Lab and AA Shanghai Visiting School. His projects and writing have been published widely.

Matthew Pryor
Matthew Pryor is a Landscape Architect, and Past President of the Hong Kong Institute of Landscape Architects. He is Assistant Professor, Head of the Division of Landscape Architecture, and Director for the BA (Landscape Studies) program at the University of Hong Kong. His research focusses on decision making and public opinion in the design of urban infrastructure, strategic landscape planning, and technical aspects of subtropical planting design in Hong Kong. He has extensive experience in strategic planning, masterplanning, design, documentation, and contract administration on landscape projects, megaprojects, and environmental remediation projects throughout China and Southeast Asia.

Brett Steele
Brett Steele is the Director of the Architectural Association School of Architecture, AA Publications, and AA Public Programs. He is the founder and former Director of the AA Design Research Lab MArch program at the Architectural Association. He is a Partner of DAL, desArchLab, an architectural office in London, and has taught and lectured at schools throughout the world. He is the editor of *Negotiate My Boundary* (London, 2002), *Corporate Fields* (London, 2005), *D[R]L Research* (Beijing, 2005), and *Supercritical*. He is Series Editor of the AA Words and AA Agendas series. His articles, interviews, and lectures have appeared in over 150 publications worldwide.

Su Yunsheng
Su Yunsheng is a CEO of Etopia, a development company based in Shanghai. He is also a Chief Planner at Shanghai Tongji Urban Planning Design Institute (TJUPDI), established in 1996, and a Professor at Tongji University College of Architecture and Urban Planning (CAUP). His TJUPDI team has completed over one thousand planning and research projects, including sixty-three prize-winning

projects at a provincial and municipal level, as well as twenty-nine at a national level in China. TJUPDI was the planning team for the World EXPO 2010 in Shanghai. He has taught at the AA Shanghai Visiting School, and is the co-founder and former co-editor of *Urban China* magazine.

Xu Feng
Xu Feng is a Principal of XWG Studio, with projects including Kai Di Technology Park in Wuhan, Yunnan Cultural Center, and the recently completed Olympic Tower Interior. Xu studied at the Design Research Lab at the Architectural Association, where he researched vector fields and fluid dynamics. He joined Zaha Hadid Architects in 2007 to work on several towers and urban masterplanning projects in Cairo, Brisbane, and Melbourne. Since 2008, he has taught design studios in London, New York, Beijing, and Shanghai. In 2008 he curated the China Section of the Beijing Biennale 2010.

Xu Weiguo
Xu Weiguo is a Professor and Head of the Architecture Department in the School of Architecture at Tsinghua University in Beijing. He received his PhD from Kyoto University and in 2007 was a visiting scholar at MIT. He has published eight books on design methodologies and new digital technologies for architecture, and his papers have been widely published. He co-curated the Architecture Biennial Beijing 2004, 2006, 2008, and 2010, together with Neil Leach. He has lectured widely in many countries, including the U.S., France, Germany, Israel, Russia, and Japan. Xu Weiguo is Principal of XWG Studio, based in Beijing.

CASE STUDIES

Associative Design Program, Berlage Institute, Rotterdam
The Associative Design Program, led by Peter Trummer from 2004 to 2010, focussed on global urbanization within late capitalism in the production of six research reports, six movies in six different global cities. Disciplinary knowledge in the field of urban design resulted from a materialist approach to urban design engagement, in the production of actual projects within the regimes of urban planning and the economic conditions of the city. Each project had a client, a particular site, and a specific economic environment in which these projects unfolded.

dotA, Beijing, Hong Kong
dotA is a cross-disciplinary practice working between architecture, engineering, and computation, led by Duo Ning, Chang Qiang and Gao Yan. dotA aims for the synthesis of hybridized architecture which can be engineered irreducibly. Their design approach fuses deterministic and nondeterministic methodologies in a rich hybridization and mutation of social, economic, ecological, technical, and political substrates. Facilitated by the application of synthetic computational techniques, dotA strives for significant and valuable design in the context of future uncertainty, and for the realization of innovative, meaningful, and sustainable propositions through information and communication.

Groundlab, London, Beijing
Groundlab is a Landscape Urbanism practice led by Eva Castro, Holger Kehne, Alfredo Ramirez, Eduardo Rico, and Sarah Majid. Comprised of a multidisciplinary team of architects, urban designers, engineers and landscape architects, Groundlab brings together diverse expertise as a response to contemporary social, economic, and environmental and infrastructural conditions. The studio approaches cities and landscapes as natural processes in constant change and evolution, thereby requiring flexible and adaptable mechanisms for the design of future urban environments. Groundlab emphasizes the analysis of existing and potential contextual conditions, and the temporal and dynamical forces which shape cities.

Group8, Geneva
Founded in 2000, and consisting of nine partners and a team comprising seventy employees, Group8 is an architectural firm whose R&D priorities are the generation of specific configurations that best fit the context, the program, and the social and environmental framework of a project. In 2007 the firm created its branch Group8asia, based in Hanoi, Vietnam. In 2010, the office was nominated for the Distinction Romande d'Architecture. Integration of economic and environmental performance, and a cultural added value within each project is derived from Group8's workshop culture and teamwork at both a local and international level.

Hong Kong Parametric Design Association, Hong Kong
The foundation of HKPDA forms a bridge between academic research, teaching, and practice, through research on parametric design methodologies integrating technology and design. Led by Sam Cho, Yang Wang, Ben Dai, and Jaenes Bong, the group was formed by an association of professors, researchers, architects, students, programmers, etc. as an umbrella organization for the sharing and dissemination of ideas, skills, and knowledge. The aim of the group is to inspire and enable a future generation of designers to be equipped with parametric capacities so that they can turn imagination into reality.

James Corner Field Operations, New York
James Corner Field Operations is an urban design and landscape architecture practice focussing on design projects across a variety of high-profile project types and scales, from large urban districts and complex postindustrial sites, to small, well-crafted, detail design projects. The practice makes a special commitment to the design of a vibrant and dynamic public realm, informed by the ecology of both people and nature. As a team with cross-disciplinary backgrounds in landscape architecture, urban design, architecture, and communication art, JCFO aims to craft ecologically smart and culturally significant built works of lasting distinction. JCFO has won numerous awards and their work has been published and exhibited internationally.

Kaisersrot, Zurich
Kaisersrot is a collaboration of architects and researchers in the field of architecture, urban design, and information technology. Kaisersrot became a

start-up company in 2008. The urban design projects of Kaisersrot highlight the dialectic opposition of top-down and bottom-up processes and systems, and the group aims to combine both strategies, oscillating between control and laissez faire. The work of Kaisersrot consists of independent projects and collaborations with other architectural offices, including recent collaborations with Herzog & de Meuron, Sauerbruch Hutton, and KCAP.

MAD, Beijing, Tokyo
MAD was founded in 2004 by Ma Yansong and is led by Ma Yansong, Dang Qun, and Yosuke Hayano. The office received worldwide attention in 2006 with the winning competition entry for a residential tower near Toronto, now nearly completed. MAD's projects, from residential complexes or offices to cultural centres, conceive future-oriented environments based on a contemporary interpretation of the eastern spirit of nature. Recent and current projects are located in cities around China, in Italy, France, and Canada. MAD has been awarded the Young Architecture Award from the New York Institute of Architects (2006) and the RIBA international fellowship (2011).

OCEAN CN Consultancy Network, Hong Kong (HQ), Beijing, Shanghai, London OCEAN CN, led by Tom Verebes, Gao Yan, and Felix Robbins, is a network of specialist design consultants based in Hong Kong, with partners in Beijing, Shanghai, and London. OCEAN CN collaborates as an integrated team of experts, amalgamated from architecture, urbanism, engineering, computational design, and manufacturing, visualization and information communication. OCEAN CN's multidisciplinary, experimental approach aims to innovate upon standard systems and methodologies, with masterplanning, urban design, architectural and interiors projects, in Asia, Europe and North America. The office has been widely published and has exhibited in some of the world's most prestigious venues.

Plasma Studio, London, Beijing, Bolzano
Led by Eva Castro, Holger Kehne, and Ulla Hell, Plasma Studio is an architecture and design practice with a portfolio of work across Europe and Asia. *Plasma*, in Classical Greek, means modeling, form, fabric, imagination, and fiction. In physics the plasma state is a unique condition of matter arising as the result of a complex overlay of external forces. Plasma Studio negotiates the nature of flows, events, and ephemera, with the rational, structural, and systemic parameters of material organization. Focussing on all scales of design, from furniture and installations to urbanism and masterplanning, Plasma's approach to tectonics sets spaces, planes, and bodies in unforeseen relationships that challenge conventional topographies and spatial codes.

Rocker-Lange Architects, Hong Kong, Boston
Rocker-Lange Architects practices architecture through designing, building, researching, writing, and teaching. Founded in 2005 by partners Ingeborg M. Rocker and Christian J. Lange, the office specializes in installations, urban interventions, and cultural and residential projects. Projects are developed through intensive research in conjunction with the use of innovative digital design

methodologies guiding the design and construction process. The office's distinctive methodology emphasizes open spatial configurations, material transformation, and refined detailing and craftsmanship. Underlying themes in the work include the conceptual use of building tectonics, components and materials, modified with both traditional and digital techniques.

Serie Architects, London, Mumbai, Beijing
Founded in 2006 by Chris Lee and Kapil Gupta, Serie has recently opened offices in China. Serie's portfolio includes projects in India, China, Singapore, Eastern Europe, and the UK, focussing on masterplanning, housing, restaurants, and the design of cultural and civic buildings. The practice is known for its theoretical position which emphasizes the study of building typologies and their evolution, and the careful study of precedents as a basis for speculating on new solutions. Their approach to design emphasizes rigorous geometry and the innovative use of materials. This design focus is complemented by a meticulous and inventive approach to construction. In 2010, Serie won the Young Architect of the Year Award.

Shanghai Tongji Urban Planning and Design Institute, Shanghai
Shanghai Tongji Urban Planning and Design Institute (TJUPDI) was established in 1996. Acting as a practice-based platform of Tongji University engaging in urban planning services, TJUPDI is comprised of over two hundred full-time urban planners, including Su Yunsheng as a Chief Planner. This team has completed over one thousand planning and research projects, including sixty-three prize-winning projects at a provincial and municipal level as well as twenty-nine at a national level in China. TJUPDI was the planning team for the World EXPO 2010 in Shanghai, and their work has been widely published and exhibited.

XWG Studio, Beijing
XWG Studio is a research-based architecture firm, operating via encoded and explicit processes across the fields of architecture, art, education, and dissemination. XWG's work aims to investigate and reflect the problems of socioeconomics and ecology within the context of rapid urbanization in China. Currently, the studio is working on a unique courtyard-based low-energy-use office building in Qinzhou, to be completed in 2013. In addition, the studio is engaged in a series of larger-scale projects in Wuhan, including the design stage for Kaidi Science Park, six office towers in the East Lakes District in Wuhan, and the design of a three-square-kilometer masterplan for a mixed-used community in Qinzhou. XWG Studio also organized and curated the Beijing Biennale in 2004, 2006, 2008, and 2010, together with Neil Leach.

Zaha Hadid Architects, London (HQ)
Zaha Hadid Architects is an award-winning practice based in London and many other cities around the world. The office works at all scales in all sectors to create transformative cultural, corporate, residential, and other spaces that work in synchronicity with their surroundings. Led by Zaha Hadid and Patrik Schumacher, the office has designed 950 projects in forty-four countries, by 350 current staff originating from fifty-five countries. Iraqi-born Hadid has been awarded a DBE by

Queen Elizabeth II (2012), the Pritzker Prize (2004), and the Stirling Prize (2010, 2011). Both Hadid and Schumacher are highly influential in shaping the next generation of young architects, through their teaching, lectures, and publications.

INDEX

adaptation 2,12, 34–37, 61–6, 89, 102–4, 111, 129, 171–2, 178, 186, 233, 235, 268
adaptability 3, 50, 71–72, 92, 129, 173, 233–35, 240, 268
Aish, R 148
Amsterdam 71
Alexander, C xii, xiii, 18, 95, 64–5, 88–9, 91–2, 105–12
Algorithm 27, 88, 107, 170–2, 186; algorithmic design 141–2, 145, 150 , 172, 179, 181, 186–7, 191; *see also* parametric design
Allen, S 112
Archigram 12, 156, 196,
Aristotle 14–15, 30–1
Architectural Association (AA) xiii, 40, 180, 226
Architecture xiii, 2–3, 8, 17, 21, 24, 26–30, 33, 37–8, 41–2, 48–52, 55–64, 69, 71, 75–6, 82, 88–9, 91–95, 100–13, 118–22, 126–7, 136, 143, 153–4, 161–2, 168–83, 189–92, 194–7, 214, 223–7, 230–3, 266–74; and complexity xi–xii, 1–3, 8, 12–13, 15, 20–1, 23–4, 27, 30, 36, 41–7, 52, 59–65, 68, 75, 78–9, 84, 88–91, 96, 99–114, 118–20, 122, 124, 129, 142–51, 153, 162, 169–74, 176, 178, 180–3, 186–7, 190–2, 195, 206, 214, 223, 226, 228, 230–1, 266, 269–70, 273; and decay 13, 36, 38, 63–4, 126, 233; and duration 2–3, 8, 13, 24, 36–7, 54, 60–5, 73, 94–5, 100, 102, 127; 223, 233–4, 273; and functionality xii, 2, 10, 13, 16, 21, 33, 35, 54–5, 58, 62–4, 80, 82, 87–88, 92, 102–7, 119–20, 126, 141, 151, 154, 173, 177–8, 182, 194–5, 227, 233, 268–9, 272; and obsolescence xiii, 2–3, 30, 35–8, 50, 52, 54, 60, 62–3, 92–3, 196, 223–255, 271; iconic architecture 51, 125, 230–1; and performance 1, 3, 8, 33, 51, 58, 61, 94, 100, , 103–108, 124–6, 141–51, 156, 173–79, 224–7, 233, 246, 269
artificial 12, 14, 16, 36, 50–3, 61–2, 68, 70, 73–4, 77, 92, 99, 103, 110, 172, 178–9, 248
artificial intelligence 52
associative model 145, 181
associative logic 7, 15–18
Athens 13
Automation 136, 150, 168, 172, 175–6, 178–80, 267, 270

Banham, R xiii, 32, 37, 61–2, 69, 169, 225
Baghdad 13
Batty, M xiii, 102, 108, 172,
Beijing 17, 29, 32, 34, 49–50, 58, 63, 82, 132, 198, 245
Berlage Institute 209–212
Biology 12, 14–15, 17–18, 61–2, 64, 77, 91, 99, 104–5, 113, 145, 169, 173, 178–9, 186, 190–2, 195, 227, 253
biological paradigm 12, 17–18, 61–2, 77, 99, 113, 145, 169, 173, 178–9, 190–2, 253
biomimetics 109, 168, 173, 175,
biomorphism 168, 173
Building Information Modeling (BIM) 52, 125, 168, 176–7, 179, 270,
Burry, M xi–xii, 8, 16–7, 56, 64, 89, 102–4, 107, 111, 142, 145, 150–1, 168, 170, 172–3, 176–8, 227, 230
Burry, J 8, 17, 56, 64, 89, 102–4, 107, 111, 145, 177–8, 227, 230

Campanella, T 29–30, 36–7, 54–5, 58
Castells, M 1, 10–11, 56–7; megacities 1, 56–7; Southern China Metropolis 56–7
Castro, E 82–4, 237–40, 287–8
city/cities; and abandonment 13, 37–8, 235; and density 36, 48–9, 54–6, 59, 71, 77, 79, 132, 159, 165–7, 198–90, 194–5, 201–2, 209, 238, 245, 259; and decline 2, 13,14, 35, 38, 223, 235; and design 3, 16, 40, 61, 76, 93, 123–6, 148, 168, 235; and complexity xii, 2–3, 12–15, 23–4, 36, 42–7, 52, 60–2, 65, 68, 75, 78, 84, 87, 93, 102–6, 109–12, 120, 129, 142, 144–51, 163, 169, 172–3, 178, 181, 186–92, 214, 223, 226, 230–5, 265–74; and countryside 7, 13, 16, 31, 33, 55–57, 62, 78 142, 193; and form 10–16, 20–1, 23–8, 30–1, 40–7, 50–3, 55–7, 59–65, 68, 71–4, 77, 87–96, 102–13, 118–22, 147–8, 150–1, 153–8, 168–73, 176–9, 182–3, 186–92, 205–6, 230, 266, 268, 273–4; and growth I, xi, 2, 8, 10, 12–16, 20–1, 27, 31–4, 37–9, 48, 58–65, 68, 72, 75–6, 87–92, 100, 103, 106–8, 112, 151, 164, 168, 172,–3, 182,–3, 187–924, 214, 274; and homogenisation 11, 23, 26, 44, 54, 57–8, 113, 158, 162, 181, 186, 196–7, 267; and industrialisation 3–4; and obsolescence xiii, 2–3, 36, 50–52, 54, 60, 62–3, 92–3, 196, 214–19, 223–35, 271; and landscape 11, 15, 17, 30–4, 43, 61–5, 71–2, 75–6, 82–5, 98–102, 112, 142, 147, 170–3, 177, 198, 201–2, 234, 237, 241, 245, 248, 253, 268; and permanence 2, 7, 8–9, 20–1, 28, 33, 56, 63–45, 88, 94, 99, 128, 183, 227–235, 268, 273; and self-organisation xii, 11–15, 35, 57, 62, 88–91, 103–5, 120, 143–4, 182, 191, 235; and systems xii, 8–18, 20–22, 24, 29, 36, 45, 53, 62–64, 82, 87–9, 91–6, 98, 99–112, 120–2, 124–7, 130–1, 141–6, 148–51, 162–3, 166, 1689–73, 176–83, 186–7, 191–7, 205, 207, 214, 223–4, 227–8, 230, 233–4, 239, 245, 253–4, 273; and utopia xi, 12–3, 21, 25, 31, 63, 89, 92; as centres of trade xi, 8, 34; as a machine 11, 13, 15–6, 25, 32, 34, 94, 147, 195; as an organism 17, 21, 33, 64, 104, 106, 124, 142, 154, 171, 173, 178, 195; and the economy 1, 10–1, 20–2, 41, 48, 56, 61, 65, 95–7, 118–9, 123, 195, 231, 259, 270; city walls 16–7, 25, 28–9, 50
Chicago 34, 36,
Childe, V. G 8, 148,
China: ancient China 28–30; and danwei 28, 58; and Deng Xiaoping 29, 48, 56; and the megablock 26; and rapid urbanisation xiii, 1, 24, 28–30, 38, 48–52, 54–9, 99, 187, 191, 193–7, 266, 268; Cultural Revolution 193; Empires 196; modern China 1, 24–6, 28–30, 34, 37–8, 48–52, 54–5, 58–9, 77–9, 80–2, 88, 92–3, 124, 128, 132–6, 193–7, 237, 241, 245, 248, 259, 267, 271–2
Chongqing 56, 110, 224, 228, 231, 234
Civilisation 7–8, 16, 32, 27–8, 97, 100, 118, 123,
complexity xii, 2–3, 12–15, 23–4, 36, 42–7, 52, 60–2, 65, 68, 75, 78, 84, 87, 93, 102–6, 109–12, 120, 129, 142, 144–51, 163, 169, 172–3, 178, 181, 186–92, 214, 223, 226, 230–5, 265–74
computation xii, xiv, 1–3, 13, 26–7, 51–2, 60, 75, 87, 91–6, 100, 105–7, 118, 121, 124–5, 132, 141–151,

168–83, 186–92, 198, 214, 223, 224–34, 238, 267 270–3
computational methodologies 2–3, 26, 51, 75, 87, 92–6, 100, 105–7, 118, 121, 125, 132, 141–151, 168–83, 186–92, 198, 214, 223, 226–34, 238; computational urbanism xii, xiv, 1, 3, 26–7, 52, 87, 92, 100, 106, 119–21, 141, 144, 150, 168–83, 186–92, 214, 226, 266, 274; and coding 96, 100, 110, 145, 158, 166, 171, 183; and design i, xii, 3, 51–2, 92–6, 105–6, 118–19, 141, 144–5, 147, 150, 168, 196, 214, 223, 228, 231, 267, 271, 273; and fabrication 51, 188–9, 196, 223, 267; computer aided design (CAD) xii, 13, 91–2, 125, 168–9, 172, 177, 270; evolutionary computation 60, 91–2, 94, 105–6, 107, 111, 124–5, 135, 142, 170, 172; software 91–2, 94–6, 100, 110, 121, 125, 168, 177, 270; computer science 103, 107, 121
Cuff, D 23–7
Culture 3, 8, 12, 16–7, 28, 36, 57, 60, 62, 65, 90, 93, 128, 142, 144, 168, 1811, 189, 196, 223, 230–1, 235, 266, 268, 270, 273
Customisation 1, 3, 136, 162, 169, 176, 223, 225
Cybernetics 13, 60, 91–3, 103, 105, 142, 182, 224

da Vinci, L 16
Damascus 13
De Landa, M xiii, 16, 88, 91, 97, 100, 103, 113, 150, 172
de Quincy, Quatremère 226,
demographics 2, 24, 28, 93, 120, 150,
Descartes 15, 88
Design: and coding 96, 100, 110, 145, 158, 166, 171, 183; and computation i, xii, 3, 51–2, 92–6, 105–6, 118–19, 141, 144–5, 147, 150, 168, 196, 214, 223, 228, 231, 267, 271, 273; and masterplanning; xi, xii, 1–3, 13, 17–18, 23–4, 28, 41, 46, 50, 63–4, 68, 71–2, 75–6, 78, 80–4, 87–113, 121–4, 129, 135, 141–51, 153–7, 162, 168–83, 186–92, 194, 198, 205, 209, 214, 237, 248, 252, 259, 266; algorithmic design 141–2, 145, 150 , 172, 179, 181, 186–7, 191; methodologies 2–3, 26, 51, 75, 87, 92–6, 100, 105–7, 118, 121, 125, 132, 141–151, 168–83, 186–92, 198, 214, 223, 226–34, 238;
Design Research Lab xiii, 27, 90, 95, 108, 143, 146, 180, 189, 267, 283–6
Detroit 38
Diagram 12, 27, 81, 92, 106, 110, 141–51, 153, 170–7, 198, 209, 227–8, 230, 245–6, 252, 254, 262; and Deleuze, G & Guattari, F 14, 113, 141–2, 148, 172, 227; van Berkel, B & Bos, C 141; Somol, R 141
Dillenberger, B 205–8
DotA 135–8, 204–8, 253–8, 285
Dubai 36–8, 68, 195
Duo, N 135–8, 204–8, 253–8, 285

Eames, C & Eames, R 225
Egypt 8
Environment: and climate 1, 37, 150; and crisis 1–2, 49–52, 54, 61, 65, 76–9,95–6; and ecology 1, 9, 13, 15, 21, 24–5, 33–7, 54–5, 60–3, 65, 71, 76–9, 81–2, 95, 97, 99–102, 104–6, 126–7 136, 173, 175–7, 233–5, 237, 253; and landscape 11, 15, 17, 30–4, 43, 61–5, 71–2, 75–6, 82–5, 98–102, 112, 142, 147, 170–3, 177, 198, 201–2, 234, 237, 241, 245, 248, 253, 268; and performance 1, 3, 8, 13, 15, 20, 33, 49–52, 58, 61, 70, 91, 94–5, 99–100, 103–8, 118, 124, 126, 141–151, 150–1, 156, 173–9, 175–7, 182, 187, 233, 224–7, 246, 269; and pollution 8, 49, 61, 76–9, 126, 150; and sustainability xi, 24–8, 37, 50, 54, 70, 75–8, 126–8, 175, 186–7, 233, 259, 268; built environment 40, 49–50, 70, 122, 129
emergence 3, 8–10, 12, 24–8, 35–6, 47, 75–8, 87–113, 153, 156, 168, 173, 182–3, 186–90, 192, 123–8, 143–5, 147, 173, 178–9, 181,
engineering 16, 21, 70, 72–3, 75, 190,
Euphrates River 7
Europe: and industrialization 8–9, 17, 30–36, 118; and urbanisation 1, 8–9 14–6, 24–6, 28–36, 55, 58, 87, 113, 194, 266, 268
European colonialism 9, 11, 30–1, 34, 37–8, 58, 68, 70, 72, 97
evolution and urbanism 1–3, 7, 9, 13, 15–18, 24, 37, 54, 57, 60, 62, 64–5, 68, 72, 76, 87–92, 99–100, 102, 104, 106–13, 118, 123, 136, 150, 168, 170, 172, 178, 186, 192, 206–7, 266, 273; and Darwin 100, 104; and planning 57, 100, 104
evolutionary computation 60, 91–2, 94, 105–6, 107, 111, 124–5, 135, 142, 170, 172

Fiori, J 40–7, 283
Fordism 1, 105, 118–20, 196, 231, 267
Form: and cities 3, 10–1, 14–6, 20–1, 23, 25–30, 36, 50–2, 55–7, 59, 64, 77, 87–113, 127, 129, 141–51, 154–7, 168–83, 186–92, 227–8, 232, 237; and generative methodologies 10, 15, 58–59, 62–3, 99, 119–21, 141–51, 172, 175–83, 227–8, 232–3; form-finding 87, 143–4; formal 25–6, 34, 46, 63, 68, 71, 72, 107, 109, 118, 129, 132, 153–7, 186, 205, 266; formation 24, 26, 62, 64–5, 87–9, 91–2, 102, 110–1, 113, 141, 144, 150, 153–8, 230, 233
Fractals 96, 110
Fraser, J 226,
Friedman, Y 15, 63
Fuller, B 61, 225
Functionalism 33, 54–5, 62, 82, 88, 105–6, 182, 194, 227, 268–9

Gao, Y 48–52, 135–8, 204–8, 253–8, 285–6
Garnier, T 88
Gaudí, A 87, 144,
Geddes, P 1, 9, 17, 31
Gehry, F O 176
Gehry Technologies 176, 283
Geometry 12, 107–113, 142, 148, 169, 190, 227
Geographical Information Systems (GIS) 150
Gerber, D J 129, 178, 186–92, 231,
Globalization 3, 7–13, 148, 196–7; and global economy 31, 57; and modernisation 57–8, 158, 226; and networks 7–13, ; history of 22, 26
Global Financial Crisis (GFC) xi, 36, 95–7, 230, 269
Go West Policy 56, 224, 228, 231
Gottmann, Jean 1, 9,
Grid 8, 17, 25, 30, 68, 109, 122, 125, 127, 130, 150, 156, 188, 194–5, 205; and China 26, 30; Jeffersonian Grid 17, 26; wet-grid 144

Groundlab 82–4, 237–240, 287
Group8 205–8, 287

Hadid, Z 122–3, 129–131, 187–91, 270, 283, 289
Harvard Project on the City 1, 8, 55, 189
Haussmann, G-E 17, 70
Hight, C xiii, 94, 113
Hilbersheimer L 17, 33, 62,
Holland, John 178
Hong Kong xiii, xiv, 27, 29, 56, 59, 68–74, 75–79, 89, 92, 158–164, 165–6, 195, 214–9, 253–65, 268, 270
Howard, E 18, 33, 88; Garden City Movement 33, 88; settlement unit 33, 58, 78

Industry 9–11, 28, 30–4, 38, 56, 62, 89, 118, 123, 125–6, 128, 142, 150, 181, 197, 223, 266, 268; and standardisation 11, 224; and mechanisation 9, 11, 62; industrial revolution 8–9, 28, 30–4, 123; industrialisation 9–10, 28, 30–4, 38, 89, 118, 150; post-industrial xi, 38, 259, 268
informal urbanism 3, 28, 40–7, 68–74, 87–9, 106, 206, 273
information 3, 8–12, 16, 26, 50, 52–3, 88, 91–3, 95–7, 99–100, 111–3, 120, 122, 124–5, 136, 141–51, 158, 168–973, 176, 179, 182, 197, 214, 227–8, 230, 270–1
innovation 1, 13, 30–1, 41, 60, 65, 78–10, 103, 107, 110, 118, 141, 150, 168–9, 175, 177, 182, 188, 223, 225, 228, 230–3, 273
Instant City 28–9, 34–7, 54, 56, 97, 124
Intelligence xii, 11–4, 17–8, 52, 77, 87, 91–3, 102–3, 105, 107, 110, 124, 126, 141–7, 169–76, 186, 191–2, 196, 224–5, 270; artificial intelligence 52, 103
interface 7, 16, 94, 106, 123, 141–2, 148, 150–1, 158–60, 181, 198, 205, 269–70
interactivity 13–4, 92, 124, 150, 179, 182, 189, 270
internet 9, 12, 29, 96, 148, 169

Jacobs, J xii, 18, 35, 63, 89, 153–4
James Corner Field Operations 80–1, 287
Jerusalem 13
Johnson, S xiii, 10, 12, 14, 99, 104, 232

Kaisersrot 205–8, 287–8
Kehne, H 82–4, 237–40, 287–8
Kipnis, J xiii, 69, 112–3, 226
Koolhaas, R xiii, 1, 14–5, 35–6, 39, 51, 55–7, 59–60, 63, 79, 156
Koralevic, B 95, 107–8, 176, 233,
Kuhn, T 94, 186
Kurokawa, K 15
Kwinter, S xiii, 1, 11, 14–5, 33, 37–8, 60, 62, 64, 96–7, 102, 105, 111–2, 142–5, 147, 169, 171

L'Enfant, P C 88–9
Las Vegas 36, 90,
Lathouri, M 20–2, 283
Le Corbusier xi, xii, 11, 33–4, 54, 60, 62–4, 88, 154, 156, 181, 224, 235, 267, 269, 271
Lee, C CM 227, 241–4, 289
Lefebvre, H xii, 10
Liang, S C 29
Liverpool 38
London xii, 31–2, 34, 38, 49, 71, 88, 126, 142

Ma, Y S 248–52, 288
MAD Architects 248–52, 288
Maki, F 59, 63,
Manchester 10, 31, 34, 38
manufacturing 8, 38, 51, 58, 65, 74, 94, 168, 176–7, 225, 259
Mandelbrot, B 96, 110–1,
Mars, N 29, 61,
Marshall, S xiii, 17–8, 61, 63–5, 88, 90, 97, 104, 106–8, 147
Marx, K xii, 16,
masterplan/masterplanning xi, xii, 1–3, 13, 17–18, 23–4, 28, 41, 46, 50, 63–4, 68, 71–2, 75–6, 78, 80–4, 87–113, 121–4, 129, 135, 141–51, 153–7, 162, 168–83, 186–92, 194, 198, 205, 209, 214, 237, 248, 252, 259, 266; and emergence 2–3, 87–92, 153–7, 186; and teleology 1, 3, 18, 23, 64, 75–6, 92–95, 186–92; and urban change (adaptivity) 1–3, 13, 46, 123–4, 186; conventional masterplanning 1–3, 17–8, 23, 41, 50, 63, 68, 75–6, 121–4, 153, 194; masterplanner 1, 17–8, 23, 71, 121; techniques of, 23, 28, 46, 63, 75, 96, 121–2, 141–51; top down masterplanning xii, 18, 24, 28, 41, 50, 63–4, 78, 87–92, 121
mechanical 7, 11, 14, 32, 62, 89, 105, 169, 195; mechanical paradigm 7, 11, 62, 105, 118, 195; mechanical and/vs. biological 14, 169, 195; mechanisation 11, 14, 32, 118
mediaeval towns 16–7, 25, 87–8
megacity 1, 10–1, 56–7, 60
megalopolis 1, 9
megastructure 59, 156,
Metabolism 12–3, 15, 63, 91
methodology 1–3, 20, 22–3, 26, 47, 75, 91, 94–6, 110–1, 113, 139–151, 168–83, 188, 198, 214, 224, 235, 237, 266–7, 269, 273
migration 7, 9, 10, 31, 61, 75, 168
military defences 8, 13, 15–7, 28, 148
Mitchell, W 94, 169,
Modernization 13, 32, 35, 55, 63, 268
Modernism 15, 18, 23, 32, 34–5, 54–5, 57, 59, 62–3, 88–90, 108–9, 113, 118–21, 179, 181, 195, 230, 267–8
morphology 51, 55, 64, 71, 106, 111–2, 120–1, 129, 134, 136, 144, 146, 153–6, 174, 181–2, 206, 209, 212, 227–8, 230, 233
Mumford, L xiii, 7, 9, 13–4, 16–8, 32–5, 58–60, 63, 65, 89, 181, 224, 233,

nature 7, 9, 12, 14–5, 18, 25, 33, 35, 50–1, 60–2, 65, 70, 77, 87–8, 92, 94–5, 100, 106–13, 173, 175, 178, 226, 248, 273; and/vs. artificial 12,51, 61–2, 70, 92, 95, 175, 226; and the city 7, 14, 25, 33, 35, 65, 70, 100, 173, 248; and mankind 9, 18, 33, 51, 60–1, 88, 273; and technology 15–16, 62, 77, 95; taming of 7, 14, 60–1
Negroponte, N 176
neighborhood unit 16, 33
neolithic 8, 16

networks 3, 7–13, 26, 31, 35–7, 45, 59, 61, 68–73, 97, 100, 105, 120, 142, 144, 147–8, 150, 170–1, 187, 190, 193, 195–6, 225, 227, 230; and globalization 7–13, 36–7, 230; and connectivity 26, 31, 45, 65–73, 100, 105, 125–6, 147, 193, 195
New Babylon 15
New Urbanism 12, 14, 25, 89
New York 25, 31, 34–6, 40, 156,
Nieuwenhuys, C 15

Obrist, H U 12, 55, 57, 63,
obsolescence xiii, 2–3, 36, 50–52, 54, 60, 62–3, 92–3, 196, 214–19, 223–35, 271
Obuchi, Y xiii, 180,
OCEAN CN Consultancy Network 132–4, 151, 158–165, 198–204, 253–265, 284–5, 288
organic 13–5, 17–8, 32, 41, 50–1, 59, 61–3, 65, 76, 90, 109, 124, 129, 151, 178, 194–5, 227, 232, 248,
organism 15, 17, 21, 33, 64, 70, 76, 103–4, 106, 109, 113, 124, 142, 154, 171, 173, 175, 178, 195,
optimization 33, 87, 108, 175–80, 191, 206, 224
optioneering 162, 168, 175–80, 192
Otto, F 9, 13, 87, 109, 145, 181, 226

paradigm 1, 3, 7, 11–8, 32, 34, 38, 54, 56, 58, 61–4, 76–7, 85–113, 121, 145, 150–1, 162, 172, 178, 181, 186, 190, 192, 195, 197, 223, 225–8, 231, 233, 270
parametric xiii, 16, 48, 51, 53, 94, 106–13, 118–22, 123–4, 132, 141–8, 151, 158–61, 168, 179, 180–3, 186–92, 197; parametric design 16, 51, 53, 94, 106, 118, 124, 141–8, 179, 180–3, 197; parametric modeling 51, 141–7, 237; Parametric Urbanism xiii, 53, 118–21, 168, 180–3, 186–92; Parametricism 118–22, 181–2
Paris 17, 31–2, 34, 49, 54, 71, 88
Pask, G 93, 103, 106, 170
pattern xii, 8, 11, 21, 25, 30, 37, 56, 58, 62–4, 73, 87, 91–2, 96–7, 100, 102, 105–13, 121–4, 129, 143, 147, 150, 155, 166, 169, 174–5, 179–83, 190, 201–23, 216, 218, 228,
Perez-Gomez, A 32
performance 1, 3, 8, 33, 51, 58, 61, 94, 100, 103–108, 124–6, 141–51, 156, 173–79, 224–7, 233, 246, 269
planning xi, xii, 1–3, 13, 17–18, 23–4, 28, 41, 46, 50, 63–4, 68, 71–2, 75–6, 78, 80–4, 87–113, 121–4, 129, 135, 141–51, 153–7, 162, 168–83, 186–92, 194, 198, 205, 209, 214, 237, 248, 252, 259, 266; and emergence 2–3, 87–92, 153–7, 186; organic planning 232; planned and unplanned urbanism 3, 28, 40–7, 68–74, 87–9, 106, 206, 273
Plasma Studio 82–4, 288
Poincaré, H 92, 227
politics xi, 1–2, 101, 17, 20–2, 25, 27, 31, 40–47, 48–9, 51–2, 73, 78–9, 87, 96–7, 113, 119, 143, 157, 169, 183, 195, 253, 273
population xi, xii, 1, 7, 10, 13–7, 21, 29, 33–4, 36–7, 46, 48, 55–6, 61–2, 75–7, 88, 99, 150, 190, 194–5, 233, 259
prediction 10, 13–4, 35, 44, 61, 65, 92–96, 102–3, 105, 107, 109, 11, 119, 121, 123–4, 145–8, 150–1, 171, 182, 192, 226, 230, 266, 269, 271; and the economy 10, 24, 96, and masterplanning 13–4, 61, 65, 92–4, 102–3, 105, 119, 121, 123–4, 145–8, 226, 230
prototype 17, 33, 54, 124, 132, 183, 196, 223–6, 230; as design methodology 124; prototyping technologies 223–6; urban prototype 17, 33, 54, 124, 182
Pryor, M 75–9, 285

rapid urbanization xiii, 1, 23, 29, 33, 48–9, 54, 56, 58, 75, 126–7, 158, 177, 268
Reas, C 173
Robbins, F xiv, 132, 158, 162, 288
Rocker-Lange Architects 162, 165–7, 288
Rome 8, 14, 31, 60, 71, 153; Roman System of city building (Vitruvius) 8, 14,
Rossi, A 18, 156, 227,
Rousseau, J-J 16
Rudofsky, B 88
rural 7, 13, 16, 31, 33, 55–57, 62, 78 142, 193
Ruskin, J 32, 141,
Rykwert, J 8

Sassens, S 1, 10–11, 57; global city 1, 10–11, 57, 105; transnational urban systems 10, 20
Schumacher, P xiii, 118–22, 129, 178, 180–1, 187–8, 190–1, 231
science(s) 2–3, 15, 16, 21, 32, 53, 62, 91–2, 94–6, 100, 103–5, 107-8, 112, 133, 142, 173, 178, 192; biology 12, 14–5, 17–8, 61–4, 77, 91, 99, 104–5, 113, 145, 169, 173, 178–9, 186, 190–2, 195, 227, 253; complexity science 2–3,15, 105, 112; computer science 2, 103, 107–8, 178; material science 143; modern science 15, 32, 62; natural science 3,15, 112; normal science and revolutionary science 23; social science 151; philosophy of 94
science fiction 59
sedentary settlements 7–8; and hunting and gathering 7–8
self-organisation xii, 11–15, 35, 57, 62, 88–91, 103–5, 120, 143–4, 182, 191, 235
Sim City 124, 150, 271
Simendon, G 225
Simon, H A 99
Singapore 29, 35, 121–3, 129–30, 187–9, Shirdel, B xiii, 226,
Shenzhen xiv, 39, 56, 80, 88, 92–3, 132, 158, 165, 197, 237, 253, 259
Shanghai 29–30, 58–9, 63, 195, 230
shape grammar 169
Shaviro, S 10–1, 13–4, 35, 150,
Solomon, J D xiii, 59, 68–74, 150, 259
Soros, G 97
Soria y Mata, A 17, 88; The Linear City 17, 88
Southern China Metropolis 56–7
space xi, xii, 2, 8–11, 15, 20–2, 29–30, 32, 34–5, 40–1, 46, 50–1, 58–9, 62–3, 68–74, 82, 88–90, 99–100, 102, 107–9, 111–3, 118–21, 123, 126, 128, 136, 141–51, 153–6, 165–6, 168–77, 182, 186, 195–6, 206, 223, 227–8, 230, 232; and differentiation 11, 99–100, 102, 111–3, 136, 142–51, 166, and hierarchy 8, 10–11, 14–5, 21,

30, 62, 71, 89, 100, 111, 145, 150, 179, 183, 209, 227; of flows 10, 35, 50, 59, 68–74, 126, 149, 153; heterogeneous space 11, 25–6, 63, 72–3, 99–100, 102, 107, 109, 111–3, 142, 166, 181, 186, 196, 206, 223, 226, 269; homogeneous space 11, 23, 26, 44, 54, 57–8, 72, 113, 267; Cartesian space xii, 227; Computational space 99, 109, 111–3, 141–51, 168–77, 186, 206, 223, 227, 230; modernist space 15, 18, 23, 32, 34–5, 54–5, 57, 59, 62–3, 88–90, 108–9, 113, 118–21, 171, 179, 181, 195, 230, 267–8; public space xi, 22, 29, 34, 46, 68, 70–4, 123, 126, 136, 165; political space 22, 35, 128, 186, 195; urban space 8, 10–1, 21, 51, 64, 68–74, 111, 144–7, 182, 228, 232
Space Syntax 147
Spuybroek, L 113, 143–4, 225
standardization 1, 3, 16, 26, 28, 32, 34, 54, 57, 105, 118–20, 151, 162, 176, 196, 223–6, 231, 267; nonstandardization 223–6, 267
Steele, B xiii, 266–72, 285
Stiny, G 169
Su, Y S 193–7, 198, 285, 289
sustainability xi, 21, 24, 37, 50, 52, 54, 60–1, 75–8, 80, 82, 126–8, 136, 186–7, 233, 235, 259, 268

Tafuri, M 31, 33, 153–4, 223,
Taleb, N 96
tabula rasa xi, 28, 30, 35, 54–8, 60, 76, 91, 124, 194, 235, 268, 272
Tange, K 63
Technology i, xii, 1, 3, 7, 9–18, 20–2, 31–2, 48, 50–2, 56–7, 59–65, 77–8, 89, 92–7, 99, 106, 118–9, 123–8, 141, 144–5, 162, 168–83, 186–93, 196, 214, 223–34, 267, 273; as infrastructure 3, 7, 9–13, 16–8, 57, 97; design technology i, xii, 3, 9–13, 20–2, 51–2, 92–6, 105–6, 118–19, 141, 144–5, 147, 150, 168–183, 196, 214, 223, 228, 231, 267, 271, 273; information technology 7, 10–11, 16–8, 20–2, 95; production technology 12; prototyping technology 141–151, 168–83, 186–92, 198, 214, 223–34, 238
Thermodynamics 91, 100,
Terzidis, K 107–9, 145, 147, 150, 168–9, 191
Thom, R 91
Thompson, D'Arcy W 144,
Tigris River 7
Timbuktu 36–7
Tokyo 34–5, 56,
Topography 9, 68, 87–8, 110, 130–1, 135–8, 141, 147, 151, 171, 180–1, 188, 218–9, 234, 253, 267
topology 8, 141–3, 161–2, 196, 226–30, 270
transformation 2, 12, 15, 17, 20–1, 25, 31, 34, 41, 44, 46–7, 56, 64–5, 75–6, 91, 94, 100, 104, 109, 112–3, 121–2, 133, 150, 162–3, 168–9, 209, 212, 223, 226–30, 235, 248, 267–8, 273
Trummer, P 153–7, 209–13, 227, 284, 286
Turing, A 178, 267
Typology 30, 35, 132–3, 141, 159, 162, 165, 194, 198, 201, 205, 209, 212, 223, 226–30, 237–8

Unger, R M 113
University of Hong Kong i, xiii, 74, 92–3, 99, 101–2, 110–1, 147, 149, 170–1, 174–5, 177, 179, 182–3, 214–9, 224–6, 228, 230–2, 234, 259–65, 284
urban: urban change 2, 12, 15, 17, 20–1, 25, 31, 34, 41, 44, 46–7, 56, 64–5, 75-6, 91, 94, 100, 104, 109, 112–3, 121–2, 133, 150, 162–3, 168–9, 209, 212, 223, 226–30, 235, 248, 267–8, 273; urban complexity xi–xii, 1–3, 8, 12–13, 15, 20–1, 23–4, 27, 30, 36, 41–7, 52, 59–65, 68, 75, 78–9, 84, 88–91, 96, 99–114, 118–20, 122, 124, 129, 142–51, 153, 162, 169–74, 176, 178, 180–3, 186–7, 190–2, 195, 206, 214, 223, 226, 228, 230–1, 266, 269–70, 273; urban design xi, 1, 3, 16, 40, 61, 76, 93, 123–6, 148, 168, 235; urban density 36, 48–9, 54–6, 59, 71, 77, 79, 132, 159, 165–7, 198–90, 194–5, 201–2, 209, 238, 245, 259; urban fabric xii, 17, 24, 30, 35, 45, 49–51, 63, 73, 75–6, 88–9, 113, 121–2, 164–5, 193–4, 225, 230, 237, 272; urban form 10–16, 20–1, 23–8, 30–1, 40–7, 50–3, 55–7, 59–65, 68, 71–4, 77, 87–96, 102–13, 118–22, 147–8, 150–1, 153–8, 168–73, 176–9, 182–3, 186–92, 205–6, 230, 266, 268, 273–4; urban growth xi, 1, 2, 8, 10, 12–16, 20–1, 27, 31–4, 37–9, 48, 58–65, 68, 72, 75–6, 87–92, 100, 103, 106–8, 112, 151, 164, 168, 172–3, 182–3, 187–924, 214, 274; urban planning xii, 57, 100, 104; urban population xi, xii, 1, 7, 10, 13–7, 21, 29, 33–4, 36–7, 46, 48, 55–6, 61–2, 75–7, 88, 99, 150, 190, 194–5, 233, 259; Urban Renewal Act (URA) 35; urban revolution 8, 10; urban sprawl 1, 17, 24–5, 28, 36, 54, 57–60, 71, 90, 194–5; urban village 88, 237
urbanization: Asian urbanization xiii, 3, 7, 9–10, 24, 28, 31, 33–4, 36, 54, 57–63, 74, 75–8, 186, 195, 266–73; rapid urbanization xiii, 1, 23, 29, 33, 48–9, 54, 56, 58, 75, 126–7, 158, 177, 268
urbanism: and decline 2, 13,14, 35, 38, 223, 235; and countryside 7, 13, 16, 31, 33, 55–57, 62, 78 142, 193; and growth xi, 1, 2, 8, 10, 12–16, 20–1, 27, 31–4, 37–9, 48, 58–65, 68, 72, 75–6, 87–92, 100, 103, 106–8, 112, 151, 164, 168, 172–3, 182–3, 187–924, 214, 274; and obsolescence xiii, 2–3, 36, 50–52, 54, 60, 62–3, 92–3, 196, 214–19, 223–35, 271; and landscape 11, 15, 17, 30–4, 43, 61–5, 71–2, 75–6, 82–5, 98–102, 112, 142, 147, 170–3, 177, 198, 201–2, 234, 237, 241, 245, 248, 253, 268; and permanence 2, 7, 8–9, 20–1, 28, 33, 56, 63–45, 88, 94, 99, 128, 183, 227–235, 268, 273; and self-organisation xii, 11–15, 35, 57, 62, 88–91, 103–5, 120, 143–4, 182, 191, 235; and systems xii, 8–18, 20–22, 24, 29, 36, 45, 53, 62–64, 82, 87–9, 91–6, 98, 99–112, 120–2, 124–7, 130–1, 141–6, 148–51, 162–3, 166, 1689–73, 176–83, 186–7, 191–7, 205, 207, 214, 223–4, 227–8, 230, 233–4, 239, 245, 253–4, 273; computational urbanism xii, xiv, 1, 3, 26–7, 52, 87, 92, 100, 106, 119–21, 141, 144, 150, 168–83, 186–92, 214, 226, 266, 274; evolutionary urbanism 1–3, 7, 9, 13, 15–18, 24, 37, 54, 57, 60, 62, 64–5, 68, 72, 76, 87–92, 99–100, 102, 104, 106–13, 118, 123, 136, 150, 168, 170, 172, 178, 186, 192, 206–7, 266, 273; informal urbanism 3, 28, 40–7, 68–74, 87–9, 106, 206, 273; Parametric Urbanism xiii, 53, 118–21, 168, 180–3, 186–92

Venice 71, 88, 162,
Verebes, T xiii–xiv, 1–3, 7–18, 23–7, 28–38, 45–65, 75–9, 87–113, 123–8, 132–4, 141–51, 158–64, 168–83, 193–7, 198–204, 214–9, 223–35, 253–73
Vitruvius 8, 14
Von Goethe, J W 227, 233,
Von Neumann, J 178

Wachsmann, K 15
Waldheim, C 11
Washington DC 9, 88
Weinstock, M 91, 99, 100, 104, 111
Wiener, N 91
Woodbury, R 107, 145, 148, 169
Wright, F L 17–8, 32,

Xu, F 48–53, 245, 286
Xu, W G 48–53, 245, 286
XWG Studio 245–7, 286, 289

Zaha Hadid Architects 122–123, 129–31, 283–5, 289
Zhang, T W 56

University of Strathclyde
Dept of Architecture
Library